Zygmunt Stojowski

Life and Music

by

JOSEPH A. HERTER

Los Angeles, 2007

Zygmunt Stojowski: Life and Music
by Joseph A. Herter

is published by

Figueroa Press
Suite 401E
840 Childs Way
Los Angeles, CA 90089
Phone: (213) 740-3570
Fax: (213) 740-5203
www.figueroapress.com

As part of the

POLISH MUSIC HISTORY SERIES
Wanda Wilk, Editor-in-Chief (vols. 1–6)
Maja Trochimczyk, Editor-in-Chief (vols. 7–8)
Linda Schubert, Editor (vols. 6–8)
Marek Żebrowski, Editor-in-Chief (vols. 9–10)

Figueroa Press is a division of the USC University Bookstore
Cover, text and layout design by USC GraphicDesign
Produced by Crestec Los Angeles, Inc.
Printed in the United States of America

Library of Congress Cataloguing-in-Publication Data
Herter, Joseph A.
Zygmunt Stojowski: Life and Music

Includes bibliographical references (p.)
ISBN-13: 978-1-932800-26-5
ISBN-10: 1-932800-26-3
Library of Congress Number: 200693358

Polish Music History Series, Vol. 10
Polish Music Center at USC
Los Angeles, 2007

To my good friend and fellow former Michigander,
John Martin Hein, Librarian Emeritus,
University of North Florida, Jacksonville,
without whose help neither the revival of Stojowski's Cantatas
nor the writing of this book would have been possible

POLISH MUSIC HISTORY SERIES

Published by the Polish Music Center at USC
(Vols. 1-5 by the Friends of Polish Music)
Flora L. Thornton School of Music
University of Southern California
Los Angeles, CA 90089-0851
http://www.usc.edu/dept/polish_music

Table of Contents

Acknowledgments

A number of people and institutions must be thanked for assisting me in my research over the past six years. First and foremost, I would like to express my deepest gratitude to John Hein, to whom this book is dedicated, a fellow Detroiter and friend since college days at the University of Michigan's School of Music in the 1960s. As Head of Technical Services at the University of North Florida Library in Jacksonville, he was my personal reference librarian when, quite frequently, I could not get questions answered here, in Poland. His indispensable help also included obtaining materials on interlibrary loan on many occasions. Another native Detroiter who must be thanked is Wanda Wilk. Founder of the Polish Music Center at the University of Southern California in Los Angeles, she was instrumental in obtaining a research grant from the California-based foundation Ars Musica Poloniae, which enabled me to travel to New York and do research in the city where Stojowski's spent the last four decades of his life. I would also like to thank Joseph E. Gore, President and Executive Director of The Kosciuszko Foundation, an American Center for Polish Culture in New York. The Kosciuszko Foundation awarded me two travel grants. The first was to present a paper on Zygmunt Stojowski at Georgetown University in Washington, D.C., in June 2002. The second—in July and August 2004—enabled me to conduct research in over half a dozen American cities. Later that same year I was invited by the Universität der Künste in Berlin to take part in a symposium entitled *Polen in Herzen* and present a paper on Stojowski as a Polish composer living abroad. I am also deeply grateful to the Polish Ministry of Culture and Minister Waldemar Dąbrowski for financial support of my research in Paris (Stojowski's home for eighteen years), and in Switzerland, where Stojowski was an annual summer guest at Paderewski's home.

My appreciation also goes to Fr. Marek Białkowski CM, pastor of Holy Cross Basilica in Warsaw, for arranging inexpensive accommodations with the

Sisters of Charity at the Dom św. Kazimerza in Paris. Similar expression of gratitude is reserved for former Swiss Ambassador to Poland Jean-Oliver Quinche and his wife Nicole, who arranged housing in Morges at the home of Genevieve Stucky to whom I am also indebted for her wonderful hospitality. The support of my many friends and relatives made "going the extra mile" possible, and I would like to thank Donald J. Lachowicz, Elizabeth Sawicki, Fr. Robert J. Witkowski, as well as my sisters Helen Perkins, and Joan Moore.

Special thanks go to the former chair of Warsaw University's Department of Musicology, Professor Irena Poniatowska, for her encouragement of my Stojowski project. Thanks to her I authored the Stojowski entries in the *Polish Music Encyclopedia* and in *Die Musik in Geschichte und Gegenwart.*

Proofreaders who graciously took the time to make corrections and suggestions are long-time Warsaw resident, the Canadian musician Michael Oczko and Henryk Polowniak, former librarian of St. Mary's College in Orchard Lake, Michigan. I am also indebted to Alfred and Henry Stojowski, the composer's sons, for answering many questions, and to Henry in particular, for opening his home to me and allowing me to turn his living room into a storage area for over 30 large boxes of manuscripts, published scores, correspondence, photos and other Stojowski memorabilia. My heartfelt thanks go to Wojciech Hulewicz, a close friend and computer expert who solved several technical problems while keeping my book intact.

The following individuals, institutions and organizations were kind enough to give me access to their archives and provide me with valuable information: Amelia Island, Florida—Antoinette Brachocki-McCarthy; Berkshire, England— Jill Kelsey at the Royal Archives, Windsor Castle; Bloomington, Indiana—Edward Auer at Indiana University; Bolton Landing, New York—Charles and Anita Behr Richards at the Marcella Sembrich Opera Museum; Boston, Massachusetts— Barbara Perkel at the Boston Symphony Orchestra; Chicago, Illinois—Halina Misterka at the Polish Museum of America, Stan Matthews, and Theodore Slabey; Cincinnati, Ohio—Linda Bailey at the Cincinnati Historical Society Library, Teri McKibben at the Cincinnati Symphony Orchestra; Cleveland, Ohio—David Krakowski; College Park, Maryland—Donald Manildi and Gregor Benko at the International Piano Archives Maryland; Cracow, Poland—The Polish Music Press (PWM) Library, Stanisław Hrabia at the Jagiellonian University's Institute of Musicology, Agnieszka Mietelska-Ciepierska at the Jagiellonian University Library; Denver, Colorado—Marcia Whitcomb; Detroit, Michigan—Jeanne Salathiel of the Music and Performing Arts Department at the Detroit Public Library; Fort Worth, Texas—Richard Rodziński, Executive Director and President of the Van Cliburn Foundation; Heidelberg, Germany—Karg-Elert-Gesselschaft;

Jackson, Mississippi—Music Director Stephen Osmond at the Jackson Symphony Orchestra; Kansas City, Missouri—pianist Ronald Brown; London, England—the BBC Orchestral Library, Polish Cultural Institute, Joanne Wainwright at Sotheby's, Mike Spring at Hyperion Records; Longwood, Florida—Gregory Gecewicz; Los Angeles, California—Director Marek Żebrowski, Office Manager Krysta Close, and former employees Maja Trochimczyk and Barbara Zakrzewska at the University of Southern California Polish Music Center, Steven Lacoste at the Los Angeles Philharmonic Archives, Senior Librarian Assistant Ned Comstock at the USC Cinema-Television Library; Lubbock, Texas—William Westney at Texas Tech University; Madison, Wisconsin—Wisconsin Music Archives at the University of Wisconsin's Mills Music Library; Manchester, England—archivist Eleanor Roberts at the Hallé Concerts Society; Mannheim, Germany—Johannes Michel; Morges, Switzerland—Cultural Affairs Officer Dr. Jean A. Konopka, Assistant Barbara Zeydler, and former librarian Rita Rosenstiel at the Paderewski Société and Museum; New Haven, Connecticut—Mateusz Zechowski at the Yale University Library, Marvin Warshaw at the New Haven Symphony Orchestra; New York City—Blessed Sacrament Catholic Church, musicologist Jeff Dane, Gino Francesconi and Kathleen Sobogal at the Carnegie Hall Archives, Assistant Director Jocelyn K. Wilk at Columbia University Archives-Columbiana Library, archivist Peter Martin at G. Schirmer, Inc., Jeni Dahmus and Jane Gottlieb at the Juilliard School Library, John Pennino at the Metropolitan Opera Archives, Richard Wandel at the New York Philharmonic Orchestra Library, Dr. Thaddeus Gromada, Joseph W. Wieczerzak and Janina Gromada Kedron at the Polish Institute of Arts and Sciences of America, Frances X. Gates of the Polish Singers Alliance of America, Gregory Moore as well as Ole and Joan Pohl, John Hunter and Harold Kooden for making those extra visits to the New York Public Library for me and for the kind hospitality; Paramus, New Jersey—Sembrich scholar Stephen Herx; Paris, France—Eva Talma-Davous, retired head music librarian at the Bibliothèque Nationale, Jean Leduc of Alphonse Leduc & Cie., composer Piotr Moss; Philadelphia, Pennsylvania—Nancy M. Shawcross, Curator of Manuscripts at the University of Pennsylvania's Rare Book and Manuscript Library, Brett Rosenau at Theodore Presser, Kile Smith at the Free Library of Philadelphia's Edwin A. Fleisher Collection of Orchestral Music and Edward Sargent; Riverhead, New York—Mary Lee at the Riverhead Free Library; San Francisco Bay Area, California—Patricia Everingham Nottingham, Janice Braun at Mills College, Robert D. Harrington; Stanford—Dr. Maciej Siekierski and Zbigniew L. Stańczyk at the Hoover Institution, Frederick Weldy at the Stanford University Music Department; Tucson, Arizona—Joseph Swinson at the University of Arizona School of Music; Venice, Florida—Louise Brachocki-Signorino; Warsaw, Poland—Archiwum Akt

Nowych, Andrzej Spóz at the Warsaw Musical Society (WTM) Library, Mariola Nałecz and Włodzimierz Pigła at the Biblioteka Narodowa, Music Reading Room of the Warsaw University Library, the Warsaw Philharmonic Orchestra and friends who have helped me with translations and typing: Richard Bialy, Krzysztof Czerwiński, Adam de Nisau, Henryk K. Grocholski, Michał Ossowski and Piotr Praczyk; Washington, D.C.—Larry Bakin and Diane Camilleri; Williamstown, Massachusetts—Douglas B. Moore, professor of cello and curator of the Willeke Collection at Williams College; Zurich, Switzerland—Mark Richli.

Joseph A. Herter
Warsaw, August 2006

Introduction

Researching the life of the pianist and composer Zygmunt Dyonizy Antoni Jordan de Stojowski[1] presented many unusual challenges. To begin with, Stojowski's music disappeared from the concert hall repertoire and with it most information about this once popular and highly esteemed post-romantic composer. When research for this book began in 1999, the last scholarly work written about him in English was an article by Frank Cooper in 1970. In Poland the situation was even worse. The last published work on Stojowski by Józef Reiss dates from 1949, and in 1950 an excellent master's thesis on Stojowski's piano works was authored by Maria Macharska-Wolańska, the late sister of the former Cardinal of Cracow. To make matters more discouraging, a legend circulated in Poland for years, purporting that all of Stojowski's manuscripts and correspondence were accidentally discarded in America, where Stojowski spent more than half of his life. When experts in Polish music history or music librarians were questioned about Stojowski, often the answer was, "Don't bother," followed by a reprise of the apocryphal story. Were it not bad enough, none of Stojowski's major works were commercially recorded, and an Internet search in 1999 brought only about thirty hits. The exploratory processes to unearth information about Stojowski often seemed closer to detective work rather than typical scholarly research.

Because of the bewilderment caused by the number of contradictory sources giving the date of his birth, it was decided to start with Stojowski's death—a date that all basic reference sources agreed upon: November 5, 1946. But even in death there was some confusion. Stojowski's obituary on the front page of Poland's largest circulating daily—*Życie Warszawy*—read, "Zygmunt Stokowski, the world-famous composer and conductor died in the United States of America, where he had lived for 40 years."[2] It would have been impossible for the average reader to ascertain if it was the composer Zygmunt Stojowski or the conductor Leopold Stokowski who had died. Although Stojowski wore many musical hats during his life—concert pianist, composer, pedagogue and musicologist—conducting was never one of his claims to fame.

Zygmunt Stojowski (1870–1946) and Leopold Stokowski (1882–1977) have been confused with each other many times, not only during their lifetimes but in recent times as well. In the French translation of a world premiere release of Stojowski's *Piano Concertos* on Hyperion Records, we find that these are "Les Concertos pour piano de Stokowski." Even the highly respected British historian Norman Davies in his 1981 *A History of Poland* had the two men confused, describing Stokowski as a Polish musician and immigrant, whose Polish name, along with many others, became well-known throughout the world. Mr. Davies might have had Stokowski in mind, but despite his Polish heritage, Leopold Stokowski was as true a native-born Englishman as there could ever be, and it is definitely wrong to categorize him as an "exile from Poland."[3] In addition to being of Polish descent, Stokowski and Stojowski had two other things in common: both immigrated to the United States in 1905 (the former from England, and the latter from Poland via Paris) and both were famous musicians: Stojowski the pianist and composer, and Stokowski the conductor.

Fate decided that they would join forces at least once during their musical careers. The coupling of talents, with Leopold at the helm of the Cincinnati Symphony Orchestra and Zygmunt at the piano, took place on February 20, 1912, at Pittsburgh's Carnegie Music Hall.[4] An amusing poem in the Pittsburgh press immortalized this musical encounter:

Stokowski and Stojowski

By Arthur G. Burgoyne [5]

Stokowski and Stojowski—oh, the combination rare!
Our music-loving folk will rush to hear the famous pair
Whose joint exploits are certain to enrapture and enthrall
Their auditors this evening at Carnegie Music Hall.
To look for standingroomski half the crowd may be compelled
When Stokowski and Stojowski do their stuntski unexcelled.

Stokowski leads the orchestra which regularly treats
The Cincinnati dilettantes to symphonies and suites
To preludes, postludes, serenades, concertos, fantasies
And other masterpieces meant to edify and please.
By himself he is a trumpski. Hence things surely ought to hum
When Stokowski and Stojowski to the frontski jointly come.

Stojowski from the ivories brings out a magic tone.
Among the pianistic sharps he nobly holds his own.
He plays glissandos, tremolos, sforzandos, trills, et cet
With dexterity that never fails excitement to beget,
Alone he is a starski. So it should be a delight
When Stokowski and Stojowski for high artski's sake unite.

A Schumann symphony is billed, an overture by Brahms,
A savage dance by Richard Strauss that causes inward qualms,
A mighty Liszt concerto—'tis a most attractive list;
But after all what makes the thing too tempting to resist
Is the knowledge that the marvelous alliterative pair
Stokowski and Stojowski in the triumphski will share.

Figure Int-1. Stojowski caricature, London, 1913. Press Clipping, ZLSC. Used by permission. All rights reserved

The musical forms and composers mentioned in the poem indicate that Stokowski conducted Stojowski in a performance of Liszt's Concerto for Piano and Orchestra No. 1. Also heard were Brahms' *Academic Festival Overture*, Schumann's Symphony No. 4, and Strauss' *The Dance of the Seven Veils* from *Salome*. This concert was the third of four Pittsburgh Series concerts which the orchestra played while on tour.[6]

Solving the mystery of Zygmunt Stojowski's date of birth is more intriguing. There are a number of possible birth years: 1863, 1869, 1870, 1871 and 1876. The choice of birthdays includes March 27, April 8, May 2, and May 14. Most Polish reference sources give the May 14 date as Stojowski's birthday.

This conundrum is actually easier to solve than the year of Stojowski's birth. The number of days between March 27 and April 8, and between May 2 and May 14 is the same: twelve days. The dates for March 27 and May 2 are obviously given in accordance with the Julian calendar. Stojowski was born in Strzelce near Kielce in the Russian partition of Poland, where the Julian calendar prevailed in daily life. The dates for April 8 and May 14 are given according to Gregorian calendar calculations, which would have prevailed in the Austro-Hungarian and Prussian partitions of Poland. The dates in May, however, can be taken out of consideration. This is an obvious error involving the sixth century Frankish king and martyr after whom Zygmunt was named, St. Sigismond, whose feast day—Zygmunt's nameday—falls on May 2, a feast observed only in the Western Church. Thus, Stojowski was born on April 8, according to the Gregorian calendar.

March 27, 1869, is the birth date given on Stojowski's 1887 high school graduation record in the former Polish capital Cracow, and thus would be the date on his first national identity card.[7] Two years later, in Paris, the date April 8, 1869 can be found on Stojowski's Paris Conservatoire certificate issued for winning the 1889 Premiere Prix de Piano.[8] This is the date Stojowski used in 1895 when completing the application form for the Anton Rubinstein Prize in Berlin.[9] On the other hand, 1870 is the year of birth given in every Stojowski résumé found in the family archives in the USA, with the exception of one, which gives 1871 as the year of birth. The digit "3" in the 1863 date must be a dyslexic substitute for the digit "9" in 1869, and it is safe to assume that the composer's widow must have given the date of 1876, the year found on Stojowski's death certificate, in a confused moment of bereavement.[10] If born in 1870, Stojowski would have been seventy-six when he died.

Sorting out the question of Stojowski's year of birth may ultimately prove impossible. Searching for his baptismal certificate in the composer's birthplace of Strzelce revealed that this village has no parish church. In fact, Strzelce—a hamlet of approximately 350 residents—does not have much of anything, except for a newsstand, small grocery store, and a fire department. The local grade school closed in 2005.[11] The nearest Catholic Church in the Diocese of Kielce is about five kilometers away, in the town of Oleśnica, where all Assumption Parish records were destroyed in a fire during World War II. It was a tragic loss for historians, since parish archives dating back to the fourteenth century were consumed by flames. The late nineteenth century church edifice also suffered fire damage. The name of the diocese is mentioned because of a nearby town, Staszów, sometimes named in placing the whereabouts of Strzelce.[12] Staszów, however, is in the Diocese of Sandomierz, which would have been a part of the Austro-Hungarian Empire at the time of Stojowski's birth. Stojowski's parents would certainly not have applied for passports just to have their son christened in Austrian territory.

It is possible that after the family moved to Cracow, Stojowski's parents falsely stated the year of his birth in order to have him start school one year earlier than normal. Stojowski quoted 1869 as the year of his birth until he left for the United States. There would be no advantage for him to fib about his age in order to become a year younger following his first transatlantic sailing. In addition to the résumés found, 1870 would be the year of his birth based on the age given on passenger ship manifests at Ellis Island, and on his son Henry's French birth certificate. It is also the year given on Stojowski's American naturalization papers. Thus, except when otherwise stated, the author uses the year 1870 as the date of Stojowski's birth when calculations of age are needed.

Figure Int-2. The composer's mother, Maria Stojowska, in the early 1920s.
Photograph courtesy of ZLSC. Used by permission. All rights reserved

Endnotes

[1] Outside of Polish circles, Stojowski was known as Sigismond rather than Zygmunt. Also, in most sources his second given name, Dyonizy, is usually given as Denis. Although it may appear to be of French origin, the name Jordan is associated with the birth of the Polish nation. Jordan (d. 982 or 984), whose date of birth or origin cannot be determined, was a bishop sent by the Church to witness the baptism of King Mieszko I, the first King of Poland, in 966. During that same year, Jordan was consecrated the first Bishop of Poland. (See: Rostworowski, vol. 11, 270–271.)

[2] Zgon Zygmunta Stokowskiego: "W Ameryce zmarł kompozytor i dyrygent światowej sławy Zygmunt Stokowski. Stokowski mieszkał w Stanach Zjednoczonych od 40-lat."

[3] Davies, 290, and Chasins, 1–2.

[4] Details of the concert program received via Internet from the archivist of the Cincinnati Symphony Orchestra and a librarian from the Cincinnati Historical Society.

[5] Pittsburgh journalist Arthur G. Burgoyne (1861–1914) was the "town poet" for nearly all of the Pittsburgh papers at various times. For more than three decades he produced daily poems—both humorous and sometimes serious—on current topics of the day.

[6] Herter, *Stokowski and Stojowski.*

[7] City of Cracow Archives (Archiwum Akt Dawnych m. Krakowa fascykuł GLN 194).

[8] ZLSC.

[9] Slonimsky. Although Stojowski was registered to take part as a pianist in the Rubinstein Competition, a contest that had categories for both composers and pianists, he never showed up. His compatriot Henryk Melcer-Szczawiński (1869–1928) became the hero of that competition, winning first prize as a composer and taking third prize as a performer. For more information, see: Melcer.

[10] Ibid.

[11] Conversation with the *sołtys* [chairman of the village council] at the local grocery store on May 1, 2006.

[12] Mechanisz, p. 160.

Zygmunt Stojowski
Life and Music

Chapter One

ANCESTRY AND CHILDHOOD

Zygmunt Stojowski was of noble descent. His paternal ancestor, Jordan Hipolit Jacenty Stojowski, received the title of nobility along with the horn featured on his coat of arms in 1838.[1] Zygmunt's parents, Alfred and Maria (née Bogdańska) came from the well-educated sphere of landowners in south-central Poland. Little is known about Stojowski's father, Alfred. He was born in 1836 and died in Poland in 1895[2] from an infected corn on his foot.[3] Zygmunt's first son—also named Alfred—was able to provide some fragmentary information about his grandfather: ". . . He was a gentleman farmer, a tall and handsome individual, conscripted into the Czar's honor guard for a time."[4] Alfred's obituary in *Le Monde musical*, states that he was a cavalry captain in the Imperial Russian Guard. In his biographical article on Paderewski, Zygmunt mentions that his father brought Paderewski's six-year-old invalid son (a child from Paderewski's first marriage) from Poland to Paris by train.[5]

Zygmunt was the younger of two boys born to his parents. His father's obituary names the two surviving sons as Zygmunt and Wacław. Henry Stojowski, the composer's second son, disagrees and is certain that Zygmunt's older brother was named Władysław, which is also Henry's given middle name. If true, it would explain the identity of Władyslaw Stojowski who lived on 19 Mokotowska Street in Warsaw and worked for the Ministry of Foreign Affairs.[6] Thus Zygmunt would stay with his older brother when visiting the capital. Unfortunately, Stojowski's surviving sons were not able to provide more information about their uncle, except for the fact that he died before Zygmunt relocated to the United States.

Much more is known about Zygmunt's mother, Maria (ca. 1850[7]–1925),[8] who outlived her husband by thirty years and played a dominant role in Zygmunt's life. She was Zygmunt's first piano teacher, before pianists Alfred Kołaczkowski and Henryk Bobiński (1861–1914) replaced her.[9] Both were on the faculty at the

Music School of the Cracow Musical Society. Musicologist Stanisław Dybowski also lists Antoni Płachecki (d. 1893) as one of Stojowski's early piano teachers.[10]

Maria's cousin, Jadwiga Bogdańska, married a politician, Tadeusz Rutkowski (1852–1918), a leader in the Democratic-Liberal Party and the future mayor of Lwów. Not only were they frequent guests at the Stojowski home in Cracow during the 1880s, but the teenage Zygmunt helped the Rutkowskis' daughter, Zosia, prepare English translations of Polish literature for publication in England which were favorably reviewed.[11]

Figure I-1. Władysław Żeleński, Stojowski's composition teacher in Cracow. Autographed photo-postcard courtesy of ZLSC. Used by permission. All rights reserved

Maria Stojowska's other important contribution to her son's development was her social network of important personalities in the world of music. She was responsible for gaining the patronage of Princess Marcelina Czartoryska (1817–

1894), a former pupil of Chopin, who became Zygmunt's sponsor in Cracow. This led to formal music lessons in piano and composition with the eminent Polish composer Władysław Żeleński (1837–1921). Princess Czartoryska's salon also became a concert venue for the fifteen-year-old Zygmunt's orchestral debut. He performed Beethoven's Piano Concerto No. 3 at a charity concert conducted by Jan Nepomucen Hock (1868–1912). The cadenza written by Stojowski for this performance was later published by Heugel. Two years later, on March 25, 1887, just prior to leaving for Paris, Stojowski played the same concerto in Cracow's Sala Saska. Between those two performances, in November 1886, Stojowski played the Piano Quartet by Saint-Saëns at the farewell concert for Józef Adamowski (1862–1930). A cellist, Adamowski left Cracow for the United States to join the Boston Symphony Orchestra, whose concertmaster, Tymoteusz Adamowski (1858–1945), was Józef's older brother.

At the age of ten (if indeed he was born in 1870), Stojowski enrolled as a private student at the Gimnazium św. Anny. Living with his family in the country where his father, a gentleman landowner, raised horses, he was tutored at home but took exams at school. His school was affiliated with the baroque church of St. Anne, and located just around the corner from the Jagiellonian University's medieval Collegium Maius. Stojowski was one of 39 students in his graduating class of 1887, and only one of eight to graduate with distinction.[12] Some of his distinguished classmates included artist and playwright Stanisław Wyspiański (who, with the exception of Polish and philosophy, was a rather poor student with mostly passing or satisfactory grades), and artist Józef Mehoffer. The final grades for Stojowski's graduation exam (*Świadectwo Egzaminu Dojrzałości*) taken on July 1, 1887 show that Zygmunt was not only musically gifted but a brilliant student as well:

> Religion – Excellent (A)
> Latin – Excellent (A)
> Greek – Praiseworthy (B)
> Polish – Excellent with Distinction (A+)
> Russian – (not taken)
> German – Excellent (A)
> History and Geography – Excellent (A)
> Mathematics – Satisfactory (C)
> Natural Sciences:
>> a. Natural History – Praiseworthy (B)
>> b. Physics – Praiseworthy (B)
> Philosophy: Excellent (A)[13]

Madame Stojowska maintained her own musical salon at home in Cracow, where visiting international celebrities such as Hans von Bülow (1830–1894),

Anton Rubinstein (1829–1894), Maurycy Rosenthal (1862–1946) and the young Józef Hofmann (1876–1956) either performed or paid a visit. It was here that Żeleński introduced Paderewski to the Stojowski family in 1884, when Zygmunt was only fourteen, ten years younger than Paderewski.[14] During his stay in Cracow in October, Paderewski gave several farewell concerts. At the end of the month, he left for Vienna to study with Teodor Leschetitzky (1830–1915). Paderewski stayed in touch with the Stojowski family and, after settling in Vienna, wrote a lively letter to Zygmunt's mother.[15]

Stojowski's mother was also responsible for a piece of musical memorabilia that became famously known as the "priceless fan." It was a hand-carved sandalwood fan with parchment folds, given to her by the Romanian Princess, Catherine Stourdza.[16] Stojowska used the fan as her personal autograph book, collecting inscriptions of leading musicians and composers. Sometimes they not only signed their names, but also added a few bars of music. By the end of her life, Madame Stojowska had collected over one hundred entries, including signatures of Eugen d'Albert, Johannes Brahms, Max Bruch, Enrico Caruso, Léo Delibes, Edward Elgar, Charles Gounod, Edward Grieg, Józef Hofmann, Josef Joachim, Édouard Lalò, Pietro Mascagni, Jules Massenet, Arthur Nikisch, Ignacy Jan Paderewski, Edward Reszke, Anton Rubinstein, Camille Saint-Saëns, Pablo Sarasate, Marcella Sembrich, Richard Strauss, Ambroise Thomas, Arturo Toscanini, Giuseppe Verdi, and many others.[17] The fan remained in the possession of the Stojowski family until the late 1980s when it was auctioned at Christie's.

Wherever the young Stojowski went, his devoted mother followed. She moved to Paris, traveled with Zygmunt to Paderewski's villa in Switzerland, and eventually followed her son to New York, where she remained the dowager of the Stojowski clan until her death. Artur Rubinstein (1887–1982), in recalling his 1902 visit to Riond-Bosson, described Madame Stojowska as an affected old lady who "amused everyone as if she was holding court" and whom Paderewski loved to tease.[18] Another account describing the mother-and-son visit at Riond-Bosson, quotes someone asking, "Where is Stojowski?" to which Paderewski reportedly answered, "With Mama, who is buttoning up his underwear."[19]

It was Żeleński in Cracow who actually shaped Stojowski's musical career by guiding him as a composer and pianist, and suggesting that he continue his studies in Paris, where Żeleński had also studied. A few years after his professor's death, Stojowski wrote:

> Żeleński…developed an unimpeachable technique, retained artistic ideals uncompromisingly pure and noble, encountered genuine and abundant inspiration. Born in 1837, he contributed a long list of works to Poland's credit, several operas . . . many symphonic and chamber works and a treasury of songs imbued with deep song feeling, conceived in a manly lyrical vein.[20]

Żeleński's admiration for Stojowski is expressed in a dedication of his *Suite de Danses Polonaises pour Orchestre,* Op. 47, published by P. Jurgenson in Moscow.

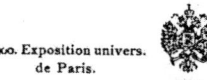

Endnotes

1 *Księga Heraldyczna Królestwa Polskiego* [The Register of Polish Heraldry]

2 *LMM*, "Nouvelles Diverses."

3 E-mail from Alfred Stojowski on November 20, 2001.

4 Ibid.

5 Stojowski, *Paderewski as I Knew Him*, 1031.

6 Stojowski *Letters to Maria Mickiewicz* (Dec 19, 1928).

7 Thirteenth Census of the United States: 1910—Population.

8 Paderewski, *Telegram of condolence.*

9 *EMTA*, "Z filharmonii.*"*

10 Dybowski, *Zapomniany Zygmunt Stojowski,* 35.

11 Kramarz, 41, 52

12 Archiwa Gimnazjum Liceum im. B. Nowodworskiego (Cracow), Folder 194 "Protokół spisany archiwa powodu egzaminu dojrzałości odbytego Archiwa Gimnazjum św. Anny Archiwa w terminie od 30 czerwca do 6 lipca 1887."

13 Archiwa Gimnazjum Liceum im. B. Nowodworskiego (Cracow), Folder 194 "Protokóły egzaminu dojrzałości, 1881–1890," 412.

14 Stojowski, *Paderewski as I Knew Him*, 1030.

15 Paderewski, *Letter to Marie Stojowska.*

16 Anon., "The Lady and the Fan."

17 Anon., "A Priceless Fan."

18 Rubinstein, 81–82.

19 Jasieński, 23.

20 Stojowski, *The Music of Poland,* 558.

Chapter Two

TRIUMPH IN PARIS

After finishing his studies in Cracow, Stojowski left for Paris in 1887, the year work on the Eiffel Tower began. The obstacles that the seventeen-year-old youth faced in getting admitted to the Conservatoire National were formidable. Although he came bearing the highest recommendation of Żeleński, Stojowski still had to endure the rigorous entrance exam audition. Before leaving for France, Stojowski wrote to Léo Delibes (1836–1891), the famous opera and ballet composer and professor of composition at the Conservatoire, for advice on taking his entrance exam. Delibes replied with several suggestions about the sight reading portion of the exam. He advised Stojowski not to play too fast and to make sure that he played with musical expression. Delibes' advice worked.[1] Of the hundred candidates who auditioned, only ten could be admitted, and only one of the ten could be a foreigner.[2] The jury's decision was unanimous: Stojowski was accepted. He became a pupil of Louis Diémer (1843–1919) in piano, Léo Delibes in composition, and Théodore Dubois (1837–1924) in harmony. In addition to his classes at the Conservatoire, Stojowski also studied history, philosophy, languages and literature at the Faculté des Lettres of the Sorbonne University, where he received his Bachelor of Letters Diploma.

Stojowski's initial year at the Conservatoire coincided with Diémer's first year as a professor there. As a teacher, Diémer produced a cavalcade of internationally famous pianists, including Édouard Risler, Alfred Cortot, Alfredo Casella, Robert Casadesus, and the organist Marcel Dupré.

Stojowski probably met Peter Ilyich Tchaikovsky (1840–1893) through Diémer and was befriended by the Russian composer. Tchaikovsky arrived in Paris to perform his *Concert Fantasy* in G Major, Op. 56 in a two piano version with Diémer on March 4 and 16, 1888. It was to Diémer that Tchaikovsky dedicated his Piano Concerto No. 3 in E-flat Major, Op. 75. Impressed by Stojowski's

Figure II-1. Stojowski in his twenties. Photograph courtesy of ZLSC.
Used by permission.

linguistic skills in Polish, Russian, French, English, German, ancient Greek and Latin, Tchaikovsky—who spoke no English—asked Stojowski to translate for the rehearsals of the British premiere of his Fourth Symphony with the London Symphony Orchestra on May 20, 1893.[3] The performance was in conjunction with Cambridge University's bestowal of honorary doctorates upon Tchaikovsky, Grieg, Max Bruch, and Camille Saint-Saëns, all conferred in a single ceremony. In return for his services, Stojowski received the copy of Tchaikovsky's marked full score, autographed with a dedication to Zygmunt in French: *A mon cher jeune ami Sigismond Stojowski, Souvenir affectueux*.[4] During his London visit, Stojowski gave a recital at Princes' Hall featuring an all-Slavic program that included the music of Tchaikovsky.[5] Stojowski was heard playing Tchaikovsky's piano works once more in a Paris recital sponsored by Tchaikovsky's French publisher, Edition Mackar et Noël, at the beginning of 1895.[6] In addition to performing Stojowski's compositions in France and abroad, Diémer collaborated with his pupil in celebrating the fiftieth anniversary of Chopin's death by performing Chopin's Rondo for two pianos in C Major, Op. 73 at a concert organized by Polish émigré circles in Paris. Diémer also appeared on Stojowski's 1891 Paris debut, performing four of his student's piano miniatures.

Figure II-2. Tchaikovsky photo with dedication in Polish to Zygmunt's mother. Photograph courtesy of International Piano Archives at the University of Maryland, College Park. Used by permission.

Stojowski graduated from the Conservatoire in 1889, the year the Eiffel Tower was officially opened. In a way, his musical education is symbolically linked with the beginning and completion of this powerful symbol of the modern age. He also won the Conservatoire's top prizes. Fourteen male pianists competed by playing *Allegro de Concert* for Piano and Orchestra by the American-born composer, Ernest Guiraud (1837–1892).[7] The First Prize was shared by Édouard Risler, who has been described as Diémer's "favorite student,"[8] Andreas Bloch and Stojowski, *trois artistes remarquables*.[9] Although Bloch quickly disappeared from Parisian musical life, Risler was active in Paris until the end of his life. He was also the dedicatee of Stojowski's *Polish Idylls for Piano,* Op. 24.

Eleven contestants competed for the school's highest honors in counterpoint and fugue. The jury included the Conservatoire's director, Ambroise Thomas[10] and other distinguished musicians: August Ernest Bazille, Henri Dallier, Théodore Dubois, Henri Fissot, César Franck, Benjamin Godard, George Mathias and Raul Pugno. Stojowski later recalled the competition:

> The candidates were locked in a room from six in the morning until twelve at night, with a few bars of a theme given by the Director to spin out, with permission to have luncheon brought in and, of course, no piano open. I must confess that when I walked out I felt a bit dizzy. My success with the fugue appeared to make Delibes very happy: I seemed to be his first student getting a prize for so serious a thing.[11]

Stojowski became the first Pole (or Russian national for that matter) to claim such distinction in the school's 82-year history. He also joined the ranks of other famous composers who won the highly coveted First Prize in counterpoint and fugue, including Franck, Dubois, Massenet, Pierné, Debussy, Dukas, and Ravel, among others.[12]

According to Stojowski, the teachers who influenced him most as a musician were violinist-composer Władysław Górski (1846–1915), and pianist-composer Paderewski.[13] Górski, who was the soloist with the Lamoureux Orchestra in Paris, offered a course on the interpretation of chamber music, *Leçons d'Accompagnement,* in which Stojowski must have participated. The two concertized together throughout Europe, and Górski was the dedicatee for Stojowski's *Variations and Fugue for String Quartet,* Op. 6 and the Violin Concerto in G, Op. 22. Stojowski credits Górski for being his guide for "extreme refinement and catholicity of taste."[14]

The friendship between Paderewski and Górski dated from Paderewski's student days (1873–1878) at the Warsaw Music Institute, where Górski was a professor. After completing his studies, Paderewski joined Górski on the Musical Institute's faculty. Later they moved to Paris. As a violinist, Górski often performed Paderewski's violin works, including an appearance on the second of two debut recitals in Paris on March 8, 1888. Later, Górski shared his talent and fame by performing with Stojowski, helping to attract audiences to the young composer's appearances.

Paderewski married Antonia Korsakówna in Warsaw in 1880. The marriage lasted less than a year, since his wife died from complications after childbirth. Their son, Alfred, died in 1901. As a widower living in Paris, Paderewski frequented the Górskis' home on Rue Boissière not only to visit his invalid son (who was cared for by the Górskis), but also for the weekly Friday musical soirées "at which Paderewski appeared whenever he was in town."[15] Paderewski also fell in love with Górski's wife Helena (née Rosen), and eventually was able to convince Władysław,

Figure II-3. Władysław Górski. Courtesy of the Paderewski Museum, Morges, Switzerland. Used by permission. All rights reserved

who could not fail to notice his wife's obvious infatuation with his younger colleague, to have his marriage with Helena annulled by the Roman Catholic Church. The grounds for annulment were that Helena married Władysław at an early age, supposedly without the permission of her father. In 1874, the year of Helena's marriage, she was only eighteen—two years too young to be married without her father's written permission under Imperial Russian law. The space on the wedding certificate for the father's permission was left blank. However, an annotation on the marriage certificate for Władysław Górski and Helena Rosen at St. John the Baptist Cathedral on Świętojańska Street in Warsaw's Old Town stated that Helena's father gave permission to his underage daughter "in person."[16] As soon as the annulment was granted, Ignacy and Helena were married on May 31, 1899, at Holy Ghost Catholic Church on the corner of Freta and Długa Streets near Warsaw's Old Town.

It was at the Górskis that Zygmunt and his mother first met the famous Polish writer Henryk Sienkiewicz (1846–1916), the author of *Quo vadis?* and Poland's first Nobel Prize laureate (1905). In a letter written from Paris in October 1888, Sienkiewicz describes an evening spent with the Górskis, Stojowskis, Władysław Mickiewicz, who is described as "the worst kind of windbag," the journalist Teodor Jeske-Choiński, and an unidentified American woman. At that time, Stojowski would have been at the beginning of his second year of studies at the Conservatoire. Although Sienkiewicz makes no comment on Zygmunt, he does refer to Mrs. Górska and Mrs. Stojowska as having been "highly courteous."[17]

Stojowski began lessons with Paderewski in 1891, after Paderewski's first triumphant tour of the United States. Prior to World War I, Stojowski was one of only four pianists who could claim that they ever took regular lessons with Paderewski over a long period of time. Initially, Paderewski's students included American pianist, Ernest Schelling (1876–1939), and Antonina Szumowska-Adamowska (1868–1938), a cousin of Paderewski's wife, Helena. British-born Harold Bauer (1873–1951), who began his musical career as concert violinist, started coaching with Paderewski in 1893. The encounter with Paderewski convinced Bauer to become a concert pianist and put the violin aside.[18] Other pianists who claimed to have studied with Paderewski in Paris included composer-pianist Józef Zygmunt Szulc (1875–1956) and Swedish pianist-composer, Lennart Lunberg (1863–1931). If they indeed studied with Paderewski, their lessons must have been rare, given Paderewski's heavy touring schedule. Unlike Stojowski, they were not honored by being invited for annual summer visits to study with Paderewski in Switzerland. Recalling those summers, Stojowski wrote "…My summer vacations would always conclude at Paderewski's villa in Morges where, in equal measure, I was subjected to unparalleled hospitality and wonderful artistic inspiration."[19] Musicologist Małgorzata Perkowska mentions Eugénie Bartholoni (1889–1940) as another Paderewski pupil. Besides several letters from her to Paderewski at the Archiwum Akt Nowych in Warsaw, no further information on her studies with Paderewski can be found.[20] In the late 1930s, Witold Małcużyński (1914–1977) also took some lessons with Paderewski. Other pianists, such as Stojowski's protégé Alexander Brachocki (1897–1948), Zygmunt Dygat (1894–1977), Stanisław Szpinalski (1901–1957),[21] Henryk Sztompka (1901–1964), and Albert Tadlewski (1892–1945), studied with Paderewski only at summer master classes held at Riond-Bosson during the years 1928–1932.[22] British pianist Adela Verne (1877–1952),[23] took four or five lessons with Paderewski, but according to a letter written by the Scranton-born Brachocki, Paderewski did not consider her to be included in the inner circle of students, nor was Harold Bauer for that matter.[24] If Brachocki's comments about who Paderewski considered a student of his are true, then Stojowski becomes one of only three, not four, early Paderewski students.

Stojowski always agreed with this assessment. The same claim is made in Charles Phillips' biography of Paderewski.[25] However, not everyone who has referred to Phillips' book has read the book's dedication:

To
Paderewski's Friend
And Mine
SIGISMOND STOJOWSKI
Musician and Scholar
Without Whose Help This
Biography Could Not Have
Been Written.[26]

Stojowski, who is mentioned more than a dozen times throughout the book, was most certainly an invaluable source of information on Paderewski for the author, and likely had a strong hand in helping him write this book.

In Stojowski's estimation, Paderewski was "the model and ideal of the virtuoso and poet-musician" and the master whose influence had been decisive in his own work.[27] Their admiration was mutual. According to Paderewski, Stojowski was "one of the few really great piano pedagogues of the present day, [who] occupies a very prominent position, for he has no superior."[28] To his mentor Stojowski dedicated the Sonata in G Major for Piano and Cello, Op. 18, Symphony in D Minor, Op. 21, Prologue, Scherzo, and Variations, Op. 32, and Lullaby for Piano (1941). In turn, Paderewski reciprocated by featuring Stojowski's music in his programs, including *Chant d'amour* and *By the Brookside* (which he later recorded), the Second Piano Concerto (which he performed with the New York Symphony and the Boston Symphony Orchestras), and *Sérénade* Op. 8, no. 3 which Paderewski first performed at the Salle Erard in Paris as a surprise name-day present for the nineteen-year-old Zygmunt on May 2, 1899, the feast of Saint Sigismond.[29]

Paris became Stojowski's home for eighteen years. At first, until more permanent living quarters could be arranged, he and his mother lived at the Hôtel Cusset at 95, Rue Richelieu,[30] the street on which the Bibliothèque Nationale is now located. In *Paderewski as I Knew Him*, Stojowski mentions that Paderewski would frequent this hotel when visiting Paris in the late 1880s. Later, Paderewski rented a ground-floor apartment at 94, Avenue Victor Hugo, and the Stojowskis moved into an apartment at 25, Boulevard Malesherbes, residing in this smart neighborhood until the autumn of 1895.[31] They were just a short walk from the magnificent Church of La Madeleine,[32] where Zygmunt's harmony professor Dubois was the organist from 1877 to 1896. Stojowski's final move in Paris was to

Figure II-4. Ignacy Jan Paderewski. Photograph courtesy of Archiwum Akt Nowych, Warsaw. Used by permission. All rights reserved

a street named after his composition teacher: 12, Rue Léo Delibes.[33] Paderewski's and Stojowski's apartments were in reasonable walking distance from each other, and were located in the now very fashionable sixteenth district of Paris on the Right Bank of the Seine. Other Polish musicians who lived in the neighborhood were Władysław Górski (first on Rue Boissière; later at 104, Rue de la Tour[34]), and Henryk Opieński (1870–1942)[35] who lived at 22, Rue Vital from 1894 to 1897.

Opieński, who graduated from the Gimnazium św. Anny in Cracow one year after Stojowski, came to Paris to study violin with Górski and theory and composition

Figure II-5. The Church of the Madeleine, Stojowski's parish church while he lived at 25, Boulevard Malesherbes. Collection of the author

with his peer, Stojowski.[36] When Stojowski left Paris in 1905, his apartment was taken over by another Polish pianist, Jadwiga Wierzbicka (ca. 1880–ca. 1945). Based on advertisements found in *Le Monde musical*, Wierzbicka appears to have lived there until the spring of 1914.[37]

Stojowski's composition teacher, Delibes, was so proud of his student that he and his wife offered to legally adopt him, so that he could compete for the prestigious Prix de Rome, a competition for which only French nationals were eligible.[38] One of Delibes' biographers described the composer as "a dedicated, enthusiastic teacher, extremely proud of his students' accomplishments," also claiming that a first prize in fugue by a student meant more to him than any other of his own successes.[39] Małgorzata Perkowska, the author of the Delibes entry in the Polish Encyclopedia of Music erroneously states that Delibes' wife was of Polish descent. All sources on Delibes confirm that Madame Delibes—Leontine Estelle Mesnage, also known as Denain—was a daughter of the former tragedian of the Comédie-Française."[40] If there was a Polish connection, it had to have been much further back in the family tree. Before Delibes' untimely death in 1891, Paderewski came to Delibes' home to look over the ballet music to his last opera, *Kasya*. According to Stojowski, Paderewski supplied Delibes with several Polish folk tunes for the opera, which is based on a Polish subject and set in the southeastern region of Poland, known as Galicia. Stojowski also recalled that Delibes had a good sense of humor:

> Again Paderewski appeared as the stern and uncompromising judge. Delighted with Delibes' harmonizations, he yet at certain times used the word "banal." "Don't say that, dear friend," Delibes objected. "Say rather, 'This is too Parisian' or 'Perhaps too Delibian.'"[41]

Delibes must have been fascinated by Poland since both *Kasya* and his more famous ballet, *Coppélia*, take place in southeastern Poland. Before writing *Kasya,* Delibes spent several months in Poland collecting folk song motives and Gypsy melodies for his opera. In addition to visiting Cracow, the ancient capital of Poland, he also visited Lwów (now Lviv), a colorful Eastern European metropolis which was the regional capital of Galicia. The population of Lwów consisted mainly of Poles, Jews, Ruthenians and Ukrainians, with other minorities—Germans, Russians, Armenians, Slovaks and Gypsies—complimenting the multi-national character of the city. Delibes also spent time in the Polish mountains, including a visit to Zakopane.[42]

Based on correspondence between Delibes and Paderewski found in Warsaw's Archiwum Akt Nowych, it is known that while Stojowski studied with Delibes, the French master occasionally sent Stojowski's compositions to Paderewski for comments. It is safe to assume that Stojowski's earliest published compositions had both Paderewski's *nihil obstat* as well as Delibes' *imprimatur.*

Stojowski paid homage to his teacher by dedicating *Le printemps,* Op. 7 to Delibes. The dedication reads : *A la Mémoire de son bien aimé Maître Léo Delibes.* Another salute to his teacher can be found in *Intermède polonaise,* the second movement of Stojowski's Suite in E-flat, Op. 9, where the music's lilting flow reminds the listener of ballet masterpieces by Delibes or Tchaikovsky.

Had Stojowski taken up Delibes' offer to become his adopted son and a French citizen, he might have never moved to the United States. Delibes' gesture may have resulted from the fact that only French nationals could teach at the Conservatoire. In Paris, Stojowski was only able to teach privately, and his advertisements for lessons in piano, composition, theory and orchestration, which took place in Stojowski's apartment, can be found in *Le Monde musical* starting from 1893. Although the Conservatoire never honored Stojowski with an invitation to serve on the competition jury (as they had honored Chopin and Paderewski), they nonetheless commissioned from him the *Fantasie pour trombone,* for the trombone class competition in 1905. Most probably, the *Romance for Flute and Piano,* written after Stojowski left Paris for New York and now lost, was also commissioned by Stojowski's alma mater.

The concert that launched Stojowski's international career as pianist and composer was his first orchestral concert in Paris at the Salle Erard in February 1891. Substituting for an "indisposed" Charles Colonne, French composer Benjamin Godard (1849–1895) conducted the Orchestre Colonne in an all-Stojowski program, including the Ballade for Orchestra (which is still unpublished), the second movement from his Suite for Orchestra and Piano Concerto No. 1, Op. 3 with the 21-year-old pianist-composer performing on the piano.[43] The program also featured Stojowski's String Quartet, two songs and four solo piano pieces.

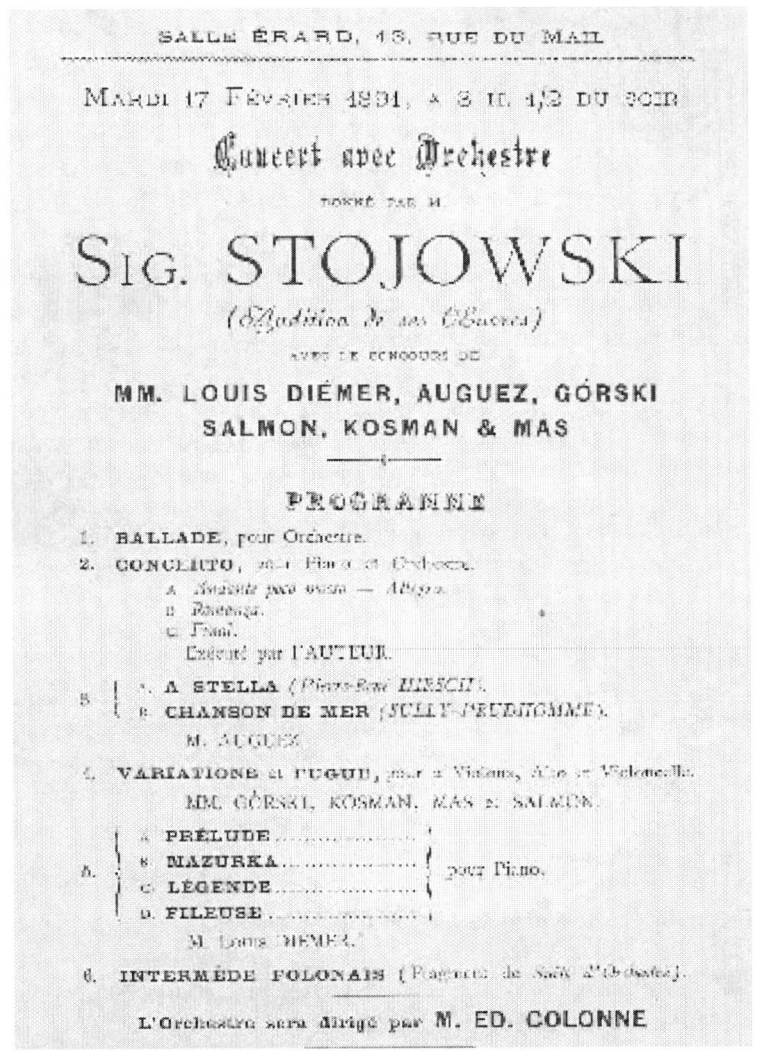

Figure II-6. Courtesy of ZLSC. Used by permission. All rights reserved.

Following his debut as a composer, Stojowski played recitals in France, Belgium, England, and Poland.[44] From that moment on, his career skyrocketed: he performed with the best orchestras and his music was played by them. In Germany he appeared with the philharmonic orchestras of Berlin, Hamburg, Leipzig and Munich; in England with Sir Charles Hallé's (1819–1895) Orchestra in Manchester, the Grand Orchestra of the Crystal Palace, and the London Symphony Orchestra. Queen Victoria's Private Band premiered the English version of Stojowski's entertaining cantata, *Le printemps,* at a command performance for Her Majesty on July 5, 1895, in Buckingham Palace.[45] In his hometown of Cracow, Stojowski was "greeted with joy as a favorite son," when he came to perform Liszt's Piano Concerto No. 1 in E-flat in January 1893.[46] Lwów's newly founded Philharmonic Orchestra featured Stojowski as a soloist in the second of three inaugural concerts that took place on September 27, 1902.

Famous playwright and music critic, George Bernard Shaw, was in the audience at Stojowski's London recital in May 1891. In the May 15 issue of *The World* he tersely praised the young pianist: "Another Pole, Stojowski, has given one recital at Princes' Hall. He can play, and that very cleverly; but he did not leave the impression that his musical ability is irresistibly specialized for the pianoforte."[47]

Stojowski's concerts in Paris were always favorably received by the critics and public throughout his eighteen years there. A 1902 review states that:

> Mr. Sig. Stojowski, already highly regarded for a long time by both the Parisian and foreign musical establishment, this year presented to the public a superb program and, rare indeed, one very well constructed. After the beautiful Variations and Fugue by Brahms, came the 8th *Novellette* and the *Nachstück* of Schumann, where the artist demonstrated the most beautiful qualities of style. The Sonata (Op. 58) by Chopin made it clear, through an impeccable and accomplished execution, that Mr. Stojowski truly understands the so distinct style of Chopin's music. Above all he played the *Largo* with a delicate touch and an admirable quality of sound. The Prelude, Aria and Finale by César Frank and the *Choeur des fileuses du vaisseau fantôme* by Wagner-Liszt was a tremendous success for the appealing artist, who also showed himself to be a talented composer (something we have already known for a long time) with the performance of his *3 Pièces romantiques* of which the last, above all, had a great success. Finally, he finished with the magnificent *Staccato Etude* by Rubinstein which earned him warm applause.[48]

Three other events in *fin-de-siècle* Paris also brought Stojowski recognition as a pianist and composer. The first was the observance of the fiftieth anniversary of the death of Frédéric Chopin, the second was the premiere of Stojowski's Violin Concerto, and the third was the World's Fair of 1900.

Chopin's anniversary celebration was organized by the Polish Society of

Arts and Literature on December 29, 1899 and held at the Salle Pleyel.[49] Stojowski not only performed Chopin's Rondo for Two Pianos with Diémer, but he also appeared on the program as soloist, playing a Polonaise, two Mazurkas and then accompanied the cellist Paul Bazelaire[50] in a performance of Chopin's *Introduction et Polonaise*. The music journal *Le Ménestrel* described Stojowski's rendition of the Polonaise in C Minor as "impeccable."[51] The concert also featured the violinist Górski and soprano Wanda Stajewska.[52]

The premiere of Stojowski's Violin Concerto once more saw Górski as the featured soloist, this time with the Orchestre Chevillard in March 1900. The critics hailed the composition, stating that this major work confirmed Stojowski's importance as a composer. The review further praised the Concerto's solid construction, several lovely themes that were skillfully developed, and the violin part that was "sustained by an orchestration of rich coloration." As to the violinist, Górski played with "laudable conviction and a consummate virtuosity."[53] Only a month before the premiere, Stojowski had taken part in a chamber music concert of his works at the Les Mathurins with the assistance of his piano professor Louis Diémer, violinist Madame Howland, soprano Mademoiselle Deshays, tenor Carl Furstenberg and pianist J. Berny.[54]

The Exposition Universelle of 1900 was a monumental international trade event which also included the music industry. The Eiffel Tower was intended to be the entrance arch for the fair, marking the centenary of the French Revolution. The Pont Alexandre III with its massive pillars and the Grand Palais with its gigantic glass cupola are two other architectural jewels connected with the World Fair that continue to grace Paris skyline between the Left Bank and Champs-Élysées. The French music industry alone had over a hundred vendors, occupying 3,000 square meters of exhibition space. The United States of America was the Fair's second largest musical representative with thirty American companies displaying musical instruments from Baldwin pianos made in Cincinnati to zithers and harps made by the Flagg Manufacturing Co. in Boston.[55] The French organized a series of five concerts, including a cantata *Le Feu celeste*, commissioned from Saint-Saëns. The other musical extravaganzas included works by Fauré, d'Indy and Massenet.[56] The Americans, on the other hand, sent John Philip Sousa and his concert band to entertain the crowds.

Coinciding with the Fair, which ran from April 14 to November 12, was an exhibition of musical autographs organized by the Bibliothèque du Musée de l'Opera. The exhibit consisted of 694 contributions by living composers who wrote out the beginning of one of their compositions on out-of-the-ordinary decorative music paper and then signed and dated the manuscript as well as including their address. Zygmunt Stojowski was one of twent-seven Polish composers represented at the exhibit of musical autographs.[57] Stojowski submitted the first 26 bars of his *Prélude* from *Deux Pensées Musicales pour piano*, Op. 1 no. 2.[58]

As a Polish composer living in Paris, Stojowski also achieved international acclaim. In Germany, his Symphony in D Minor, Op. 21 won First Prize and 1,000 Rubles[59] at the 1898 Paderewski Competition for Polish Composers in Leipzig. This Symphony (with a revised last movement) was part of the November 5, 1901 inaugural concert of the newly formed Warsaw Philharmonic Orchestra.[60] Another competition in 1901 brought Stojowski Second Prize (First Prize was not awarded) for his *Fantazja Polska* [Polish Fantasy for Piano and Orchestra] at the Maurycy Zamoyski Competition in Warsaw.[61] In 1894, Stojowski signed an exclusive contract with the publisher Stanley Lucas, Weber, Pitt & Hatzfeld Ltd., in London that lasted until 1900. After that, Schott & Co. in England, Peters in Germany, Heugel in France, Gebethner & Wolff in Poland and Arthur P. Schmidt in Germany and America, and G. Schirmer in the United States published his compositions.

Stojowski was also hailed as Poland's foremost symphonist, based on European rather than provincial or nationalistic standards. His name can be found in every Polish music history book dealing with the late nineteenth and early twentieth centuries. With Noskowski, Nowowiejski, Paderewski and Karłowicz, he was included in every list of outstanding post-romantic composers, and his Symphony has been referred to as "a jewel of the Polish symphonic literature."[62] The Symphony's fantastic *Scherzo* was frequently performed separately by such conductors as Nikisch, Młynarski and Fitelberg.

Unfortunately, the Symphony was not universally acclaimed. Following its performance in Paris with Emil Młynarski conducting the Orchestre Colonne in 1903, Claude Debussy wrote about Stojowski's composition and Polish music in general. He was unsympathetic to both. Debussy's review, *At the Concert Colonne* reeks of cynicism and snobbery:

> A very fine concert where French music found itself in the company of Polish. (Long live Poland, sir!) Naturally, I am not going to speak to you of the French music. It was represented by Lalo, Massenet, and Bruneau. Just to quote their names means I need say no more. As for the Polish music, until now I have had only a prejudiced viewpoint. The Symphony in D Minor by S. Stojowski won a prize (inaugurated by Paderewski) over all other works by Polish composers. It doesn't make one want to know the rest. We were told in advance that it had been enthusiastically received and heralded as a highly important work. If anyone asks, I will agree with this opinion as it was given to me in the program. As for the rest, I must admit that Noskowski's *The Steppe* had a certain flow, and it seemed that Cossacks were circling around giving out apache cries. Mme Bolska[63] sings very well, and M. Mlynarski,[64] conductor of the Polish orchestra, dampened his shirt collar with dignity.[65]

CONCERTS-COLONNE

THÉATRE DU CHATELET

Dimanche 29 Mars 1903, à 2 h. 1/4

(Vingt-unième Concert de l'abonnement)

AVEC LE CONCOURS DE Mme

BOLSKA

de l'Opéra Impérial de Saint-Pétersbourg

M.

MLYNARSKI

Chef d'orchestre de la Société Philharmonique
et de l'Opéra Impérial de Varsovie

ET DE M.

BARCEWICZ ET STOJOWSKI

Première partie

SOUS LA DIRECTION DE

M. ED. COLONNE

OUVERTURE DU « ROI D'YS »........... ED. LALO.

ESCLARMONDE.................................. J. MASSENET.
a) *Hyménée.*
b) *Scène (D'une longue torpeur).*

Mme BOLSKA.

LA BELLE AU BOIS DORMANT (2e Aud.).. ALFRED BRUNEAU.
Poème symphonique.

Deuxième partie

SOUS LA DIRECTION DE

M. MLYNARSKI

SYMPHONIE EN RÉ MINEUR, Op. 21... STOJOWSKI.
I. *Andante mesto, Allegro.* — II. *Andante.*
III. *Scherzo.* — IV. *Allegro con fuoco.*

ADAGIO ET FINALE DU 2e CONCERTO. WIENIAWSKI.
M. BARCEWICZ.

QUATRE MÉLODIES POLONAISES :

a) LE MESSAGE............................. ZELENSKI.

b) J'AI TANT ENDURÉ, TANT SOUFFERT PADEREWSKI.

c) MIGNON.................................... MONIUSZKO.

d) POUR TOI SEUL.......................... CHOPIN.

Mme BOLSKA.

LA STEPPE, Poème symphonique. Op. 66... NOSKOWSKI.

PIANO ÉRARD

CE PROGRAMME EST DISTRIBUÉ GRATUITEMENT

Prière de ne pas entrer ni sortir pendant l'exécution des morceaux.

Figure II-7. Courtesy of ZLSC. Used by permission. All rights reserved

Fortunately for Stojowski, Młynarski believed in this exceptional work. He not only conducted it at the inaugural concert of the Warsaw Philharmonic in 1901, but also gave repeated performances of the Symphony in Great Britain and Denmark. In addition, he conducted the *Scherzo* movement with the Vienna Philharmonic at a program of Polish symphonic music in March 1921. The Austrian critic, Dr. Walther Klein, began his review of that concert by stating that the Viennese had been so busy with their own musical revolution, which they thought was taking on a worldwide scale, that they became totally unaware of what was happening on the other side of the Carpathian Mountains. Stojowski was described as a brilliant member of a completely different musical world. The critic found the *Scherzo* to be ingenious and full of French flair. "Stojowski's music is extremely witty. The composer knows well how to ensure that everything new and significant is also endearing." Among other composers on the program, including Szymanowski, Noskowski and Karłowicz, apparently only Stojowski showed any musical sense of humor. The critic went on to praise Młynarski's talent, writing that he belonged to a small group of truly great conductors.[66]

Figure II-8. Stojowski on the S.S. Isle de France in late 1920s. Courtesy of ZLSC. Used by permission. All rights reserved

Endnotes

[1] This undated letter is in the possession of the composer's great granddaughter, Lisa Stojowski, who purchased it on eBay in 2005. It had originally been one of many letters from famous composers that once belonged to the collection. To mention only a few, among the correspondence that was sold, there were letters from Brahms, Delibes, Debussy, Paderewski, Saint-Saëns and Tchaikovsky. Sold to various collectors by Henry Stojowski over the years, with the exception of the Tchaikovsky letters, Henry did not have the letters transcribed or copied for posterity's sake.

[2] Reiss, *Stakowski, Melcer, Młynarski, Stojowski,* 20. In ZS' *Untitled Resume,* the composer writes that there were over 250 (!) candidates.

[3] Stojowski was in England with pianist Antonina Szumowska and violinist Władysław Górski, who were accompanying Paderewski on his tour. Paderewski also arranged concerts there for all three musicians. See: *EMTA* (May 29, 1893), 272.

[4] Stojowski, *Untitled Résumé,* ZLSC. The Tchaikovsky score was auctioned at Sotheby's in December 2000. The score played an important role in the musical career of Stojowski's student Antonia Brico.

[5] *MT,* Jul 1, 1893, 408.

[6] *LMM,* "Edition Mackar et Noël."

[7] At this time in history, there were two faculties at the Conservatoire based on gender: one for the female students and one for the male students. Paderewski served as a juror for the women's piano competition in 1889.

[8] Bongrain, 71.

[9] *LMM,* "Conservatoire de Musique," (July 30, 1889).

[10] The French have a saying about Thomas' music which goes, "Il y a de la bonne musique, de la mauvaise, et celle d'Ambroise Thomas". [There's good music, bad music, and there's the music of Ambroise Thomas.]

[11] Armstrong.

[18] "Biographical Sketch" in *The Harold Bauer Collection*. Washington, DC: The Library of Congress, 1995, http://www.loc.gov/rr/perform/special/bauer.html (April 3, 2005).

[19] Stojowski, *Paderewski in Light of My Recollections and Beliefs,* online English translation, paragraph 11.

[20] Perkowska-Waszek, *O Paderewskim*, 626.

[21] See Stojowski Catalogue for piano works edited and arranged by Szpinalski.

[22] Zamoyski, 220–221.

[23] Adela Verne was the mother of the composer and pianist John Vallier (1920–1991). Verne also composed and is credited for a march which she wrote for Queen Elizabeth, the Queen Mother, during World War II, entitled *H.M. Queen Elizabeth's March*. The Queen Mother had been taught to play the piano by Verne's sister Matilda (1865–1936).

[24] Brachocki, *Letter to Wife*: August 7, 1932.

[25] Phillips, 173.

[26] Phillips, dedication page, not paginated.

[27] Stojowski. *Biographical Data.*

[28] Paderewski. Letter of Recommendation.

[29] *LMM*, "Deuxième et troisième recitals Paderewski." This performance of the *Sérénade* is not listed in Perkowska-Waszek's *Dariusz koncertowy Paderewskiego.*

[30] One hundred and twenty years later, there still exists a hotel at this sight now called the *Cusset Opera*, part of the Mercure-Accord hotel chain. Number 95 is found in the second *arrondisement* on the corner of Rue d'Amboise and Rue de Richelieu, near the Richelieu-Druot Metro station.

[31] Stojowski. *Paderewski…*, 1032.

[32] *LMM,* Advertisement, (May 1895), 323.

[33] There is a "Polish connection" to the Madeleine. In Poznań (Posen), Poland on December 2, 1806, Napoleon signed a decree ordering the building of a temple to the glory of the French armies on the sight of the unfinished Madeleine Church. After his defeat during the Russian campaign of 1812, Napoleon reverted to the original plan of building a church.

[34] *LMM,* "Advertisement," (October 15, 1895), 194.

[35] Polish composer Alexandre Tansman also lived on this same street prior to World War II.

[36] Like Stojowski, Opieński first studied composition with Władysław Żeleński in Cracow. After he finished his studies in Paris, Opieński further studied composition in Berlin under Heinrich Urban, thanks to financial aid from Paderewski. Opieński wore many musical hats. He was a violinist, a member of the original Warsaw Philharmonic Orchestra from 1901 to 1904; a conductor, the first conductor of the Warsaw Philharmonic Orchestra Chorus; a teacher and a prolific composer. He was able to combine his conducting and composing skills when he became the first music director of the Teatr Polski in Warsaw (1913–1914). He was also a music critic and musicologist who wrote numerous articles on Polish music. In 1926, Opieński relocated to Morges, where he not only became involved in the musical life of the Swiss canton in which Morges is located, but where he also became a regular

bridge player with Paderewski at his Riond-Bosson villa. The municipality of Morges has remembered its former Polish residents by naming streets after them: Avenue Ignace Paderewski and Allée Henri Opienski. The city also has memorial plaque to Opieński and his wife on the Grand Rue as well as a monument and museum dedicated to Paderewski which is run by an active Paderewski Society.

[37] Morawska, 164.

[38] *LMM,* "Wierzbicka Advertisements." Wierzbicka is the dedicatee of Stojowski's *By the Brookside* (*Près du ruisseau*), Op. 30, no. 3. This Parisian address is also the one that the Stojowskis gave on their son Henry's birth certificate of 1921. Luisa and Zygmunt were in France that summer when she prematurely gave birth to Henry at Fontainebleau.

[39] Stojowski. *Biographical Data.* Actually, three students of Delibes won the *Prix de Rome*: Charles René (1884), Camille Erlanger (1888) and Alexis Fournier (1891).

[40] Boston, 39–40.

[41] De Curzon, 73.

[42] Stojowski, *Paderewski as I Knew Him,* 1031.

[43] *EMTA*, "Kasia."

[44] Colonne is listed as the conductor on the printed program. A review of the concert, however, listed Godard on podium. "M. B. Godard a conduit l'orchestre en l'absence de M. Colonne retenu chez lui par une indisposition." *LMM,* "M. S. Jordan de Stojowski."

[45] Preyss, 1.

[46] *State Concert Program.* The Royal Archives, Windsor Castle.

[47] Reiss. *Almanach Muzyczny Krakowa,* 65.

[48] Shaw, 234–235.

[49] *LMM,* "M. S. Stojowski" (May 15, 1902).

[50] Chopin died in October of 1849. For some reason the Polish émigrés in Paris were not able to observe the anniversary closer to the actual date of his death.

[51] Paul Bazelaire (1886–1958) won first prize in cello at the Paris Conservatory at the age of eleven. In addition to being a performer, he was also a composer, the author of books on the cello and professor of cello at the Conservatoire for almost forty years.

[52] Anon., "Paris et Départaments."

[53] *LMM,* "Cinquantennaire de Fréderic Chopin."

[54] *LMM,* "M. Ladislas Gorski."

[55] Flyer for February 16, 1900 concert (Stojowski File, Music Reading Room, Bibliothèque Nationale, Paris.)

[56] Woollett.

[57] Talma-Davous, 611.

[58] Talma-Davous, 616–617.

[59] An album containing facsimiles of the twenty-seven Polish contributions to this exhibit is currently being prepared for publication and edited by Irena Poniatowska, retired Professor

of Musicology at Warsaw University, and Eva Talma-Davous, the former head librarian of the Music Division at the National Library in Paris.

[60] At the end of 1897, one ruble was worth $0.51 dollars (based on the French franc/Russian ruble and then the French franc/American dollar exchange rates found in the *New York Times)*. Thus, the value of the prize in American dollars was $510.00. The purchasing power of this amount in 1897 would have been the same as $11,231.04 in 2003. A year earlier in 1896, Paderewski donated 55,000 French francs (the sum reported by *Le Monde musical* in 1897) to establish a similar competition in New York for young American composers, administered by Steinway House. At that time there were 5.225 francs to one dollar and Paderewski's donation converted into $10,527.00. Its purchasing power in 2003 would have been $231,699.27. (Courtesy of the University of North Florida Library Reference Department.) According to musicologist Małgorzata Perkowska in her *Diariusz Koncertowy Ignacego Jana Paderewskiego* [The Concert Diary of Ignacy Jan Paderewski], however, the amount mentioned in *Le Ménestrel* was 50,000 francs. The most reliable source is the letter of April 21, 1896 which Paderewski sent to Mr. Steinway. The amount that Paderewski mentions is $10,000. There were three prizes to be given every three years for the best chamber music and symphonic compositions. First prize in the 1890s was $500, but by the mid-1930s it had increased to $1,000. The award was known as the Paderewski Prize of the Paderewski Fund Competition. It should not be confused with the Paderewski Testimonial Fund (1939–1959), also mentioned in this book, or with the Paderewski Foundation (1948–2001), which, for approximately the last twenty years of its existence, gave an annual Paderewski Memorial Concert at Princeton University. Some of the Paderewski Prize winners included Horatio Parker, Arthur Bird, Henry Hadley, Arthur Shepherd, Wallingford Rieger, Rubin Goldmark, Hans Heniot Levy, Paul Allen, David Stanley Smith, Allan Arthur Wilman, Herbert Elwell, William Helfer, Morris Mamorsky, David Diamond, Gardner Read, Phyllis Sampson Hoffman, David Stock, Donald Martino, Robert Wykes, Norman Krieger and Robert Kurka. [Phillips, 223–224, and various online reference sources.]

[61] During that historic first season, in addition to having his symphony played at the inaugural concert, Stojowski appeared twice as a soloist, and he had a monographic program of his works performed. Unfortunately, the Warsaw Philharmonic Orchestra not only ignored Stojowski's music during their centennial concert in November 2001, but they also neglected to program any of his music during their centennial concert season.

[62] This work was either withdrawn from the composer's catalogue or was renamed as *Rhapsodie symphonique pour Piano et Orchestre,* Op. 23, which was premiered a year before the competition.

[63] Śledziński, 440–441.

[64] Pseudonym for soprano Adelajda Skąpska (1874–1930). Bolska studied in Moscow and Milan and debuted at La Scala in 1889. She also performed with the opera companies of Bayreuth, London, Moscow, Paris, Barcelona, Vienna and Warsaw. From 1898 to 1918, she was a soloist of the Bolshoi Opera. She spent the last five years of her life in Warsaw.

[65] Emil Młynarski (1870–1935), one of Poland's most internationally famous conductors of the first half of the twentieth century. In Warsaw, he was the first conductor of the Warsaw

Philharmonic Orchestra and later served as the director of Teatr Wielki [Opera House] and the capital's music conservatory. In 1929–1931, he was the conductor of the Curtis Institute's orchestra in Philadelphia. His daughter, Aniela, married pianist Artur Rubinstein, and his other daughter, Wanda, married pianist-composer Wiktor Łabuński.

[66] Debussy, 161–162. When translated from the original French *Monsieur Croche et autres écrite* and published in Polish, Debussy's criticism did not include this derogatory review. One can only wonder if this omission was the editor's choice or an order given by the communist regime's censor.

[67] Klein. The concert, for which Młynarski had only two short rehearsals with the orchestra, also included Noskowski's *The Steppe,* Szymanowski's Second Symphony and an unidentified work by Karłowicz.

Chapter Three

PIANIST AND PROFESSOR IN AMERICA

In October 1905 (not 1906, as given in many sources), Sigismond Jordan de Stojowski sailed alone to the United States on the S.S. Moltke. His first address in the New World—12 Fifth Avenue—was in Greenwich Village, about a block and a half from Washington Square Park.[1] Stojowski came to America on the invitation of Frank Damrosch (1859–1937), founder and director of the newly formed Institute of Musical Art (IMA), to head the piano department. The Institute was located at the corner of 12th Street and Fifth Avenue, only a few blocks away from Stojowski's apartment. Damrosch interviewed Stojowski in Paris, because he was highly recommend for the position by Harold Bauer and Pablo Casals (1876–1973). Bauer was a fellow Paderewski student and Stojowski dedicated his *Rapsodie symphonique* to him. Stojowski's association with Casals began with a joint performance of his Sonata for Piano and Violoncello, Op. 18 on May 7, 1900 at the Salle Erard in Paris. After hearing Stojowski play Schumann's Sonata in F-sharp Minor, Op. 11 at his apartment, Damrosch immediately offered him the post.[2]

Although he had come to New York to teach, it did not take long for Stojowski to display his talents as a concert pianist. By January 24, 1906, he had appeared not only as a recitalist at IMA's Mendelssohn Hall, as an accompanist with violinist Willy Hess in Washington, D.C. on Christmas Day, and as a chamber musician with the Boston Symphony Quartet, but also as a concert soloist with the New York Symphony Society Orchestra, with Frank Damrosch conducting, at Carnegie Hall on Epiphany 1906, playing Saint-Saëns' Concerto No. 4 in C Minor, Op. 44.[3] This was the first of Stojowski's six appearances with the New York Philharmonic or the New York Symphony Society Orchestra during his lifetime. On January 25, 1906, music critic Richard Aldrich of the *New York Times* wrote in his review of the solo recital that the large audience had "found abundant reason for congratulation that so excellent an artist has been added to the list of musicians resident in New York." Stojowski's performance of Schumann's Sonata was described as "a superb outpouring of youthful passion and romantic ardor."[4]

New York City.

Institute of Musical Art
OF THE CITY OF NEW YORK
Endowed and Incorporated
FRANK DAMROSCH, Director
OPENS OCTOBER 11TH
At 53 5th Ave., N. E. Cor. 12th St.

Offers a thorough Musical Education to every serious student of music, professional or amateur in all branches of the art.

THE FACULTY INCLUDES :

Singing—Mme. Etelka Gerster, Mme. Hess-Burr, Mlle. Madeleine Walther, Georg Henschel, and M. Alfred Giraudet.

Sight-Singing, Chorus and Pedagogy—Mr. Frank Damrosch.

Pianoforte—Mr. Sigismund Stojowski.
Stringed Instruments—The Kneisel Quartet.

Organ—M. Gaston M. Dethier.

Theory and Composition—Mr. Percy Goetschius, Mr. Louis V. Saar.

TUITION FEES MODERATE.

For prospectus and information, apply to

THE REGISTRAR, 53 Fifth Avenue

Figure III-1. Display advertisement from the October 1, 1905 issue of *The New York Times* p. 19.

1905   EIGHTH SEASON   1906
CARNEGIE HALL

SYMPHONY CONCERTS
FOR
Young People
FRANK DAMROSCH, Director

THIRD CONCERT
Saturday Afternoon, January 6th, 1906

Mr. Sigismund Stojowski, Soloist

Programme

SYMPHONY in E Major "Lenore"
JOACHIM RAFF
(1822-1882)

Part I, Happiness of Love
Allegro; andante quasi larghetto

Part II, Separation
Tempo di marcia; agitato

Part III, Reunion in Death
Allegro; un poco più mosso (quasi stretto)

Programme continued on second page following

Figure III-2. Carnegie Hall program from Stojowski's American orchestral debut. In the upper right-hand corner, notice the advertisement for a novel by Rupert Hughes about the love life of a Polish pianist. Courtesy of ZLSC. Used by permission. All rights reserved

In addition to the orchestras of the New York Philharmonic and New York Symphony Society, other American orchestras with whom Stojowski would perform as soloist included the Metropolitan Opera, the New York Women's Symphony, the Cincinnati Symphony, the Boston Symphony, the Boston Opera Company, the Buffalo Symphony, the Indianapolis Musikverein, the New Haven Symphony, the San Francisco Symphony, and the Antonia Brico Orchestra. His concerto repertoire was relatively limited, and featured several of his own works for piano and orchestra:

Beethoven: Concerto No. 3 in C Minor, Op. 37
Beethoven: Concerto No. 4 in G Major, Op. 58
Chopin: Concerto No. 2 in F Minor, Op. 21
Liszt: Concerto No. 1 in E-flat
Rubinstein: Concerto No. 4 in D Minor, Op. 70
Saint-Saëns: Concerto No. 4 in C Minor, Op. 44
Stojowski: Concerto No. 1 in F-sharp Minor, Op. 3
Stojowski: Concerto No. 2 in A-flat Major, Op. 32
Stojowski: *Rhapsodie symphonique*, Op. 23

What impressed Stojowski the most about America? In a 1906 interview for *Musical America,* Stojowski answered by saying:

There can be only one answer to that after all the cordiality and kindness I have met with here on every side. Americans are nothing if not hospitable, and another national characteristic that has impressed me deeply is the enthusiasm that seems to be innate in each individual. I notice it so often in your business men, especially. The European business man finds his own work prosaic and tedious, and goes to it in a grumbling spirit; but the American puts his heart into it and takes genuine pleasure out of it. Love for work seems to be in the air here. The American's capacity for it is prodigious. This struck me immediately when I came here last year, just as the same thing in smaller measure had impressed me when I first went to France from Poland, for I am forced to admit that my fellow countrymen are just a bit—lazy," he laughed frankly, "and the French are really an industrious people. I know that the opposite impression prevails here, but that is because you cannot form a just estimate of them during a short stay in their capital. It is now eighteen years since I first went to Paris, and I remained there until I came to New York. As my mother lives there it is really my home still.[5]

Clearly, Stojowski had a superb command of the English language. Years later, a reporter covering Stojowski's first master classes in Los Angeles in 1924, wrote, "A Pole by birth, French in manner and gesture, he speaks with polished English which in its delicate shades of expressiveness might be the envy of many a college professor."[6]

Stojowski's domestic arrangements were settled when, in 1907, his mother sailed to America to join him. Henceforth, she supervised the household and watched over her son's career from their residence in New York's West Side at 45 West 71st Street. By 1910, Zygmunt and his mother were living at 249 West 74th Street, between Broadway and West End Ave.[7]

In the meantime, helping Stojowski down the road of fame and popularity were his friend Paderewski and America's finest music magazine, *The Etude*, which had a monthly subscriber circulation of nearly 200,000 during the Great War.[8] *The Etude* published Stojowski's *Gondoliera* from *Quatre Morceaux pour piano*, Op. 5, no. 3, and *Mélodie* from *Deux Pensées,* Op. 1, no. 1 in musical supplements to their August and December 1906 issues respectively. This was only the beginning of a thirty-five year association with the periodical for which Stojowski would supply articles, interviews, and many of the magazine's popular *Master Lessons*.

During the season following Stojowski's arrival in America, Paderewski programmed his friend's *Chant d'amour*, Op. 26, no. 4, performing it over fifty times from coast to coast.[9] By doing so, Paderewski helped establish Stojowski's name throughout America's musical centers. Thereafter, Stojowski would be introduced as "the world famous composer of *Chant d'amour*."[10] Paderewski recorded it for Victrola, and Stojowski's recording on piano roll for Ampico was still available for purchase on the Internet from the Keystone Music Roll Company in 2002. Even the flamboyant Liberace (1919–1987) came out with an arrangement of the work with the George Liberace Orchestra on his 1955 Columbia LP, *Moonlight Sonata*.[11]

Stojowski taught at IMA until the spring of 1911. Before he left IMA, he presented a set of five historical piano lecture-recitals beginning on February 4 and ending on April 1 at IMA's Mendelssohn Hall. The first was dedicated to the Baroque masters: Couperin, Daquin, Rameau, Paradisi, Scarlatti, Handel and Bach. The second, given on February 18, featured works of Haydn, Mozart and Beethoven. Stojowski's March 4 program was devoted to compositions by Weber, Schubert, Mendelssohn and Field. The fourth, performed on March 18, focused on the music of Schumann and Chopin. His last recital included contemporary music by Debussy, Saint-Saëns, Paderewski, and Moszkowski as well as works by Liszt, Brahms, Franck, Rubinstein, Grieg and MacDowell.[12] Following the opening recital, *The New York Times* praised once again Stojowski's considerable undertaking:

> He showed excellent musicianship in his appreciation of its style as can be made available upon the modern pianoforte . . . Before he began his performances he spoke at length upon some of the historical features which such a program offers for consideration in a truly embarrassing richness."[13]

The fact that Stojowski had a full teaching load and could still prepare and perform five different and demanding programs within two months is nothing short of extraordinary. His accomplishments become even more amazing when we learn that he also had performances with orchestras during the same period of time. One day after the March 18 concert, Stojowski played the American premiere of his Symphonic Rhapsody, Op. 23 with Walter Damrosch conducting the New York Symphony Society Orchestra at the New Theater,[14] and a day after his April 1 recital Stojowski gave the American premiere of his Piano Concerto No. 1 with the Metropolitan Opera House Orchestra under the direction of Josef Pasternack.[15] How many piano professors would have the courage and stamina to endure such a feat today! According to the Polish illustrated weekly *Świat*, Stojowski's historical lecture recitals were repeated in Buffalo and Chicago.[16]

Frank Damrosch offered Stojowski a three-year contract to continue as IMA's piano department head in 1911. Damrosch acknowledged that Stojowski was an excellent teacher and that he produced many of the best graduates of the school in its beginning years.[17] Stojowski turned down the offer, possibly because IMA moved to the Upper East Side on Claremont Avenue near Columbia University in 1910, while he had moved to the upper West Side. It is also possible that Stojowski did not want to commit himself for a three-year period. Whatever the reason, he began to teach at the Von Ende School of Music, located at 44 West 85th Street and recently chartered by the University of the State of New York. He worked there until 1918. At the Von Ende School, he enjoyed the distinction of being one of the highest paid teachers on the faculty. While the fee for other faculty members averaged between $25–30 for ten private half-hour lessons, Stojowski's fee was $60. Ten private one-hour lessons with Stojowski were available for $120.[18]

Stojowski taught until the end of his life. According to Stojowski's son Henry, his father also took on some private students in addition to the ones he had at IMA or the Von Ende School. Eventually, in October 1923, because of the great demand of students who wished to study with him, Stojowski was able to open his own studios in a brownstone that he bought on West 76th Street. Beginning in 1924 and lasting into the 1940s, Stojowski spent his summers giving recitals and teaching master classes throughout North America, visiting Buffalo, Chicago, Denver, Detroit (Detroit Foundation School of Music), Hartford (Hartford School of Music), Los Angeles (UCLA; West Lake School of Music), Pittsburgh, Portland, San Francisco (University of California, Berkeley; Mills College, Oakland), Seattle (University of Washington—Cornish School Summer Colony) and Washington, D.C. (Washington College of Music), as well as Manitoba, Canada (University of Manitoba), and South America (Havana, Lima, Mexico City, and Rio de Janeiro). Sometime before 1925, Stojowski also made regular trips to give lessons at The

Academy of the Holy Names, a private girls' school in Albany, New York.[19] During the summers of 1932 and 1940–1946, Stojowski was also on the faculty of the Juilliard School of Music, established in 1926 by merging IMA with the Juilliard Graduate School.[20] His Juilliard classes in the 1940s were interpretative courses on Chopin's music, with Stojowski lecturing and performing. Finally, as a septuagenarian, Stojowski traveled twice a month on the weekends to teach at the Hartford School of Music in Connecticut.

Figure III-3. Courtesy of ZLSC. Used by permission. All rights reserved

A new chapter in Stojowski's life was opened with the end of World War I. He married, and became a father. He also performed less frequently in public. Concert programs found in the Stojowski Collection at the Polish Music Center in Los Angeles indicate a hiatus of eight years (1916–1923) as an orchestral soloist. That is a very long time for a concert pianist to be off-stage, out of the limelight, and out of the minds of concert goers and impresarios. Although afterwards Stojowski continued as a recitalist, he focused more and more of his time on teaching.

Nevertheless, Stojowski's talents as a world-class pianist were required for the 1921 Testimonial Concert in Carnegie Hall. It was held to assist pianist-composer Moritz Moszkowski (1854–1925), a Polish Jew born in Breslau, Germany (now Wrocław, Poland). Stojowski and Moszkowski knew each other. In his short biography on Paderewski, Stojowski recalled Moszkowski's sense of humor:

> One time, on my way to Morges by train, I encountered the composer Moritz Moszkowski. He was a great wit... On saying that the object of my journey was a lesson with Paderewski, he observed, "Then you must have paid a lot for excess baggage—you must be carrying some heavy pieces with you." A few days later he came to Morges, and I remember a corking time between those two flashing wits.[21]

Later in their careers, Moszkowski and Stojowski dedicated works to each other: Moszkowski dedicated his 1911 Prelude and Fugue in D Minor for string orchestra, Op. 85 to Stojowski,[22] and Stojowski reciprocated with his *Fantasie* for piano, Op. 38, published in 1912. Stojowski also dedicated his first opus, *Deux Pensées Musicales pour piano,* to Moszkowski's wife, Henriette.

The Testimonial Concert for Moszkowski, held at Carnegie Hall on December 21, 1921, was one of the great pianistic extravaganzas of the twentieth century. Organized by Ernest Schelling to help the ailing and financially impoverished Moszkowski who lived in Paris, Schelling recruited fourteen of the most famous pianists living in America for this gala benefit. In addition to Schelling and Stojowski, the following pianists performed under the direction of Willem Bachaus, Harold Bauer, Alfredo Casella, Walter Damrosch, Ignaz Friedman, Ossip Gabrilowitsch, Percy Grainger, Ernest Hutcheson, Alexander Lambert, Joseph Lhèvinne, Elly Ney, Leo Ornstein, and Germaine Schnitzer. Stojowski contributed to the program by taking part in performances of Saint-Saëns' Variations for Two Pianos on a Theme by Beethoven, Schumann's *Carnaval*, Moszkowski's *Spanish Dances for Four Hands*, and Schubert's *Marche Militaire*.[23] The box office receipts came to about $9,000. The sale of autographed programs by an array of artists, autographed etchings of Moszkowski, money brought in from auctioning items during intermission, and donations from individuals and organizations brought the fund for Moszkowski to well over $20,000.[24]

Three years later, the outcome of the second attempt to present a similar program on December 30, 1924 was less successful. Once again, the concert was organized by Schelling and took place at the Metropolitan Opera House as a benefit for the Association for Improving the Condition of the Poor (AICP). In addition to Stojowski, Schelling, Bauer, Hutcheson, Lhèvinne, Gabrilowitsch and Schnitzer, the star-studded cast also included Myra Hess, Ethel Leginska,[25] Yolanda Mérö, Guy Maier, Carl Friedberg, Lee Pattison, Guiomar Novaes, Mischa Levitzki, Olga Samaroff, Alexander Brailowsky, and Alexander Siloti—eighteen pianists in all.[26] Stojowski's contribution to the program was augmented this time to include *Berceuse* by Rimsky-Korsakov for piano, four hands, a variation on *Chopsticks* from *Paraphrase sur un thème favori et obligé*.[27] Stojowski performed this variation with his student, Novaes. News of the concert was mentioned in the January 12, 1925 issue of *Time Magazine* in an article entitled "Pianos." The article ended by stating that the performances of the various *Chopstick* variations were recorded on a piano roll which was then auctioned at $2,000 to Mr. Cornelius N. Bliss.[28]

AICP allowed the proceeds of the concert ($9,700) to be used to buy an annuity for Moszkowski from the Metropolitan Life Insurance Company. He was to receive an annual income of $1,275.96 for life, payable in monthly installments of $106.33 beginning on March 1, 1925. Unfortunately Moszkowski died on March 4, without having received the first installment. To make the situation even more tragic, despite Schelling's insistence, the Metropolitan Life Insurance refused to refund part of the sum in view of the exceptional circumstances, returning only $350.00[29] to cover the expenses Schelling incurred while closing the Moszkowski estate. In a letter to all the pianists who took part in the benefit, Schelling explained the situation and ended it by stating, "I regret exceedingly that our efforts to help Moszkowski was [sic!] not more successful but he knew that we did make this effort and I am sure it cheered him to know that so many great artists had come forward on his behalf."[30]

Two years later, on March 28, 1927, Stojowski once more joined forces with his fellow pianists. This time, however, it was mainly a social event, organized by the Beethoven Association in New York. Other pianists included Harold Bauer, Alexander Brailowsky, Artur Bodanzky, Walter Damrosch, James Friskin, Rudolph Ganz, Ernest Hutcheson, Joseph Lhévinne, Yolanda Mérö, Benno Moisseiwitsch, Harold Randolph, and Ernest Schelling. The program consisted of the *Diabelli Variations* with each player performing the variation assigned to him.[31]

Endnotes

[1] Stojowski, *Letter to Paderewski*, October 19, 1905.

[2] Damrosch, *History of The Institute of Musical Art,* 26.

[3] Two days later at Carnegie Hall, Artur Rubinstein made his American debut with the Philadelphia Orchestra.

[4] Aldrich, 129.

[5] Anon., "Stojowski Admires American Energy."

[6] *LAT*, August 24, 1924.

[7] Thirteenth Census of the United States: 1910—Population.

[8] E-mail letter from Brett Rosenau of Theodore Presser, May 3, 2002.

[9] Perkowska, *Diariusz Koncertowy I. J. Paderewskiego,* 235.

[10] An unidentified Philadelphia press clipping from 1915, ZLSC.

[11] At the age of seven, Władziu (the endearing form of Władysław) Valentino Liberace also was able to arrange an audition with Paderewski. Unlike the other Paderewski "auditioners" mentioned in this book, Liberace did not have the good fortune of being advised to study with Stojowski.

[12] Anon., "Stojowski Historical…" ZS recorded MacDowell's *Woodland Sketches,* Op. 51: No. 4, *In Autumn* and No. 2: *Will-o'-the-Wisp* on piano roll for Ampico Recordings.

[13] Aldrich, 320.

[14] NY Philharmonic Archives, Lincoln Center.

[15] The Metropolitan Opera had no record of this Stojowski performance because all their programs for the 1910–1911 Season were lost when the company moved to Lincoln Center in the 1960s, including the one for the world première of Puccini's *The Girl of the Golden West.*

[16] Anon., *Koncerty Zygmunta Stojowskiego w Ameryce*, 1, [Press clipping, ZLSC]. As far as can be ascertained, Stojowski visited Chicago six times, four of which included public appearances: In 1910 for the Chopin Centennial at the Auditorium, in 1911 for a recital at Northwestern University, in 1935 for Paderewski's Diamond Jubilee at the Auditorium, and a Chopin lecture-recital introduced by Rudolph Ganz, president of the Chicago Musical College, in April 16, 1945. There were also private visits in June 1930 and in November 1943.

[17] Damrosch, *History of The Institute of Musical Art— Appendix,* 6.

[18] The Von Ende School of Music. *Bulletin 1915–16*, p. 8, ZLSC.

[19] Oliver.

[20] Gottlieb, 18.

[21] Stojowski, *Paderewski as I Knew Him*, 1034.

[22] Based on the MARC Record for this work in the catalogue of the Free Library of Philadelphia's Fleisher Collection.

[23] Concert Program, ZLSC.

[24] Anon., "Fourteen Pianists Join Forces…"

[25] Leginska (1886–1970) was born "Ethel Liggins." She changed her name on the advice of an impresario who advised her that the best known pianists of her time either had Polish or Russian surnames.

[26] Concert Program, ZLSC.

[27] The other variations are by Borodin, Cui and Liadov.

[28] Cornelius N. Bliss (1874–1949), financier who was chairman of his father's firm, Bliss, Fabyan & Co., until 1932. He succeeded his father as chairman of the Republican National Committee, during the ill-fated candidacy of Charles Evan Hughes. In World War I he was a member of President Wilson's War Council, and in World War II, was chairman of the Red Cross advisory council on war activities. *NYT,* "Cornelius Bliss, 74, Financier, Is Dead."

[29] The valuations are given in the historic amounts.

[30] Letter from Ernest Schelling to Stojowski.

[31] Leedy, 203–204.

Chapter Four

TEACHER AND STUDENTS

S tudents of Stojowski could trace a Viennese pianistic tradition stretching back at least to Beethoven. Stojowski's teacher, Paderewski, studied with Theodore Leschetizky (1830–1915), who was a student of Karl Czerny (1791–1857). Czerny, in turn, was one of the most famous students of Ludwig van Beethoven (1770–1827), and Beethoven was—of course—a student of Haydn!

Leschetizky's teaching combined the technically demanding skills required by Czerny with the *cantabile* tone of Chopin. Stojowski's philosophy on merging the two was simple and direct:

> In music, the purpose of technique is simply to facilitate the fluent expression of musical meaning. When it carries beyond that, into a vainglorious chase after mere effect, it becomes an actual obstacle to human development as well as to the searching out of musical values. For that reason, we must guard against allowing a mere pianistic mentality to block the highroad into music. Technique is simply the means of expressing musical meaning; music is not a vehicle for displaying technical skill.[1]

Stojowski coached hundreds of pianists, many of whom had illustrious musical careers or became highly esteemed piano teachers. Former students showed their unparalleled loyalty and admiration for their teacher by organizing themselves into the Stojowski Students' Association, and publishing regular news bulletins. By the mid 1930s, the Stojowski Students' Association numbered over 260 members.[2] Stojowski was known to say, "There are no good teachers, but only good pupils."[3] A listing of some of the "good pupils" who were fortunate to study with Stojowski reflects the remarkable musical lineage they represented. Six of the seventeen students described here can be found in the 1924 class photo with Stojowski and Paderewski: Brachocki, Johnson, Levant, Loesser, McGlinchee and Schachter.

Elenore Altman (1887–1980), an American pianist and teacher. She studied with Stojowski at the Institute of Musical Art at the same time as Arthur Loesser in the late 1900s. One source refers to her as having been of Polish descent. In 1926, a *New York Times* critic described her as "a player of intelligence and facile technique." In 1929, Altman left New York to teach in Arizona.

In his history of the University of Arizona's School of Music, Dr. James R. Anthony has written that,

> Madame Elenore Altman commuted over rough roads from Phoenix to Tucson in 1929–1930 to teach piano part-time at the University of Arizona. In 1930… [she] was hired as Professor of Piano. With her red hair and her gravely voice, Elenore Altman was an aggressive and vital presence on the School of Music faculty for 38 years, retiring in 1967 at the age of 79. She died in Tucson in 1980 at age 93. Although she claimed not to like the title "Madame," by which she was always addressed in Tucson, she did little to discourage its use. Plagued in later years by increasing deafness, Mme Altman inhabited a world of her own distinctive sounds; the noise of her old Buick heralding her daily arrival at the old College of Fine Arts as she hit the driveway into the adjacent parking lot at too fast a speed; the incessant banging of her long cigarette holder to punctuate some strong opinion; and the hum of the batteries of her hearing aid. Nonetheless, she must not be remembered just as an eccentric. She was an intelligent musician who battled constantly to curb her enthusiastic interpretations of the Romantic piano repertory with rigorous harmonic and formal analysis of the music itself.[4]

Alexander Brachocki (1897–1948). Polish-American pianist and composer. At the age of seventeen, Brachocki auditioned for Paderewski in New York. Paderewski declared Brachocki a "genius" and sent him to study with Stojowski, paying for the young man's lessons. The coaching began in 1915 and lasted for many years. From October 1919 to May 1924, Brachocki also studied theory with Percy Goetschius at the Institute of Musical Art,[5] winning the Institute's coveted Isaac N. Seligman Award of $500 for composition.[6] Sometime during this period, Brachocki made his orchestral debut with the New York Symphony Society Orchestra while it was on tour. Playing in his hometown of Scranton, Brachocki dazzled the local audience. The *Scranton Times* wrote, "No artist created the *furore* that Alexander Brachocki did when he appeared here for the first time as soloist with the New York Symphony Orchestra."[7]

Brachocki continued his studies during the summer of 1921 in Europe, where he was in the first class of the Conservatoire Américaine in Fontainebleau. Brachocki's teachers included Nadia Boulanger in harmony and Paul Vidal in composition.[8] Aaron Copland also studied at Fontainebleau that year. In a letter

Figure IV-1. Alexander Brachocki. Courtesy of Louise Brachocki-Signorino and Antoinette Brachocki-McCarthy.

written to his parents, he mentioned Brachocki and the concert on which both their works were played. In his translation of several French reviews, Copland wrote, "The compositions presented to the public by Aaron Copland and A.[lexander] Brachocki, were full of life and French qualities, which ought to be played and appreciated in the U.S.," and "The composers A.[aron] C.[opland] and Alex[ander] Brachocki worship in their fashion our dear Claude Debussy."[9] Brachocki also wrote in Polish about his studies in France to Paderewski, "Thanks to people of goodwill, I was able to obtain the funds that succeeded in my getting there, where I benefited [from studies] mostly in composition."[10]

Thanks in part to Stojowski, Brachocki became one of a select group of Polish pianists who participated in summer master classes with Paderewski at his villa in Morges, Switzerland, during the late 1920s and early 1930s. Brachocki studied with Paderewski free of charge for three summers in 1930–1932. In a letter to his mother-in-law Brachocki wrote, "[Paderewski] said that I have been excellently prepared by Stojowski for work with him and that he is greatly pleased with the ease with which I can imitate Paderewski's expressions."[11]

Paderewski arranged for Brachocki to have his debut with the Warsaw Philharmonic Orchestra, playing the inaugural concert of the 1932–1933 Season. On September 16, Brachocki performed Paderewski's Concerto for Piano and Orchestra, Op. 17, under the direction of Grzegorz Fitelberg. Brachocki's colleague from Morges, Henryk Sztompka, performed Paderewski's Polish Fantasy for Piano and Orchestra, Op. 19, on the same program. After a few recitals and a repeat performance of Paderewski's Concerto with the Warsaw Philharmonic in November, Brachocki returned to the United States, where he spent the rest of 1933 getting ready to return to Poland on a permanent basis.

Brachocki moved to Poland in 1934 and took the post of professor of piano and composition at the Silesian Conservatory of Music in Katowice.[12] He arrived alone in February. His wife, Florence, and twin daughters Antoinette (named after Paderewski's sister) and Louise (named after Stojowski's wife) followed in the spring. Brachocki loved his work in Katowice. He was also on the founding faculty of the School of Music in Cieszyn, located on the Polish—Czech border. As a composition teacher he could take pride that one of his first students at the Conservatory, Michał Spisak, later became one of Nadia Boulanger's most outstanding students, and one of the leading representatives of Polish neo-classical school.[13]

In July 1939 Brachocki returned to the United States, intending to perform Paderewski's Piano Concerto in conjunction with the Polish arts festival taking place at New York World's Fair. Unfortunately, the concert never took place. With another war on the horizon, funds earmarked for cultural activities were diverted into Poland's defense buildup. On August 23 Brachocki's family gathered at the pier to bid him farewell for his return to Poland on board the S.S. Batory. His wife's tears so overwhelmed him that, even though he was already on board, he decided to postpone his return for two weeks and remain in New York with his family. As history bore witness, the outbreak of World War II on September 1 made Brachocki's return impossible.

His situation was truly terrible—he was penniless, had no immediate work prospects, and a family to feed. Brachocki's piano, furniture, manuscripts and all published music were still in Poland. He lived out the war residing in Brooklyn's Park Slope district, teaching at a private music school on Long Island, performing on the radio, and giving benefit concerts for Polish relief whenever possible. He never returned to Poland. At the end of the war, Brachocki came down with a debilitating and painful kidney disease which took his life in January 1948. His widow traveled to Poland after his death to collect his manuscripts and musical scores. However, after she died in 1994, the music could not be found. Brachocki's legacy as a composer has been lost, and the only recording of his playing that remains is a piano roll on AMPICO (no. 66431), performing Stojowski's *Légende,* Op. 8, no. 1.[14]

Antonia Brico (1902–1989). American conductor of Dutch origin. The long association between Brico and Stojowski began at a piano recital given by Paderewski during the summer of 1923 at the University of California in Berkeley. Brico completed her musical studies there that same year.   Apparently Brico purchased a standing room ticket for Paderewski's concert and sneaked in a camp stool wrapped in paper into the auditorium. Once there, she placed it about four feet from the piano, right in the front row aisle, perching herself upon it in order to get a better view.

The following year, when Stojowski taught a summer class in Berkeley, one of the California professors related the Paderewski recital episode to him. Stojowski's response was "that anyone with such determination and sincere desire should be recognized."[15] He requested a meeting with Brico at which he not only proposed that she come to New York to study with him, but also invited her to become part of the Stojowski household, living with the family in one of the guest rooms on the fourth floor of their brownstone on West 76th Street. Brico agreed and spent two years studying with Stojowski in New York prior to her departure for Germany in 1927.

Brico's visit in Europe was very successful. Armed with a letter of introduction to Karl Muck from Stojowski,[16] she became the first American to graduate in the master conducting program at the Berlin State Academy of Music, where she studied with Muck, the former musical director of the Boston Symphony Orchestra. In 1930 she became the first woman to conduct the Berlin Philharmonic Orchestra. That same year she conducted the Hamburg Symphony as well as several other European orchestras and then returned to the United States where she appeared with the Los Angeles and San Francisco symphony orchestras.

On August 26, 1930, at the San Francisco Civic Auditorium, Stojowski performed his Symphonic Rhapsody for Piano and Orchestra, Op. 23 with Brico conducting. It was the first of their several artistic joint ventures. In 1931 Brico returned to Europe, becoming the first woman to conduct the Warsaw Philharmonic Orchestra and Poznań Philharmonic Orchestra[17] during the autumn of that year. A critic for the Polish women's weekly magazine *Bluszcz* wrote of the Warsaw concert:

> The sensation of the season was the conducting of Sunday afternoon's [October 18] concert by Antonia Brico. Unfortunately, not much of an audience was present. Women's solidarity was not at work, and, at the outset, the feeling among the males present at the concert was one of distrust for this woman conductor. Brico, however, proved to be a very experienced and energetic

conductor. Her tempos were so well controlled, even at rapturous times as in Beethoven's *Leonora* [Overture] or Strauss' *Don Juan*. Her unfailing sense of rhythm and convincing sensitivity for shading dynamics, though, were qualities that were mainly manifested in Tchaikovsky's symphony.[18]

The year 1931 marked the 30th anniversary of the Warsaw Philharmonic Orchestra. It would not be surprising if Stojowski, who was a member of the Philharmonic's 30th Anniversary Committee, had a hand in arranging Brico's guest appearance with the orchestra.[19]

Figure IV-2. Antonia Brico. Photo from *Bluszcz* magazine, October 24, 1931, p. 13. Used by permission. All rights reserved

Stojowski was also the unsung hero for Brico's triumphant New York debut as guest conductor with the Musicians' Symphony Orchestra at the Metropolitan Opera House on January 10, 1933. One of the works that Brico conducted was Tchaikovsky's Symphony No. 4 in F Minor, Op. 35. The New York critics praised her performance, with the *New York Times* critic Olin Downes going so far to say that Brico's insight into the piece was deeper than most of her male colleagues.[20] The score she used was the same annotated score that Tchaikovsky used for the May 1893 premiere of his Symphony in London, and later gave to Stojowski in appreciation for translating for him at rehearsals. The score remained in Brico's possession for several decades until it was returned to the Stojowski family, who auctioned it at Sotheby's in 2000.

Brico eventually returned to New York, and in late 1932 moved into an apartment at 137 West 75th Street, only a block away from Stojowski's home on West 76th Street. In New York and San Francisco in the 1930s, there would be several more concerts with Brico at the helm of the orchestra, either conducting the music of her esteemed professor or conducting concertos in which Stojowski was the featured soloist. The first of these artistic collaborations took place in August 1930 with Stojowski performing his Symphonic Rhapsody with the San Francisco Symphony Orchestra at the Civic Auditorium. The second was in March 1935, when Stojowski performed Chopin's Concerto No. 2 in F Minor, Op. 21, at the debut concert of the New York Women's Orchestra at Town Hall. He was not only a soloist at this standing-room-only concert, but also addressed the audience during the intermission.[21] In addition to sharing his musical talents with Brico, Stojowski and his wife were sponsors of the Women's Symphony Orchestra, along with Bruno Walter, Harold Bauer, Ossip Gabrilowitsch, Mayor and Mrs. Fiorello La Guardia, Eleanor Roosevelt, members of the Vanderbilt and Rockefeller families, and many others.[22]

The next Brico-Stojowski appearance was with the San Francisco Bay Region Festival Orchestra on August 16, 1938, with Stojowski performing Liszt's Piano Concerto in E-flat Major. This concert took place only one month following Brico's historic accomplishment, when she became the first woman to conduct the New York Philharmonic Symphony Orchestra. Back in New York on January 25, 1939, Brico conducted Stojowski's Suite in E-flat Major for Orchestra, Op. 9, at a Carnegie Hall concert with the Brico Symphony Orchestra.[23] This performance, given as a benefit concert for the relief of infantile paralysis, had the good fortune of being recorded by the Carnegie Hall Recording Co. on 78-RPM records. The original disc and its CD transfer can be found in the Stojowski Collection at the Polish Music Center at the University of Southern California in Los Angeles.

On at least one occasion, Brico called on the artistry of Stojowski's wife, Luisa, who joined forces with Antonia and two other pianists, Lee Pattison and

Joyce Barthelson, in performance of J. S. Bach's Concerto in A Minor for Four Harpsichords with the New York Women's Orchestra.[24] Brico also led the January 18, 1938 Carnegie Hall concert, and the four harpsichords were supplied by Steinway & Sons!

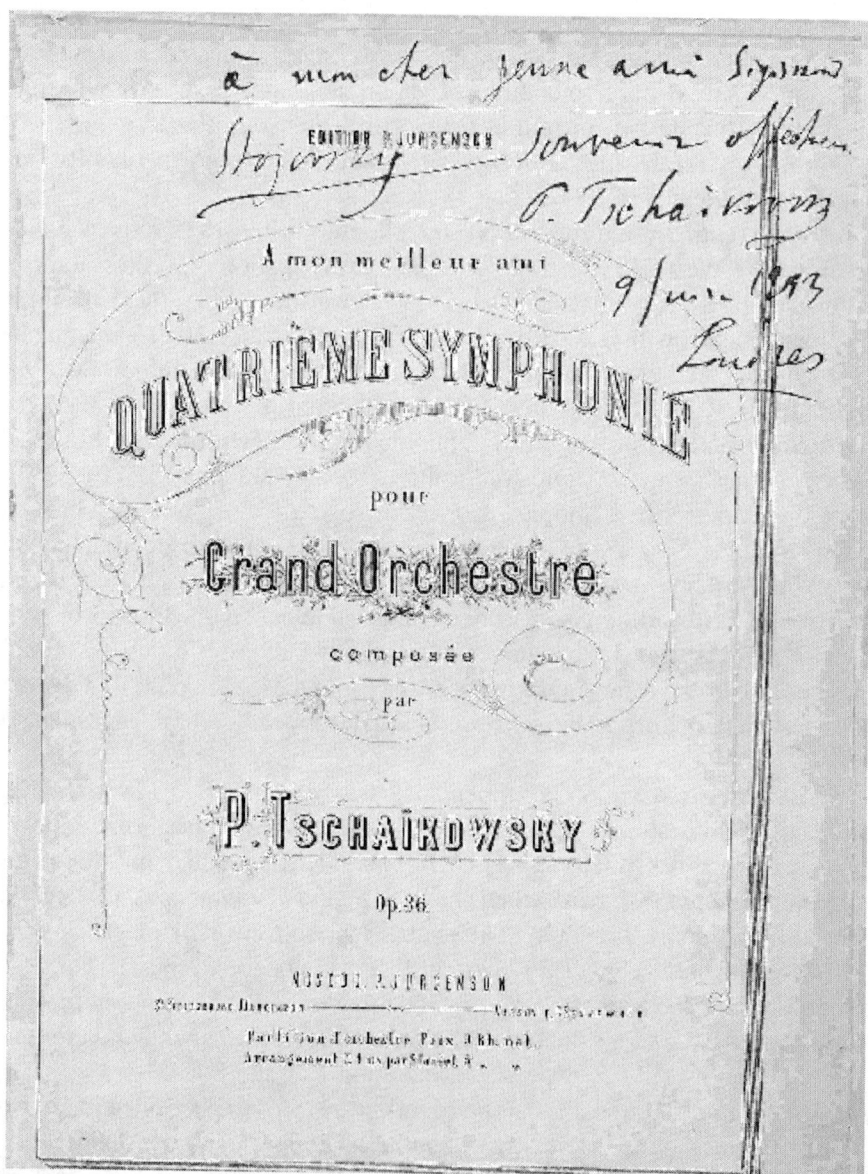

Figure IV-3. Cover of the full score to Tchaikovsky's Fourth Symphony with a dedication to Stojowski. Courtesy of Sotheby's. Used by permission. All rights reserved

During the war years and in the twilight of his life, Stojowski spent much of his time giving lecture-recitals on Chopin's music. Once again, Antonia Brico (who had lived in Denver since 1942), helped her former teacher by arranging master classes and an all-Chopin recital at Denver's Central Christian Church. She also returned the hospitality that Stojowski once showed her in New York by hosting him and his wife Luisa in Denver between March 23 and April 9, 1945.

Antonia Brico's musical influence also extended to Stojowski's sons, Alfred and Ignatius. During Alfred's medical studies at Columbia University in 1938, he accepted Brico's invitation to join the choir in a performance of Verdi's *Requiem*. This Carnegie Hall concert by Brico and the New York Women's Symphony Orchestra was held on April 26, 1938. Ignatius' musical association with Brico lasted much longer. Following Brico's invitation, "Lou" went to Denver where he taught Latin, French and Spanish for the Denver Public Schools from 1952 to 1955. At the same time he also studied the piano, bassoon and French horn, taking theory and conducting with Brico.

In the 1974 Oscar-nominated documentary film *Antonia: A Portrait of the Woman*, Brico recalls Stojowski with affection, and his photo is prominently displayed in her studio. She mentions his reaction to her artistic plans to become a conductor: "Ridiculous," was Stojowski's initial reply. Brico also recalls Stojowski's and Bruno Walter's help in inviting Artur Rubinstein to join them in observing her in a specially arranged orchestra rehearsal at Carnegie Hall. She was determined to get Rubinstein to write a letter of recommendation that she could send to Finnish composer, Jean Sibelius. She succeeded not only in obtaining the Rubinstein letter, but also in being invited by Sibelius to Finland in 1946 to study his symphonic works with him and conduct the Helsinki Symphony Orchestra. According to the documentary, Sibelius proclaimed her the best interpreter of his orchestral opus. After Stojowski died in 1946, Brico kept in touch with Luisa Stojowska by corresponding and sending Christmas cards for several decades until the late 1970s.

Shura Cherkassky (1909–1995). Ukrainian-born Russian pianist. In a brochure advertising Stojowski's summer master classes at the University of Washington in Seattle from July 23 to August 24, 1928,[25] Cherkassky is listed among Stojowski's prominent pupils. Although Stojowski is not mentioned in Elizabeth Carr's 2006 biography on Cherkassky published by Scarecrow Press, on learning of Stojowski's death, Cherkassky wrote to Luisa Stojowska, "That outside of the fact that I studied under him for some time, I was very fond of him as a man, as well as an admirer of him as a musician."[26]

Cherkassky probably studied with Stojowski upon arriving in the United States, directly after his escape from the Bolshevik Revolution. He also played an audition for Paderewski. Quite probably, Paderewski gave Cherkassky his usual advice to go and study with Stojowski. In any case, Cherkassky's studies with Stojowski must have taken place prior to his work with Józef Hofmann. Shura Cherkassky's American debut in 1923 was followed by concerts on six continents and a professional career that lasted for nearly seventy-five years.[27]

Barbara Custance (1909–1985). Canadian pianist and teacher. After early musical training in Vancouver, Custance went to England for further studies, and made her debut at Wigmore Hall in 1928. She returned to America to study piano with Stojowski in 1929–1933, and made her Town Hall debut in 1943. According to Jacqueline Droz, a retired piano teacher living on Vancouver Island, Custance had small, fattish hands when she came to Stojowski. Apparently he recommended that she systematically flatten them on a table to stretch them. As painful as it sounds, it must have worked as Custance had a successful career, concertizing throughout Europe and North America as well as performing as soloist with the Toronto Symphony Orchestra and with the orchestras in Winnipeg, Vancouver, Seattle, Buffalo and the Little Symphony of Montreal. From 1960 to 1968, she was on the faculty of the University of British Columbia.

Figure IV-4. Paderewski, Phyllida Ashley, and Stojowski in California, July 1927.
Photo: Paderewski Museum, Morges. Used by permission. All rights reserved

Phyllida Ashley (Everingham Cheek) (1894–1975). A San Francisco Bay Area resident, Phyllida was one of Stojowski's favorite pupils and one of Paderewski's favorite bridge partners. Her name frequently appears in Stojowski brochures as an example of one of his "rising stars" or "famous" students. At the age of five, she had the privilege of playing for Paderewski in his Pullman car while he was in San Francisco. She appeared as soloist with the San Francisco Symphony Orchestra several times and, for many years in the 1920s and the 1930s, had her own weekly Thursday evening duo-piano radio program with pianist Aileen Fealey, first on station KGO and, after 1930, on NBC's Pacific Coast network. The program, *Piano Paintings,* brought fame for the two pianists through its transcontinental broadcasts.[28] She also taught privately. Stojowski's *Romance for Piano,* Op. 43, no. 1 is dedicated to her. Phyllida raised two daughters, Anne (b. 1919) and Patricia (b. 1924). Anne Everingham Adams was the harpist of the San Francisco Symphony Orchestra and Opera as well as harp teacher at Mills College for over 40 years. Anne also lived with the Stojowski household while she was completing her harp studies at Juilliard. Anne's younger sister, Patricia Nottingham, was trained as a pianist and would often accompany her sister in concert.[29]

Esther Johnson (1901–1982). American pianist and ethno-musicologist. Esther Johnson was born in Ishpeming, Michigan. Her early music training was with her father, who was the organist at the Swedish Lutheran Church in Chicago. After completing her studies in 1929 at the University School of Music in Lincoln, Nebraska, she went to New York to study with Stojowski and then to London, Paris and Vienna for further musical studies. Her professional debut as a pianist took place in Paris with the Orchestre de la Société des Concerts du Conservatoire, with Philippe Gaubert conducting. She became the first American chosen as an "official soloist" at the 1931 Salzburg Festival. Although she gave concerts in the United States and in Canada, she became better known in Europe, where she won special acclaim for her playing of Mozart.

In the late 1930s, she became interested in Slavic folk music and spent much time in Serbia, recording the folk songs of villagers and visiting places where radio had not yet appeared. She spent the rest of her life specializing in the music of the Balkans. The results of her research can be found in the Traditional Music Archives at Indiana University. In 1941, she married Arthur A. Garlinghouse, and later moved to Amarillo, Texas, where she died.

Oscar Levant (1906–1972). Composer, pianist and entertainer. Levant was one of the more colorful figures among Stojowski's pupils. Born to a Jewish family in Pittsburgh, Levant came to New York in 1921 as a fifteen-year-old child to study with the fifty-one-year-old Stojowski.

Figure IV-5. Oscar Levant in the 1930s. Photograph courtesy of
the Oscar Levant Collection, USC Cinema-Television Library.
Used by permission. All rights reserved

In spite of his four-year classical music training under Stojowski, Levant
became a famous jazz pianist specializing in the music of George Gershwin. In
the late 1920s, he had the distinction of being the first pianist after Gershwin to
record *Rhapsody in Blue*, and later the first pianist to record all of Gershwin's
major works for the piano.[30] Still, he did not abandon classical music completely.
He turned to composing, studying first with Joseph Schillinger in 1934 and Arnold
Schoenberg in 1935–1936. He became popular as a jazz pianist after performing
in nine motion pictures from 1929 to 1953.[31] They have been described by
Public Broadcasting System's Roger Rosenblatt as "a display of talent devoted
to genius that could render a work of art powerful, beautiful and everlasting."[32]
His keen wit, coupled with neurotic phobias, chain smoking, and superstitions
made him a favorite TV talk show celebrity, not only hosting his own local Los
Angeles show in 1958–1960, but also as a frequent guest on Jack Parr's *Tonight
Show* in the early 1960s.[33] Levant's unique sense of humor was also recorded

in several entertaining books, including *A Smattering of Ignorance* (1940), *The Memoirs of an Amnesiac"* (1965) and *The Unimportance of Being Oscar* (1968).

Levant describes his years with Stojowski with both fondness and humor. In his first book, Levant credits Stojowski with the famous one-liner referring to Saint-Saëns' Second Piano Concerto: "It begins like Bach and ends like Offenbach." In that same book Levant paints the following portrait of his beloved piano professor:

> However, a good deal of what I know of music and also what I feel about it owes its origin to Sigismond Stojowski (please, NOT Stokowski), who is not only a brilliant pedagogue but a warmly sympathetic human being. The several years I spent studying piano in New York with him remain among the most profitable and worth remembering of my life. He provided the best summation of that period when he asked me what music I was going to play at a student recital for which he was preparing the program. "I think I'll play Debussy's *Reflets dans l'eau* or *Poissons d'or*," I answered. He looked at me intently for a moment and then said, "Your piano playing is not improving but your French is."[34]

Levant also recalled Stojowski's qualities as a teacher with sincere praise, extolling him as:

> . . . a magnificent pedagogue who has the art of transporting his pupils into that state of inspiration and admiration that makes them want to do their best. That is the best kind of teaching. The man who teaches you to play scales, teaches you simply to play scales; but the man who makes you want to do your best, gives you music."[35]

In *The Memoirs of an Amnesiac* Levant remembers Stojowski's reaction to his playing of Gershwin's *Fascinating Rhythm* from the musical *Lady Be Good* following one of the studio master classes. In the hallowed home of the author of *Chant d'amour*, it "was practically an act of musical blasphemy."[36] Even though he became one of the best-known jazz pianists and Gershwin interpreters of his time, Levant seems to have had some sort of neurotic guilt and inferiority complex that left him in fear of his distinguished teacher. As late as 1940, fifteen years after studying with the famous Pole, Levant recalls seeing Stojowski on the streets of New York.

> I saw Mr. Stojowski on the street the other day. I would have given a lot to have a good talk with him. But my recollections of what he would have wanted a pupil to accomplish made me see all I have not accomplished; so I crossed the street and got out of his way.[37]

Although working with Stojowski might have been less advantageous than studying in a large music school, where recitals and performances with student orchestras were the norm, Stojowski had the great advantage of being able to arrange, from time to time, student recitals at which Paderewski would be present. This was the case with Levant. Following an all-Paderewski program at Carnegie Hall on May 5, 1924, Stojowski arranged a recital of his students for Paderewski at the Hotel Plaza, where Levant played Paderewski's *Légende*. Levant remembers this being his first encounter with a world famous musician and that Paderewski had an "imposing, magnetic personality." Levant's description of the event is quite insightful:

> [Paderewski] . . . would congratulate the performer with a handshake and some words of praise. A girl who had cried when she made a mistake got a special kiss on the forehead—something she wouldn't have received if she'd played correctly... We also had a group picture taken with him. Stojowski confided to me that Paderewski had said that I was very talented but years later I made light of this remark by saying that while Paderewski patted me on the head he restrained his foot from kicking me.[38]

Mischa Levitzki (1898–1941). Ukrainian pianist. Levitzki was a favorite of American audiences in the 1920s and the 1930s. Prior to coming to America, he studied for a year with Aleksander Michałowski (1851–1938) at the Warsaw Conservatory. Levitzki's studies with Stojowski at the Institute of Musical Art from 1906 to 1911 were followed by tutelage with Ernö von Dohnányi in Berlin for three years. Mischa Levitzki's recording of Stojowski's *Valse Humoresque*, Op. 12, no. 2, for Ampico Piano Rolls was stunningly transferred to a Klavier LP recording in 1970.

Arthur Loesser (1894–1969). American pianist and a child prodigy, Loesser became one of Stojowski's first students at the age of 11 in the 1905 class of the Institute of Musical Art. Stojowski recommended Loesser for the Institute's "Faculty Free Scholarship" for the academic year of 1910–1911[39] and was responsible for Loesser's audition for Józef Hofmann on January 28, 1912 at the Vanderbilt Hotel in New York.[41] Eventually, Loesser joined the IMA faculty in 1919.

In 1926, Loesser moved to Cleveland and became affiliated with the Cleveland Institute of Music for the rest of his life. A highly respected teacher, he chaired the piano department there from 1953 to 1969. Between 1927 and 1967, Loesser made almost thirty appearances with the Cleveland Orchestra, performing the concertos of Bach, Beethoven, Brahms, Chausson, Chopin, Dohnanyi, Liszt, Mozart, Poulenc, and Saint-Saëns. In addition to his role as soloist, he also served as the Orchestra's program annotator from 1936–1941. From 1938 to 1956 he also wrote reviews for the now defunct *Cleveland Press*.[42]

Figure IV-6. Photo of the Stojowski Class, taken at the Hotel Plaza, New York, May 6, 1924. Photograph courtesy of ZLSC. Used by permission. All rights reserved. Pictured in the photo, standing from left to right: Alexander Brachocki, Oscar Levant, Nils Nelson (became an accompanist working with such artists as tenor Jan Kiepura, contralto Gladys Swarthart and soprano Florence Austral), Sidney Schachter, Manuel Funes (Cuban pianist), William Sauber (winning pianist of the William W. Naumburg Foundation Competition in 1927). Seated in center row: Miss Julia Levine (dancer?), Mrs. Albert Vertchamps, Mr. Paderewski, Mr. Stojowski. Mme Conrad-Korzeniowska (the wife of Joseph Conrad), Miss Esther Johnson. Seated below: Miss Constance McGlinchee, Miss Lois Maer. (Maer moved to Memphis where she was also an organist. The city's Beethoven Club Competition has a $2,500 award named after her.)

A man of many talents, Loesser was also a linguist, specializing in Japanese. He was an intelligence officer in the United States Army during World War II in Japan, where he became the first foreigner to perform with the Nippon Symphony in Tokyo after the war. Arthur's half brother, Frank Loesser, was the famous Broadway composer and librettist, who wrote *Brigadoon* and *Guys and Dolls*.[43]

Loesser spent much of his career as an accompanist and a duo-piano performer. He authored the well-known book *Men, Women and Pianos,* an informal social history of the piano. James Methuen-Campbell, in his book *Chopin Playing*, considers Loesser to have been one of the truly great interpreters of Chopin and bemoans the fact that Loesser was little known outside the United States. He writes:

Loesser's strengths in Chopin were very much those one identifies from the accounts of the composer's playing: infinite variety of nuance, the most delicate *piano* and *pianissimo* playing, and an overall control of the emotional content of the music. . . . Loesser's effects are always highly idiomatic and perfectly judged, and it is lamentable that he did not record more Chopin, since he was a very great performer.[44]

In his two-disc CD recital recording released by Marston Records, prior to playing Paderewski's *Légende* at his 1967 Town Hall recital, Loesser addresses the audience and recalls his learning the piece under the tutelage of Zygmunt Stojowski.

Constance McGlinchee (1897–1986). Hailing from Newtonville, Massachusetts, McGlinchee first studied piano with Carlo Buonamici (d. 1932) in Boston before moving with her family to New York and studying with Stojowski. In New York, she made her debut at Aeolian Hall on December 2, 1920. She performed Schumann's Concerto for Piano and Orchestra Op. 54, with the Boston Symphony Orchestra at Sanders Theatre in Cambridge on April 10, 1924. A review in *The New York Times* dated February 21, 1928 described her as "a sincere musician of native temperament, sound technique and musical understanding." McGlinchee recorded

Figure IV-7. Alfred Newman. Photograph courtesy of the Alfred Newman Collection, USC Cinema-Television Library. Used by permission. All rights reserved

Brahms' Romance Op. 118, No. 5, for Duo-Art Piano Rolls (7412). She also had a studio in New York City in the 1920s. A music fellowship was named after her at Radcliffe College by her sister Claire's family in 1990. Claire (1898–1990) was a 1921 Radcliffe alumna who became a professor of English at Hunter College.[45]

Alfred Newman (1901–1970). Hollywood composer. A student of Stojowski at the Von Ende School during World War I, Newman won nine Academy Awards as composer and music director, more than any other musician in the history of Hollywood.[46] He also held the record for the most Oscar nominations—forty-five—a record which was finally matched by John Williams in March 2006. At the age of twenty Newman met Gershwin, and conducted some of his shows. He also arranged some of Chopin's Nocturnes for a ballet performance. Newman's colleague and a distinguished film composer, David Raksin, summed up Newman's musical beginnings as follows:

> The story of Alfred Newman's life is one of those rags to riches tales that are supposed never to happen outside the novels of Horatio Alger or the wistful fantasies of children. He was born in New Haven, Connecticut in 1901, the eldest of ten children. The family was terribly poor, but somehow the mother was able to get piano lessons for her six-year-old son, for twenty-five cents, that's per lesson, of course. The teacher was a house painter by trade, and the boy quickly outgrew his tutelage and progressed to a scholarship with a professional. A year later he gave his first recital, and soon some kind friends brought him to the attention of the great Polish pianist, Sigismond Stojowski, who offered him a scholarship. Before long, Alfred had won a silver medal and a gold medal in a competition; among the judges were the German conductor Karl Muck and the renowned composer-pianist Ferruccio Busoni. But, prodigy or not, there was no escaping hard reality: Al's father could not find work, and the boy had to earn a living for his family. Once again friends intervened, and he found a job as piano soloist at the Strand Theatre in New York City. He was now thirteen.[47]

Guiomar Novaes (1896–1979). Brazilian pianist who first studied with Luigi Chiafferelli in São Paulo and later with Isidore Philipp in Paris. In New York City, she studied with both Luisa and Zygmunt Stojowski. His 1945 *Dumka for Piano* is dedicated to her. Stojowski said that "Novaes is the greatest pianistic talent I have ever encountered."[48] She was the last person to benefit from studies with Stojowski, returning to him in the autumn of 1946 for work on piano literature she studied with him earlier.[49] Payment for coaching consisted of tutoring in Portuguese in return for piano lessons. She had an extraordinary career and performed in the United States for nearly 57 years. Covering her American debut, Henry T. Finck (1854–1926), the music critic of the *New York Evening Post*, humorously referred to Novaes as "the Paderewska of the Pampas." Novaes married Brazilian composer and architect Octavio Pinto. Correspondence between Luisa Stojowska and Novaes is found in ZLSC.

Figure IV-8. Guiomar Novaes-Pinto. Photograph courtesy of ZLSC. Used by permission.

Sidney Schachter (1906–1988).[50] A Canadian-born pianist, Schachter also had the good fortune of playing for Paderewski as an eighteen-year-old when the Polish virtuoso visited his home town of Winnipeg in 1924. Paderewski's advice was again the same: "Come to New York and study with Stojowski." Schachter was an exquisite performer, as may be heard on the Polish Music Center's CD transfer of the 1947 radio broadcast of the Stojowski Memorial Program on station

WNYC. Following his studies with Stojowski, he was a laureate of the MacDowell Club Young Artists Contest on November 3, 1935,[51] and had his New York debut performing Paderewski's Piano Concerto with the Bronx Symphony Orchestra at the Brooklyn Museum later that month. He played many radio broadcasts and recitals in the New York City area, dozens of which are mentioned in *The New York Times*, the last being a 1967 recital at the Brooklyn Museum. A bachelor, Sidney lived with his sister in a Brooklyn apartment. He would go to the homes of his students to give piano lessons. According to one of his students, Vicky Guadagno, Schachter enjoyed reminiscing about Stojowski and Oscar Levant during her lessons.[52]

Harriet Ware (1877–1962). American pianist and composer. Born in Waupun, Wisconsin, Ware attended the Pillsbury Conservatory of Music in Minnesota and later piano with William Mason in New York. She then traveled to Paris where she studied both composition and piano with Stojowski.[53] She performed with many American orchestras and her tone poem *The Artisan* was programmed by the New York Philharmonic and the Philadelphia Orchestra. A prolific composer of songs, she gained national recognition in 1908 when her composition *Boat Song* sold more than a million copies. In 1945, her song, *This Is My Day*, was performed over 200 times by polio-stricken Metropolitan Opera soprano Marjorie Lawrence in concerts throughout the United States.[54]

Luisa Mathilde Moralès-Macedo (1890–1982). Peruvian-born pianist and wife of Zygmunt Stojowski. Born to a wealthy family in Lima, Peru, Luisa began her musical career at the age of six, and at the age of sixteen became the first woman to play in concert with an orchestra there. The future Madame Stojowska came to America in 1913, a year before the outbreak of World War I, in hopes of studying with Paderewski. Like many talented pianists who were lucky to be granted the opportunity to meet with Paderewski, Morales-Macedo was advised to "Go and study with Stojowski."[55] She did, and the rest became history. She described her first lesson with Stojowski as being a frightening experience. "He was gruff and severe and the first thing he said to me was, 'Are you here to build or reconstruct?' and he made me throw out my entire repertoire."[56]

"Thanks to a push from his mother," as Henry Stojowski relates, Zygmunt finally ended forty-eight years of bachelorhood. Although his bride was twenty years younger, Stojowski married Luisa on October 2, 1918. The wedding took place at the Church of the Blessed Sacrament at 152 West 71st Street which became their parish church for the next two decades. The 1918–1919 New York City Directory has Stojowski listed as living at 249 West 74th Street, squarely within the parish boundaries. According to Alfred Stojowski, his parents and grandmother lived for several years in an apartment on Riverside Drive near 86th Street before finally relocating to 150 West 76th Street, a few blocks down the street and around the corner from the residence of the great soprano, Marcella Sembrich (1858–1935)[57] who lived at 151 West Central Park.[58]

Luisa Stojowska was a teacher and performer in her own right. She not only taught privately, but she also gave a popular course, "The Art of Piano Practicing," at the Juilliard Summer School from 1940 to 1952. Van Cliburn (b. 1934) was among the legion of students who took her class. She also offered her course in conjunction with Stojowski's master classes throughout North America in the 1920s and the 1930s. During the academic year 1948–1949 Luisa Stojowska taught at Juilliard's Extension Service.[59] She periodically returned to her native Peru, where she had the distinction of being the first concert pianist to introduce the Steinway Piano in Western South America. She later served on the Steinway Artists Centenary Committee in 1953.[60] After Stojowski's death she performed more on her own, playing radio broadcasts and recitals, including a New York Town Hall recital as well as a London Wigmore Hall recital during the 1950s. Her programs always featured music by her beloved husband. Luisa Stojowska also served on many international and domestic juries for all manner of piano competitions.

Polish-American pianist and composer Wiktor Łabuński (1895–1974), who spent most of his American career teaching and performing in Kansas City, described Luisa as "an excellent pianist and teacher" and "a charming lady." Recalling a visit to New York City after Stojowski had died, Łabuński mentions how Luisa enjoyed showing an autographed photo of Tchaikovsky. Dedicated to Luisa's mother-in-law Marie, the dedication and signature were written in Polish. Łabuński also pointed out that Tchaikovsky, like Stravinsky and Shostakovich, was of Polish ancestry.[61]

Endnotes

[1] Stojowski, "What the Pianist of Tomorrow Must Possess," 730.

[2] Index card mailing list, ZLSC.

[3] Stojowski, Résumé *Biographical Note.*

[4] Anthony, 6.

[5] Juilliard School Archives.

[6] Damrosch, *History of the Institute of Musical Art 1904–1926,* 44. Isaac Newton Seligman (d. 1917) had been on the Board of Trustees of the Institute of Musical Art. In 1919, his widow established an annual prize in memory of her husband to the student offering the best composition for chamber music or orchestra.

[7] "Comments of the Press" in *Concert Program*, Aeolian Hall, New York, November 6, 1923. Brachocki Family Archives. According to the New York Philharmonic Archives, the New York Symphony Society Orchestra did not keep complete records of the concerts they played on tour.

[8] *LMM,* "Fontainebleau."

[9] Aaron Copland, *Letter to Parents*, October 3, 1921, Washington, D.C., Aaron Copland Archives, Library of Congress.   http://lcweb2.loc.gov/music/copland/letters.txt.   One review which Copland missed was one that commented on Brachocki's and Copland's "modern style." See: Anon., "Conservatoire de Fontainebleau."

[10] Brachocki, Letter to Paderewski, December 13, 1921, Warsaw: Paderewski Archive, Folder 553, no. 1–4, AAN.

[11] Brachocki Family Archives, *Brachocki to Maria Linke*, July 27, 1930.

[12] The school, founded in 1929, celebrated its 75th anniversary during the academic year 2004–2005. Now the Szymanowski Academy of Music, the school's website history includes Brachocki among the school's first famous group of pedagogues: http://www.am.katowice.pl/Strony/uczelnia_historia.html.

[13] Michał Spisak (1914–1965) moved to Paris in 1937 to study on a Silesian Conservatory Grant and remained in Paris until his death.

[14] At the time of publication of this book, Brachocki's daughters (b. 1931) were living in Florida, Toni (Mrs. Joseph McCarthy) on Amelia Island and Lu (Mrs. John Signorino) in Venice. The daughters are in possession of dozens of letters written by their father to Paderewski, their mother and grandmother. They give invaluable information about studies with Paderewski at Morges and life in Poland in the early 1930s. In addition to the correspondence, they also possess priceless home-made silent movies which their father took of Paderewski while studying with him in Morges.

[15] Reprint from *Treble Clef Chorus Program*, Contemporary Club, White Plains, New York, January 15, 1937, Brico Clipping File, New York Public Library, Mid-Manhattan Branch.

[16] Roberts.

[17] Kassern, "Poznań…"

[18] Anon. "Antonia Brico…"

[19] Filharmonia Warszawska, 37.

[20] Olin Downes in an undated review from the *New York Times* found in the Brico press clipping file of the music division of the Mid-Manhattan New York Public Library.

[21] Anon., "Woman's [sic!] Symphony under Brico…"

[22] *NYT*, "Women's Symphony Orchestra of 80 Will Make Its Debut Here Monday" and Jane Bowers, 361.

[23] This orchestra evolved from the New York Women's Orchestra, which, after allowing men to join the orchestra in January 1939, changed its name to the Brico Symphony Orchestra. This was probably the orchestra's first concert under that name.

[24] Concert flyer from 1938, ZLSC.

[25] ZLSC.

[26] Cherkassky.

[27] According to an e-mail to the author dated April 6, 2006, neither does Mrs. Carr remember Cherkassky ever mentioning Stojowski in conversation or his stating that Paderewski recommended study with someone in particular.

[28] Anon., "Popular Pacific Coast Piano Duo."

[29] Based on a January 2002 telephone conversation with Phyllida Ashley's daughter, Patricia Nottingham.

[30] *Rhapsody in Blue, Second Rhapsody, Concerto in F, Variations on 'I Got Rhythm,' Preludes.*

[31] *Dance of Life* (1929), *Rhythm on the Range* (1936), *Nothing Sacred* (1937), *Made for Each Other* (1939), *Rhythm on the River* (1940), *Humoresque* (1946), *The Barkleys of Broadway* (1949), *An American in Paris* (1951) and *The Band Wagon* (1953).

[32] Rosenblatt.

[33] Levant's talk show was supposedly taken off the air because of a racy anecdote he told about Mae West's sex life.

[34] Levant, *A Smattering of Ignorance,* 266.

[35] Levant, *The Odyssey of Oscar Levant,* 316.

[36] Levant, *The Memoirs of an Amnesiac*, 63.

[37] Ibid.

[38] Levant, *The Memoirs of an Amnesiac*, 64.

[39] The list of names was found on a paper with a Stojowski Studios letterhead; it accompanied the copy of the photo found at the Paderewski Museum in Morges.

[40] Stojowski, *Letter to Arthur Loesser* (May 17, 1910).

[41] Stojowski, *Letter to Arthur Loesser* (January 27, 1912).

[42] Courtesy of the Cleveland Orchestra Archives.

[43] *NYT,* "Arthur Loesser, 74, a Concert Pianist."

[44] Methuen-Campbell, 208–209.

[45] Based on information from the Harvard University Music Department, *The New York Times*, Social Security Records and the archives of Radcliffe College and the Boston Symphony Orchestra.

[46] Dane.

[47] From American Composers' Orchestra: *David Raksin Remembers His Colleagues*. Full text at: http://www.americancomposers.org/raksin_newman.htm

[48] Stojowski, Résumé *Biographical Data.*

[49] Stojowski, Résumé *Biographical Note.*

[50] Dates taken from Social Security records.

[51] Stojowski was one of the jurors. *NYT,* "Activities of Musicians."

[52] Most of the information on Schachter came via e-mail from Mrs. Guadagno whose Website, which makes mention of "the phenomenal Sidney Schachter," caused the author to write to her. Further information came from a Schachter recital program given at The Brooklyn Museum, November 14, 1948 [ZLSC].

[53] Howard.

[54] *NYT,* "Harriet Ware, Concert Pianist and Composer, Is Dead at 84."

[55] Stojowski, Luisa.

[56] Milne.

[57] Praxede Marcella Sembrich (1858–1935), Polish diva and one of the world's legendary great coloratura sopranos of all-time. She received her musical training at the Lwów Conservatory, studying violin and piano, the latter with Wilhelm Stengel whom she later married. According to legend, she once sang for Liszt who recommended that she become

a singer. Whether or not the story is true, she refocused her attention on her voice and went to Vienna and Italy for vocal training. After her operatic debut as Elvira in Bellini's *I Puritani* in Athens in 1877, she performed with the opera companies of Berlin, Budapest, Dresden, Frankfurt, Lisbon, London, Lwów, Madrid, Milan, Monte Carlo, Moscow, New York, Paris, St. Petersburg and Warsaw. She gave her Metropolitan Opera debut in the company's inaugural season of 1883, singing the part of Lucia in Donizetti's *Lucia di Lammermoor.* From 1898 to 1909, Sembrich sang at Metropolitan Opera where she sang 25 roles in 253 performances. She retired from the operatic stage in 1909 and from the concert stage in 1917. She spent the rest of her life teaching at the Curtis Institute in Philadelphia and at the Juilliard School of Music in New York as well as giving summer master classes at her home in Bolton Landing on Lake George in upstate New York, where the Sembrich Opera Museum, operating every summer since 1937, exists today. [Kutsch, 4348 and Herz.]

[58] Stojowski was one of the 12 honorary pallbearers at Sembrich's funeral service at St. Patrick's [Haughton, 17.]

[59] Juilliard School Archives.

[60] Letter from Edward Johnson to Percy Grainger (June 15, 1953) on Steinway Artists Centenary Committee stationery. Percy Grainger Collection, Steinway Folder, Library of Congress, Washington, D.C.

[61] Łabuński, 411. For more on Wiktor Łabuński, see *Remembering Wiktor Łabuński*: http://www.usc.edu/dept/polish_music/news/sep04.html#labunski. Although the original Tchaikovsky photograph could not be traced, a copy of it was found at the International Piano Archives at Maryland in College Park and is reproduced in the illustration section.

Chapter Five

FAMILY

In the six years following their marriage, Luisa and Zygmunt created what he referred to as his "three best compositions," Alfred (b. 1919), Henry (b. 1921) and Ignatius (1923–1985).[1] According to Henry Stojowski's daughter, Nancy, Luisa once told her that her mother-in-law, Marie, was quite furious when she found out that Luisa was pregnant with her first child so soon after her marriage to Zygmunt. Apparently Marie insisted that Luisa and Zygmunt sleep in separate bedrooms for a year after their wedding, holding that it was unbecoming to a Polish family of aristocratic origin to have a child too soon. If Marie had her way, she would have been happy to see the first child come during the fourth year of marriage.[2] Of course, these were days when many married Catholics would find it intimidating or be embarrassed to undress in front of each other before going to bed, so Marie's attitudes were really not that uncommon. Nevertheless, the fact that she wanted to keep her son chastely tied to her apron strings after decades of bachelorhood seems quite amazing even for that time.

Stojowski's eldest son, Alfred Charles Marian Jordan, was baptized in New York City and had Marcella Sembrich and Józef Hofmann for his godparents. A year later, he was taken to Lima, Peru, and—by his own account—his family was given a special Church dispensation to have him receive the Sacrament of Confirmation at such an early age. They gave him the name Stanislaus as his confirmation name, and were able to please the Peruvian relatives with a quasi-christening party of their own.[3]

Henri Sigismond Ladislas Jordan[4]—prematurely born in Fontainebleau while his parents were touring Europe—was christened in honor of the French kings who have Fontainebleau as their final resting place. Coincidentally, the first summer session of the Conservatoire Américaine in Fontainebleau was held in 1921, the year of Henri's birth. Stojowski's pupil, Alexander Brachocki, was enrolled at the Conservatoire and Stojowski's sojourn in Fontainebleau was likely connected to visiting Brachocki and possibly performing or giving a master class there as well. Stojowski may well have been trying to ascertain if he could get a post at the school. Nothing seems to have come of it, and after six weeks the family sailed back to America.

Figure V-1. October 2, 1918. Zygmunt, who was 5'6" tall, was one inch shorter than his newlywed, Luisa. Photograph courtesy of ZLSC. Used by permission. All rights reserved

The youngest son, Ignatius, was named after his godfather, Ignacy Jan Paderewski, and baptized Ignaś Louis (the baptismal register shows his first name as Iguan). His godmother was Paderewski's wife, Helena. Ignatius was called "Lou" by his family and friends.[5]

Figure V-2. Left to right: Ignacy, Henry and Alfred Stojowski. Photograph courtesy of ZLSC. Used by permission.

"Best compositions" aside, the sons were not musically talented. Tongue in cheek, Stojowski wrote in a letter to Paderewski that when people asked him if his children were musical, he would reply, "No, they sing."[6] Actually, the oldest,

Alfred, was a singer. When he was studying medicine at Columbia University, he joined forces with the Choral Arts Society of New Rochelle and Queens Choral Society of Jackson Heights in a performance of Verdi's *Requiem*, conducted by Antonia Brico. Upon completing medical school in 1944, Alfred joined the Army Medical Corps and was wounded in the jungles of the South Pacific during World War II. Appropriately enough, Captain Stojowski would later sing the leading male role in a production of Rogers and Hammerstein's *South Pacific* at Music Theater Wenatchee in Washington. Alfred Stojowski has lived in Wenatchee since 1953, working for many years as an Associate Clinical Professor for the University of Washington School of Medicine, and serving for sixteen years on the Washington State Arts Commission as well as co-founding the Wenatchee Valley Symphony Board. Following his parents' example, he and his wife Alice also raised their own Stojowski trio—two boys (Peter and Jordan) and a girl (Pamela).

The second son, Henry, vividly remembers his only serious attempt at the piano as a child. The Stojowski boys had their living quarters on the third floor of their home on West 76th Street, with each boy having his own room. His parents' teaching studio and master bedroom were located on the floor below. The fourth floor was the living quarters for Stojowski's boarding students. Each of them had a separate room with an upright piano. Henry recalls being bombarded almost daily with the sound of piano music being played from above and below. One day he took the opportunity to imitate the sounds he was hearing daily. His father, who was receiving a guest in the first floor salon during this artistic attempt, broke into the teaching studio and shouted, "Would you please stop that infernal racket!" That was the end of Henry's career as a performer.

After graduating with honors from Yale University Architectural School, Henry had a very successful career. He too saw action during World War II, serving in the Navy in both the Atlantic and Mediterranean theaters, and finishing his military career with the rank of Lieutenant. He and his wife, Sarah, created a Stojowski quartet—three girls (Susan, who is now deceased, Christine and Nancy) and a boy (Stephen). After the death of his mother and youngest brother in the 1980s, Henry became the custodian of the family archives. It is thanks to him that the musical world can once more rediscover the treasures that his father left behind and help renew a very long overdue interest in the music and lives of his parents. Henry, a widower, currently lives in Baldwin, New York, on Long Island.

Ignatius—or "Lou" as he was called—took his given name seriously. After he finished high school in 1942, he entered the Jesuit Order, founded by his godfather's patron, St. Ignatius of Loyola. He left the Jesuits in 1949, after graduating from Woodstock College in Maryland in 1948. He also received his M.A. from Iowa University.[7] Ignaś (as he would sign his letters to Paderewski) was already contemplating the priesthood while he was in grade school. In one of them, he wrote to his famous godfather about his desire to become a priest, mentioning that his father had already started to give him Latin lessons at home.[8] Although Ignatius did not become a priest, he was a Latin teacher and published some articles on Latin in a classical studies periodical.

It is hard to find out what musical talents Lou had as a child. Between 1952 and 1955, while teaching Latin, Spanish and French for the Denver Public Schools, he took private lessons in piano, bassoon and French horn. He also studied theory and conducting with Antonia Brico. Ignatius took an active interest in trying to promote his father's music. While working as Latin teacher at the Chestnut Hill Academy in Philadelphia (1970–1972), one of his promotional successes was convincing Albert Conkey (1923–2000), the choir director at the Academy to give a performance of Stojowski's cantata, *Prayer for Poland*, Op. 40, with the Chestnut Community Chorus.[9] A letter found at the Paderewski Museum in Morges gives us some insight on what kind of person Ignatius was. "He seems more of a person of the nineteenth century than the twentieth . . . [he gave me] the impression of someone with not too much experience in the complexities of present day life."[10] "Lou" the linguist (his résumé also lists Polish as one of his languages) never married. In 1985, he died of cancer. Just as with his parents, the Requiem Mass for Lou took place at St. Ignatius Loyola Church in Manhattan.

The Stojowski family was multilingual. Spanish was not only spoken with Luisa but also with the housekeeper and cook, who lived with her family in the basement of Stojowski's four-story brownstone. For the boys, of course, English was the language of the neighborhood and school, as well as means of addressing their father. French and Polish were most often used when guests arrived. Madame Stojowska, who actually taught French in a private school when she arrived in America in order to help make ends meet, also became fluent in spoken and written Polish. Pianist Lidia Grychtołówna (b. 1928), a laureate at the Fifth International Chopin Competition in Warsaw in 1955, remembers Luisa's excellent command of the Polish language. The two first met in Rio de Janeiro where Luisa was on the jury of a piano competition in which Lidia participated. Two years later, in 1960, both pianists met again in Warsaw, where Grychtołówna entertained Stojowski's widow in her Warsaw apartment and remembered her as one of "the most interesting and most likeable" guests she ever had in her home. She recalled Luisa's "beautiful" Polish, stating that she would hesitate from time to time in order to search for the right word or declension. After all, it had already been almost two decades since her husband had passed away.[11]

When Nancy asked her grandmother in what language she formed her thoughts, she received a surprising answer, "In Polish." Nancy expected that the answer would be Spanish but Luisa told her that when she thought in Polish, she felt closer to her husband. In a letter to the author, Nancy Stojowski wrote, "When they first knew each other, they communicated mostly in French until she gained proficiency [in Polish]. . . . they would switch from one language to another so that they could have private conversations in front of the children."[12]

Figure V-3. Luisa Stojowska in the 1960s. Photograph courtesy of ZLSC. Used

Endnotes

[1] In one of Stojowski's letters to Maria Mickiewicz, Stojowski refers to his three sons as his *Trzech Budrysów* (*Three Lithuanians*), a literary reference to the title of a ballade written by Maria's grandfather, poet Adam Mickiewicz.

[2] Conversation with Nancy Stojowski in Richmond, Virginia, in 2003.

[3] E-mail letter from Alfred Stojowski to the author, August 18, 2002.

[4] Bulletin de Naissance, no. 211, Ville de Fontainebleau, September 9, 1921, ZLSC.

[5] Church of the Blessed Sacrament (New York City) Baptismal Register 1922–1938, 8.

[6] Stojowski, Letter to Paderewski, April 20, 1938.

[7] Stojowski, Ignatius L. *Data Sheet.*

[8] Stojowski, Ignatius L. *Letter to Paderewski.*

[9] Conversation with Edward Sargent, graduate of Chestnut Hill Academy, Philadelphia, June 2002.

[10] Dunham.

[11] Dybowski, *Laureaci konkursów chopinowskich*, 219. Probably one of the reasons that Luisa came to Poland was to collect royalties from the Polish Music Press (PWM) made from the sale of several editions of her husband's works that were published in Poland during the 1950s.

[12] E-mail letter to the author, December 5, 2005.

THE GREAT WAR

The despair felt by Poles as a result of their loss of sovereignty throughout the nineteenth century is best described by the English writer of Polish birth, Joseph Conrad. In his short story from 1911, *Prince Roman,* Conrad wrote:

> The speaker was of Polish nationality, that nationality not so much alive as surviving, which persists in thinking, breathing, speaking, hoping, and suffering in its grave, railed in by a million bayonets and triple-sealed with the seals of three great empires.[1]

It was during Stojowski's tenure at the Von Ende School of Music that World War I broke out. Just before the onset of hostilities, Stojowski was in Riond-Bosson attending Paderewski's annual name-day celebration[2] with such artists as Marcella Sembrich, Felix Weingartner (1863–1942), Tymoteusz Adamowski (1858–1943), Józef Hofmann, Rudolph Ganz (1877–1972), Gustave Doret (1866–1943), and the leader of the National Democratic Party in Poland, Roman Dmowski (1864–1939).[3] During the party on the evening of July 31, 1914—the feast of St. Ignatius of Loyola—it was announced that Germany gave an ultimatum demanding the demobilization of Russia. The next day, for the first time in 120 years, Poland's enemies—Austria, Prussia and Russia— who had wiped Poland off the map of Europe, were at war with each other. This was a war that all Poles secretly wished for. The seed of hope for an independent Poland had been sown, and a double task at hand stood clear: "Save the Poles for future Poland, restore a free Poland for those saved."[4]

During this "war to end all wars," Paderewski epitomized the true Polish patriot fighting for Polish independence. As his weapons he used the piano works of Chopin, those "Cannons buried in flowers," as Schumann once described them.[5] Paderewski's performances of Chopin were able to overwhelm the hearts of statesmen and commoners as well as overturn opposition to the rebirth of a sovereign Polish State. ". . . Fiery oratory seconded the sounding beauty of his art. Hearts melted, and purse-strings loosened at his appeals—and, in time—doors of chanceries opened to the great gentleman-artist that were closed to professional politicians," Stojowski recalled.[6] Violinist, composer, musicologist and conductor Henryk Opieński described Paderewski's use of Chopin as "a peaceful sword," which—according to Stojowski—sounded "beauty for his country's salvation" and created "a magic spell that set human hearts vibrating."[7] Indeed, it was this peaceful sword that helped forge an independent Poland for the first time in over a century. Through music Paderewski would lead his people into a land of freedom.

In America, the first to respond to the need of assistance for Poland was Marcella Sembrich. Traveling on a German passport, she and her husband returned to New York from Europe in October 1914. At the end of November, Sembrich was named the honorary president of the Polish National Relief Fund that operated under the auspices of the Polish-American Ladies of New York. Less than two weeks later, the organization changed its name to the American Polish Relief Committee (APRC) and Sembrich became its president. Zygmunt Stojowski served as one of its vice-presidents and a member of its executive committee.[8]

In this capacity Stojowski helped to co-produce the 1915 production of Marcella Sembrich and Ernest Schelling's musical pageant *A Night in Poland,* picturing a peasant wedding with songs and dances.[9] This was a high-society fundraiser to benefit Sembrich's organization, APRC. Stojowski orchestrated Chopin's Polonaise in F-sharp Minor, Op. 44, the Mazurka in D Major, Op. 33, no. 2, and the Mazurka in B-flat Major, Op. 7, no. 1 for the spectacle. He also wrote the pageant's spoken prologue, *Glimpses of Polish History.* While Schelling trained a chorus of American ladies to sing in Polish, Stojowski coached them, phonetically spelling Polish words in English. Schelling and Stojowski spent weeks rehearsing the performers, including the amateur chorus, and arranging the music—Polish patriotic tunes and folk songs—for the show.[10] Schelling also composed an original mazurka to function as the show's overture.

Ryszard Ordyński (1878–1953), who had just arrived in America in January 1915, was the stage director for the pageant. By 1917 he became the head stage director at the Metropolitan Opera Company, a post he held until 1920. Sets and costumes were designed by the painter Władysław Benda (1873–1948) and made by his family, including Emilia and Jadwiga Benda.[11] The spectacle, accompanied by Nahan Franko (1861–1930)[12] and his orchestra, included the following stars: soprano Marcella Sembrich, bass Adam Didur (1874–1946),[13] violinist Tymoteusz Adamowski,[14] baritone Albert Janpolski and pianist Rudolph

Figure VI-1. Sembrich as "Ulana," the role she created in Paderewski's opera, *Manru* (1902). Photograph courtesy of the Marcella Sembrich Opera Museum in Bolton Landing.

Ganz (1877–1972). This quasi-folk opera took place in the ballroom of the Hotel Biltmore on April 8, and, as a fundraiser, it brought in $10,000 for Polish war relief.[15]

Stojowski wrote of the show's musical success and called Sembrich's performance "incomparable in song, mimicry and dance."[16] In paying tribute to Schelling following his early death in 1939, Stojowski wrote, "In the ensuing campaigns for Polish Relief and for Polish Independence, Schelling was an ardent and able helper, a better Pole than many a real one."[17] In 1917, Schelling joined the United States Army Intelligence Corps, served in Europe and was later decorated by the governments of the United States, Poland, Spain, and France. His outstanding musical contribution was the symphonic tone poem, *A Victory Ball,* based on the anti-war poem of the same title by Alfred Noyes. Schelling's composition celebrates the signing of the Armistice. Following the introduction, the ball begins with a polonaise and ends with a frenzied krakowiak as "...the dead men grin from the wall, watching the fun of the Victory Ball." The music fades into the distance and the work ends with an offstage trumpet playing taps.[18]

As the war continued, there was much pressure put upon Sembrich to stop her relief work under the auspices of APRC and to consolidate her efforts with Paderewski's Polish Victims' Relief Fund (PVRF). Paderewski's PVRF worked as the American branch of the General Committee for Polish Relief in Switzerland, founded by Henryk Sienkiewicz, the organization's president, and Paderewski, its vice president. Sembrich was named one of PVRF's vice presidents as a peace offering. According to Sembrich scholar, Stephen Herx, "Sembrich was 'strong-armed' into working with the PVRF and later tried to sever that connection."[19]

Some sectors of the American Polonia were very critical of Sembrich's efforts on Poland's behalf. She was accused of being excessively ambitious and trying to be in the forefront of all initiatives, because of her own desire for glory and fame. In the conclusion of a letter to Mr. Stanisław Osada of Chicago, dated March 13, 1915, APRC's secretary, Dr. Lewiński-Corwin writes that, in confidential documents from Mr. Osada he has read Osada's accusations of Sembrich's ambitions, and he assures him that Sembrich's motives are only to help Poland and that his criticisms only bring her harm.[20]

During the summer of 2002 at the Polish Institute of Arts and Science's 60th anniversary meeting in Washington, D.C., the author had the honor to deliver a paper on Stojowski at Georgetown University. Also present at this conference was the eminent Polish-American historian, Professor Mieczysław Biskupski, who painted a harsh picture of Stojowski. In his paper *The War of Maestro and Diva: Sembrich, Paderewski and the Politics of Polish Relief, 1914–1918,* Dr. Biskupski reported that, in spite of his magnanimity, Paderewski could be a shrewd politician who would stop at nothing to get his way. The historian went so far as to accuse Stojowski of being Paderewski's henchman. Stojowski's "dirty work" supposedly included authoring a letter discrediting Sembrich and asking Polonia groups to send their donations to Paderewski rather than to her. More shocking was the accusation that Stojowski helped supervise the robbery of the safe at Sembrich's APRC headquarters, so that the money could be diverted to Paderewski's PVRF. According to Sembrich scholar Stephen Herx, who was also a participant at the same meeting, "the financial records of Sembrich's APRC are pretty much in order at Lincoln Center and no monies seem to have gone

POLISH VICTIMS RELIEF FUND

Figure VI-2. Postcard designed by Władysław Benda during World War I. A booklet of six different postcards sold for twenty-five cents. Courtesy of ZLSC. Used by permission. All rights reserved

missing."[21] Another aspect to consider is that if Stojowski was implicated in his campaign against Sembrich, why would she ever agree to be the godmother of his first-born son just a few years later?[22]

In any case, the feuding took its toll on Sembrich's health. Doctors ordered her to resign from her Polish relief work. On November 12, 1915, Sembrich left the presidency of APRC. The healing process took months and, among the reports on her health, *The New York Times* wrote that she had suffered a nervous breakdown.[23]

Stojowski continued his work for Polish relief under the wings of his mentor and teacher, Paderewski. With Tadeusz Wroński[24] and Wacław O. Górski (Helena Paderewska's son from her first marriage), Stojowski became the co-director of *Polskie Biuro Koncertowe,* a Polish concert agency in New York. Supported by Paderewski, it organized benefit concerts and shows for the PVRF.[25] In addition to innumerable benefit recitals that Stojowski and others played for the fund, he also engaged his students from the Von Ende School in the effort. Among the many programs in the Zygmunt and Luisa Stojowski Collection, a May 19, 1916 benefit recital for the Polish Victims' Relief Fund clearly stands out, with some of Stojowski's more famous students playing: Brachocki, Zygmunt's future wife Luisa, Arthur Loesser and the fifteen-year-old "Master" Alfred Newman.[26] The students must have been thrilled by the presence of Maestro and Madame Paderewski at their performance.[27]

Stojowski also used the power of his pen to gain sympathy for the Polish cause of independence by writing a series of articles on Polish history and culture for the *New York Evening Post* during the Great War.[28]

Stojowski's cantata, *Modlitwa za Polskę* [Prayer for Poland], Op. 40, was another important musical wartime endeavor. Set to a poem by the Polish romantic poet Zygmunt Krasiński (1812–1859), it is one of the few national works dating from World War I with a spiritual base. In writing about music as a voice of war in his book on twentieth-century music, the noted American musicologist Glenn Watkins states:

> At various junctures throughout the twentieth century, man's search for spiritual values has surfaced in opera, symphony, and Mass; mystery play, ballet and cantata. Yet the period before the beginning of World War I to the conclusion of hostilities was not noticeable for a musical corpus with a pronounced spiritual base, and while the anxiety of a society on the eve of global conflict has frequently been seen as the root of the Expressionist movement, the number of musical statements that speak directly of the war of 1914–1918 are few.[29]

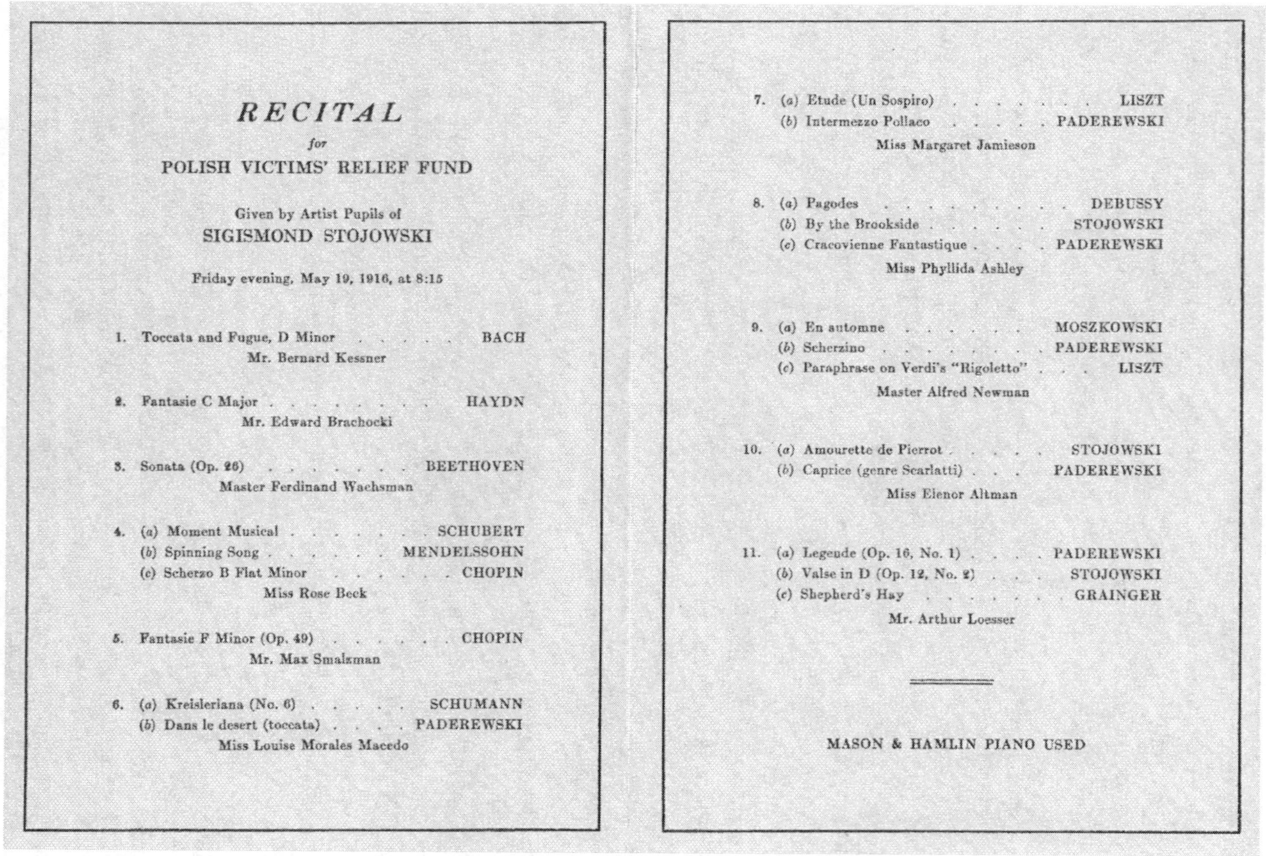

RECITAL

for

POLISH VICTIMS' RELIEF FUND

Given by Artist Pupils of

SIGISMOND STOJOWSKI

Friday evening, May 19, 1916, at 8:15

1. Toccata and Fugue, D Minor . . . . . . BACH
   Mr. Bernard Kessner

2. Fantasie C Major . . . . . . HAYDN
   Mr. Edward Bruchocki

3. Sonata (Op. 26) . . . . . . BEETHOVEN
   Master Ferdinand Wachsman

4. (a) Moment Musical . . . . . . SCHUBERT
   (b) Spinning Song . . . . . . MENDELSSOHN
   (c) Scherzo B Flat Minor . . . . . . CHOPIN
   Miss Rose Beck

5. Fantasie F Minor (Op. 49) . . . . . . CHOPIN
   Mr. Max Smalcman

6. (a) Kreisleriana (No. 6) . . . . . . SCHUMANN
   (b) Dans le desert (toccata) . . . . . . PADEREWSKI
   Miss Louise Morales Macedo

7. (a) Etude (Un Sospiro) . . . . . . LISZT
   (b) Intermezzo Pollaco . . . . . . PADEREWSKI
   Miss Margaret Jamieson

8. (a) Pagodes . . . . . . DEBUSSY
   (b) By the Brookside . . . . . . STOJOWSKI
   (c) Cracovienne Fantastique . . . . . . PADEREWSKI
   Miss Phyllida Ashley

9. (a) En automne . . . . . . MOSZKOWSKI
   (b) Scherzino . . . . . . PADEREWSKI
   (c) Paraphrase on Verdi's "Rigoletto" . . . . . . LISZT
   Master Alfred Newman

10. (a) Amourette de Pierrot . . . . . . STOJOWSKI
    (b) Caprice (genre Scarlatti) . . . . . . PADEREWSKI
    Miss Elenor Altman

11. (a) Legende (Op. 16, No. 1) . . . . . . PADEREWSKI
    (b) Valse in D (Op. 14, No. 2) . . . . . . STOJOWSKI
    (c) Shepherd's Hay . . . . . . GRAINGER
    Mr. Arthur Loesser

MASON & HAMLIN PIANO USED

Figure VI-3. Courtesy of ZLSC. Used by permission.

The Cantata is dedicated to the composer's mother, and it is Stojowski's last major work. It was first performed in New York on Tuesday, March 7, 1916 with the Schola Cantorum and the Symphony Society of New York under the direction of Kurt Schindler at Carnegie Hall.[30] The work is addressed to the Virgin Mary, who is called upon as the Queen of Poland to "End...for Poland her deep anguish."

The cult of the Virgin has been widespread in Poland for centuries, embracing generations of Polish Roman Catholics. The Marian appellation "Queen of Poland" dates from the seventeenth century, following the defeat of the Swedish invaders at Częstochowa, the site of the shrine of Poland's miraculous icon of the Black Madonna. To celebrate that victory, King Jan Casimir dedicated the entire Polish nation to Mary as the Queen of Poland in a special ceremony at the Roman Catholic Cathedral of the Assumption in Lwów (now Lviv, Ukraine). Later, the Vatican gave its permission for the Church in Poland to use this appellation during the recitation of the Litany of the Blessed Virgin. Polish Catholics also credit Mary for the "Miracle on the Vistula," the battle where Poles defeated the invading Bolsheviks on the outskirts of Warsaw on the feast of the Assumption, August 15, 1920. Stojowski, too, was engulfed in this devotion to the Madonna. In addition to his Cantata, other Marian influences can be seen in Stojowski's *Suite for Orchestra*, which uses the Polish hymn *Witaj, Królowo nieba* [*Salve Regina*] as the theme for the first movement's set of variations and in his art song, *Invocation*, which uses the incipit of the solemn version of the Gregorian chant *Salve Regina* in its introduction and coda. There is also Stojowski's harmonization of the chant *Bogurodzica* [Mother of God], Poland's oldest poem and composition, dating from the thirteenth century.

Figure VI-4. Stamps sold in aid of Paderewski's Polish Victims Relief Fund. An entire book of stamps sold for $1.00. Courtesy of ZLSC. Used by permission. All rights reserved

Although little known in Anglo-Saxon countries, Zygmunt Krasiński was one of Poland's great romantic poets of the early nineteenth century. His dramatic poems *The Undivine Comedy* and *Iridion* confront the plight of humanity and outline a philosophy where Poland's messianic role in history was suggested.[31] In Krasiński's *Prayer for Poland*, dating from 1839, the suffering of Poland becomes the suffering of Christ. During the soprano solo, Mary, the Queen of Poland is reminded of the role she played as the *mater dolorosa* at her son's passion. Likewise, the baritone solo symbolically recalls Christ's rising from the dead, and the Cantata itself ends by asking Mary to have Poland share in the glory of her son's resurrection.

Stojowski also shared Krasiński's belief in Poland's messianic role, holding it until his death in 1946. He saw World War II as a conflict where Poland was first crucified by the Nazis and the Soviets, and then entombment by the communists for nearly fifty years. Dying from cancer, Stojowski wrote to his son Ignatius, a Jesuit seminarian, on April 11, 1946:

My Dearest Ignatius,

. . . Time has a way of speeding that baffles and frightens us poor mortals. . . . And what of our upset and confused world, of poor Poland sold down the river by would-be friends while devastated by wicked foes?! When and how can she recover? I do earnestly hope you also pray and induce others to pray for that unfortunate country, of which you have but had a glimpse in childhood[32] on which [it] should remain dear to your heart because of its loyalty to the Faith and its ideals.

The picture of Christ with the enumeration of your offerings on my behalf,[33] I have put into my Polish prayer-book. —Thank you, Dearest Son, and thank others for me, and as the book is to the picture, so let Poland be the framework of salvation for many more than your humble and deeply loving

Tata [Dad][34]

While available in a piano-vocal reduction, the orchestral score and parts for *Prayer for Poland* were never published. This, in addition to the ensemble requirements (including organ and/or antiphonal brass) helps explain why this work did not enter the concert repertoire. Like Elgar's *Polonia*, (written for the Polish cause), or *Carillon* (written for the suffering Belgians during World War I), it was inevitable that *Prayer for Poland* was an esoteric concert item, even if the full score had been published and its composer had not fallen into obscurity. On the other hand, those of a strong spiritual inclination might prefer to believe that Stojowski's setting of Krasiński's prayer was actually heard at its performance in 1916 by the heavenly powers. In any case, believers and non-believers must admit that the text was prophetic. Poland's independence as a sovereign nation was restored in 1918, obviating—at least for the time being—the further use of this work! Certainly, following World War I, there would have been no need or inclination in Polish musical circles to program a piece that implored for an independent Poland since, by then, Poland was a sovereign state. This status quo lasted about twenty years, after which Poland once again fell under the heel of the conqueror.

As the years went by, the lack of a published orchestral score of *Prayer for Poland* placed the work in an even more precarious position: it fell into the category of Stojowski's works that were rumored to have been discarded. A three-year search for the Cantata's manuscript triggered this author's interest in Stojowski and happily led to the score's rediscovery in January 2002.[35] This book is the culmination of that journey. When *Prayer for Poland* was performed during World War II in Chicago and in the 1970s in Philadelphia, it was done with piano accompaniment only.[36] The first performance with orchestra since the 1916 world premiere took place in May 2003 in Warsaw at a Stojowski May Festival organized and conducted by the author. The parts and score were prepared by John Hein of the University of North Florida in Jacksonville, and are currently available from the University of Southern California's Polish Music Center in Los Angeles. Hopefully, since the orchestral score and parts have been edited and are available, *Prayer for Poland* will enter the repertoire of Polish ensembles. The work is ideal for anniversary concerts commemorating the outbreak of World War II (September 1), Polish Independence Day (November 11), or any other memorial concerts marking the upcoming hundredth anniversary of World War I in 2014.

As a composer, Stojowski was not terribly productive during the years of World War I. Besides the Cantata, he wrote *Aspirations*, Op. 39 (a set of piano pieces), and *Concertstück for Cello and Orchestra*, Op. 31. He was, however, in great demand during the war both as a composer and performer, gaining the unique distinction of being the first Polish composer to have an entire concert of his works performed by the New York Philharmonic Orchestra. This historical concert took place on March 1, 1915, at Carnegie Hall in New York with Josef Stransky conducting, and featured the following works:

Symphony No. 1 in D Minor, Op. 21
    (American premiere)

Concertstück for Cello and Orchestra, Op. 31
    (World Premiere), with Willem Willeke, cello

Second Piano Concerto (*Prelude, Scherzo and Variations*), Op. 32
    (American premiere) with Sigismond Stojowski, at the piano. [37]

To my beloved Mother, Ukochanej Matce

Prayer for Poland
Modlitwa za Polskę

Poem by
Sigismund Krasinski
English version by
Geo. Harris, Jr.

Sigismond Stojowski. Op. 40

Andante con moto

Piano

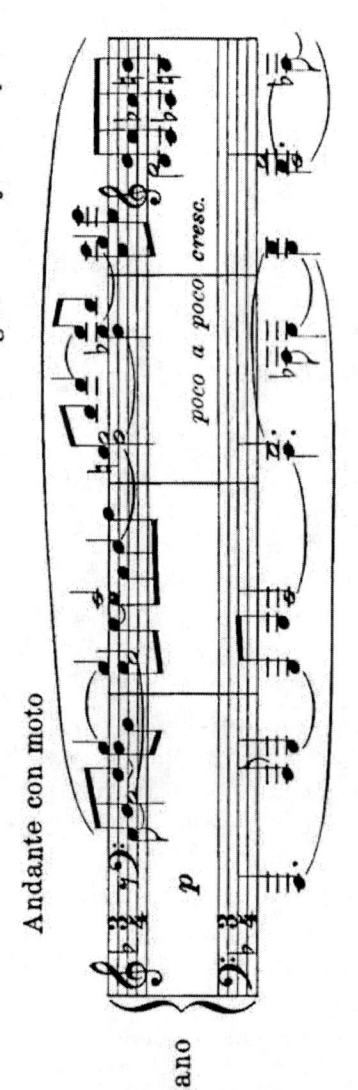
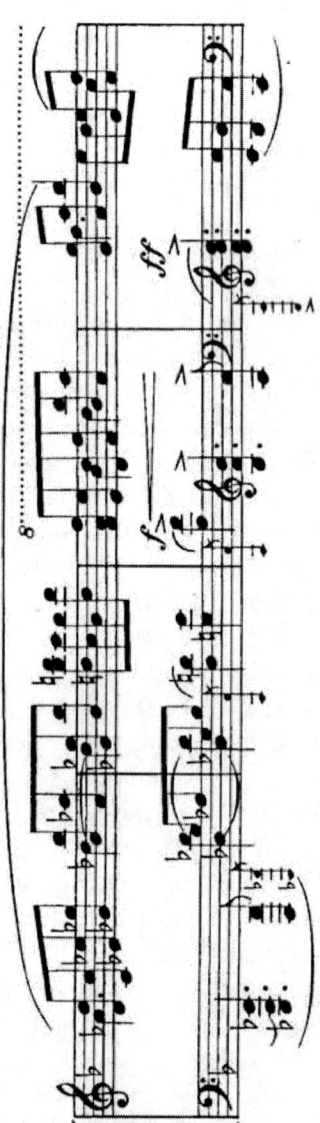

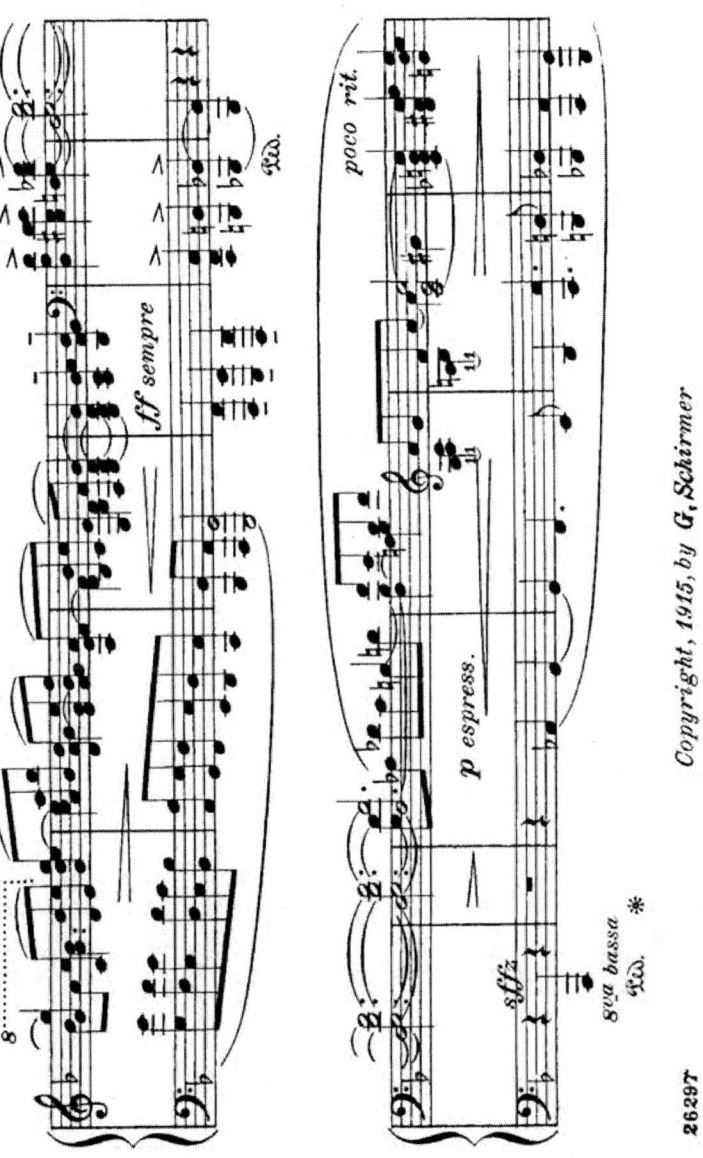

Figure VI-5. Sigismond Stojowski, *Prayer for Poland*, Op. 40. Page 1 of the piano-vocal score. Published by G. Schirmer, 1915. Downloaded from the Sibley Music Library Website at the Eastman School of Music, Rochester. Used by permission. All rights reserved

An idea of how much in demand Stojowski and his music were during the World War I can be gained by taking a look at his calendar for March 1916:

- March 2 & 4, Carnegie Hall: Performance of Second Piano Concerto with pianist Ignacy J. Paderewski, New York Philharmonic, Walter Damrosch conducting
- March 7, Carnegie Hall: World premiere of *Prayer for Poland.*
- March 10 & 11, Orchestra Hall: Performance of Second Piano Concerto, I. J. Paderewski, Boston Symphony Orchestra, Karl Muck conducting
- March 15, Carnegie Hall: Gala Benefit Concert. Stojowski performs with pianists I. J. Paderewski and Ernest Schelling, tenor Lucien Muratore, the Trio de Lètuce (flautist Georges Barrère, harpist Carlos Salzedo, cellist Paul Kéfer), and the Flonzaley Quartet (Aldolfo Betti, Alfred Pochon, Ugo Ara, Iwan d'Archambeau) to aid the artists of the Paris Conservatoire who had been crippled or made destitute by the war[38]
- End of March, Aeolian Hall: a benefit concert for the Polish Victims' Relief Fund[39]

Because of his charitable and patriotic service for Poland World War I, on November 28, 1926, Stojowski was awarded the medal of *Polonia Restituta (Odrodzenia Polski),* the highest distinction the Polish government could confer upon a civilian.[40] He was also awarded a Distinguished Service Medal from the United States Treasury Department's Liberty Loan Committee and War Savings Committee for his "faithful and loyal services in the Polish Division of the Foreign Language Bureau of the United States Loan Operation".[41] Clearly, Stojowski worked untiringly, championing the cause of freedom of both America and Poland, as well as raising funds for his wounded colleagues in Paris.

Endnotes

[1] Conrad, p. 144.

[2] July 31 is also the name-day for Helen. Thus, it was a joint name-day celebration for both husband and wife.

[3] Phillips, 290. Dmowski was a nationalist who held anti-Semitic views. Both he and Paderewski represented Poland at the signing of the Treaty of Versailles. Although both men collaborated together for Poland's independence, Paderewski did not share Dmowski's anti-Semitic feelings.

[4] Stojowski, *Paderewski Anniversary 1945*.

[5] From Robert Schumann's *Gesammelte Schriften über Musik und Musiker* [Complete Writings on Music and Musicians], 5th ed., 2 vols. Leipzig, 1914.

[6] Stojowski, *Paderewski Anniversary 1945*.

[7] Stojowski, *Paderewski, the Unique*, 223.

[8] American Polish Relief Committee of New York stationery letterhead. Archives, the Polish Museum of America, Chicago.

[9] The full score and set of parts for *A Night in Poland* may be found in the Stojowski files at the Polish Institute of Arts and Sciences of America in New York. A missing part or two as well as stage directions are found in Box I, Case III, Folder 8 at ZLSC.

[10] Some of Stojowski's arrangements found their way into his anthologies of Polish song, *Memories of Poland* and *Chansons Polonaises*.

[11] Komorowska.

[12] Violinist and conductor, Franko was the concertmaster of the Metropolitan Opera Orchestra from 1883 to 1907. He became the first native-born American to conduct with that company in 1904.

[13] One of Poland's greatest basses, (1874–1946). His musical training took place in Lwów and Milan. After singing with the opera houses of Lwów, Cairo, Milan, Warsaw and South America, Didur made his debut with the Metropolitan Opera in 1908. There he performed

for 25 seasons, singing 54 roles, for a total of 690 performances. Following World War II in 1945, he moved to Katowice, where he established the Silesian Opera Company in neighboring Bytom. (Kutsch, 1163–1164.)

[14] Adamowski was concertmaster of the Boston Symphony Orchestra from 1884 to 1908.

[15] "Society Revives Poland's Past as a Spectacle." *The Herald* (April 9, 1915). On that same day, however, *The World* reported receipts of only more than $6,000. [The Marcella Sembrich Scrapbooks on microfilm at the New York Public Library for the Performing Arts.]

[16] Stojowski, "A Tribute to Ernest Schelling," 2.

[17] Ibid.

[18] Schelling, *A Victory Ball*.

[19] E-mail letter from Stephen Herx to the author, October 17, 2003.

[20] Archives, the Polish Museum of America, Chicago.

[21] E-mail letter from Stephen Herx to the author, October 17, 2003.

[22] Trochimczyk, "Music at PIASA's 60th Meeting."

[23] Herz, unpublished biography; *NYT,* "Mme. Sembrich Must Rest."

[24] Tadeusz (Thaddeus) Wroński (1887–1965), Polish bass and impresario. Wroński studied voice in Warsaw, Milan and Paris, and made his operatic debut in Bagnacavallo, Italy, in 1910. He came to America to sing with the Boston Opera Company in 1913. During his operatic career he also sang with the opera companies of Paris, Venice, Milan, St. Petersburg and Warsaw. During World War I, he was also one of the music directors for the Columbia Gramophone Co. for whom he not only recorded but was also in charge of the production of its foreign records. He is listed as the copyright owner on the score of Paderewski's 1918 edition of *Hej, Orle biały*, the battle hymn of the Polish Army in America. [See: Paderewski *Hey, Orle biały*.] A good friend of Stojowski's, he was the best man at his wedding in 1918. In 1921, he moved to Detroit where he founded the city's first professional opera company, the Detroit Civic Opera, becoming its executive director and conductor of the opera chorus and the "Father of Detroit Opera." He authored a book on singing entitled *The Singer and His Art* which was critically acclaimed. He spent the last years of his life in San Diego.

[25] Pływawko, 219–220.

[26] Brachocki's given name, Alexander, is mistakenly printed as Edward.

[27] Anon. "Stojowski Artist-Pupil Recital for Polish Victims Relief Fund."

[28] Anon. "Stojowski to Return to Concert Field after Six Year's Interval."

[29] Watkins, *Soundings*, 464.

[30] Carnegie Hall Archives. *Słownik muzyków polskich,* v. 2 incorrectly gives the date as March 6.

[31] Program Notes for *Prayer for Poland…*

[32] The entire Stojowski family came to Poland during the autumn of 1929.

[33] These were known as "spiritual bouquets" in the American Catholic world and were given to friends and relatives as spiritual gifts. They would include the number and kind of prayers that would be said by the giver for the receiver.

[34] Ignatius Stojowski, Letter to father.

[35] The Cantata was actually found by Barbara Zakrzewska from the University of Southern California's Polish Music Center, who came to New York to create a preliminary catalogue of the Stojowski material that had been already found by the author.

[36] The Chicago performance took place at a local district convention of the "United Polish Choral Societies," which is probably a misnomer for the Polish Singers Alliance of America on May 3, 1941. *Bulletin of the Stojowski Students' Association*, February 1941.

[37] Carnegie Hall Archives.

[38] *Ibid.*

[39] Anon. "Hopes of Poland Crystallized in Stojowski's New Cantata."

[40] *Księga Kawalerów orderu 'Odrodzenia Polski,' Obywatele Cudzoziemscy.* Marcella Sembrich was also granted the same order on the same day as Stojowski's was awarded.

[41] Letter from Joseph Hartigan [sp?], Manager of the Foreign Language Bureau, Second Federal Reserve District, Treasury Department, New York, July 10, 1919 [ZLSC]. Stojowski's obituary in *Musical America* states that he was awarded the medal "for his welfare work."

Chapter Seven

THE COMPOSER IN DECLINE

W hen Stojowski arrived in America, he was best known as a composer, pianist and a teacher. At the time of his death, he was remembered as being a renowned teacher, an excellent pianist, and an occasional composer. Of the forty-three opus-numbered compositions, twenty-seven were written by the time he arrived in America in 1905 at the age of thirty-five. Stojowski lived for another forty-one years, adding only sixteen works with opus numbers to his catalogue. Additionally, there are two sets of Polish folk songs which he arranged, one which contains five exquisite settings of Polish Christmas carols for mixed chorus and piano, as well as a handful of published works that do not bear opus numbers.

The reason for his inactivity as a composer was primarily due to a change of priorities in his life. After all, Stojowski came to America to teach. Nonetheless, thirteen new works were added to his catalogue between 1906 and 1915. Stojowski's teaching obligations and his performing schedule reduced his composing activities to the summer months. This was certainly not a unique predicament—Gustav Mahler found himself in a very similar situation just a few years earlier. Until the outbreak of World War I in 1914, Stojowski spent each summer in Europe, except for the summer of 1911. Afterwards, there is a six-year hiatus from 1916 to 1922 when nothing was added to Stojowski's catalogue of compositions, except for a piece for solo violin published in 1920, a piano piece *Intermède lyrique pour piano*, Op. 41, no. 1, composed in 1922, and a song *Ce furent là des heures douces*, published that same year.[1] This period included the war years as well as Stojowski's settling down and raising a family. With the exception of the Polish folksong arrangements, *Chansons Polonaises*, there is a nine-year break until he composes *Scherzo-Caprice pour piano*, Op. 41, no. 2, in 1931. *Variations et fugue sur un thème original pour piano*, Op. 42, dedicated to his wife, dates from 1933. The Romance for Piano, Op. 43,

Figure VII-1. Stojowski ca. 1910. Photograph courtesy of ZLSC. Used by permission.

dedicated to Stojowski's student, Phyllida Ashley Everingham, was composed three years later but not published until 1941.[2] From 1933 to 1941, only the publication of his Polish folksong arrangements, *Memories of Poland* fill in the gap. While the responsibilities of being a husband and father may have caused the initial six-year hiatus in composing and performing, the later creative interruptions were caused by Stojowski working actively as a leader of the New York Polonia, writing numerous articles on music and his native land, traveling and teaching around the country each summer, and concert touring including foreign tours in France in 1921 and 1925, as well as taking the entire family to Poland in 1929 and South America in 1934. These activities certainly replaced the once sacred time for composing, for which Stojowski's summers were heretofore reserved. Finally, with the outbreak of World War II, Stojowski's patriotic fervor was once more rekindled, and he plunged headlong into his favorite cause of coming to the aid of Poland. One work, however, was written in 1941, *Lullaby,* based on a South American folksong. The work, dedicated to Paderewski *in memoriam,* appeared in an anthology of piano works entitled *Homage to Paderewski* published by Boosey & Hawkes. His next and last work was *Dumka for Piano*, dedicated to another former student, Guiomar Novaes-Pinto, and published in 1945.

Stojowski considered being a composer a "luxury." His correspondence with one of his publishers, Arthur P. Schmidt, preserved in the Library of Congress, shows Stojowski complaining about copyists and their high fees. Perhaps most contemporary composers would agree that not much has changed since then. However, according to a conversation that took place during the summer of 2005 in Paris, the publisher Jean Leduc told the author that Stojowski was one of Heugel's highly paid authors, and that he received handsome amounts for his compositions. For example, in 1910, he received 1,000 francs for his *Six melodies,* and in 1912, 1,200 francs for his *Quatre Morceaux pour piano* (also known as *Poème d'été* in the American edition published by G. Schirmer), Op. 36[3]. In 1913, his fee for *Aspirations—Poèmes pour piano*, Op. 39 was 1,200 francs.[4] It is important to remember that until World War II most European publishers did not pay royalty fees on the number of copies sold. Composers received a one-time honorarium. Since in 1913 $1.00 was worth 5.18 French francs, 1,200 Francs represented a sum of $231.66 at that time. Converting it to the current prices (at the ratio of a 1913 dollar equal to $18.99 in 2004), Stojowski's 1913 honorarium for *Aspirations* had the purchase power of $4,399.22 in 2004.[5]

Naturally, Stojowski supplemented his income by writing, teaching or performing. He also received royalties from the sales of piano rolls that he recorded for Ampico, but based on annual Ampico invoices found in ZLSC, they amounted to only a few dollars each year. Certainly, Stojowski was not alone in this predicament of trying to make a living as a composer. One only needs to look to Igor Stravinsky, who supplemented his income by conducting his own works, just like many other musicians who engaged in a variety of side activities in order to boost their earnings.

Stojowski believed in Mendelssohn's observation that a composer should write every day. When he returned to composing after a long stretch of teaching and performing, it would take him usually three days before ideas would begin to flow and take hold of him. As a composer, he had to reconcile himself with the toll composing would take upon his career as a pianist. In an article based on an interview with the composer for *Musical America,* Stojowski said:

> I have found it difficult to maintain harmony in the relation between composition and virtuosity. The former is likely to encroach upon the latter, and, although

the importance of technique in piano playing is frequently over-estimated, it is true that the pianist must keep his technique constantly exercised. When I met [Anton] Rubinstein, he asked me: 'What do you do?' I answered: 'I play the piano like a composer and compose like a pianist." This seemed to amuse the old master, who laughingly retorted: 'That's what I have been trying to do all my life.'[6]

Another reason which might have carried much weight in influencing him to make composing the least of his musical priorities—especially during the last two decades of his life—was the awareness that the music he wrote was no longer in tune with the times. While musical tastes changed, Stojowski remained a diehard romantic at heart, and his audiences knew it. Works by such composers as Albéniz (d. 1909), Debussy (d. 1918), Granados (d. 1916), Scriabin (d. 1915) and Szymanowski (d. 1937) represented the limit of modernity in Stojowski's repertoire. He held the music of Florent Schmitt (his exact contemporary) in high esteem, and thought that his music was unfairly underestimated. Even though Ravel's *Pavane pour une infante défunte* was in Stojowski's repertoire, he considered Ravel's music, for the most part, to be overestimated.[7] Stojowski's oeuvre, although beautifully imbued with rich lyricism and skillfully crafted, is unadventurous for the period, although his later works show the influence of impressionism. Some of Stojowski's most adventurous music is found in the seventh variation of the last movement in his Second Piano Concerto. Canonic in structure, the thematic motive is based on a rising fifth followed by two descending minor seconds. This theme is sequentially repeated until all 12 tones of the chromatic scale are employed, and then descends chromatically in a fragmented pattern consisting of two notes followed by rests. It is played in canon, first at the major third below and then at the minor sixth above, creating a feeling of polytonality while major sevenths and ninths are heard as harmonic suspensions, adding their own dissonance. In this variation, Stojowski also abandons tertian harmony and instead uses the fourth, fifth and diminished fifth to create this unusual harmonic texture.

At first, the new wave of music sweeping the globe prior to World War I was not threatening him. A recollection of Paderewski's 1913 name-day party at Riond-Bosson has Stojowski entertaining the guests with a lecture on the 30,000 natural noises that were used in contemporary music. Joining Stojowski to help demonstrate these contemporary techniques were Józef Hofmann and Rudolph Ganz, who—dressed as piano tuners—provided musical examples on the piano.[8] A few years later, when being posed the question, "What is the future of futurism?" Stojowski became politely philosophical, answering that everything is relative— even modern music—and that a lot of it must be taken *cum grano salis.*[9] In the press, Stojowski was even being praised for sticking to his guns and not breaking away from tradition nor turning to "tonal ugliness"[10]:

Figure VII-2. Zygmunt Stojowski: Second Piano Concerto (*Prologue, Scherzo & Variations*, Op. 32). Var. VII

The Stojowski muse does not lose itself in a chase after supermodernity, and therein lies the composer's real value, for he says what he has to say in a straightforward style which is always attractive and appears to express spontaneously the musical thoughts that spring up in Stojowski's fancy.[11]

By the 1930s, he was no longer hiding his feelings towards contemporary music. In 1932, the New York press accused Stojowski of musical censorship in his summer piano class at the Juilliard School of Music by quoting the summer school bulletin and stating that Stojowski will not allow works of some Moderns to be played when their music is "of an experimental nature or devoid of serious artistic purpose."[12] In an August 1934 interview in the Peruvian newspaper *El Comercio*, one can certainly sense that the composer feels as though he has been left out of the contemporary picture as he answers a question on modernism by saying:

But 'modernism,' in so far as [sic!] it stands for an idiom now in fashion, makes us unjust to many contemporaries that have not broken away from tradition and whose various works still could enrich and diversify our programs. [13]

It is hard to believe that Stojowski spent the first month of that summer on the ten-member music faculty of Mills College in California. He worked with futuristic composer Henry Cowell (1897–1965) who taught a contemporary music appreciation course.[14] It is a pity that Stojowski was so adamant about his dislike for such music. Who could not fall under the magic spell of Cowell's music when hearing *The Banshee*? It is probably safe to presume that Stojowski never dropped in to hear one of his colleague's lectures and thus missed an opportunity of being able to experience the worth of "experimental" music that could be seriously abundant in artistic purpose.

Whatever his opinions on the music of his contemporary American colleagues may have been, Stojowski took an active role in the formation of the American Grand Rights Association, Inc. (AGRA). It was the classical music equivalent to ASCAP. AGRA's purpose was to "promote, protect and police the performing rights of serious music" in the United States. At one promotional meeting in May 1936, among others, Stojowski shared the podium with Aaron Copland and Virgil Thomson.[15] AGRA was short-lived, but it became the forerunner of the American Composers Alliance (ACA) which was organized in December of the following year.

As a judge of contemporary music, Stojowski sat on the jury of the Paderewski Prize of the Paderewski Fund for Composers on at least two occasions. He is mentioned, along with Deems Taylor and Edward Burlingame Hill, as a member of the 1935 jury which awarded Chicagoan Allan Arthur Wilman (b. 1909) first prize of $1,000 for his symphonic poem *Solitude*, premiered by Serge Koussevitzky and the Boston Symphony Orchestra on April 20, 1936.[16] Again in 1938, Stojowski, Quincy Porter and Hans Lange were the jurors who voted to bestow the Paderewski Prize upon Hunter College faculty member William Helfer and Yale University graduate Morris Mamorsky. It is not known how often Stojowski served in this capacity. However, other composers who won the prize in the early 1940s, for example, were David Leo Diamond (1915–2005) and Gardner Read (1913–2005).

Even though his popularity faded as musical tastes changed, Stojowski could pride himself in knowing that his music was performed by the greatest musicians of his time. Paderewski paid Stojowski the greatest respect by performing his works, and so did his piano teacher in Paris, Louis Diémer. A review in *The Daily Graphic* of Diémer's May 19, 1893 recital at London's St. James Hall reported, "Louis Diémer gave a brilliant rendering of two clever pieces by Stojowski." Other notable pianists who featured Stojowski's works on their concerts included Ignacy Friedman (1882–1948), Rudolph Ganz, Boris Goldowsky (1909–2001), Percy Grainger (1882–1961), Myra Hess (1890–1965), Elly Ney (1882–1968), Alec Rowley (1892–1958), Olga Samaroff (1882–1948), Ernest Schelling, Stanisław Szpinalski (1901–1957), Antonina Szumowska, and Józef Hofmann, who kept Stojowski's hair-raising *Caprice-Orientale*, Op. 10, no. 2, in his concert repertoire for 40 years. Stojowski's songs were programmed by sopranos Marcella Sembrich and Maria Bogucka,[17] Greta Torpadie (who also sang the 1923 American premiere of Arnold Schoenberg's *Pierrot lunaire* and Charles Ives' Symphony No. 3), Povla Frijsh[18] and contralto Marie Delna.[19] Violinists who performed Stojowski's violin works included Arthur Argiewicz (1881–1966), Mischa Elman (1891–1967), Georges Enesco (1881–1955), Władysław Górski, Jascha Heifetz (1901–1987), Willy Hess (1859–1939), Sascha Jacobsen (1895–1972), Paweł Kochański (1887–1934), Émile Sauret (1852–1920), Jacques Thibaud (1880–1953), and "the German Paganini" August Wilhemj (1845–1908). Cellists who played Stojowski included Pablo Casals, Joseph Salmon (1864–1943), Herman Sandby (1881–1965), Herman Sandby (1881–1965), Alwin Schroeder (1855–1920), Mila Wellerson, and Willem Willeke (1880–1950). Famous conductors who incorporated Stojowski's orchestral works in concert included Sir Thomas Beecham, Jerzy Bojanowski, Antonia Brico, Hans von Bülow, Frank and Walter Damrosch, Grzegorz Fitelberg, Benjamin Godard, Sir Charles Hallé, Willem van Hoogstraten, Emil Młynarski, Pierre Monteux, Karl Muck, Arthur Nikisch, Josef Pasternack, Sir Malcolm Sargent, Ernest Schelling and Josef Stransky.

Endnotes

[1] Stojowski also disappeared from the New York concert stage for six years (1915–1921). According to an article in *Musical America* (June 11, 1921), "Stojowski to Return to Concert Field after Six Years' Interval," the composer supposedly completed his Second Symphony during this time. Unfortunately, only the Symphony's *Scherzo* survives in ZLSC.

[2] In the author's article "The Life of Zygmunt Stojowski," which appeared in the Winter 2002 issue of the *Polish Music Journal*, some of these dates were given in error, including mistaken information that there had been an eighteen-year hiatus in the composer's career. Lack of access to the manuscripts stored in New York, while the article was being written in Poland, was the cause.

[3] With this composition Stojowski enjoyed the best of all possible worlds. Not only did he receive an honorarium to compose the work for Heugel in Europe, but he also received 10% in royalties for copies sold in North America. [Courtesy of G. Schirmer Archives, New York.]

[4] Letter from Jean Leduc to author, April 10, 2006.

[5] "How Much Is It Worth Today?" Website http://eh.net/hmit/.

[6] Clark. "Hopes of Poland Crystallized in Stojowski's Cantata."

[7] Anon. "Day of Mediocrity in Piano Music."

[8] Phillips, 289.

[9] Stojowski, *The Future of Futurism* and an unidentified news clipping *Polish Pianist Greets Old Pupils after Concert at Albany Institute,* November 1923, ZLSC.

[10] Elson, "Paderewski and Symphony Concert."

[11] Review. Press clipping, *Music Courier*, February 10, 1915.

[12] Cushing.

[13] *Stojowski Students' Bulletin*, February 1935, 4.

[14] *Mills College Bulletin,* 23, 25.

[15] *NYT,* "Composers Form Promotion Group."

[16] Leichtentritt, 108.

[17] Maria Bogucka (1884–1957), Polish soprano. Her operatic debut took place in 1903 in Moniuszko's *Verbum nobile* at the Teatr Wielki in Warsaw. From 1906 to 1924, she sang with the National Theater in Prague. She guest performed in the opera houses of Paris, Vienna, Lwów, St. Petersburg, the Teatro Regio Turin and Teatro Communale Bologna. Her repertoire consisted of over 70 operas. She created eight roles, including that of Lygia in Jean Nouguès's opera *Quo vadis?* in Warsaw in 1910. She relocated to the United States and taught in New York. [Kutsch and Riemens, 477 and transcript for the 1949 WNYC Stojowski Memorial Program.]

[18] Povla Frijsh (1881–1960), Danish soprano. Trained in Copenhagen, Frijsh specialized in singing art song. She frequently performed with Alfred Cortot at the piano. In 1910, she sang in Paris under Gustav Mahler. During World War I, she performed for the French troops, and when she relocated to the United States in 1915, she gave benefit concerts with Stojowski for Polish relief. At the end of her concert career in 1940, she taught at the Juilliard School of Music. [Kutsch, 1576.]

[19] Marie Delna (1875–1932), French contralto. Delna's debut took place at the Opéra-Comique as Dido in *Les Troyens* by Berlioz in 1892. She sang at the Opéra-Comique for many seasons, creating eight roles. Her American debut took place at the Metropolitan Opera where she performed only in 1910. She also guest appeared with the opera companies of Monte Carlo Opera, La Monnaie in Brussels, La Scala, and the Grand Theatre de Parme. Despite a successful career, she died a pauper and was buried by the State. [Online: Historic Opera, http://www.historicopera.com/jsingerd_D1_page.htm.]

Chapter Eight

PROUD TO BE POLISH[1]

After the Great War, Stojowski became a champion of the newly independent Polish nation. According to a letter found in the Stojowski file at the Juilliard School Archives, Paderewski invited Stojowski to become a member of his government when he became premier.[2] Stojowski, however, found other ways to work for Poland and Polish culture by staying in the United States. In 1920, he took over the presidency of the Polish political and cultural club Koło Polskie [Polish Circle] of the local Society of Engineers and Merchants. This club, which Stojowski led for over twenty years, was a "round table" at whose meetings politics and cultural events were discussed in a non-partisan way.[3] Koło Polskie also functioned as an intermediary between the New York Polish community and the homeland, and was responsible for a wider understanding of Polish culture in American society.[4] The Polish press made note of Stojowski's contribution to the Polish cause in America and his efforts which often put "Country first, then Art."[5]

> The events of the past years have often torn Stojowski away from the piano and artistic output, forcing him into civic and patriotic work in the role of a lecturer. The many papers which he read, whether in university auditoriums or at artistic or scientific gatherings, were papers that informed the American public about the problems and meaning of Poland, and were remarkably instrumental in rolling away the clouds of ignorance and indifference in the spheres of Polish issues and nationality.[6]

Regarding the university auditoriums mentioned, Stojowski appeared at Columbia University both as a lecturer on Polish issues and as a performer of Polish music. Two such appearances took place in 1919, the first a lecture on "Poland's Share in the Rebuilding of Europe" on February 8, and the second a lecture-recital entitled "The Development of Polish Music" on December 19. For the latter, Stojowski was assisted by his pupil Alexander Brachocki, and a fellow countryman, the singer Tadeusz Wroński. Several hundred people turned out for the event.[7] Two years later, on December 13, 1921, Stojowski, joined by bass Adam Didur, violinist Paweł Kochański,[8] composer Karol Szymanowski and dancers from Warsaw's Municipal Auditorium shared a program at Columbia's Horace Mann Auditorium, billed as "An Evening of Polish Music."[9] The concert was sponsored by the University's Institute of Arts and Sciences and the Department of Slavonic Languages. In fact, it appears that an annual "Polish Night" might have taken place at Columbia University during the late 1910s and the early 1920s. In a letter to pianist Percy Grainger dated November 28, 1923, Stojowski sends his apologizes for not being able to attend a forthcoming Grainger recital because it conflicted with "a Polish evening at Columbia, in which I always take an active part."[10]

If there was an event that called for Polish music, Stojowski was always ready and willing to offer his services. On at least two occasions Stojowski was a guest artist for national conventions of the Polish Singers Alliance of America (PSAA). Founded in 1880, PSAA is today the oldest Polish cultural organization in North America. Stojowski participated in the opening concert of PSAA's 1923 Convention in Detroit,[11] performing as a soloist at Orchestra Hall, playing Chopin and works of his own, and once more accompanying bass Tadeusz Wroński as well as Metropolitan Opera contralto Ina Bourskaya.[12] Again, in 1929, PSAA hosted Stojowski at its national convention in Cleveland, where he performed works by Chopin, Paderewski and his own. He also accompanied soprano Maria Bogucka, former soloist of the Prague and Warsaw Opera Houses, in a selection of art songs and folk songs, including original compositions and his own arrangements.[13]

Also in 1929, Stojowski made his only return to Poland after the reestablishment of Polish independence in 1918, performing with the Warsaw Philharmonic Orchestra, playing recitals in Lwów and Poznań, and visiting Kraków and Zakopane. Based on letters from 1928 and 1929 that Zygmunt wrote to Maria (also known as Mariotka) Mickiewicz, both Paderewski and Opieński had approached him on the subject of directorship of the Warsaw Music Conservatory. His feelings on the subject were further tested during his visit in Warsaw. Had Stojowski accepted the position, he would have replaced Karol Szymanowski as the Conservatory's rector, a position that Szymanowski held in 1927–1929 and 1930–1931. In his October 1929 letter to Maria Mickiewicz, written as he sailed to America and following the Stock Market crash, Stojowski voices some frustration that his musical goals in the United States were never completely fulfilled. He contemplates whether or not a return to Poland would allow the fulfillment of these ambitions. Of course, Stojowski mentions his children and wonders how he could provide for them on a Polish salary.

Stojowski returned to America at the outset of the Great Depression. The financial crisis took its toll on the Stojowski family as well. In search of a better paying teaching position, Stojowski wrote to his friend and compatriot Józef Hofmann, who was then the director of the Curtis Institute of Music in Philadelphia, to see if anything was available. Hofmann wrote that, "…I am very much grieved to inform you that there is no possible chance of availing ourselves of your very good services because, as everyone knows, the tendency these days is to reduce and not to increase, which is also true of our Institute."

Back in New York, Stojowski continued to promote Polish culture. In the autumn of 1931, he performed at the opening of an exhibition of Polish arts and crafts at the Grand Central Palace, a large exhibition hall on Lexington Avenue, near Grand Central Station. His former student, Alexander Brachocki, first performed works by Chopin, Paderewski and Stojowski; then Stojowski accompanied Maria Bogucka in a group of his own songs.[14]

Stojowski had the distinction of being one of the founders of the short-lived Polish Institute of Arts and Letters (PIAL), incorporated in 1932 and active for five years. The Institute was founded "with the aim of presenting all phases of Polish culture to the American people, and in the belief that if the American public were familiarized with the great intellectual and artistic achievements of Poland, mutual benefits would result."[15] This approach was—and still is—unique for the Polish community. Most émigré Polish cultural organization are formed to do just the opposite, serving only the needs of the Polish community and preserving Polish heritage for its own people—or "Polonia," as the Polish diaspora refers to itself—and not function as a representative voice in non-Polonia circles.

The Institute became the American prototype for the Polish Institute of Arts and Sciences of America (PIASA), founded during World War II to function in exile as the Kraków-based Polski Instytut Umiejętności. Stojowski's Polish Institute of Arts and Letters was much more arts-oriented than today's PIASA. During its first three years, PIAL presented twenty-six programs—recitals, concerts, lectures and radio talks, art exhibitions and memorial programs—saluting illustrious Poles, including Metropolitan Opera tenor Jean de Reszke,[16] radiologist Madame Marie Skłodowska-Curie (1867–1934), Shakespearean actress Helena Modjeska (1842–1909), and author Joseph Conrad (1857–1924).[17] Honorary patrons of the PIAL at its founding included the Polish Ambassador and Consul General, Ignacy Paderewski, Marcella Sembrich, and many other leading persons in the world of politics, business and the arts, including Stojowski himself.[18] The Polish Institute of Arts and Letters was located in the Roerich Museum at the corner of 310 Riverside Drive and West 103rd Street,[19] and directed by Edith Bramhall Cullis-Williams[20] from its founding to dissolution.

Between the wars, Stojowski was a charter associate member of the American Polish Chamber of Commerce & Industry and a contributor of articles on Poland and Polish music to the Chamber of Commerce's *Poland America* magazine. Stojowski wrote on both Polish music and history, including such titles as *Paderewski, the Unique* and *[An] Outline of Polish Music.* During the 1920s Stojowski also served on the National Council Advisory Board for the newly formed Kosciuszko Foundation in New York.

Stojowski did not limit himself to writing on Polish topics. Over seventy of his articles and addresses in English and Polish have been found. According to one of the Stojowski résumés, he also wrote articles in French, German and Spanish; these efforts have not yet been researched or used in writing of this book. As a pianist and pedagogue expressing himself in writing, there are Stojowski's articles on piano performance and interpretation, as well as many *Master Lessons* which appeared in *The Etude* magazine. As a composer, we find him authoring articles that reflect his philosophy of music and give his opinion on the contemporary music of his day. Stojowski collaborated with the editors of *The Etude* for thirty-five years, about a half of the monthly's seventy-five-year history, spanning the years 1883–1957.

In addition to writing for music magazines, Stojowski also served on the advisory boards of two of them. The first was *Tempo*, a periodical published by the Music Education League in New York in 1934–1935. Rachmaninoff, Sembrich, Albert Spalding and Harold Bauer also served on its advisory board. The other magazine, *Keyboard*, was a professional magazine for piano teachers. Stojowski served on its advisory board in the early 1940s and wrote articles for it as well.

As a scholar, Stojowski was at his best writing about the music of his native land. His unpublished fifty-page commentary intended to accompany his also unpublished edition of Chopin's *Mazurkas*, was a project that occupied him for the last two years of his life.[21] As if this were not enough for a dying man in his mid-seventies, he was also helping the Klub Polski at Columbia University prepare for the sesquicentennial anniversary of poet Adam Mickiewicz's birth by gathering song settings of Mickiewicz's verse. The anthology, published a year after Stojowski's death, bears a dedication to Stojowski, without whose help the book's publication would not have been possible.[22] While living in Paris, Stojowski befriended the poet's son, Władysław and his daughter, Maria. Correspondence between Zygmunt and Maria is found at the Polish Library in Paris and at the Polish Music Center in Los Angeles.

Significantly, the Polish qualities of Stojowski's music should not be forgotten. They resonate throughout his Suite for Orchestra, the last movement of Symphony No. 1, and the patriotic Cantata *Prayer for Poland*. Stojowski's settings of Polish folk songs in two anthologies and his art songs—including two song cycles set to Polish poetry—are also based on Poland's musical heritage.

Finally, there are Stojowski's piano compositions. Two works not bearing opus numbers as well as twenty-four of his opus-numbered compositions form seventy-eight piano miniatures. Nineteen of them—or nearly twenty-five percent—are based on Polish melodies or dances, including the krakowiak, kujawiak, oberek, mazurka and polonaise as well as the dumka, a Slavic song form originating in Russia. Many of the piano pieces are also imbued with Chopinesque influences, including those not based on Polish dances and themes, such as the *Fantasie*. The *Rhapsodie symphonique* for Piano and Orchestra is still another composition based on Polish dance forms: the *Allegro moderato* uses the krakowiak rhythm, and the *Allegro vivace* is inspired by the mazurka. When mentioning Stojowski's piano works based on Polish dance forms, the early twentieth-century music critic Adolf Chybiński wrote, "They are full of honest sentiment joined with the great finesse of a pianist-composer who excellently knows how he must bring out the desired effect."[23]

The Suite for Orchestra in E-flat, Op. 9, proves Stojowski to be an accomplished orchestral composer, as well as a Polish patriot. National dances or melodies influence each of the Suite's three movements. The third movement contains a krakowiak, the second movement is an animated mazurka, and the first is a set of theme and variations based on the Polish Marian hymn *Witaj, królowo nieba* [*Salve Regina*].[24] Dating from 1891, the Suite is dedicated to the German conductor Hans von Bülow who conducted it on one of his last concerts in Hamburg. Around that same time, Stojowski showed the Suite to Brahms in Vienna, who looked at it, exclaiming, *Donnerwetter! Sie instrumentieren aber raffiniert!* [By Jove! You orchestrate with finesse!][25] Tchaikovsky was still another famous composer who took a fancy to the work and planned to conduct the Suite on January 15, 1894, at a concert featuring works by young composers in St. Petersburg.[26] Tchaikovsky's sudden death in November 1893 unfortunately prevented that from happening. Tchaikovsky, Brahms, and von Bülow were not alone in their admiration for the work. British composer Edward Elgar and conductor Sir Thomas Beecham programmed the Suite on the concert that featured the world premiere of Elgar's *Polonia* which was performed with the London Symphony Orchestra at Queen's Hall on July 6, 1915.[27]

Two musical examples from the Op. 9 Suite are given in order to show Stojowski's remarkable craftsmanship. The first is the melody for the Theme and Variations, which is intoned by the clarinet and bassoon and played in two periods of three-measure phrases. The second example is the exposition of the fugato which begins the last variation of that movement. The subject is based on the thematic material found in bars seven, eight and the first note of bar nine.

SUITE.

I. Thème varié.

Figure VIII-1. Stojowski: Suite in E-flat for Orchestra, Op. 9. The opening theme, *Witaj, królowo nieba*. Stanley Lucas, Weber, Pitt & Hatzfeld Ltd., 1891. Public domain

Figure VIII-2. Zygmunt Stojowski: Suite in E-flat for Orchestra, Op. 9 The fugato at the beginning of the Fourth Variation. Stanley Lucas, Weber, Pitt & Hatzfeld Ltd., 1891. Public domain

Endnotes

[1] Herter, *Zygmunt Stojowski—Polish Composer and Patriot.*

[2] Gamble.

[3] Preyss, Adele and Joanne Stefanik, 5.

[4] Adrianowska, 6–7.

[5] Quotation attributed to Paderewski.

[6] Anon., *Polska w Ameryce*, 8.

[7] Lecture File Card, Beginning of the Twentieth Century, Courtesy of Columbia University Archives—Columbiana Library. Stojowski also received a $35.00 honorarium for his first lecture on February 8.

[8] Stojowski would be one of the honorary pallbearers at Kochański's funeral in January 1934 at the Juilliard School of Music. [Anon. "Paul Kochanski, Noted Violinist Passes Away after Long Illness."]

[9] Program, ZLSC.

[10] Stojowski, *Letter to Percy Grainger.*

[11] Program, ZLSC. For some reason this concert is not mentioned in the otherwise thorough history of the Polish Singers Alliance of America by the late Stanislaus A. Blejwas.

[12] Born of Polish descent as Janina Burska in Zhytomir, Ukraine in 1888, Bourskaya gave her operatic debut in Kiev in 1913. For the next four years she sang in Russia where she changed her surname to a Russian-sounding one. After the Bolshevik Revolution, she toured China, Singapore and Indonesia and then relocated to New York City, where she had her debut in 1922 as Maddelena in *Rigoletto*. She continued to sing at the Metropolitan Opera until 1937, performing 37 roles and appearing 400 times. She also guest starred with the opera companies of Chicago and San Francisco. She died in Chicago in 1954. [Kutsch, 547.]

[13] Blejwas, 270.

[14] "Alexander Brachocki, New York," *Bulletin of the Stojowski Students' Association,* Mid-Winter Edition, Dec 1931, p. 3.

[15] Polish Institute of Arts and Letters, 1.

[16] Jean de Reszke (1850–1925), Polish tenor. Reszke came from a family of opera singers. His brother Édouard was a bass and his sister Joséphine was a soprano. Starting as a young boy, he sang for twelve years in the choir at St. John Cathedral in Warsaw. His operatic debut under the name of Giovanni di Reschi as Alfonso in Donizetti's *La Favorita* took place in Venice in 1874. He sang in the opera houses of Austria, England, France, Italy, Russia, Spain and the United States. In 1890, he debuted at the Metropolitan Opera and sang 17 roles and gave 227 performances during his career there. [Kutsch, 1116–1117.]

[17] Polish violinist Bronisław Huberman's December 16, 1934 lecture on the Pan-European Problem can be found on the internet at http://www.huberman.info/literature/pan_europa/pan_europe_problem/. The original typewritten copy is in the Edith Cullis-Williams Collection, The Kosciuszko Foundation Archives, New York.

[18] PIAL stationery letterhead, Edith Cullis-Williams Collection, The Kosciuszko Foundation Archives, New York.

[19] The Roerich Museum was founded by Nicholas Roerich (1874–1947), a Russian artist and peace activist who also wrote books and articles on art, education, culture, philosophy and humanitarianism. He was a classmate of Sergei Diaghilev, who engaged Roerich to design the sets and costumes for Rimsky-Korsakov's *Ivan the Terrible* and Borodin's opera *Prince Igor*. Together, the two of them collaborated with Igor Stravinsky on the world premiere of the ballet *Le Sacre du Printemps*. The museum changed its name to the Riverside Museum in 1936, due to quarreling among Roerich's followers. Although the Art Deco building which Roerich built for his museum still stands today, the Nicholas Roerich Museum is currently located a few blocks away at 319 West 107th Street. For more information, see: www.roerich.org.

[20] Kosciuszko Foundation Archives. Edith Bramhall Cullis-Williams (d. 1955), a woman of non-Polish descent, was stationed as an American Red Cross nurse in Poland in 1919. It was there that she became interested in Polish culture, causing her to also become a great friend of Poland. She returned to Poland several times in the 1920s and the 1930s. After her work with PIAL, she was actively involved with the Kosciuszko Foundation from 1947–1954, donating over 1,000 books to the foundation and providing shelves for them.

[21] Only the Mazurka in C Minor, Op. 30, no. 1 was published in Frank Cooper's article *Stojowski 100 Years Later.*

[22] Coleman, dedication page.

[23] Chybiński, 322.

[24] The Polish equivalent of the eleventh-century hymn *Salve Regina*.

[25] Stojowski, *Recollections of Brahms,* 149.

[26] Poznansky, 29.

[27] A year later the American premiere of Elgar's *Polonia* shared the program with Paderewski in Stojowski's Second Piano Concerto.

Chapter Nine

TWILIGHT OF A GREAT MUSICIAN

There is a Polish saying, *Starość nie radość*. Translated literally into English (and losing its rhyme), it means, "There is no joy in getting old." The same was true for Stojowski. He and his wife sold their four-story brownstone on West 76th Street and moved into the ten-room, fourth-floor apartment at 16 East 96th Street, formerly occupied by Pablo Casals. Henry was away at Dickinson College and Ignatius was in a seminary, leaving only Alfred, who was studying at Columbia, at home. At their new residence there were no stairs to climb. The move was made in 1939, when Stojowski was sixty-nine years old.

Because teaching now took priority in his professional life, Stojowski's output as a composer decreased tremendously, just like his concert appearances. Except for a couple of performances of his *Rhapsodie symphonique* and Liszt's Piano Concerto No. 1 during the late thirties, Stojowski basically limited his playing to lecture-recitals on Chopin's music. The audiences for these programs were either the academic or the Polish émigré circles, and the general public had only rare occasions to admire Stojowski's music or his pianistic prowess.

One thing that Stojowski never tired of—even in his old age—was coming to the rescue of his native land. The outbreak of World War II on September 1, 1939 on Polish soil provided the opportunity to demonstrate his patriotism. Stojowski also realized that his son, Henry, born to a Polish national on French soil on the same day eighteen years earlier, could be eligible for the draft into both the French and Polish armies. Worrying about the fate of their son, Zygmunt and Luisa finally decided to apply for United States citizenship.[1]

Just two months after the Nazi and Soviet invasion of Poland, Stojowski helped to organize the Commission for Polish Relief, an organization that sponsored a Polish Relief Concert at Carnegie Hall on November 14, 1939, featuring tenor Jan Kiepura (1902–1966) and Artur Rubinstein.[2] In his memoirs *My Many Years*, Rubinstein mistakenly states that the concert was held at the Metropolitan Opera.[3]

According to the stationery letterhead of the Paderewski Testimonial Fund, Inc., which can be found in PIASA archives, Stojowski was a committee chairman and sponsor of this organization. Created to honor the memory of Paderewski, who died in June 1941, the Fund was intended to relieve the suffering of the Polish population, much as the World War I Polish Victims' Relief Fund did. The Paderewski Testimonial Fund was a participating service of the Polish War Relief through the American National War Fund.[4]

There is still another letterhead of the New York City Committee for the Paderewski Fund for Polish Relief on which Stojowski is listed as one of the organization's many vice-chairmen.[5] Written during the war, it is a draft of a letter to Dr. Samuel T. Arnold, the first provost of Brown University. In the letter, written in pencil and very difficult to read, Stojowski asks Arnold to meet with him with at PIASA to see if there was a possibility of Arnold cooperating with the Paderewski Fund. Dr. Samuel T. Arnold (1892–1956) was the man responsible for hiring the scientists who worked on the Manhattan Project (1942–1946) which produced the atomic bomb. Although the two had met earlier in the spring of that year, it is not known if the meeting at PIASA ever took place.

Stojowski became actively involved with PIASA shortly after its founding in 1942. In a letter dated June 22, 1942, Wacław Lednicki, the Chairman of PIASA's Commission on the History of Arts and Music, offered Zygmunt the position of Vice-Chairman.[6] Stojowski declined. Nevertheless, in 1943, he served on the Commission's subcommittee, which planned a series of lectures, the first of which was Feliks Łabuński's *Six Centuries of Polish Music*, and in 1944 he chaired the committee which organized the May 4 Carnegie Hall concert of Polish music, also sponsored by PIASA.

Stojowski's other wartime activities included serving as the president, in 1945, of the *Polish Review,* a weekly magazine published with the assistance of the Polish Government Information Center, as well as founding and chairing the Polish Musicians' Committee (PMC).[7] Members of the Committee included conductor Grzegorz Fitelberg (1879–1953), pianist Mieczysław Horszowski (1892–1993), violinist Bronisław Huberman (1882–1947), composer-pianist and music critic Feliks R. Łabuński (1892–1979), harpsichordist Wanda Landowska (1877–1959), pianist Witold Małcużyński, composer Karol Rathaus (1895–1954), pianist Artur Rubinstein and Stojowski. Composer and music critic Michał Kondracki (1902–1984) joined the Committee after he arrived in New York in 1943, but resigned after what seems to have been a disagreement with Rubinstein. In his diary for December 18, 1943, Horszowski writes, "Rubinstein voted against Kondracki who left the committee."[8]

Looking at the membership list of this Committee, two things can be quickly ascertained. One is that no one could ever accuse Stojowski of being anti-Semitic. Over half of the members on his committee were Poles of Jewish extraction. The other is that all members resided on America's East Coast at the beginning of World War II. Musicians like conductor Artur Rodziński, who was then conductor of the Cleveland Orchestra, Jerzy Bojanowski, a Polish conductor who was based in Milwaukee, and pianist-composer Wiktor Łabuński, the director of the Kansas City Conservatory of Music, were probably not asked to join.[9]

However, there were some prominent musicians, who lived or worked on the East Coast, whose names are absent from the list: Leopold Stokowski and Josef Hofmann, for example. At the outbreak of World War II Stojowski was in Los Angeles for five weeks of master classes. He contacted Stokowski, asking him to become chairman of the committee he was about to form, an offer which the conductor immediately accepted. Two days later Stokowski wrote to Stojowski, stating that he had second thoughts of becoming a member, because it was "going to be difficult to keep politics out of people's thoughts." Stokowski was obviously afraid of what the American public might think of his taking a stand as an American in a war that America was not yet involved.[10]

In spite of his full teaching load, the exhausting heat wave with temperatures soaring into the 100s that Los Angeles was experiencing, and enduring the only tropical storm to hit California in its history, the 69-year-old Stojowski found the time and energy to contact people who empathized with him over the fate of Poland. In a matter of weeks, the Hollywood Committee for Polish Relief, Inc., was formed. At its outset, the committee tackled the problem of caring for the 30,000 Polish refugees who escaped to Romania. The committee also planned to expand their relief work and carry on the same task with Polish refugees in Hungary. Although Stojowski could not convince Stokowski to become involved with the committee's administration, he did obtain his consent to conduct the October 19, 1939[11] benefit concert for Polish relief. Since it was between the Hollywood Bowl season and the regular concert season, the concert was played by an *ad hoc* orchestra called "The Augmented Symphony Orchestra" made up of members of the Los Angeles Philharmonic. A total of 110 instrumentalists played in the orchestra.

An appeal by novelist Rupert Hughes was included in the program. Hughes wrote the 1905 novel *Żal,* a love story of a Polish pianist, which was advertised in Stojowski's Carnegie Hall debut program of January 6, 1906 (see Fig. III-2, p. 54). Hughes was now writing about how President George Washington had wept "when in 1798 a Polish poet described to him the sufferings of Poland turned asunder." Both Stokowski with Zygmunt and Luisa Stojowski are listed among the concert's 106 patrons. Stojowski, who helped form the committee, is also listed among the forty-seven members of the Board of Governors.

The committee had a star-studded cast, including film directors Cecil B. DeMille, Ernst Lubitsch and Joseph Pasternak; Polish-born Harry Warner (one of the founders of Warner Brothers Pictures); motion picture producers Walt Disney and Sol Lesser; composers Irving Berlin, Bronisław Kaper and Victor Young; actresses Joan Crawford, Kay Francis and Doris Kenyon; actors Ralph Bellamy, Douglas Fairbanks and his son Douglas Fairbanks Jr., Robert Montgomery, Basil Rathbone, Edward G. Robinson and Charles Chaplin. Stojowski's World War I volunteers are found too: Ernest Schelling and Thaddeus Wroński. Polish Metropolitan Opera star and tenor-turned-actor Marek Windheim, pianist Józef Hofmann (who was originally scheduled to be a soloist on the concert) and violinist Bronisław Gimpel are also found, the first as patron, concert committee member and board of trustees' member, the second as a patron, while the latter was both a patron and one of the concert's four soloists.

The program was both patriotic and mindful of a wartime atmosphere. The tragedy of death was reflected in soprano Rose Bampton's performance of *The Song of the Wood Dove* from Arnold Schoenberg's *Gurrelieder*,[12] and baritone Nelson Eddy's aria *Pauvre martyr obscure* from the patriotic opera *Patrie* by Emile Paladilhe (1844–1926), as well as the performance of Liszt's *Funerailles* by pianist Dalies Frantz.[13] According to reports carried in the *Los Angeles Times* on October 20, the concert raised $6,000 for Polish relief.[14]

Stojowski probably did not ask Hofmann to join his Polish relief efforts because of at least two rejections regarding proposals to help with Polish causes in America. When, in 1915, Stojowski sent Hofmann a letter reminding him that he had not yet answered Paderewski's appeal to raise ten million dollars in one month for the Polish cause, Hofmann replied that he saw no place for an independent Poland after the war. Being a political pessimist, Hofmann was convinced that Poland's autonomy would not be advantageous to any of Poland's three partitioning powers, Prussia, Russia and the Austro-Hungarian Empire that had been administering Polish territory since the late 1790s.[15] Hofmann also added that if the Russian-controlled capital of Poland would fall into the hands of the Germans, they would cause much more harm than the Russians ever could. As it turned out, Hofmann's deeply pessimistic scenario predicted with chilling accuracy the tragic fate of Poland during World War II.

In 1926, Stojowski asked Hofmann to join his Koło Polskie. Hofmann replied with a letter stating that he had better things to do with his life than just chitchat, and that he would never join a Koło Polskie in New York or anywhere else for that matter. He then asked condescendingly, "Would it please you if I became a 'passive' member of the Koło Polskie?"[16] As a result, Stojowski did not take him up on his offer to only lend his name to the organization.

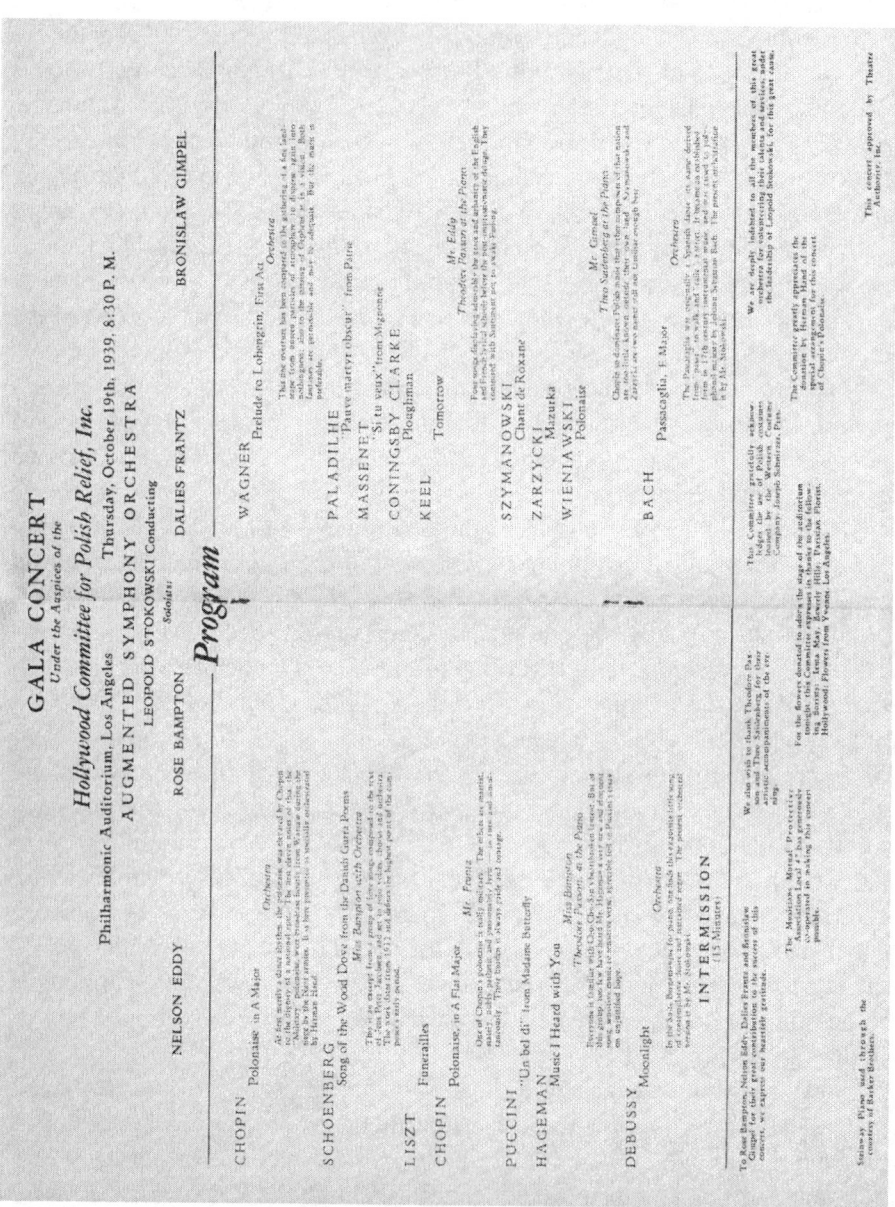

Figure IX-1. Program for the benefit concert of the Hollywood Committee for Polish Relief, Inc., an organization that Stojowski helped found. Courtesy of ZLSC. Used by permission. All rights reserved

The Polish Musicians' Committee sponsored two concerts of Polish music in 1944. The first (mentioned earlier as having been presented with the help of PIASA) was the May 4, 1944, concert of Polish orchestral music at Carnegie Hall with "members of" the New York Philharmonic-Symphony, led by Grzegorz Fitelberg.[17] The concert included music by Stojowski, Łabuński, Paderewski and Szymanowski.[18] Soloists included Huberman in Szymanowski's Violin Concerto, and Małcuzyński in Paderewski's Piano Concerto.[19] The US State Department recorded the concert for later radio broadcast to Europe.[20] The second concert, which PMC also presented that year, was a concert of contemporary Polish chamber music at Times Hall, 240 West 44th Street, on December 18. The program featured works by Antoni Szałowski (1907–1973), F. Łabuński, Karol Rathaus and Jerzy Fitelberg (1903–1951), the son of the conductor Grzegorz Fitelberg.[21] Performers for the chamber music concert included the Gordon String Quartet, clarinetist Simon Bellison, pianists Mieczysław Horszowski and Karol Rathaus, violinist Boris Schwarz and flautist John Wummer.[22]

The activities of PMC also included charitable work. Based on correspondence between Zygmunt Stojowski and Feliks Łabuński, who took over as PMC chairman when Stojowski was hospitalized with cancer of the colon in the spring of 1946, the committee sent packages to needy Polish musicians living in Western Europe following the war.[23] Correspondence found at Warsaw University's Library in the Archives of Twentieth-Century Polish Composers makes clear who benefited from the packages sent out in 1945 and 1946. They included composers Antoni Szałowski (1907–1973), Michał Spisak (1914–1965), Alfred Gradstein (1904–1954), conductor Ignacy Neumark (1888–1959), pianist Zygmunt Dygat and composer and music critic Zygmunt Mycielski (1907–1987). For example, Spisak received ten packages and Szałowski fourteen from May through September 1945. On at least one occasion, Stojowski's wife, Luisa, actually did the packing and mailing. In a letter from Grzegorz Fitelberg to Antoni Szałowski dated February 2, 1946, Fitelberg wrote, "Did the packages arrive? Five were sent—two for you, two for Dygat, and one for Spisak... Mrs. Stojowska sent the packages."[24] There are also other bookkeeping records for the Polish Musicians Relief found in ZLSC dating from 1941–1942 that testify to the same kind of aid given to Polish musicians earlier in the war.[25] Other Polish musicians living in the United States who were not on the committee also contributed financially to its activities. One of the most generous was Hollywood composer Bronisław Kaper (1902–1983), who became an Academy Award winner in 1953.[26] PMC ceased operating in the summer of 1947. The committee transferred the remaining funds of $1,428.22 to the Polish Institute of Arts and Sciences of America on July 27, and PIASA was to use that capital for helping Polish musicians in the USA and abroad.[27]

One more wartime activity of Stojowski's seems to have been forgotten. In a letter written by Frederick Gamble found in the Juilliard School Archives, it is mentioned that, at the outbreak of World War II, the Polish Government-in-Exile in London requested Stojowski to help oversee the management and protection of millions of dollars in Polish gold on deposit in the United States of America. This claim seems to be confirmed in a letter found in the family archives from the New York law firm of Sullivan & Cromwell. The letter, dated March 22, 1944, and addressed to Sigismond J. Stojowski and Roman Józef Majewski, informs them that the Polish gold reserves had been returned to the Bank of Poland. Further correspondence in the Stojowski Collection indicates that he was also involved in saving Polish gold deposits in France. A letter from Bank Polski c/o Bank of England, London, EC 2, typed in Polish, dated September 12, 1941, thanks Stojowski for his efforts in America related to the recovery of Polish gold reserves held by the Banque de France.[28]

At the close of 1944, with the end of World War II on the horizon and an ominous political future for Poland in sight, Stojowski was on the podium giving speeches condemning the West for its plans for Poland. According to Stojowski, Western leaders were allowing Poland to fall under "the mighty fraternal embrace of the big [Russian] bear" along with her "two cubs," the Union of Polish Patriots—a Communist substitute for the legitimate Polish Government-in-Exile in London—and the "Free Germany Committee." He decried the decision to change Poland's western and eastern borders which would mean "Herding people like cattle across frontiers arbitrarily traced, new migrations enforced upon an unhappy lot, to the tune of appeasement of the powerful." He also felt that it was Poland who lost and was forced into "unconditional surrender" at the end of the war.[29] On December 16, Stojowski, in the name of the Koło Polskie of New York, sent a Christmas cable to President Franklin D. Roosevelt. Stojowski's holiday greetings open with his expression of trust in Roosevelt's high moral authority, and express hope that forcing a unilateral solution upon gallant Poland can be "averted in the very interest of amity between neighbors and a trusted world order." He ends the telegram by wishing the President, "May this Christmas remind our would-be friends that peace was promised to men of good will, and may God inspire your leadership to make power just and justice strong for our children's sake in a better world."[30] If only Stojowski could have had the same political clout with President Roosevelt that Paderewski had had with President Wilson!

Endnotes

[1] Conversation with Henry Stojowski in January 2002.

[2] *Bulletin of the Stojowski Students' Association*, New York, (Jan 1940), 7.

[3] Rubinstein, Artur, *My Many Years*, 466.

[4] Schelling, Mrs. Ernest.

[5] ZLSC.

[6] Lednicki.

[7] Not to be confused with today's *The Polish Review*, a quarterly published by the Polish Institute of Arts and Sciences of America in New York.

[8] Horszowski, 332.

[9] Although Rodziński was not a member of the Polish Musicians' Committee, Stojowski and Rodziński were in contact with each other during World War II regarding a possible performance of Karol Szymanowski's *Stabat Mater*. (The American premiere of the work took place in New York on January 29, 1931 with the New York Schola Cantorum and the New York University A Cappella Choir and New York Philharmonic Symphony.) Because the full score and parts would have had to have been hired from Universal Edition, the composer's publisher in Nazi-controlled Vienna, Rodziński's performance did not take place until after the war. In a letter dated December 30, 1944, Rodziński apologizes to Stojowski for having to postpone a 1945 performance because of a conflict with recording sessions and promises to perform it a year later. The letter was found in 2004 in the unsorted and not yet catalogued Arthur Rodziński Collection at the Library of Congress, Washington, D.C.

[10] Stokowski.

[11] Oakley, 6. Oakley gives the date as October 18. The concert actually took place on October 19.

[12] The first orchestral performance of *Gurrelieder* in 1913 featured Polish soprano Marya Freund (1876–1966), the mother of bass-baritone Doda Conrad (1905–1998).

[13] Program of the Hollywood Committee for Polish Relief, Inc. Benefit Concert, ZLSC.

[14] *LAT,* "Noted Artists Play and Sing for Charity."

[15] Hofmann would respond musically to the tragedy of the war by composing a song set to the poem *In Flanders Fields* by Canadian John McCrae and an arrangement for piano of the American national anthem, *The Star-Spangled Banner.*

[16] Correspondence from the Josef Hofmann Archives, International Piano Archives, College Park; currently on loan to Gregor Benko.

[17] Gregorz Fitelberg (1879–1953), Polish conductor and composer of Latvian-Jewish descent. His family moved to Warsaw in 1896 so that he could study the violin with Stanisław Barcewicz at the Warsaw Music Institute where he also studied composition with Zygmunt Noskowski. As a conductor, he made his debut with the Warsaw Philharmonic Orchestra in 1904. As a composer, he was a member of a group of Polish composers known as *Młoda Polska* [Young Poland].

[18] The program: Stojowski—*Intermède polonaise* from Suite in E-flat Major, Op. 9; Łabuński—the NY premiere of his Suite for Strings; Paderewski—Polish Fantasy for Piano & Orchestra, Op. 19; and two works by Karol Szymanowski (1882–1937)—the ballet *Harnasie,* Op. 55, and First Violin Concerto, Op. 35.

[19] Carnegie Hall Flyer of May 4, 1944 concert, Carnegie Hall Archives.

[20] A 78-RPM recording of the second movement of Stojowski's Suite from this concert with a US State Department label exists in ZLSC. Unfortunately, conductor Grzegorz Fitelberg performed it at such an outrageously fast tempo that the clarity of the composer's writing is completely blurred by the inability of the musicians to play the work at such speed. One can compare Fitelberg's performance with the live-concert recording of Antonia Brico's devoted and masterful interpretation. Both recordings are found in ZLSC and have been transferred onto CD.

[21] Exact program: Szałowski—Third String Quartet; F. Łabuński—Divertimento for Flute and Piano; Rathaus—world premiere of Trio for Violin, Clarinet and Piano; Szymanowski—Four Mazurkas, Op. 50, and *Tantris le Bouffon* from *Masques,* Op. 34; J. Fitelberg—American premiere of Third String Quartet.

[22] Times Hall Concert Flyer for December 18, 1944, ZLSC.

[23] Stojowski, *Letters to Feliks Łabuński.*

[24] Fitelberg, 84.

[25] Stojowski, *Polish Musicians Relief.*

[26] Kaper, who would have been 100 years old in February 2002, won the 1953 Academy Award for the best motion picture song of the year, *Hi Lili, Hi-Lo.* Sadly, the centennial of his birth was ignored not only by Polish musical circles

in the USA, but also, for the most part, by those in his native Poland. As this book goes to print, Polish film director Anna Ferens plans to produce a documentary film on Kaper.

[27] Feliks Łabuński, *Correspondence* K-LXXXIV/14.

[28] These transfers, of course, were to the Polish Government-in-Exile in London.

[29] Stojowski. *Eastern Europe and the American Dream.*

[30] Stojowski, *Telegram to President Roosevelt.*

Chapter Ten

REMEMBERING STOJOWSKI

Stojowski died on November 5, 1946 and was buried on November 8 following his funeral at St. Ignatius Loyola Church on Park Avenue and East 84th Street. Later his wife, Luisa, and the youngest son, Ignatius, also had their requiems sung at this church. For someone who refused to break from musical tradition, Stojowski would surely be happy to know that his parish church continues to preserve the rich musical heritage of the Roman Catholic Church, and escaped the post-Vatican II invasion of musical mediocrity into liturgical music. The church's High Mass on Sunday mornings has gained national acclaim for its superior musical standards—it is a service that no Catholic musician should miss when visiting New York City. The church has the largest mechanical action organ in the city, and its organist, Kent Tritle, is also the organist for the New York Philharmonic Orchestra and is on the faculty of The Juilliard School.

Stojowski's burial took place in the gigantic Calvary Cemetery Woodside in Queens County, New York, where his remains are interred alongside those of three million New Yorkers. Horszowski, who attended the funeral, recorded in his diary that Stojowski's casket was placed in the same grave as his mother.[1] When Luisa died in March 1982, her casket was placed upon her husband's. Only Stojowski's mother, Marie, however, has a tombstone.

Until 1953, annual memorial concerts on May 2 (Zygmunt's name-day) were broadcast on station WNYC. The 1949 concert, for example, featured Sidney Schachter and the composer's widow, Luisa, at the piano as well as the soprano Maria Bogucka. The concert was prepared in part by composer Tadeusz Kassern (1904–1957) who came to the United States in 1945 as the cultural attaché for the People's Republic of Poland. Kassern was responsible for making arrangements with the radio station, writing the program's introduction and sending a press release to the New York papers.[2] It is very doubtful that Stojowski, whose political leanings were 'better dead than red," would have had anything to do with a Polish communist regime official in order to promote Polish culture. Nonetheless, two years after Stojowski's death, in December 1948, Kassern not only resigned from the diplomatic corps, but he also applied for political asylum in the United States. Kassern's assistance on Stojowski's memorial program was perhaps a way of paying respect to the composer who was the senior figure among Polish musicians living in America at the time of his arrival.

After these concerts concluded, Stojowski practically disappeared from the concert stage and the media. For the centennial of Stojowski's birth in 1970, the biographical article by Frank Cooper in *Clavier* was the only major commemoration of the anniversary. A quiet celebration of this historical landmark may have been due to Luisa's serious illness and hospitalization for treatment of ulcers. A few years later, in 1976, the International Piano Archives (co-founded by Stojowski's student, Arthur Loesser), came out with a LP of transfers of Stojowski's radio broadcasts and Luisa's performances of her husband's compositions.

At the moment, Stojowski's music seems to be enjoying a modest revival. After a hiatus of several decades, his orchestral music was once again heard in Poland's capital when British pianist Jonathan Plowright performed the First Piano Concerto with the Warsaw Philharmonic Orchestra in October 2003. The Lutosławski International Cello Competition now lists Stojowski's Cello Sonata as one of twelve repertoire works for the second round of the competition. In October 2004, Universität der Künste in Berlin presented an International Symposium entitled *Polen im Herzen: Komponieren in der Fremde* [Poland in the Heart: Composing Abroad], during which a paper on Stojowski's music was read and his Second Violin Sonata performed. The Szczecin Philharmonic Orchestra performed Stojowski's Suite for Orchestra in December 2005.

Other significant milestones in the rekindling of interest in the music of this extraordinary musician were the releases (in 2001, 2002, 2004, 2005 and 2006) of six commercial recordings of Stojowski's three compositions for piano and orchestra, a selection of his solo piano works, the First Violin Sonata, the Cello Sonata, and the complete works for cello and piano. The first included a recording of *Rhapsodie symphonique* with pianist Ian Munro and the Tasmanian Symphony Orchestra on ABC Records Australia. The second and third CDs were Hyperion Records' release of the two piano concertos with Jonathan Plowright and the BBC Scottish Symphony Orchestra, and Plowright's interpretation of Stojowski's solo piano works. Both of Hyperion's CDs became award-winning recordings. The fourth CD, a recording of the First Violin Sonata, was released in Poland on Acte Préalable with violinist Barbara Trojanowska. In 2006 two other recordings were issued on Polish labels. The first was Michał Dmochowski's interpretation of

Stojowski's Sonata for Piano and Cello on DUX, and the second was once more on Acte Préalable, featuring cellist Jarosław Domżal in Stojowski's complete works for cello and piano. The latter recording, released in November, marked the sixtieth anniversary of the composer's death. In 2007 Acte Préalable also plans to record Stojowski's Symphony and Suite for Orchestra with the Rzeszów Philharmonic Orchestra, Jerzy Kosek conducting. Abroad, the German classical music label EDA from Klassik Center Kassel also plans to release a Stojowski CD in the future.

Archival radio recordings also took place in 2006. The National Polish Radio Symphony Orchestra in Katowice recorded the Cello Concerto (*Concertstück*) with cellist Tomasz Strahl and both the Violin Concerto and the *Romanze* for violin and orchestra with Tomasz Tomaszewski, the concertmaster of the Deutsche Oper in Berlin. Łukasz Borowicz was the conductor for both recordings.

Musicologists, historians and even political scientists will be interested in the Stojowski items that were donated by the New York Philharmonic Orchestra Library to the Polish Music Center in Los Angeles in October 2006. Representing the New York Philharmonic, Hanna Lachert, a violinist with the Orchestra since 1972, transferred the Stojowski memorabilia to the Polish Music Center. This brief ceremony took place at the beginning of a lecture on Stojowski given by the book's author at the Kosciuszko Foundation in New York. The Stojowski materials that were donated come from the Harold Lineback Collection, purchased by the Orchestra in 2002. Harold Lineback, a collector from St. Louis, Missouri, received the items from Luisa Stojowska in 1972.

In addition to such memorabilia as programs and correspondence, the collection also contains scores of small notebook pads in which the Polish musician recorded his philosophical thoughts on music and life. Of equal interest are nearly a dozen articles and addresses which Stojowski either published or presented. Some of the articles from the Great War period were published under the pseudonym Anthony D. Jordan.

One of the Collection's most interesting speeches is one that was given in New York on May 25, 1919, only six months after Poland's return to independence. Entitled *The Poles, the Jews and the World's Peace*, it shines like a light in the darkness of the many accusations made against Poland for being anti-Semitic. Stojowski—as a leader of the New York Polonia—calls upon the acceptance of Jews in Poland as true Poles and not as aliens on Polish soil. He recalls Poland as once being a "torchbearer of liberty and justice" for all. He reminds his listeners of the rights given in the Polish constitution of May 3, 1791, which decreed, "Every man who sets foot on Polish soil is free." "By that bidding," Stojowski continues, "the new Poland must and will provide." He continues by supporting the idea that Polish schools be open to Jews, going so far as demanding that Polish schools be compulsory for Jewish children. Stojowski, however, puts the political leanings of American Jewry to the test, admonishing them for supporting German control over northern Silesia and for being against Polish control of the western part of the Ukraine. Stojowski calls upon the American Diaspora to give newborn Poland a chance by stating, "...No one more than a Pole could sympathize with the sufferings of the Jew [and] no one more than a Jew would rejoice at the rebirth of Poland." How unfortunate that Stojowski never had the opportunity to give this speech in his native Poland!

However much has been already accomplished, still more must be done to keep Stojowski's music alive. A critical step was the donation of the Stojowski family archives—officially known as the Zygmunt and Luisa Stojowski Collection—to the Polish Music Center at the University of Southern California. The official presentation of the Collection to the University took place on October 11, 2006. The next day the annual Paderewski Lecture, devoted to the life and music of Zygmunt Stojowski, was given by the author. The Lecture was followed by a recital of Stojowski and Paderewski's music by pianist Jonathan Plowright, who repeated the program at the Cass Winery in Paso Robles (the town where Paderewski had his vineyards) and at Weill Hall in Carnegie Hall in New York.

The musical taste of artistic directors and conductors of orchestras will be one of the most significant factors in continuing the revival of Stojowski's music. When Stojowski was ignored by the Warsaw Philharmonic during their centennial season, one of the reasons cited for that omission was that he was just "too old-fashioned" for contemporary tastes. Stojowski was not the only composer who was ignored. The music of Władysław Żeleński and Zygmunt Noskowski (who shared the 1901 Warsaw Philharmonic inaugural program alongside works by Paderewski and Moniuszko) was also ignored. How ironic indeed, that the recent interest in Stojowski's music actually began outside of Poland! As Stanisław Dybowski pointed out in his four-page review of Plowright's recording of Stojowski's piano concertos in 2002, this is not the first time that foreigners have discovered what hidden jewels the Poles possess. Plowright's future recordings with Hyperion Records will feature more Polish music of the period, including compositions by Paderewski (Sonata, and Theme and Variations in E-flat Minor) and a recording of the Second Piano Concerto by Henryk Melcer. At long last, for the first time in decades, Warsaw's Philharmonic Hall will once more echo with the sounds of Stojowski's Symphony. This time it will be during a guest performance by the Rzeszów Philharmonic Orchestra on February 9, 2007.

Like Stojowski's Cantatas *Springtime* and *Prayer for Poland*, whose full scores and parts were prepared by John Hein in a new edition available from the Polish Music Center, many other works still need to be made widely available.

They include the following unpublished works: the Cantata *Automne*, the orchestral version of *Concertstück* for Cello, the brilliant *Scherzo* from Stojowski's unfinished Second Symphony and the *Ballade*, Stojowski's first orchestral work which contains thematic material that he later used in his Symphony in D Minor. Perhaps some present day conductors will follow in the footsteps of Fitelberg, Młynarski, Damrosch, Hallé, Nikisch and von Bülow and consider programming Stojowski's symphonic music for their audiences. If Stojowski's massive Symphony is too rich a sampling of his musical genius, there is the more compact Suite for Orchestra in E-flat. If it was a sure bet for Tchaikovsky and Brahms, it can be a winner for musicians today. The catalogue of Stojowski's works included with this publication also lists works orchestrated by others, such as the outstanding *Fantasie pour trombone*. Choral conductors will find five beautifully arranged *Polish Christmas Carols* for mixed chorus and piano that will prove very rewarding in concert. Many of Stojowski's works written before 1923, those which are considered public domain, can be downloaded free of charge from the website of the Sibley Music Library at the Eastman School of Music. Finally, pianists will find an amazing treasure trove of well-written, effective and truly charming compositions that could grace many a recital program. One can only hope that musicians and the public will finally see the true value of Stojowski's fascinating and deeply felt music and sustain the legacy of this eloquent musician, articulate man of letters, and most passionate Polish patriot. Hopefully, Zygmunt Stojowski's time has come.

Figure X-1. Stojowski in Paradise Valley, Rainier National Park with Mount Rainer in the background, 1926. Photograph courtesy of the Stojowski Family. Used by permission.

Endnotes

1. Horszowski, 342.

2. Kassern, *Letter to Luisa Stojowska*.

3. Paderewski is credited with introducing the Zinfandel grape to America.

4. Dybowski, "Zapomniany Zygmunt Stojowski" [The Forgotten Zygmunt Stojowski], 34.

5. Request for Public Domain Scores: https://urresearch.rochester.edu/handle/1802/291

Annotated Catalogue of Compositions
by Zygmunt Stojowski

ABBREVIATION GUIDE

Entries with asterisks (*) denote compositions analyzed in the 1950 unpublished master's thesis by Maria Macharska-Wolańska, *Twórczość fortepianowa Zygmunta Stojowskiego* [The Piano Works of Zygmunt Stojowski], at the Jagiellonian University, Cracow.

Alec Rowley's comments on Stojowski's compositions are taken from his article, *The Pianoforte Works of Siegmund* [sic!] *Stojowski, A Short Survey.*

AAN:	Archiwum Akt Nowych (State Archives, Warsaw)
Anon. Per.:	Anonymous Performer
ASU:	Arizona State University (Tempe)
BBC:	BBC Music Library (London)
BJ:	Biblioteka Jagiellońska (Cracow)
BL:	British Library (London)
BNP:	Bibliothèque Nationale (Paris)
BNW:	Biblioteka Narodowa (Warsaw)
BPL:	Boston Public Library (Massachusetts)
BR:	Brandeis University (Waltham, Massachusetts)
BRU:	Brown University (Rhode Island)
CAM:	Chopin Academy of Music (Warsaw)
CBN:	Centralna Biblioteka Nutowa (Warsaw)
CC:	Connecticut College (New London)
CLP:	Carnegie Library of Pittsburgh
CML:	Columbus Metropolitan Library (Ohio)
CPL:	Cleveland Public Library
CSB:	College of St. Benedict (Minneapolis)
CSU:	California State University (Hayward)
CT:	Curtis School of Music (Philadelphia)
CU:	Cambridge University (England)
DPL:	Detroit Public Library
EAST:	Eastman School of Music (Rochester, NY)
EMTA:	*Echo Muzyczne, Teatralne i Artystyczne*

EU:	Edinburgh University (Scotland)
FLP:	Free Library of Philadelphia (Fleisher Collection)
FSU:	Florida State University (Tallahassee)
GAM:	Gdańsk Academy of Music
HPL:	Hartford Public Library (Connecticut)
HVU:	Harvard University, Loeb Library (Massachusetts)
ICA:	Interlochen Center for the Performing Arts (Michigan)
IPA:	International Piano Archives (New York)
IPAM:	International Piano Archives at Maryland, College Park
IU:	Indiana University (Bloomington)
KSU:	Kansas State University (Manhattan)
LAT:	*Los Angeles Times*
LC:	Library of Congress (Washington, D.C.)
LMM:	*Le Monde musical*
LS:	Luisa Stojowski
MC:	Mills College (Oakland, California)
MCM:	Mannes College of Music (New York)
MO:	Musica Obscura (Johnson City, Tennessee)
MSM:	Manhattan School of Music (New York)
MT:	*The Musical Times*
NU:	Northwestern University (Evanston, Illinois)
NYPLPA:	New York Public Library for the Performing Arts
NYT:	*The New York Times*
OSU:	Ohio State University (Columbus)
OU:	Ohio University (Athens)
PC:	Paris Conservatoire (Conservatoire National)
PIASA:	Polish Institute of Arts and Sciences of America (NYC)
PR:	Polish Radio (Warsaw)
PWM:	Polskie Wydawnictwo Muzyczne (Cracow)
QCC:	Queensborough Community College Library (New York)
RPL:	Richmond Public Library (Virginia)
SAM:	Szymanowski Academy of Music (Katowice)
SC:	Smith College (Northampton, Massachusetts)
SMU:	Southern Methodist University (Dallas, Texas)
SU:	Stanford University (California)
SZCZ:	Biblioteka Książąt Pomorskich (Szczecin)
TU:	Tulane University (New Orleans)
TX:	Texas Wesleyan University (Fort Worth)
UC:	University of Colorado (Boulder)
UCN:	University of Cincinnati (Ohio)
UG:	University of Georgia (Athens)
UI:	University of Illinois (Urbana-Champaign)
ULB:	Université Laval Bibliotheque (Quebec)
UM:	University of Michigan (Ann Arbor)
UMC:	University of Maryland (College Park)
UMK:	University of Missouri (Kansas City)
UO:	University of Oxford (England)
UP:	University of Pennsylvania (Philadelphia)

UPI:	University of Pittsburgh (Pennsylvania)
USC:	University of Southern California (Los Angeles)
UTA:	University of Texas (Austin)
WP:	*The Washington Post*
WSU:	Wichita State University (Kansas)
WSU:	Wright State University (Dayton, Ohio)
WTM:	Warszawskie Towarzystwo Muzyczne (Warsaw)
WU:	Warsaw University
WVW:	West Virginia Wesleyan (Buckhannon)
ZLSC:	Zygmunt and Luisa Stojowski Collection (Family Archives), Polish Music Center, USC
ZS:	Zygmunt Stojowski

Figure Cat-1. Stojowski in the 1930s. Photograph courtesy of ZLSC. Used by permission.

I. Published Works with Opus Numbers

The following information accompanies each entry:

- Title and Date of Composition
- Dedication and information on the dedicatee when possible
- Movements and/or Tempo Markings
- Manuscript, editions and libraries
- Orchestration
- Additional remarks (analysis, a list of historic performances, excerpts from reviews, etc.)
- Recordings

Regarding the manuscripts found in ZLSC: The Collection's list of Stojowski's manuscripts is based on three inventories. The first was made by Barbara Zakrzewska on November 5, 2001, after the Stojowski documents were found in New York. In 2003, the second was created by Maja Trochimczyk, former director of the Polish Music Center, in preparation for shipping the Collection from New York to California. The last inventory was made by current Polish Music Center Director, Marek Żebrowski, and it is based on the contents of the Collection which arrived at the university in December 2004. This final inventory is included in the Appendix of this book.

Opus 1: *Deux Pensées Musicales pour piano* (1889)

- **Dedication**

  A Madame Henriette Moszkowska (née Chaminade).
  Henriette was the wife of the pianist and composer, Moritz Moszkowski, and the sister of the composer Cécile Chaminade.

- **Movements**

  No. 1 *Mélodie—Andantino*
  No. 2 *Prélude—Alegretto moderato*

- **Editions**

  Manuscript for the first 26 bars of No. 2 is found at the Bibliothèque Musée de l'Opera in Paris.

  V. Durdilly, Paris, 1889: BNP. This edition mistakenly lists the work as Opus 2.

  Costallat & Cie., Paris, 1891: WU.

Pitt & Hatzfeld, London, 1891 (Edited by C.P. Scott): BL, EAST. A digitalized score can be downloaded at:

http://hdl.handle.net/1802/2380

Theodore Preser, Philadelphia, 1891: ZLSC.

Schott & Co. Ltd., London, 1901: BNW No. 2; WU; ZLSC no. 1.

No. 1 also appeared in the December 1905 issue of *The Etude.*

Arrangements and editions of No. 1 for violin and piano:

Wilhemj, August (arr.) in *Professor A. Wilhelmj's Newly Revised Edition of Violin Music*, No. 72, Schott & Co., London, 1901: Fontys Hogescholen, Amsterdam.

Lifka, Ch. B. (arr.), Schott & Söhne, Mainz, 1905: BL, LC, ZLSC.

Wilhemj, August (arr.), Schott & Söhne, Mainz, 1907, "dedicated to Miss Frances Jude": WU.

Ambrosio, W.F. [pseud. of Gustav Sanger] (ed.), a revised edition of the Wilhemj arrangement, C. Fischer, New York, 1910: BR.

Elman, Mischa (ed.). *Mischa Elman Concert Folio.* C. Fischer, New York, 1920: LC, MC.

Elman, Mischa. *Concert Favorites: Music Minus One – Violin* (printed music and two CD recordings, one with and one without solo violin part). Music Minus One, Elmsford, New York, 1999: CML.

Arrangements and editions of No. 1 for organ:

Goss-Custard (arr.), Schott & Co., London, 1891: ZLSC. Reissued in an anthology edited by Custard ca. 1905: BL.

Schott & Co.'s Brown Album of Twenty Pieces for the Organ, Vol. 4. Schott & Co., London, 1910-1919?: CLP, EAST.

Rodgers, James H. (arr.). *Thirty Offertories for the Organ.* Oliver Ditson, Boston, 1914: CPL, EAST, FLP.

Wier, Albert E. (ed.). *Modern Organ Pieces the Whole World Plays.* D. Appleton-Century Co., 1934: CPL, EAST, UI.

Arrangement for orchestra:

Andrée, Alfred (arr.), Schott & Co., London, 1909: BL.

• **Remarks**

Mélodie is a delicious work, fresh and warm, with every piano sonority felt and catered for. Only moderately difficult, this is teachable and playable in every degree. *Prélude* suffers somewhat from a likeness to one by Pachulski; nevertheless it is well worked out and playable in every degree." [Rowley] Henryk Pachulski (1859-1921), was a student of Strobl, Moniuszko and Żeleński. He lived in Moscow from 1880 to the end of his life.

Upon hearing a performance of Stojowski playing his *Prélude*, Saint-Saëns embraced the young composer, kissed him on both cheeks, and said. "This is fine. We expect (great things from you)." [From Radio Station WNYC Stojowski Memorial Program of Jan 13, 1947, ZLSC.]

The MS for No. 2 in Paris bears the tempo marking *Andantino con moto;* the Durdilly edition lists *Andantino malinconico*. Later editions indicate *Allegretto moderato*.

The arrangements for violin have been transposed to G Major, a half-step lower than the original version for solo piano.

Jascha Heifetz played the Wilhemj arrangement of *Mélodie*, including a performance at Carnegie Hall in Jan 1920. The arranger and violinist August Wilhemj (1845-1908) was often referred to as "the German Paganini."

The organ arrangements of *Mélodie* were probably heard more frequently at the cinema during the screening of silent movies than they were heard in church during worship.

In the *Prélude* at bar 114 there is an F-flat the left hand of the second eighth-note chord. It should be F-natural.

The performance of the *Prélude* by Stojowski's pupil Sidney Schachter on the 1947 Stojowski Memorial Program includes an additional E-flat played an octave higher on the ultimate chord of the piece.

Deux Pensées Musicales were written when Stojowski was in his late teens and studied with Léo Delibes at the Conservatoire National. Delibes' correspondence with Paderewski at the Archiwum Akt Nowych in Warsaw indicates that Delibes sent Stojowski's compositions to Paderewski for approval and comments. Both must have agreed on the merits of these works before they went to print. Opus

1 shows Stojowski's prodigious gift for beautiful melodies and great skill in creating an exquisite accompaniment.

- **Recordings**

No. 1 recorded by ZS for Ampico (piano roll) Recordings 67863H under the title of *Musical Thought.*

No. 1 recorded on radio by ZS, October 15, 1944, NY, transferred onto LP: Desmar IPA 115, *Sigismond Stojowski Plays Chopin, Paderewski and Stojowski,* 1976.

No. 1 recorded by Boris Goldovsky, Allegro Royale 1402, c. 1955.

No. 2 recorded by Sidney Schachter, Carnegie Hall Recording Co., Station WNYC, 78-RPM: Jan 12, 1947, ZLSC.

No. 2 recorded by LS, Desmar IPA 115, 1976.

Nos. 1 and 2 recorded by Jonathan Plowright for Hyperion Records, CDA67437: *Stojowski, Music for Piano,* London: 2004.

See *Music Minus One* edition in arrangements for violin and piano. Recorded by Daniela Stereva, MMO CD 3163.

Opus 2: *Deux Caprices-Etudes pour piano* (1889)

- **Dedication**

A mon cher Maître Louis Diémer. The 1889 edition also gives the abbreviation «M» for *Monsieur* before Diémer's given name. Louis Diémer (1843-1919) began teaching piano at the Conservatoire National in 1887, Stojowski's first year at the school. Many of Diémer's students became professors at the Conservatoire, passing down the "Diémer tradition" to future generations of pianists. More information on Diémer is found in Chapter 2.

- **Movements**

  *No. 1 *Fileuse—Vivace*
  *No. 2 *Toccatina—Presto*

- **Editions**

  E. Hatzfeld, London & Leipzig, 1892 (edited by C. F. Scott): BJ no. 2; BL no. 2; WU; UT, WSU no. 1; WTM.

Bruneau & Cie, Paris, 1889: BNP, WTM This edition lists the work as *2 Morceaux pour piano*, Op. 3.

No. 1 printed by G & B, Warsaw, 1900 and reprinted in 1903, 1910 and 1912 (fingering by Rodolphe Strobl): BNW, BJ, WTM.

Augener & Co., London, 1903: BL no. 2; ZLSC no. 1.

No. 1 Theodore Presser, Philadelphia, 1906, in *Standard Concert Etudes for Advanced Study*, edited by W. S. B. Matthews: CLP, CSB.

No. 1 also appeared in Theodore Presser's graded series entitled *Morceaux pour piano par Sig. Stojowski* ca. 1890.

Augener's Edition, London, No. 1 1935, No. 2 1932: PWM.

No. 1 of the 1892 Hatzfeld edition reissued by Musica Obscura, Johnson City, 1988: SMU.

- **Remarks**

The former (*Toccatina*) is a smaller edition of the great Schumann *Toccata* and, as such, is negligible as music of originality, but *Fileuse* is individual and a most exacting test for the fingers. Played *vivace* it should be most effective. [Rowley]

- **Recordings**

No. 1 recorded by Zygmunt Lisicki for PR under the title *Etuda— kaprys*, RII 88716-A, 1957.

*Opus 3: *Concerto en fa # mineur pour Piano et Orchestre* **(1890)**

- **Dedication**

Hommage à Antoine Rubinstein. Anton Rubinstein, (1829-1894) Russian pianist and composer whom Stojowski knew personally. Rubinstein, the co-founder of the St. Petersburg Conservatoire, had been a guest at Stojowski's home in Cracow in the 1880s.

- **Movements**

Andante poco mosso
Romanza - Andante sostenuto e molto cantabile
Allegro con fuoco

- **Editions**

Manuscript: Northwestern University Library, Moldenhauer Archives, acquired in 1972 along with two printed copies. Hardbound score in ink on 19-stave paper, 201 pages; signed "Sigismond Stojowski, Paris, 1890." Purchased by Moldenhauer from the publisher, Louis Hatzfeld, on March 20, 1934.

Manuscript: First draft of two-piano arrangement in ZLSC. See Appendix Inventory.

S. Lucas, Weber, Pitt & Hatzfeld Ltd., London & Leipzig: 1893.
Full score: BBC, BL, EAST, LC, WAT. A digitalized full score can be downloaded at: http://hdl.handle.net/1802/2378

Full score & parts for hire: CBN, FLP.

Augener, London: between 1905–1910. Full score: UO (PWM has 1935 reprint).

H. B. Stevens Co., London; E. Hatzfeld, Leipzig, 1893.
Arrangement for two pianos by the composer: EAST, LC, NYPLPA, WU, ZLSC.

Augener's Edition, London, 189?, Full Score: PWM.

Augener, London, Two Pianos, (edited by C. P. Scott), 1935: BL.

- **Orchestration**

Pno-2.2 (2nd alt. E.H.).2.2.-4.2.3.0-timp.perc-str

- **Remarks**

First performance took place in Paris on February 17, 1891, at the Salle Erard with the Orchestre Colonne. Although the program lists Édouard Colonne as the conductor of the concert, the Concerto was performed under the direction of composer Benjamin Godard, who replaced the ailing Colonne. Other early performances included Stojowski and the Berlin Philharmonic on February 19, 1892, at the Singakademie, and British performances with Sir Charles Hallé's Orchestra in Manchester. The first American performance took place with the New York Metropolitan Opera Orchestra on April 2, 1911, with Josef Pasternack conducting and the composer performing.

The work opens with a mysterious theme given out without harmony by the orchestra—(was the composer thinking of a certain slow movement of Beethoven's in one of his Quartets?)—it constitutes the principal theme of the movement, and it is treated with great skill and variety. The second theme, in the orthodox relative major, which is evolved from it, forms an admirable contrast. The second movement, *Romanza*, is in D-flat, the enharmonic equivalent of C-sharp. The opening *cantabile* theme, of Chopinesque character, has much charm; it is first given out by the orchestra. After a middle section, *piu mosso*, of some power, a return is made *via* a short but showy *Cadenza*, to the opening theme, which is now presented in ornamented fashion. The closing movement is an *Allegro con fuoco*, full of storm and stress; except in the hands of a great pianist it would stand but a poor chance. It is hoped that Sigismond Stojowski will soon have an opportunity of presenting his work before an English audience. [*MT*, "Concert in fa sharp."]

Beautifully laid out for the piano. Somewhat dated but contains some beautiful melodies. Virtuosic in places. [Hinson]

The piano part is very virtuosic, making use of all the sound possibilities of the instrument. Thus, we have double note figurations, triplets in the inner voices, high tremolos which are several times reinforced by the octave, wide octaves and chords, and frequently displayed passages of chords and arpeggios. [Macharska]

At the age of 16, German pianist Elly Ney won first place in the Ibach Competition performing Stojowski's First Piano Concerto. [Ney, 71]

Polish pianist Józef Stompel had the concerto in his repertoire from the mid 1960s to the late 1980s. [Bias]

This work was most probably submitted by Stojowski at the Rubinstein Competition in Berlin in 1895. Stojowski did not win any prizes. The first-prize laureate that year, both as composer and pianist, was another Pole, Henryk Melcer [see Introduction, Endnote 9].

• **Recordings**

Recorded by Józef Stompel for PR, PB 974, The Polish Radio & TV Orchestra in Katowice, Jerzy Salwarowski, conductor; 1979.

Recorded by Piotr Łoboz for PR, DR 184 (See original: mo 95955) The Polish Radio & TV Orchestra in Cracow, Krzysztof Missona, conductor.

Recorded by Jonathan Plowright and the BBC Scottish Symphony Orchestra, Martin Brabbins, conductor; Hyperion Records CDA67314, in 2002.

Opus 4: *Trois Intermèdes pour piano* **(1891)**

- **Dedication**

    1. *A mon ami Paul Braud.* Paul Braud (b.1860), French pianist. Born in Paris, he won first prize in piano at the Conservatoire in 1882. He was one of the piano teachers of the Cuban-born American pianist and composer Joaquin Nin-Culmell (1908-2004). César Franck died of injuries incurred in an automobile accident which took place as Franck was on his way to attend one of Braud's rehearsals.

    2. *A mon ami Pierre-René Hirsch.* Hirsch (1870–1891) French pianist and poet. Born in Paris, Hirsch won first prize in piano at the Conservatoire in 1886. He is the poet for two of Stojowski's songs: *A Stella* and *La flûte muette*.

    3. *A mon ami Lennart Lundberg.* Lennart Lunberg (1863–1931), Swedish pianist and composer. He studied in Paris at the same time as Stojowski, living in the same hotel as Stojowski and Paderewski around 1887.The online Swedish Music Information Center lists him as a pupil of Paderewski from 1888 to 1891. Earlier, he had studied with Mme Camille Dubois, who was a student of Chopin. He taught piano at the Stockholm Conservatory from 1903-1928, becoming Professor in 1913. He composed exclusively and prolifically for the voice and the solo piano.

- **Movements**

    *No. 1 in G Major—*Allegretto moderato e con fantasia*
    *No. 2 in E Minor—*Andantino capriccioso, più tosto allegretto*
    *No. 3 in B-flat Major — *Moderato*

- **Editions**

    Schott & Co., London, 1891: WU

    No. 3 printed by Theodore Presser, Philadelphia, in the graded series *Morceaux pour piano par Sig. Stojowski*: 1891.

    E. Hatzfeld, Leipzig, 1891: WTM no. 1.

    E. Hatzfeld, Leipzig, 1894: CLP, WSU, BNW no. 2 and 3.

    Shott, Mainz, ca. 1900: Listed in Hofmeister.

- **Remarks**

    The first is best and is a sheer delight, with its flute-like melody and its suggestive pizzicato bass. The rising sevenths at the end must have caused a certain consternation in 1891. [Rowley]
    BJ has an autographed copy of the printed score with a dedication ending in

a Polish proverb to Stojowski's composition teacher in Cracow, Władysław Żeleński:

> *Kochanemu Tatusiowi muzycznemu*
> *'czem chata bogata, tem rada.'*
> *Zygmunt*
> [To my beloved musical Father:
> 'Frugal the fare, but yours to share.'
> Zygmunt]

- **Recordings**

No. 1 recorded by Anon. Per. on Aeolian Co. (piano roll) AEOL T 30316, London, ca. 1905 and on The Orchestrelle Coy (piano roll) AEOL L 2387, London, 1905-08.

No. 3 recorded by Józef Śmidowicz for PR, 88716-C, 1957.

Opus 5: *Quatre Morceaux pour piano* (1894)

- **Dedication**

1. *A Sir Charles Hallé.* Charles Hallé (1819-1895), German-born British conductor and pianist. In 1836 he moved to Paris where he befriended Chopin, Liszt and Wagner. Twelve years later, he moved to England where he settled in Manchester in 1849. Under his directorship, the Hallé Concerts became the leading music event of that city. Stojowski performed his First Piano Concerto with Hallé's orchestra in February, 1894.

2. *A Mademoiselle Clotilde Kleeberg.* Clotilde Kleeberg (1866-1909), Parisian-born German pianist. At the age of eleven she won first prize in piano at the Conservatoire in 1878. She later studied with Clara Schumann and recorded two Welte piano rolls.

3. *A Mademoiselle Augusta Bennich.* Possibly related to the Polish-Jewish Bennich family of Łódź, where the family was known for its textile factories.

4. *A Mademoiselle Hilda Thergerström.* Hilda Thergerström was professor of piano at the Conservatory of Music in Stockholm.

- **Movements**

No.1 *Berceuse—Lento*
No.2 *Scherzo—Molto vivace*
*No.3 *Gondoliera—Andantino con moto*
No.4 *Mazurka—Vivace*

- **Editions**

  Manuscripts: All four pieces are found in ZLSC. See Appendix Inventory. The opus number on the MS is written as "11" instead of the published "5." The dedicatee for No. 2 also differs. On the MS the dedication reads, "A Monsieur Alexandre Michałowski, Professeur en Conservatoire de Varsovie."

  Stanley Lucas & Co., London, 1894: BL; ZLSC no. 1.

  Schott & Co., London, 1894: BNP, WU, BJ, PWM no. 1; BNW, BJ nos. 3 and 4; ZLSC no. 1.

  No. 3 appeared in the August 1905 issue of *The Etude* and under the title *Barcarolle* in Theodore Presser's 1905 anthology *Modern Drawing-room Pieces*. Presser also released it as a separate work under its original title in a graded series *Morceaux pour piano par Sig. Stojowski*.

  It was also arranged for organ by R. Goss-Custard and appears in the anthology *Buff Album of Twenty Pieces for the Organ* published in London by Schott & Co., Ltd., ca. 1933.

  No. 4 appeared as "Supplément au No. 3047" in *L'Illustration* (July 20, 1901), 101-104. It was a reprint of the Schott edition: BL, BNW.

- **Remarks**

  Of these the *Berceuse* is delightful, with enchanting harmonies and a swaying tune that is not quite like anything one has heard before (even now!) *Gondoliera* has a most captivating rhythmic swing throughout. The *Mazurka* is not very distinguished. [Rowley]

  The *Gondoliera* is a revised version of a piece found in the composer's juvenilia, *Petite Barcarolle,* written in Cracow in 1885. The latter is written in G-flat Major, but for Op. 5 the composer uses its enharmonic equivalent of F-sharp Major.

  Also see the review of Opus 5 under Opus 10, *Deux Orientales.*

Opus 6: *Variations et Fugue pour deux Violons, Alto et Violoncelle* (1890)

- **Dedication**

  A Monsieur Ladislas Górski. Władysław Górski (1846-1915), Polish violinist, teacher and composer. He studied violin with Kazimierz Baranowski at the Warsaw Institute of Music. Afterwards he continued studying composition with

Friederich Kiel in Berlin. Back in Warsaw, Górski became the solo violinist of the Warsaw Opera (Teatr Wielki) and a professor at the Warsaw Institute of Music where he befriended Paderewski. In 1885, he relocated to Paris, where he joined the Lamoureux Orchestra, and later became instrumental in promoting the career of the young Stojowski. For more information on Górski, see Chapter 2.

- **Movements**
  Theme—*Andante*
  Variations—*L'istesso tempo*
  > *Poco più mosso e con fantasia*
  > *Con fuoco*
  > *Tempo del Thema*
  > *Più mosso e con espressione*
  > *Allegro feroce*
  > *Andantino grazioso*
  Fugue—*Allegro scherzando*

- **Editions**
  Full score and parts:
  London, Leipzig: Pitt & Hatzfeld, 1891: BL (set of parts only), BJ; BNP (set of parts only); EAST (set of parts only); FSU, LC. A digitalized set of parts may be downloaded at: http://hdl.handle.net/1802/2736

  Full score:
  London: The Standard English Edition, ca. 1910: BL.

- **Remarks**
  One of the most appealing of the violinists belonging to the Parisian foreigners' colony, Mr. Górski counts many enthusiastic admirers who never miss a chance each year to come and applaud him. One can only congratulate the eminent violinist on his beautiful virtuosity, all the while regretting its use in the performance of works with so little musicality as the acrobatics of Paganini. [*LMM,* "M.L. Górski."]

  First known performance: Salle Erard in Paris, February 17, 1891 with Górski as the leader of the quartet. Further performances followed (Berlin, February 19, 1892), and other European cities. The work was also featured during the Stojowski Festival in Warsaw on May 2, 2003, and played by students from the Academy of Music, with Michał Osmycki as leader of the quartet.

  The fugue is based on an original theme and lends credence to the jury's decision to award Stojowski first prize for counterpoint and fugue.

- **Recordings**

  Recorded for PR, DR 186, Quartet from Polish Radio & TV
  Orchestra in Cracow, 1957.

Opus 7: *Le printemps, d'après une Ode d'Horace pour choeur et orchestre* **(1895)**

- **Dedication**

  A la Mémoire de son bien aimé Maître Léo Delibes. Léo Delibes (1836-1891), French composer. Delibes was Stojowski's composition teacher at the Conservatoire in Paris. He is remembered for his operas and ballets. For more information on Delibes, see Chapter 2.

- **Editions**

  Full score manuscript: ZLSC (missing p. 15). See Appendix Inventory.

  Choral Score (French *Le printemps*): Stanley Lucas & Co. London &Leipzig, 1895: BL.

  Choral score (French and German *Der Frühling*): Stanley Lucas & Co., London, 1895: ZLSC.

  Choral score (German and Polish *Wiosna*): Stanley Lucas & Co., London, 1896: BL, CBN.

  Piano-vocal score *Spring-Time*: Novello & Co., London, 1905 (English ed.): BL, EAST, LC, UO, WU (Polish text by L. Marjańska is handwritten in the score.)

  Full score (in French & German): Stanley Lucas & Co, London, 1895: BBC, BL, BNP, LC, PR.

  Full score (French & English) and parts, edited by John M. Hein: Polish Music Center at USC, 2003: USC.

- **Orchestration**

  2*.2.2.2.-4.2.3.1.-timp-perc-chorus SATB-hp-str

- **Remarks**

  Text: From Fourth Ode of Horace, Book I: *Salvitur acris hiems...* The French text by Jules Barbier ("L'aimable printemps ramène dans la plaine...") is the same as

Debussy's Cantata of the same title for 4-part chorus and orchestra. It was his Prix de Rome submission in 1884, catalog number L56.

French translation by Jules Barbier, German by Alfred Nossie. English by Mrs. Malcolm Lawson, and Polish by J. Czubek.

"Spring," the Ode by Horace in a translation by J. Czubek, is very charming in its use of musical images. The composer, with the help of the orchestra, strives in detail to represent the scenes written in each verse. The very beginning has an idyllic character and is full of serenity. This is why the same idea is repeated at the end, rounding out the entire work well. Although there are several closing modulations that are entertaining, they nevertheless strengthen the mood of serenity. [From a review for *Kurjer Warszawski* by the composer Zygmunt Noskowski (1846-1909)]

Noskowski's lengthy review closes by giving a description of how the thirty-one-year-old Stojowski was idolized by Warsaw's concertgoers. He received three wreaths (one from the Philharmonic and two from fans), a basket of white roses presented by a group of young ladies as well as flowers thrown from the audience onto the stage. [*Kurjer Warszawski* press clipping in the Paderewski Archives, 570 no. 41, AAN.]

A review of the printed English choral score in England read, "Mr. Stojowski's music reflects it jocund vein, and light heartedness and graceful spirits. The work only occupies 18 octavo pages, and while artistic in design is simple in character." [*MT*, "The Wreck of the Hesperus...Spring-Time."]

No delusions of grandeur or highbrow composition here. This is Victorian, light classical music at its best. Entertainingly written and a bit campy at times (as when Vulcan starts blowing and the anvil in the percussion begins playing), it is all great fun, fit for a queen.

By command of Queen Victoria, the Cantata was premiered in English at a State Concert held at the Buckingham Palace on the evening of Friday, July 5, 1895. The orchestra and chorus, conducted by Sir Walter Parratt, consisted of 160 performers and comprised Her Majesty's Private Band, assisted by members selected from the principal orchestral and choral societies of London.

Le printemps was performed in Warsaw at an all-Stojowski program given by the Warsaw Philharmonic Orchestra in January 1902. It was sung in Polish by the Warsaw choir *Lutnia*, an amateur choral ensemble, which is still in existence.

The first American performance took place on March 21, 1906, with the Boston Singing Club at the Boston Opera. In New York, the Cantata was first heard on December 11, 1912 with the Schola Cantorum under the direction of Kurt Schindler at Aeolian Hall.

During World War II, the Polish Army Choir in England joined forces with the Women's Choir of the Dunfermline Music Institute, giving two performances of *Spring-Time* on April 15 and 16, 1942, under the direction of Lieut. Kołaczkowski. [*MT*, "Music in the Provinces."]

The score and set of parts at Centralna Biblioteka Nutowa in Warsaw had been miscataloged for over 50 years and been listed among the works written by Léo Delibes, the dedicatee of the Cantata. The mistake was not discovered until June 2003, explaining why the work was not performed in Poland after World War II. The work was heard in Warsaw for the first time in 101 years in a performance at the Zygmunt Stojowski May Festival by the Szczecin Boychoir, Bożena Derwich, conductor, the Warsaw Archdiocesan Cathedral Men's and Boys' Choir, Cantores Minores, and the Stojowski May Festival Orchestra in May 2003 at Holy Cross Basilica under the direction of the author.

Opus 8: *Trois Morceaux pour piano* **(1891)**

- **Dedication**

  No. 1. *A Monsieur Joseph Schloss*
  No. 2. *A Monsieur Constantin Hartong*
  No. 3. *A Madame Frédérique Hertzka.* Hertzka was a pianist who lived in Vienna and possibly the wife of Emil Hertzka (1869-1932), the Austrian music publisher. She was a friend of Paderewski and the Stojowski family. [Paderewski, Letter to Maria Stojowska.]

- **Movements**

  *No.1 *Légende—Andantino con moto*
  *No.2 *Mazurka—Con spirito*
  *No.3 *Sérénade—Andantino con moto*

- **Editions**

  Schott, London, 1891: WTM no. 1.

  Pitt & Hatzfeld, London, 1892: BJ; EAST no. 3; BNW nos. 1 and 3; WU nos. 1 and 2, ZLSC nos. 1 and 2. A digitalized score for no. 3 can be downloaded at: http://hdl.handle.net/1802/2464

  Schott, London, 1892 and 1907 reprint: WTM no. 3.

Légende.

Figure Cat-2. Stojowski, *Legende* Op. 8, no. 1. Pitz & Hatzfeld, Ltd., 1892. Public domain

Theodore Presser, Philadelphia: nos. 2 & 3, (date?)

Gebethner & Wolff, Warsaw, c. 1910: no. 3, fingering by A. Michałowski: WTM, WU.

Schott & Co., London; B. Schott & Söhne, Mainz, 1900: BL no. 3; PWM. No. 3: Schott, London, 1907: UPI.

No. 3 also appeared in the November 1907 issue of *The Etude.*

Arrangement of No. 1 for violin and piano:

Under the title of *Aubade*, No. 1 was arranged for violin and piano by A. Kaiser, Schott & Co., London, 1910: ZLSC, SAM.

Arrangement for orchestra:

In 1955, No. 1 was arranged for clarinet and string orchestra by Arnold Rezler (1909-2000), PR.

• **Remarks**

It [*Légende*] contains one of the longest opening melodies that I have ever come across—22 bars. Just when you think it is about to end, Sigismond adds another layer to it, so the effect is always of moving forward on to the next section. Also, it's quite a dreamy melody..." [Pianist Jonathan Plowright in an e-mail letter to the author, June 25, 2006.]

Here we have a work [*Légende*] of difficulty. It would be a hard matter to forget the opening melodic phrase, which battles itself up and grows and grows until it becomes almost a work in itself. To concert pianists I recommend this without reserve. *Mazurka* is quite ordinary in matter and construction, but *Serenade* is graceful and (although technically difficult) full of charm and lilting phrases. [Rowley]

The arranger Arnold Rezler's career as a conductor included directorships of the Polish Radio Orchestra in Bydgoszcz (1945-56), the Warsaw Philharmonic (1956-58), Teatr Wielki in Warsaw (1958-65), and the Polish Army Orchestra (1965-75). He also arranged Stojowski's *Fantasie pour trombone, Polnische Idyllen,* and *Chant d'amour* for orchestra.

• **Recordings**

No. 1 recorded by Alexander Brachocki for AMPICO (piano roll) Recordings (no. 66431). A Midi recording of this performance can be found on the Internet at:

http://www.kunstderfuge.com/midi-s.htm

Opus 9: *Suite en Mi bémol pour Grand orchestre* (1891)

• **Dedication**

Hommage à Hans von Bülow. Hans von Bülow (1830-1894), German conductor, pianist, composer, teacher and writer. He conducted the world premiere of Wagner's *Lohengrin* in Weimar. As a teenager, Stojowski first met von Bülow in Cracow during the 1880s.

- **Movements**

  Thème varié
  Theme—*Andante*
  >   Variation 1—(*Andante*)
  >   Variation 2—*Poco più mosso*
  >   Variation 3—*Con brio ma non troppo allegro*
  >   Variation 4—*Molto tranquillo e con espressione*
  >   Variation 5—[*Fugato-Finale*] *Allegro molto moderato; Poco più*
  >   *mosso; Intermède polonais—Tempo di mazurka,*
  >   *con anima; Rêverie et Cracovienne—Lento, Allegro*

- **Editions**

  London: S. Lucas, Weber, Pitt & Hatzfeld Ltd., 1893
  Full score: BL, EAST, EU, LC, NYPLPA, PR. Digitalized full score can be
  downloaded at: http://hdl.handle.net/1802/1548

  Full score and parts: BBC, FLP

- **Orchestration**

  3.3*.2.2.-4.4.3.1-timp.perc-hp-str

- **Remarks**

  The first movement is a theme with variations. The theme is a rather melancholy
  tune sung by clarinets and bassoons over a meager string accompaniment. For
  the first variation the woodwind preserve the theme more or less intact but a
  peculiar texture is woven from melodic fragments on solo strings, beginning
  with the viola. After this the theme in any easily recognizable shape departs, and
  the second variation is a jolly intermezzo. The brass enters [sic!] in the third
  variation and add strenuousness to jocosity. A solo horn reminds us of the theme
  in the fourth variation while moving figures on flutes, harp and strings point to the
  direction *molto tranquillo e con espressione.* A solo viola plays some part in its
  expressiveness. The finale begins, *fugato*, with a transformed snatch of the theme
  but ends with a massive and forceful treatment in chorale style with the full brass
  reinforced by occasional drum and cymbal strokes.

  The second movement, *Intermède polonais*, is a mazurka and the whole
  thing is skilfully developed from the theme that makes it way out of violas and
  bassoons after two preliminary bars, with the exception of a short contrasting
  section with a soulful song on the *cor anglais.*

  The last movement, *Rêverie et Cracovienne*, opens mistily as befits a
  reverie, and a flute swings softly downwards in a phrase which other instruments
  are not slow to pick up—the viola being especially favoured among the strings.
  Then the mutes are off and the violas race away with the dance tune (it should

be said here that there is little typical of the traditional Polish dance about this specimen, since the rhythm has been altered from 2/4 to common time and the usual syncopations transplanted). For a time violas and bassoons have the theme between them but the other instruments are infected by the gay spirits and compelled to join in. The bassoons have a new tune, no more sober, and when this has been worked up to a boisterous climax the slow "reverie" mood returns, and strings and wood-wind voice their individual thoughts. It passes out in a long drawn sigh and the Cracovienne theme comes back, albeit a trifle hesitant, but speedily to work up to its former boisterousness and after some vicissitudes to bounce to the end in streperous energy. [From the *Analytical Notes* by John F. Russell for the Hallé Orchestra concert of May 3, 1942. Used with permission of the Hallé Concerts Society, Manchester, U.K.]

The author would like to differ with Mr. Russell in his description of the Suite's second variation. This variation is clearly based on the first three bars of the theme, played in syncopated rhythms, alternating between the strings and woodwinds.

The variations are decidedly clever. The second movement is entitled *Intermède polonais*, and is, in fact, an animated Mazurka. There is a certain waywardness about the music that gives to it the appearance of an improvisation; the middle section *menno mosso*, which opens with a refined but melancholy solo for the *cor anglais*, is highly characteristic. The third movement is... full of strange rhythms and striking harmonies... The instrumentation is of an elaborate character, and the music, generally, polyphonic. [*MT*, "Suite en mi bémol... "]

The Stojowski Suite asked more of the different choirs of the orchestra. It is very well composed and was played with devotion. It is genuine music. Repeatedly the composer was obliged to bow his acknowledgement from a box. [*NYT*, "Brico Orchestra at Carnegie Hall," review by Olin Downes]

The theme of the first movement's variations is based on the Polish Marian hymn tune *Witaj, Królowo* [Salve Regina]. Since World War II, the hymn tune used by Stojowski has lost its popularity in Polish urban centers. However, the tune is still very popular in the North American Polonia where it almost always sung at the gravesite following a Polish funeral.

Although the second movement was first heard on February 17, 1891 at Stojowski's debut concert in Paris, the first complete performance was probably given by the Berlin Philharmonic Orchestra on February 19, 1892 in Berlin. Hallé conducted the Suite with his orchestra in Manchester on February 1, 1894. Von Bülow, the dedicatee, conducted the piece on one of his last concerts in Hamburg in 1894. The Lamoureux Orchestra performed the Suite in Paris on March 30, 1895. In St. Petersburg, Tchaikovsky planned to conduct the Suite during the spring of 1894 at a concert featuring music of young composers. His death in November 1893 prevented that from happening. Stojowski showed the work to Brahms in Vienna, who exclaimed, "Donnerwetter! Sie instrumentieren aber raffiniert!" [By Jove! You orchestrate with finesse!] According to Stojowski, Brahms was instrumental in arranging performances of the Suite in London and Vienna that were conducted by Hans Richter. [Poe] London performances took place at Queen's Hall with the London Symphony Orchestra on June 14, 1914, Emil Młynarski conducting, and again at the world premiere of Edward Elgar's symphonic prelude *Polonia* on July 6, 1915, with Thomas Beecham conducting. In Poland, another 1915 performance took place in Wilno on July 2. Adam Wyleżyński (1880-1954) conducted the second movement with the local orchestra.

In America, the first performance took place at Carnegie Hall with the New York Philharmonic Society on February 5, 1915, Josef Stransky conducting. Ernst Schelling also programmed the second movement with the New York Philharmonic Orchestra at a Young People's Concert at Carnegie Hall on December 29, 1930, and conducted the first movement with the Baltimore Symphony Orchestra on February 7, 1937. The Brico Brico Symphony Orchestra under Antonia Brico gave a performance of the Suite on January 25, 1939 at Carnegie Hall.

During World War II, the work was performed on both sides of the Atlantic. On the anniversary of Polish Constitution Day, May 3, 1942, the Suite was heard on the all-Polish program conducted by Malcolm Sargent with the Hallé Orchestra at the Manchester Opera House. Members of the New York Philharmonic performed the Suite's second movement on the all-Polish concert on May 4, 1944 at Carnegie Hall.

More recently, the Suite's first movement was given at the May 2003 Stojowski Festival at Holy Cross Basilica in Warsaw (at which the composer's son, Henry, and granddaughter, Nancy, were present); the entire Suite was also performed by the Szczecin Philharmonic Orchestra in December 2005. Both performances were conducted by the author. Also, the Rzeszów Philharmonic Orchestra is southeastern Poland has tentative plans for a performance and recording of the work during the 2006-2007 concert season.

- **Recordings**

Recorded by Brico Symphony Orchestra, Antonia Brico conductor, Carnegie Hall; Carnegie Hall Recording Co., 16-inch 78-RPM: Jan 25, 1939; ZLSC.

Second movement recorded by members of the New York Philharmonic Orchestra, George Fitelberg conductor, Carnegie Hall, U.S. Department of State, International Broadcasting Division, 16-inch 78 RPM: May 4, 1944, ZLSC. Recorded for PR, 81620-621, The Grand Symphony Orchestra of Polish Radio in Katowice (WOSPR), Jerzy Kołaczkowski, conductor, 1953; second recording with Kołaczkowski for PR, PA 1417 A, 1969.

Opus 10: *Deux Orientales* **(1894)**

- **Dedication**

  1. *A mon ami Paul Bergon.* Paul Bergon (1863-1912), French musician and photographer. He studied music at the Conservatoire National where he won second prize in harmony in 1886. As a photographer, he was one of the rare pictoralists to take up color images when autochrome appeared in 1907.

  2. *A mon ami Joseph C. Hofmann.* Józef Kazimierz Hofmann [better known outside Polish circles as Josef C. Hofmann] (1876–1957), Polish pianist, composer and inventor. A child prodigy, Hofmann became one of the few to study with Anton Rubinstein. He also studied composition with Moritz Moszkowski and, at first, published his compositions under the pseudonym Dvorsky. He was the first musician recorded by Thomas Edison and, as an inventor himself, he is credited with inventing windshield wipers. In 1924, he became the first director of the Curtis Institute of Music in Philadelphia. For his relationship with Stojowski, see Chapters 5 and 8.

- **Movements**

  No. 1 *Romance—Sostenuto e con molto espressione*
  *No. 2 *Caprice—Allegro assai*

- **Editions**

  Manuscripts: ZLSC. See Appendix Inventory.

  Stanley Lucas & Co., London & Leipzig, 1894: BL.

  E. Hatzfeld, Leipzig, 1894: WU.

  Augener & Co., London, 1903: BL.

  Gebethner & Wolff (fingering by Rodolphe Strobl), Warsaw: 1903.

  Musica Obscura, Johnson City, 198-: SMU, UC, UMK.

  No. 2, Polish Music Center, USC, 2004: Digitalized score may be downloaded at http://www.usc.edu/dept/polish_music/news/jan04.html

  The online score in PDF format was prepared by Mr. Frederic Dannen and based on the manuscript found at PMC. This edition includes the two A-Minor arpeggiated chords used by Hofmann for an introduction.

• **Remarks**

Of these I do not care much for the *Romance*. The *Caprice*, however, is another story. Original and breathless, like a wild dance, this would bring down the house if played as it should be. (But it isn't easy!) [Rowley]

None of these pieces are difficult or long; they require, however, a considerable amount of taste from the players who undertake to reveal their beauties, which, though not perhaps of the rarest order, are nonetheless many. Chief among their merits are a certain vein of originality—of quaintness, indeed, in the case of the two pieces first named—and a degree of refinement and grace that is very welcome. The *Scherzo* is mostly written in canon, and, though the chief theme is, to our thinking, too constantly present, is very pretty. The *Oriental* Romance is perhaps the most striking of the series. All these pieces may be recommended for teaching purposes–that is, if the pupil has musical feeling and a good instrument by which to reveal it. Otherwise, Clementi will be safer. [A review of Opus 10 and *Quatre Morceaux pour piano*, Op. 5 which appeared in the June 1, 1895 issue of *The Musical Review*, p. 386.]

For sheer virtuosic bravura and unleashed power, Hofmann's performance of Sigismond Stojowski's little known *Oriental* is about as exciting as anyone could wish for. The piece itself is quite remarkable and wonderfully idiomatic. It is a worthy substitute for, and welcome relief from, Balakirev's *Islamey*. [From Rafael Kammerer's liner notes for Hofmann's recording on the Veritas Records label.]

Hofmann's performances of the *Caprice* included two added arpeggiated chords in A Minor to function as an introduction. These chords can be found in the Polish Music Center online edition.

These two musical impressions of the Orient—Deux Orientales by the twenty-four-year-old Stojowski living in Paris in the late nineteenth century totally differ from each other in mood and character. The cantabile style and the effects of Oriental-sounding scales make the Romance (*Sostenuto e con molto espressione*) quite striking. Ending the cadenza of the first section, Stojowski creates an interesting colouristic effect with the ascending Oriental-sounding passage held by the sostenuto pedal. Without re-striking the keys, the performer is instructed to hold down the seven keys which form a G Minor chord, quickly clear the pedal and then release the keys one at a time. A brief contrasting, impassionate middle section is followed by the closing section, similar in style to the opening section. The composer makes use of mixed meters, alternating between duple and triple in the key of F Major.

If the opening Romance creates an impression of being somewhere in the Middle East, the Caprice Orientale brings the listener much closer to Constantinople. Stojowski's "Turkish" opus is a wild and exciting bacchanalia, full of power and virtuosic bravura. A rhythmic ostinato:

leads the piece to its frenzied climax and dominates it from beginning to end. Józef Hofmann kept this highly original pianistic *tour de force* in his repertoire for over 40 years.

- **Recordings**

No. 1 recorded by LS, Desmar IPA 115, 1976.

No. 2 recorded by Józef Hofmann. A recording of the live performance of the April 7, 1938 Casimir Hall Recital at the Curtis School of Music is found on Veritas Records VM 101: New York, 1967; LC, PR. It is also available in *The Complete Joseph Hofmann* vol. 1 no. 6, CD 2, Marston 52-014-2, 1998.

No. 2 recorded by Irena Szynkorek for PR, R II 93910-B, 1960.

Nos. 1 and 2 recorded by Jonathan Plowright for Hyperion Records, CDA67437, *Stojowski, Music for Piano,* London: 2004.

No. 2 recorded in concert by Jonathan Plowright, Danacord Records, "Rarities of Piano Music at *Schloss vor Husum*," vol. 16, DACOCD 649 [DDD], Copenhagen: 2004.

Opus 11: *Pięć Pieśni—Cinq Mélodies* (1895)

Poems by Adam Asnyk, translated into French by Stéphan Bordèse

- **Dedication**

A Madame la Comtesse Anna Branicka née Comtesse Potocka, J. W^néi Pani Annie z hr. Potockich hr. Branickiéj. Countess Anna Branicka (1876-1953), daughter of Julia Potocka (1854-1921). An aristocratic family, the Potockis played an important role in Polish history during the eighteenth and nineteenth centuries.

Movements

No. 1. *Letni wieczór - Soir d'eté* [e–a']
No. 2. *Wędrowało sobie słonko - Le Soleil emplit la voûte* [e–g#']
No. 3. *Nie będę cię rwała - Pourquoi te cueillir* [d–g']
No. 4. *Ach, jak mi smutno - Pleure mon âme* [e–g']
No. 5. *Siedzi ptaszek na drzewie - Sur le branche l'oiseau* [f–f#']

Editions

Manuscripts: ZLSC. See Appendix Inventory. The manuscript copy of No. 5 claimed by the Biblioteka Narodowa in Warsaw does not appear to be in Stojowski's hand.

E. Hatzfeld, Leipzig, 1895: BL, BJ, BNP, LC.

Schott, Mainz, 1910: Listed in Hofmeister.

Schott & Co., London: ZLSC.

Remarks

No. 4: *Pleure mon âme*, a very beautiful lament by Stojowski that the interpreter [Mlle Delna] had to encore in the company of the author. The remarkable pianist Stojowski also had a great personal success with his refined playing of *Warum* and *Papillons* by Schumann... [*LMM*, "M.L. Górski."]

An autographed copy of the 1895 edition with a dedication in Polish to "Marcella Sembrich-Stengel," dated September 28, 1908, Paris, exists at ZLSC. The dedication ends with the same Polish proverb found in the dedication to Władysław Żeleński, "Frugal the fare, but yours to share," has a September 1908 dedication to Edouard Risler's wife.

Nos. 1 and 5 were first performed by soprano Mira Heller and No. 4 by tenor Carl Furstenberg in May 1896 at the Salle Erard. No. 4 was also sung by Mlle Deshays at the Salle Erard in February 1900.

• Recordings

No. 2 recorded by baritone Janusz Kowalski for PR, R II P-5164-G, 1989.

Nos. 3, 4 and 5 recorded by soprano Maria Bogucka (1879-1958) and pianist LS for the 1948 Stojowski Memorial Program on radio station WNYC, New York. A 78.26 RPM record as well as a CD transfer of the recording exists in ZLSC.

Nos. 1 and 3 recorded by soprano Wiesława Ćwiklińska, for PR, PA-2097 G and PA-2097 J respectively, 1971.

Opus 12: *Danses Humoresques pour piano* (1893)

• Dedication

1. *A Monsieur Théodore Jelowicki*. Théodore Jełowicki (1828 or 1831-1905), Polish lawyer and musician, the third son of Michał Jełowicki (b. 1780) and

Antonina Iwaszkiewicz. From Łanowiec in the former Eastern territories of Poland, Jełowicki was forced to sell his land, which the family had owned for several centuries, and emigrate.

2. *A Madame Ladislas Mickiewicz*. An accomplished pianist and wife of Władysław Mickiewicz (1838-1936), the son of the famous poet, Adam Mickiewicz (1798-1855). Władysław was a leader of the Polish émigrés in Paris. For 21 years he directed the Luxembourg Bookstore which specialized in the publication and sale of Polish authors, and for the last 47 years of his life he was the director of the Polish Library and Adam Mickiewicz Museum in Paris. Twenty-six letters from Stojowski to their daughter Maria (Mariotka) can be found at the Polish Library in Paris.

3. *A Mademoiselle Sophie Gabryszewska*.

4. *A Monsieur Louis Morelowski*. Louis [Ludwik] Morelowski (1847-1916), a Stojowski student. By profession a court clerk in Cracow, he was also a trained composer. His *Barcarolle,* Op. 10, for solo piano is dedicated to Stojowski, and his *Danses à l'antique,* Op. 4, is dedicated to Stojowski's mother, Maria.

5. *A Mademoiselle Antoinette Szumowska*. Antoinette Szumowska (1868-1938), Polish pianist. A pupil of Paderewski's, she was a cousin of Paderewski's second wife Helena. She married Józef Adamowski, a cellist with the Boston Symphony Orchestra, whose brother Tymoteusz, a violinist, was the orchestra's concertmaster. In 1896, the three of them formed the Adamowski Trio, and all three taught at the New England Conservatory of Music. As a soloist, she performed over a dozen times with the Boston Symphony Orchestra. She was known in Polish circles as Antonina Adamowska-Szumowska.

6. *Princess Catherine Stourdza*. A Rumanian princess who lived in Paris at the same time as Stojowski. She gave Stojowski's mother the famous parchment fan that Madame Stojowska used as an autograph book.

- **Movements**

  *No. 1 *Polonaise—Poco maestoso*
  No. 2 *Valse—Allegretto con moto*
  *No. 3 *Mazurka—Allegretto capricioso*
  No. 4 *Cracovienne—Allegretto con fantasio*
  No. 5 *Mazurka—Allegro moderato*
  No. 6 *Cosaque fantastique—Molto vivace*

- **Editions**

  B. Schott's Söhne, Mainz, 1893: WU no. 2.

  E. Hatzfeld, Leipzig; Stanley Lucas, Weber, Pitt & Hatzefld Ltd., London, 1893-1894 (edited by C.P. Scott): BL, LC; WU nos. 4; BNW nos. 1, 3, 5 and 6; BJ nos. 1, 2, 3 and 5; WTM nos. 3, 5 and 6; ZLSC no. 4 and 6.

Augener Edition, London, 1894: WU nos. 1, 2, 3, 5 and 6.

Augener Reprint of 1903: BL no. 6; ZLSC no. 4.

No. 2 and 3 published in Philadelphia by Theodore Presser ca. 1893.

Figure Cat-3. The cover of a piano miniature composed by Louis Morelowski and dedicated to his teacher. Courtesy of Biblioteka Narodowa, Warsaw, Poland. Call no. MUS III. 66.246. Used by permission. All rights reserved

- **Remarks**

The *Polonaise* has not much to recommend it. The *Valse* is one of his most popular works. It is delightfully made, and practically plays itself. Here we have the maximum effect with minimum means. *Mazurka* is really warm and rhythmic. I do not care for this form as a rule, but Stojowski manages to infuse interest and variety to a high degree in this work. *Cracovienne* has a delightful theme which is worked out in very clever fashion. The last two are not very striking. [Rowley]

The dances were an "*immense succès*"; from a review of a performance by Louis Diémer at the Salle Erard in Paris in May 1895. [*LMM*, "Salle Erard, Mme Conneau."]

Pianists who wish to add a striking and characteristic piece to their repertory may be recommended to purchase this composition. It requires a firm touch and spirited style for its effective performance, but presents no exceptional executive difficulties." [From a review of the published score of No. 6 in *MT*, January 1, 1895, p. 30.]

- **Recordings**

No. 2 recorded for Ampico (piano roll) Recordings by Mischa Levitzki 57423 also 10027, later released on an excellent Mason-Hamlin Ampico reproducing piano recording entitled *Mischa Levitzki Plays Beethoven, Mendelssohn and Brahms,* Klavier Records KS-H6, North Hollywood, California: 1970.

No. 2 recorded by Marguerite Volavy on Welte-Mignon 6982.

No. 2 recorded by Herma Merth on Artrio-Angelus (piano roll) 8103.

No. 2 recorded by Sidney Schachter, Carnegie Hall Recording Co., Station WNYC, 78-RPM and CD transfer: January 12, 1947, ZLSC.

No. 2 recorded by Zygmunt Lisicki for PR, 88716-B, 1957.

No. 2 recorded by LS, Desmar IPA 115, 1976.

No. 5 recorded by Michael von Zadora on Welte (piano roll) 3655, ca. 1920–1921.

Opus 13: *Sonate (en Sol majeur) pour Piano & Violon* (1893)

- **Dedication**

A mon cher Maître Ladislas Żeleński. Władysław Żeleński (1837–1921) Polish composer, pianist and teacher. Żeleński was Stojowski's piano and composition teacher in Cracow. He was also the father of the famous Polish writer Tadeusz Boy-Żeleński. In 1888 he organized the Conservatory of the Cracow Musical Society and became its director, a position he held until his death. Żeleński dedicated his *Suite de Danses Polonaises pour Orchestre*, Op. 47 to Stojowski.

- **Movements**

  Allegro non troppo
  Allegretto capriccioso
  Thème varié—Andante maestoso

- **Editions**

  E. Hatzfeld, Leipzig, 1894: WU.

  Stanley Lucas, Weber, Pitt & Hatzfeld, Ltd., London, 1894: BL, BJ, CC, CPL, DPL, LC, NYPLPA, SAM.

  Schott, London, 1894: EAST. A digitalized score and part can be downloaded at: http://hdl.handle.net/1802/2704

  B. Schott Söhne, Mainz, 1910: NYPLPA, PWM.

- **Remarks**

  The first performance took place in May 1893 with Stojowski accompanying Górski at the Salle Erard in Paris. Émile Sauret performed the Sonata with the composer in London at the turn of the century.

  The only piece of any length, however, was a Sonata in D [sic!] for pianoforte and violin, from Mr. Stojowski's own pen, in which he was assisted by his compatriot, Mr. Gorski. It is a bright and animated work in three movements, of which the last, a theme with variations, is the cleverest, Slavonic character being perceptible throughout its phraseology. [From a July 1, 1893, London review, "Pianoforte Recitals" in *The Musical Times*, p. 409; the program included music by Paderewski, Tchaikovsky, Żeleński, Moszkowski, and Stojowski.]

  The Paris correspondent of the Warsaw daily *Kurjer Warszawski* wrote in a review of the Sonata that it should be named the *Chłopska* [Peasant] Sonata, because of the composition's opening theme. [From an undated press clipping in the Paderewski Archives, 570 no. 56, at the AAN]

  The first American performance took place on Christmas Day 1905 in Washington, D.C. The soloist was Willy Hess, the concertmaster of the Boston Symphony Orchestra from 1904 to 1910 and the leader of the Boston Symphony Orchestra Quartet. The composer accompanied. [*WP*, "Sigismond Stojowski."]

  Stojowski has had some attention from Hyperion. Both his piano concertos have been recorded as has an anthology of his piano solos. Like the Żeleński, this is a recording premiere for his Violin Sonata. The first movement is another high water mark example of late-romantic plunging ardour. It has a touch of salon sentimentality about it too; something Żeleński steered well clear of. What the two composers have in common is a folk accent which is clearly to the fore in the drone and slow dance of the *Allegro capriccioso*. Amid the wood-smoke there is also a hint of Mephistophelean enchantment. The sentimentality comes out again for the finale which veers towards Bruch.

It is interesting to compare master and pupil as represented by these works. Żeleński would never drop his guard and allow in sentimentality. Clearly Stojowski had a more accommodating faculty. However when you hear that soft-chiming Brahmsian piano at 2:02 in the finale of the Stojowski you know that it spells a suave melody for the violin. And so it arrives with the sob and the smile of a spiritual. Then again Stojowski steels himself for a stern determined ascent at 6:12 in the finale. Sparks fly to the four winds in the stamping last three minutes of the Stojowski Sonata. Such is the savagery of this music I several times thought of Bartók. [From a MusicWeb internet review by Rob Barnett of Barbara Trojanowska's recording found at: http://www.musicwebinternational.com/classrev/2005/Nov05/ZELENSKI_STOJOWSKI_sonatas_AP0112.htm (March 25, 2006)]

The first movement begins with the usual sonata allegro form. The second movement, however, uses the Polish dance form mazurka for its formal structure as a Scherzo and introduces Polish mountaineer music just prior to the second movement's *Da capo al fine*. The Sonata ends with a set of variations based on a lush-sounding theme played in the violin's lower register.

Ruth Breton, a New York violinist and former student of Leopold Auer who made her debut in 1924, performed the Sonata during the opening concert of the Polish Institute of Arts and Letters on April 7, 1932.

* **Recordings**

Recorded by Lidia Kmitowa, violin, and Jerzy Lefeld, piano for PR, 94165, 1959

Recorded by Barbara Trojanowska, violin, and Elżbieta Tyszecka, piano, for Acte Préalable, AP0112 in 2005.

Opus 14

* **Remarks**

A manuscript copy of the violin and piano part of the unpublished and unfinished Violin Concerto in D in the ZLSC has the designation "Op. 15" in the manuscript. It might be the missing Op. 14.

Opus 15: *Trois Morceaux pour piano* **(1896)**

- **Dedication**

  1. *A Mademoiselle Angela Anderson.* Angela Anderson was a Stojowski student in Paris. See Remarks.

  2. *A Madame Henry Singer.*

  3. *A Mademoiselle Ivana Meedintiano.* Meedintiano was a pianist who made several recordings accompanying the American-born French mezzo-soprano, Claire Croiza.

- **Movements**

  *No.1 *Rêverie—Andante*
  *No.2 *Intermezzo–Mazurka—Allegretto*
  No.3 *Au soir—Andante con moto*

- **Editions**

  E. Hatzfeld, Liepzig; Stanley Lucas, Weber, Pitt & Hatzfeld, London, 1896: BL nos. 1 and 2; BNW no. 2; ZLSC no. 3.

  Schott & Co., London, 1896: WU nos. 1 & 2; BJ nos. 1 & 2, BNW no. 2.

  Schott & Co., London, 1898: PWM, WU no. 3.

  No. 2 published in the anthology *Mazurkas* by Biblioteka Narodowa, Warsaw, 1995.

- **Remarks**

  Rêverie, in his favorite key (A-flat), has all the characteristics we now associate with this writer. Melody, with chordal accompaniment off the beat; enharmonic changes, a new version of the theme on its re-appearance. *Au Soir* [is] rather like Moszkowski, only deeper in musical thought. The last page is difficult, and somewhat needlessly involved, perhaps, but a charming work altogether. [Rowley]

  Student of Mr. Stojowski, Mlle Anderson cannot help but make considerable strides each year. Her concert this year marks, as it were, the progress made since that of last year, and I cannot but endorse an elegant public's unending applause produced by her execution of the *Fantasie et fugue* of Bach-Liszt, three Pieces of Chopin, *Barcarolle* of Fauré, Caprice and *Légende* of Stojowski and *Valse* of Moszkowski. [*LMM*, "Mlle A. Anderson."]

- **Recordings**

  No. 2 recorded by Anon. Per. for The Orchestrelle Coy. (piano roll) AEOL L1048, Great Britain, 1903–1908.

Opus 16: *Deux Caprices pour piano* (1898)

- **Dedication**

  A mon cher Maitre M. Louis Diémer.
  See Opus 2 for information.

- **Movements**

  No. 1 *Allegretto moderato*
  *No. 2 *Allegro molto*

- **Editions**

  Stanley Lucas, Weber, Pitt & Hatzfeld Ltd., London & Leipzig: 1898: BJ, BNW, PWM, WU; WTM no. 2; ZLSC no. 2.

  Schott, Mainz, ca. 1900: Listed in Hofmeister

- **Remarks**

  Deux Caprices are rather cut up into little bits, quite difficult and not very interesting musically. The same remarks apply to *Arabesque,* Op. 19, no. 2. Not quite spontaneous, one feels. [Rowley]

Opus 17: *Doumka* (c. 1910)

- **Dedication**

  [*A*] *Mlle Sophie Gabryszewska.* Gabryszewska might have been related to Antoni Marian Gabryszewski, a well known anatomist of the time.

- **Tempo Marking**

  Andante con moto

- **Editions**

  Gebethner & Wolff (fingering by ZS), Warsaw, 1911: BNW, PR, PWM, WTM

- **Remarks**

  This is the only work by Stojowski that was first published in Poland. Stojowski, like many of his Polish colleagues—Paderewski, Młynarski, Różycki and Wertheim—had foreign publishers. [Jasiński, *Na przełomie epok*, 431.]

  Also spelled *Dumka*, this is a form of Slavic folk song that originated in Russia. Its main characteristics are the shifts between the nostalgic and boisterous moods. Stojowski wrote two other works that bore this title: a very short unpublished composition for voice and chamber orchestra and another solo piano piece without opus number, published in 1945 by G. Schirmer in New York. The latter is a revised version of Opus 17.

Opus 18: *Sonate pour Piano et Violoncelle* **(Kissingen and Paris, September–November 1895)**

- **Dedication**

  A mon très cher Maître I. J. Paderewski. Ignacy Jan Paderewski (1860–1941), Polish pianist, composer, statesman, patriot and philanthropist. Paderewski studied piano with Theodore Leschetizky in Vienna and composition with Friederich Kiel in Berlin. He was Poland's first prime minister following World War I. As a pianist he amassed a huge fortune for his time—$10 million—most of which was spent on Polish relief and countless other causes around the world. He was Stojowski's teacher and mentor who performed and recorded his pupil's compositions.

- **Movements**

  Andante
  Allegro
  Allegro con fuoco

- **Editions**

  Manuscript: ZLSC. See Appendix, Inventory, Box 1 Case Va, Folder 3, no. 3.

  Schott & Söhne, Mainz, 189–: BJ.

  H. B. Stevens, London, 1895–1896: ZLSC, Printed with wrong opus no., i.e., Op. 17.

  Stanley Lucas, Weber, Pitt & Hatzfeld Ltd., London, 1898: BJ, CA Rare Book Room, NYPLPA, WU.

  Schott, London, 1900: EAST, LC, SAM. A digitalized score and part can be downloaded at:http://hdl.handle.net/1802/2161.

- **Remarks**

The first performance took place with French cellist Joseph Salmon accompanied by the composer at the Salle Erard in Paris in May 1896. [*LMM*, "M. Sigismond Stojowski," May 30, 1896.]

The Sonata was composed in Kissingen and Paris and designated as "Op. 17" on the manuscript. It is more virtuosic for the pianist than for the cellist. The work explores the *cantabile* character of the violoncello, and is cyclic in form. Stojowski uses sonata allegro form for the first and last movements, while the second movement is A B A1 B1 A2. The opening theme of the first movement and the second movement's contrasting theme (B) are based on the rhythm of the Polish folk dance, *kujawiak.* The thematic material is based on modal scales. The first is a pentatonic scale (e–f#–a–b–c#) and the second is the hypolydian scale (g–a–b-flat–c–d–e–f–g). [Suchecki, 204, 215, 218.]

A performance with Stojowski accompanying the 24-year-old Pablo Casals took place in Paris at the Salle Erard on May 7, 1900. [*Le Figaro,* May 2, 1900 press clipping in Paderewski Archives, 570 no. 43, AAN.]

As a composer, Mr. Stojowski limited himself to playing for us a Sonata for Piano and Violoncello. This work is abundant in beautiful melodic ideas that are not banal. Personally and skillfully treated in the *Andante,* Mr. P. Casals phrased and nuanced with artistic feeling, which explains the rapid success of this young Spanish cellist in Paris. [From a review in *LMM,* "M. Sig. Stojowski." vol. 12.]

Along with pianist Harold Bauer, Casals recommended Stojowski to Frank Damrosch for the position of professor of piano at Damrosch's newly created Institute of Musical Art in New York City in 1905. (The IMA was later incorporated into the Juilliard School of Music). The Stojowski family moved into Casals' former ten-room apartment at 16 East 96th Street after selling their four-story brownstone at 150 West 76th Street in 1939.

A concert of Polish music was given yesterday afternoon in Mendelssohn Hall by Mr. Sigismund Stojowski, who is himself a Pole, and has taken part in the creative work of contemporaneous musical Poles. He began his concert with a Sonata for Piano and Violoncello, in which the violoncello part was played by Mr. Alwin Schroeder, by the hand of a master. The Sonata shows the traits of Polish melody as it has been made known by Paderewski's earlier compositions. One of the most characteristic of these is the opening theme of the first movement, foreshadowed in the slow introduction, which returns in the last. Many of Mr. Stojowski's themes, however, do not seem striking or pregnant upon a first hearing. He has developed them often at too great length, and the Sonata suffers somewhat from prolixity. The slow movement has genuine feeling and poetic quality. But it is skillfully written throughout by one who understands and intelligently uses the true idiom of the violoncello, and never forces it to the uncouth tricks of agility that some composers and performers delight in. Its utterance is always noble and dignified, and the work is one which, excepting for its too great length, gives pleasure. [From a review of the first American performance in *NYT*, "Mr. Stojowski's Recital."]

Principal cellist of the Boston Symphony Orchestra, Alwin Schroeder, performed the work with the composer at the piano at the Colony Club in New York in March 1910.

Danish cellist, Herman Sandby (1881–1965), the principal cellist of the Philadelphia Orchestra, performed the work with Stojowski at Witherspoon Hall in 1917.

• **Recordings**

Recorded by cellist Thaddeus Brys and pianist Luisa Stojowska for the WNYC-FM Stojowski Memorial Program of April 30, 1952; Five 12-inch 78.26 RPM records as well as one 10-inch 33 RPM and a CD transfer: ZLSC. Before switching to the cello, Mr. Brys (b. 1929) studied the piano with both Zygmunt and Luisa Stojowski. Currently professor emeritus at the University of Louisiana in Baton Rouge, Brys is a graduate of the Mannes College of Music. He coached with Pablo Casals in France during the summer of 1951.

Recorded by cellist Tomasz Strahl and pianist Edward Wolanin for PR, PC-1039, 1992.

Recorded by cellist Jarosław Domżal and pianist Joanna Ławrynowicz for Acte Préable AP0144, *Complete Works for Cello*, November 2006.

Figure Cat-4. Thaddeus Brys, July 1949. Photograph courtesy of
Mr. Brys.

MINIATURES

№ 2
Moment musical.

A Mlle Geneviève Emile Ollivier.

Sigismond Stojowski.
Op. 19 – № 2.

Figure Cat-5. Stojowski: *Moment musical* Op. 19, no. 2. Hatzfeld & Co., 1905. Public domain

Opus 19: *Cinq Miniatures pour piano* **(1900)**

- **Dedication**

  1. *To Miss Maude Hatzfeld.* Miss Maude Hatzfeld was probably the daughter of Stojowski's British publisher, Louis Hatzfeld.

  2. *A Mlle Geneviève Emile Ollivier.* Geneviève Emile Ollivier was probably the wife of Emile Ollivier (1825–1913), a French statesman.

  3. *A Miss Sallie F. Acken.*

  4. *[A] Mlle Paulette Denisane.*

  5. *A Madame la Comtesse Antoine Potocka.* Another member of the aristocratic Potocki family. In 1904, Marcel Proust wrote an article "Le Salon de Comtesse Potocka" in *Le Figaro* on May 13.

- **Movements**

  No. 1 *Feuillet d'Album—Andantino semplice*
  No. 2 *Moment musical—Andantino quasi allegretto*
  *No. 3 *Arabesque—Allegretto moderato*
  No. 4 *Barcarolle—Andantino con moto*
  *No. 5 *Mazurka—Allegretto grazioso*

- **Editions**

  Hatzfeld & Co., London, 1905: In this edition the order of works differs from the Heugel edition given above. The *Barcarolle* is listed as a *Berceuse*. BJ and LC nos. 3, 4 and 5 become 1, 2 and 3; BNW no. 3 and 4 become nos. 1 and 2. The order in the Hatzfeld edition is the following:
  No. 1 *Arabesque—À Miss Sallie F. Ackens,*
  No. 2 *Berceuse (Barcarolle)—A Mademoiselle Paulette Denisane,*
  No. 3 *Mazurka*
  No. 4 ?
  No. 5 ?

  Heugel & Cie., Paris, 1912: BNP, LC, OSU, WU, ZLSC.

  No. 1 arranged for organ: Plant, Arthur B. (arr.) *Modern Masters for the Organ,* vol. III, London: Edwin Ashdown, 1900–1940?: SC.

- **Remarks**

  No. 1 is a revised version of *Feuillet d'Album* which Stojowski wrote at the age of fourteen. Instead of four-bar phrases used that are used in the early work, the music flows in five-bar phrases in Opus 19.

Unlike most of Stojowski's works, No. 2 is technically easy to play. It must have been written to meet the dedicatee's abilities. Of interest are the syncopated rhythmic *ostinato* in the left hand (lasting 67 bars, from the beginning to the antepenultimate bar of the piece), and the irregular phrasing, starting with the first seven-bar phrase.

- **Recordings**

  No. 5 recorded by Stojowski for Ampico (piano roll) 60501H.

  No. 5 recorded by Stojowski for a New York radio broadcast on October 15, 1944. Transferred onto LP: Desmar IPA 115, *Sigismond Stojowski Plays Chopin, Paderewski and Stojowski,* 1976.

Opus 20: *Romanze für Violine mit Begleitung des Orchesters oder des Pianoforte* **(1901)**

- **Dedication**

  Herrn Jacques Thibaud gewidmet. Jacques Thibaud (1880–1953), French violinist, who won first prize in violin at the Conservatoire National in 1896. By the end of 1899, he had performed as a soloist with Concerts Colonne over 50 times. Like Stojowski, he was a soloist during the inaugural season of the Warsaw Philharmonic Orchestra (1901–1902). He is best remembered for his trio recordings with cellist Pablo Casals and pianist Alfred Cortot.

- **Tempo Marking**

  Andante ma non troppo

- **Editions**

  Orchestral score manuscript: ZLSC. See Appendix Inventory.
  Leipzig: C. F. Peters, 1901
  Full score: CU, DPL, LC, MCM, UP
  Full score and parts: FLP, ZLSC
  Violin/Piano score: BJ, WU

- **Orchestration**

  2.2.2.2-4.2.3.0-timp.cym-hrp-str

- **Remarks**

  This is a one-movement work in E-flat Major, duple meter. In Poland, it was performed by Michał Osmycki at the Stojowski May Festival in Warsaw in 2003. As this book prepares to go to print there are plans to make an archival recording of the work with violinist Tomasz Tomaszewski, concertmaster of the Berlin Deutsche Oper, and the National Polish Radio Symphony Orchestra in Katowice.

Opus 21: *Symphonie in D moll für großes Orchester* (1898)

- **Dedication**

  I. J. Paderewski gewidmet. See Opus 18 for biographical information. "To be or not to be" is written on the title page of the manuscript score.

- **Movements**

  Andante mesto
  Andante
  Scherzo: Molto vivace
  Finale: Allegro con fuoco, ma non vivace

- **Editions**

  Full score manuscript: ZLSC. See Appendix Inventory.
  C. F. Peters, Leipzig: 1901.
  Full score: BL, BNW, DPL, LC.
  Full score and parts: BBC, CBN, FLP, NYPLPA, SAM, and (on hire) from C. F. Peters.

  Arrangement for Piano/Four Hands by Juliusz Spangler, 1902: BJ, BNW, LC, WSU.

- **Orchestration**

  3*.3*.3*.2-4.2.3.1-timp-harp-str

- **Remarks**

  The Symphony won first prize on July 9, 1898 at the Paderewski Competition in Leipzig. Arthur Nikisch, director of the Leipzig Gewandhaus Orchestra, presided over the jury, whose other German members included composer Karl Reinecke, critic F. R. Pfau, and cellist Julius Klengel. [Piber, 254–255]. The quotation from Shakespeare, "To be or not to be," found on the manuscript score, was Stojowski's anonymous identification code for submitting the composition to the jury.

  In spite of his leaning towards the national idioms, of which he has made ample use in his minor works, the composer of this Symphony, in attempting the largest form of instrumental music, evolved along the traditional lines and most universal in its appeal, has refrained from what may be termed 'genre-music.' Barely the theme of the last movement with its proud, chivalrous character, especially when accompanied by some characteristic rhythmical figures in the bass, carries a suggestion of Poland. The work, voluntarily sober in harmony and instrumentation, maintains in formal structure the main lines of the classical symphony. Nor did the composer choose to deprive himself of that source of riches and variety which came to the classical symphony from the use of different themes for the different movements. But if every movement possesses its own themes, a sort of unity is attempted by the recurrence of some themes, more or less modified, but always recognizable, in the various movements. So, for instance, the theme of the finale is announced in the slow movement, where it breaks in twice upon the tender mood by a dramatic appeal from the horns. In the scherzo, again, the main theme of the first movement suddenly emerges, in a subdued and altered form, from the bubble of the swiftly moving runs, shakes and tremolos. The whole movement is dipped in a phantastic atmosphere, which suggests hustling and dancing elfs [sic!] in a moonlit dance. It has been described by foreign critics as an effective bit of orchestra writing and has often been played separately, namely, by Mr. Arthur Nikisch. There is no programmatic pretense to this Symphony, to which, however, Hamlet's 'to be or not to be' might serve as a motto. In the opening bars a bass-clarinet, like some enigmatic personage, voices the second subject in a sort of reflective mood, and the whole movement, with its sombre and violent main theme and its alternatives of light and shade, seem to depict the struggle between the 'to be or not to be'—until the final assertion of the triumph of light. [From Philip Hale's English translation of Charles Malherbe's notes for a program of the Paris Colonne Orchestra. The English version appeared on pp. 739–740 of the Boston Symphony Orchestra Program of January 16 & 17, 1920, under Pierre Monteux.]

The bass clarinet solo, which opens the Symphony, is the same bass clarinet solo that opens the composer's unpublished *Ballade for Orchestra*, Stojowski's first orchestral work.

Stefan Śledziński in *Zarys dziejów symfonii polskiej w XIX wieku* [A Historical Sketch of the Symphonic Genre in Nineteenth-Century Poland] writes that the first performance also took place in Leipzig at the Competition. No other information verifies this so-called premiere in Leipzig. However, Stojowski revised the last movement, and the first performance of the new version took place with the Berlin Philharmonic Orchestra under the Czech conductor Josef Řebiček (1844–1904) on November 15, 1900, in Berlin's Beethoven-Saal. The first Polish performance took place at the inaugural concert of the Warsaw Philharmonic Orchestra with Emil Młynarski conducting on November 5, 1901. Other performances followed in January 1903 (Arthur Nikisch and the Gewandhaus Orchestra in Leipzig), and on March 24, 1903 (Emil Młynarski and the Colonne Orchestra at the Théâtre du Châtelet in Paris). Carnegie Hall was the site of the Symphony's American premiere with the New York Philharmonic playing an all-Stojowski program on March 1, 1915, conducted by Josef Stransky. This concert marked the first time in the orchestra's history that an entire program was dedicated to the music of only one Polish composer.

The composer Feliks Nowowiejski (1877–1946) conducted a performance of the Symphony in 1911 in Cracow, where he was the artistic director of the Cracow Musical Society until 1914. Since Cracow did not have its own symphony orchestra, Nowowiejski organized amateur musicians—instrumentalists from two army ensembles as well as students and professors from the Musical Society—for the performance. The following year, when Nowowiejski's cantata *Quo vadis?* received its American premiere at Carnegie Hall, Stojowski was in the audience. [Nowowiejski, 78, 91]

Also in 1911, the Warsaw Philharmonic included the Scherzo of the Symphony on its tenth anniversary concert of November 15 with Józef Ozimiński conducting. Stojowski was a member of the Philharmonic's 10th Anniversary Committee. [Filharmonia Warszawska, 14–15, 37]

The Symphony was featured at the festival *Tydzień Muzyki Polskiej* [A Week of Polish Music] in Poznań on October 7, 1938.

Nikisch, Młynarski, Ozimński, and Fitelberg separately programmed the Symphony's brilliant *Scherzo* on numerous occasions.

During the depression, one of the New York W.P.A. orchestras performed Stojowski's Symphony six times during the winter of the 1935–1936 Season. [Stojowski. Letters to Arthur P. Schmidt.]

The Rzeszów Philharmonic Orchestra plans to perform and record the Symphony during the 2006–2007 concert Season.

For more information on the Symphony, see Chapter 2.

- **Recordings**

Recorded for PR, 95732 A: The National Polish Radio Orchestra in Katowice (WOSPR): Włodzimierz Ormicki, conductor, 1962.

Recorded for PR, PB-5284: The Polish Radio & TV Orchestra in Cracow, Zbigniew Chwedczuk, conductor, 1983.

Opus 22: *Concert in G für Violine* **(1899–1908)**

- **Dedication**

  À monsieur Ladislas Gorski, au maître – collaborateur, au premier interprète, témoignage de reconnaissance artistique pour le précieux concours qu'il m'a prêté lors de la composition de cet ouvrage. For more information on Górski see Opus 6 and Chapter 2.

- **Movements**

  Allegro deciso
  Andante non troppo
  Allegro giocoso

- **Editions**

  Manuscripts: ZLSC. See Appendix Inventory. The opus number on the MS is "20" rather than the published "22."

  Arthur P. Schmidt, Boston & Leipzig: 1908.
  Full score: BBC, BL HVU, LC, UI, ZLSC.
  Full score and parts: BJ, FLP.
  Violin/Piano score: BL, BJ, CPL, DPL, UMC, WU, ZLSC.

- **Orchestration**

  vn-2.2.2.2-4.2.3.0-timp-hp-str

- **Remarks**

  The first performance took place in Paris (Orchestre Chevillard) in March 1900. Subsequent performances took place in Berlin (Berlin Philharmonic) and Cracow in November 1900 with Górski as the soloist for all three performances. In Cracow, the concerto was performed with piano accompaniment only, and the composer at the piano.

  "M. Ladislas Gorski – The renowned Polish violinist gave his annual concert with the assistance of the *Orchestre Chevillard*. Having found in Mme Howland a remarkable partner, M. Gorski began with the Bach Concerto for Two Violins, played in an excellent style. But the big attraction of the evening was the premiere performance of the Concerto for Violin by M. Sig. Stojowski. This major work confirms the importance of the composer, several of whose pieces for voice and piano we already knew. Very solidly constructed, the Concerto contains several lovely themes, skillfully developed, and the violin part is sustained by an orchestration of rich coloration. Let us hope that M. Colonne or M. Chevillard will not be long in scheduling this work for one of their Sunday programs. M. Gorski performed it [the Concerto] with a laudable conviction and a consummate virtuosity. The warm reception that he received was reaffirmed with [his performance of] the *Berceuse* of his own composition and the *Airs Hongrois* of Ernst. M. Stojowski performed two pieces by Chopin, executed with the brilliant pianistic qualities for which we have come to know his playing. He was obliged to add the Serenade by Schubert-Liszt." [From a review of the world premiere in *LMM,* "M. Ladislas Gorski"]

The first American performance took place in 1909 with Willy Hess as soloist. In a letter to Arthur P. Schmidt dated January 26, 1909, Stojowski writes that the premiere will take place April 18, 1909 at Carnegie Hall in a concert sponsored by the American Music Society. [See: Stojowski, Letters to Arthur P. Schmidt]. Although a concert sponsored by this organization did take place on that date, the Carnegie Hall archives do not have any record of Stojowski's Concerto being played on the program.

The concerto was performed with violinist Tomasz Tomaszewski and the Poznań Philharmonic Orchestra on November 10 and 11, 2006, Lukasz Borowicz conducting. An archival recording of the work is planned with the same two artists performing with the National Polish Radio Symphony Orchestra in Katowice.

Opus 23: *Rapsodie symphonique pour Piano et Orchestre* (1900)

• **Dedication**

A Monsieur Harold Bauer. Harold Bauer (1873–1951), British-born American pianist. Although first trained as a violinist, coaching with Paderewski convinced Bauer to become a pianist. In 1894 he debuted in Paris, and in America in 1900 with the Boston Symphony Orchestra. Bauer became an American citizen in 1917 and founded the Beethoven Association in 1918. He was the head of the piano department at the Manhattan School of Music and later taught at the University of Miami. He is also the dedicatee of Ravel's *Ondine.*

• **Editions**

C. F. Peters, Leipzig: 1904–1907.
Full score: BL, CLP, DPL, FLP, LC, NYPLPA.
Full score and parts (on hire): C. F. Peters.
Arrangement for Piano/Four Hands by composer ca. 1925: BJ, BL, CLP, BNW.

• **Orchestration**

Pno-3*.3*.2.2-4.2.3.0-timp.perc (4)-hp-str

- **Remarks**

Symphonic Rhapsody for Piano and Orchestra is a big concert work, which somehow does not seem, characteristically Stojowski. We feel that it is rather 'made.' [Rowley]

The *Rhapsodie Symphonique* begins with an introductory movement, *Andante con moto*, which admirably fulfils its purpose by exciting expectation. This is accomplished at the outset by a solo passage for the *cor anglais,* and ten bars later by the entrance of the pianoforte, also without orchestral support. This part gradually increases in importance, growing more florid, and ultimately working-up to a climax crowned with the impressive statements in full chords, accompanied by *arpeggi*, of the first phrase of the principal subject of the *Allegro moderato*; but before this is commenced the pianoforte has a *cadenza* consisting chiefly of a series of shakes. On the *Allegro moderato* being reached, its chief subject is announced by the oboe and bassoon, supported by *pizzicato* chords from the strings. When the solo-instrument re-enters, it is with a series of double trills, which lead to its emphatic delivery of the principal theme. After this, animation prevails, the music becoming joyous in nature, albeit the second subject-matter is flowing and *legato*. The clever manner in which the composer has treated the characteristic phrases of this thematic material will be noticed, for the design is clear and the scoring picturesque. Attention may be drawn, however, to an effective passage of song-like suggestiveness for the celli and the ingenious combination of themes in the *Molto vivace*, which brings the work to a brilliant conclusion. [From the analytical notes for the Sunday afternoon, June 7, 1908 program of the London Symphony Orchestra at Royal Albert Hall with Emil Młynarski, conductor, and the composer at the piano.]

Selected reviews of Stojowski's March 19, 1911 performance with the New York Symphony Orchestra, Walter Damrosch conducting:

Mr. Stojowski writes with strong originality and in the idiom of Poland, his own country. This work is essentially of that country, with its poetic line of melody, its strong rhythms that almost suggest the mazurka, and behind it is a fine imagination and a thoroughly skilled pen. The orchestration is exceedingly well done, and the concise form in which it is written makes it doubly interesting and worthy, not one hearing alone, but many of them. It was received with enthusiasm. [*New York Evening Mail*]

The great advantage of hearing a work for the first time played by the composer, especially when he is a soloist of distinction, is an unusual one, and this is what happened yesterday. Mr. Stojowski has made an addition to current pianistic literature of genuine worth and merit, and it is to be hoped he will have an opportunity of playing it again and letting the public become familiar with it. He has unusually original ideas, even in the art of programme making, and such an artist should be encouraged. The Rhapsody was very well received. [*Brooklyn Standard Union*]

Sigismond Stojowski provided the novelty and was the soloist in his own new symphonic Rhapsody, a work of much beauty yet simple refinement. Some of the orchestral passages were exceptionally brilliant. [*New York Evening Sun*]

Stojowski's Rhapsody received mixed reviews in Paris in 1925. Many critics did not even mention Stojowski's links to Paris and his distinguished scholarly record at the Conservatoire. Mr. J. Himonet wrote that the work was "a mediocre composition, without musical interest and color, and even though the cantilena solo played by the English horn at the very outset sounded promising, it failed to live up to its promises." The critic also referred to Stojowski's "dry hammering" at the keyboard and regretted that there was not more music in the piece. [Himonet]

The first performance was with the Berlin Philharmonic Orchestra with the composer performing and Josef Rebicek (Řebiček) conducting at the Beethoven-Saal on November 15, 1900. [Taken from a review of the Berlin concert in *Le Figaro* on November 19, 1900, Paderewski Archives, 570 no. 46, AAN.] This is probably the same work as the *Fantazja polska* [Polish Fantasy], which one year later won the 250-ruble second prize (no first prize given) for the best composition for soloist and orchestra at the Count Zamoyski Competition in Warsaw, on October 20, 1900. [See: *Echo Muzyczne i Teatralne,* October 19, 1901.] If this is not the case, Stojowski withdrew the *Fantasy* from his catalogue.

In January 1902 Stojowski performed *Fantazja polska* for the first time in Poland with the Warsaw Philharmonic. In September of that same year, Stojowski played the work at the second inaugural concert of the Lwów Philharmonic Orchestra, Ludwik Heller conducting. In June 1908, he performed it with the London Symphony Orchestra under Emil Młynarski. Later, the work was performed with the New York Symphony Society at the New Theatre on Sunday afternoon, March 19, and again at Carnegie Hall on December 1, 1911, with Walter Damrosch conducting both concerts. Still another performance took place at the Boston Opera on January 26, 1913. This composition was programmed in the 1920s and 1930s with the Buffalo Philharmonic, the San Francisco Symphony Orchestra, and the Orchestre Colonne of Paris. All performances featured Stojowski as soloist.

The work begins and ends in D Major but passes through many keys during its five sections:

1. *Andante con moto*
2. *Allegro moderato*
3. *Allegro vivace e giocoso /quasi mazurka/*
4. *Poco maestoso*
5. *Molto vivace*

It is based on two subjects. The first is heard at the outset and played in succession by the English horn, oboe, flute, and piano; the second—which dominates the entire composition—is intoned by the flute and oboe in the following *Allegro moderato* section.

An autographed copy of the score with a dedication to pianist Rudolph Ganz is found at the Music Library at Roosevelt University in Chicago. "To Mr. Rudolph Ganz in token of sincere artistic admiration and personal sympathy. [signed] On board of *La Provence* Oct 2, 1907."

• **Recordings**

CD Recording: ABC Classics 465 424-2; Pianist Ian Munro with the Tasmanian Symphony Orchestra, David Porcelijn – conductor; Vol. 1 of *Concerto Symphonique, Virtuoso Works for Piano and Orchestra*, Australia: 2001.

Opus 24: *Polnische Idyllen für das Pianoforte—Polish Idylls for Piano* (1901)

• **Dedication**

Eduard Risler freundschaftlich zugeeignet. Eduard [also Édouard] Risler (1873–1929), German-born French pianist, who shared first prize in piano with Stojowski at the Conservatoire in 1889. Examples of Risler's artistry exist on 1917 Pathé recordings that have been transferred onto CD by Marston Records.

• **Movements**

No. 1 *Einsamkeit—Solitude—Andante quasi allegretto*
No. 2 *Auf zur Ernte—L'appel des moissoneurs—Allegro con spirito*
No. 3 *Dorfcoquette—Coquette de Village—The Village Flirt—Allegretto moderato e grazioso*
No. 4 *Tanz-Vision—Vision de danse—Vision of the Dance—Vivace, ma non assai*
No. 5 *Fest-Nachklänge—Souvenirs de fête—Allegro con fuoco*

• **Editions**

C. F. Peters, Leipzig, 1901: BJ, BNW, EU, LC, NYPLPA, SU, WTM, WU.
Nos. 1, 2 and 4, Gebethner & Wolff (fingering by Rodolphe Strobl), Warsaw,
1901 WTM, printed under the title of *Idylles Polonaises*. WTM.

No. 1 also appeared in the December 1970 issue of the *Clavier*. Reissued in
1993 by MO: SMU, UC.

Nos. 1 and 3, arranged by Stanisław L. Szpinalski under the titles of *Samotność*
and *Wiejska zalotnica,* appeared in *Utwory fortepianowe kompozytorów*
polskich, published by Czytelnik, Warsaw, 1952: USC.

No. 4 is an *oberek*, a lively Polish dance in triple meter.

Nos. 4 and 5, arranged by Stanisław L. Szpinalski under the titles of
Wizja taneczna and *Po kiermaszu*, appeared in *Pedagogiczna Biblioteka*
Fortepianowa, number 64 and 73 respectively, PWM, Cracow, 1952: BJ, BNW,
SZCZ, UC, USC.

No. 4 reprinted in the anthology *Neue Meister des Klavierspiels, V. 1* by Schott,
Mainz, 19–: HPL.

• **Orchestrations**

Entire suite arranged by Arnold Rezler (b. 1909) for small orchestra. Score and
parts: PR
1.1.1.1.-1.1.1.0.-timp-perc-pn-str

No. 4 *Wizja Taneczna* [Vision of the Dance] arranged for orchestra by Michał
Baranowski (1935–1963), former director of the Polish Radio Symphony
Orchestra in Katowice. Score and parts: CBN
2.2.2.2-2.2.2.0-timp-str

• **Remarks**

Polnische Idyllen have a French flavour, of which the best is the *Coquette of the*
Village. (Most male pianists that I know would fall for this!), and *Solitude*, a sad
picture indeed. [Rowley]

The Suite of five pieces that make the *Polish Idylls* is of lighter character, and
well done in its genre. The audience liked the *Coquette de Village* so well that it
was repeated. For the writer the most original and interesting movement was the
Vision de danse, with its true smack of the Polish soil.

This concert at the end of the day filled with music was a pleasure to hear. The pleasure proceeded from the healthy musical, emotional interpretations, the excellent piano style, the unassuming sincerity, but, at the same time, authority of the performances. Once more it was shown that nothing is necessary in giving a concert, save to convey the composer's message with all the heart. There was a good-sized audience, and Mr. Stojowski was applauded with much enthusiasm. [From Olin Downes' review of a performance given by the composer in New York's Aeolian Hall on February 21, 1925. The concert also included works by Beethoven, Chopin, Schumann and another piece by Stojowski.]

Polish Idylls form an impressionistic suite depicting life in the Polish countryside. The pieces alternate between duple and triple meter from beginning to end. The tonal scheme: B-flat Minor, B-flat Major, E-flat Major, G Major, C Major, and E Major.

- **Recordings**

No. 3 recorded by ZS for Ampico (piano roll) Recordings 67863H. This piano roll recording was later released on the LP, *Famous Composers Play Their Own Compositions*, by Allegro, New York, 195–: IU, KSU.

No. 3 recorded by Sidney Schachter, Carnegie Hall Recording Co., Station WNYC, 78-RPM and CD transfer: Jan 12, 1947, ZLSC.

No. 1 recorded by Stanisław L. Szpinalski, LP *Słynni Soliści Polscy* [Famous Polish Soloists], MUZA L 0152: 1959.

No. 1 recorded by LS, Desmar IPA 115, 1976.

No. 1 recorded by Nina Sapiejewska for PR, R II P-4844-B (also PB 633 B0, 1979.

Nos. 1 & 3 recorded by Lidia Kozubek for PR, PA 5192-A and PA 5192-B respectively, 1977.

Nos. 1 & 3 recorded by Lidia Kozubek for PR, R-II P5219-C, 1981.

Nos. 1 & 3 recorded by Lidia Kozubek, LP *Neo-romantic Polish Piano Music*, Pronit SX1433, 1982, BNW; later reissued on CD by Polskie Nagranie, PNCD630, 2003.

No. 3 recorded by Boris Goldovsky, LP Allegro Royale 1402, c. 1955, ZLSC.

No. 4 recorded by Regina Smendzianka for PR, R II 91314-A, 1958; also recorded for MUZA Records, LP Muzyka, *Płytoteka dla powszechnej szkoły średniej (3)*, MUZA SX 1723: 1982, BNW.
Nos. 1–4 recorded by Elżbieta Karaś—Kasztel for PR, PB 5031-B, 1982.

Orchestral version (first four movements only) recorded for PR, PA-5693: The Polish Radio & TV Orchestra in Cracow, Krzysztof Missona, conductor, 1977.

Orchestral version recorded for PR, 98253 D: The PR Orchestra in Cracow, Stanisław Has, conductor, 1964?

Orchestral version of No. 3 recorded for PR: R II P-4454-A: The Polish Radio Orchestra in Bydgoszcz, Arnold Rezler, conductor, 1953.

Opus 25: *Romantische Stücke für das Pianoforte* (1902)

- **Dedication**

  Frau Sadi Fuller Burchard in verehrungsvoller Freundschaft Zugeeignet.

- **Movements**

  No.1 *Geständnis—Confidence—Andantino con molto*
  No. 2 *En valsant—Allegretto con molto*
  No. 3 *Idylle—Andantino*
  No. 4 *Barcarolle—Moderato*
  No. 5 *Frülingserwachen—Réveil du printemps—Spring's Awakening—Molto vivace*

- **Editions**

  C. F. Peters, Leipzig (fingerings by Adolph Ruthardt), 1902: CAM, EAST, HVU, LC, NYPLPA, PR, WU; WTM 1927 reprint. A digitalized score can be downloaded at: http://hdl.handle.net/1802/2214

  No. 3 arranged and edited for harmonium by Sigfrid Karg-Elert (1877–1933). No. 11 in *Harmonium Album /28/ ausgewählte Stücke*. Leipzig: C. F. Peters, 1914 / 1915: HVU, SC.

Figure Cat-6. Stojowski's greatest hit, *Chant d'amour*. Peters Edition, Public Domain. From the author's collection

- **Remarks**

  Confidence is full of Schumannesque charm, and is not difficult. *Idylle* has a theme which is quite unforgettable (although the work is overlong). *Barcarolle* (in 5/4 time), flowing and rather well made for the fingers. This last one—full of Spring 'feels.' [Rowley]

- **Recordings**

  No. 1 recorded by LS, Desmar IPA 115, 1976.

Opus 26: *Quatre Morceaux pour piano—Vier Stücke für das Pianoforte* **(1902?)**

- **Dedication**

  1. *A Madame la Comtesse Jeanne Des Fossez.*
  2. *A Madame Sadi Burchard.*
  3. *Dedicated to Miss Julia Appleton Fuller* (in Schirmer edition) and *A Mademoiselle Julia Fuller* (in Peters edition).
  4. *A Madame Marie Panthès-Kutner.* Marie Panthès-Kutner was born in Odessa in 1871. She took first place in piano at the Conservatoire in 1888.

- **Movements**

  *No.1 *Mélodie*
  *No.2 *In tempo di Minuetto*
  *No.3 *Chant d'amour —Andante*
  *No.4 *Thème cracovien varié* (See Remarks)

- **Editions**

  Manuscript for no. 2: ZLSC. See Appendix Inventory.

  Manuscript for no. 3: NYPLPA; microfilm of MS at HVU. The dedication on this holograph is "To Wesley Weyman, with highest regard . . . Sigismond Stojowski New York, May 1907."

  Manuscript for no. 3: ZLSC. See Appendix Inventory.

  Manuscript for no. 4: ZLSC. See Appendix Inventory.

  C.F. Peters, Leipzig (fingering by Adolf Ruthard), ca.1903: BJ, BNW, CAM, EAST, LC, NYPLPA, UT, WU. A digitalized score can be downloaded at: http://hdl.handle.net/1802/2214

No. 3: Reprint of the 1903 Peters edition in *Sang und Klang im XIX/XX Jahrhundert Ernstes und Heiteres aus dem Reiche der Tone*. Musikverlag Sang und Klang, Berlin-Basel, 1903, pp. 97–100, SZCZ.

C.F. Peters 1910 reprint BNW; 1917 reprint BNW, WTM; 1930 reprint BNW; 1936 reprint appeared in *Gradations*, a series of graded modern piano pieces selected by Alec Rowley, BNW. See illustration.

G. Schirmer, NY: 1908. Composer's fingering. English subtitle *Love Song,* EAST, LC, NU, UG, USC, ZLSC. From 1917 to 1933, this edition was reprinted six separate times. (Courtesy of G. Schirmer Archives.)

Carl Fischer, New York: 1912. Fingering by Maurice Gould: EAST, LC.

B. F. Wood Co., Boston: c. 1920, with wrong notes in the left hand in m. 9, ZLSC.

Carl Fischer, New York: 1922, edited by Hans Semper, ZLSC.

Bendix Publishing Co, Lincoln, Nebraska: ca. 1929 & 1940. Edited and fingered by Basil Darrah: CSU.

Theodore Presser, Philadelphia, also subtitled *Love Song*: 190–, KSU, ZLSC.

Czytelnik, an arrangement by Stanisław L. Szpinalski entitled *Śpiew miłości* in *Utwory fortepianowe kompozytorów polskich*, Cracow: 1952, pp. 18–21, SZCZ.

Willis Music, Cincinnati: 1984, edited and fingered by Duncan Stearns, LC.

Hinds, Hayden & Eldredge, NY: 1912, arr. by E.R. Kroeger for piano/four hands in *The Most Popular Piano Duets*, SU, UI, ULB.

- **Orchestrations**
Chant d'amour was also arranged for chamber orchestra by Gottfried Huppertz, C. F. Peters, Leipzig: 1930.

Score and parts: BBC and an incomplete set of parts at CAM.

Another orchestral arrangement of *Chant d'amour* under the Polish title *Pieśń miłości* was made in 1951 by Arnold Rezler. The arrangement is transposed a minor second lower to the key of F.
1.1.1.1.-1.1.1.0.-timp-perc-pn (hp)-str

Score and parts: PR.

- **Remarks**

The *Mélodie* (which requires large hands for its manipulation) is characteristic and warm. The *Minuetto* is rather too long, but *Chant d'amour* is a gem of the first water. A ravishing melody, with harmonies that thrill one—romantic to a degree. [Rowley]

Probably no piece is more frequently played by Paderewski than the *Chant d'amour* of Sigismond Stojowski, an exquisitely melodious composition piquantly harmonized—a piece that should be in the repertory of every pianist, professional or amateur. [From the review "A Stojowski Concert" in *The New York Post*, March 2, 1915. Stojowski Clipping File, NYPLPA.]

Regarding *Chant d'amour*: The piece is in the key of G-flat, and is marked by a formal feature of an original nature: The principal melody dies away in a cadenza in D-flat, leading to a middle part of a duet-like character, which, after working itself up to an impassioned climax, gives way to a return of the first theme by means of the same cadenza, this time in G-flat. [From the program notes of Paderewski's 1907–1908 tour. Krehbiel]

Regarding the editions: The author feels that Stojowski's G. Schirmer revised edition with his own fingering is the best. The original Peters 1903 edition has a wrong note in the left hand of the final chord in the seventh bar: instead of "C-flat" there should be a "C-natural." The 1912 Fischer edition by Maurice Gould omits some of Stojowski's expressive markings. The B. F. Wood edition of 1920 has wrong notes in the ninth bar. The 1984 edition for Willis Music by Stearns is very heavily edited and fingered, and, although the editor's markings are quite sensible and musical, there is no indication which markings come from the editor and which are Stojowski's.

The *Variations on a Cracovian Theme* is based on the delightful melody of the Polish folksong "Bartoszu, Bartoszu" (also known as *Pobudka Krakusów*), written in the Polish *krakowiak* dance form.

The text of this song is both patriotic and religious. The title refers to Wojciech Bartos, a hero of the Battle of Racławice. This victorious battle for the Poles, led by Tadeusz Kościuszko, was fought against their Russian oppressors in April 1794. Thus, the folksong is sometimes referred to as the *Kościuszko Krakowiak*:

Bartos, Bartos, do not give up hope.
God will bless us and save the Fatherland.
There, on the hill, look to God.
His love is greater than the power of the enemy.

The piece, which begins and ends in the key of G Major, is a set of nine variations on this theme. There is a gradual increase of tempo in the first five variations: 1. *Allegretto moderato*; 2. *Con grazia, un pochettino piu animato*; 3. *Piu mosso*; 4. *Leggiero e veloce* and 5. *Molto vivace*. The fifth variation is also marked by a change to compound duple metre and staccato articulation. A sudden change of tempo, metre, key and mood take place in the sixth variation as Stojowski modulates to the parallel key of G Minor, switches to compound triple metre, gives the tempo marking as *Andante con moto* and replaces the staccato articulation with the markings *sempre legato* and *ben cantato*. Another sudden change of tempo takes place in variation 7, *Con moto*. Here the music reverts to duple metre and uses the opening figure of the theme in canonic imitation, briefly modulating to B Minor before ending in G Minor. In variation 8, *Allegretto capriccioso, ma non vivace*, Stojowski returns to the original key of G Major, changes to triple metre and switches the dance form to a mazurka.

In comparison to the other variations, variation 9, *Allegro vivo*, is the longest and most developed of the set. It forms an effective coda for the work. The opening motif is masterfully braided into a sixteenth-note configuration heard throughout. Here the harmonies are more complex than those used in previous variations, and the melodic progression is strongly chromatic.

• **Recordings**

No. 3 recorded by Stojowski on Ampico (piano roll) Recordings 63923H, January 1925.

No. 3 recorded by James Whittaker on Ampico (piano roll) 5220.

No. 3 recorded by Antoinette Szumowska on Welte (piano roll) 3664.

No. 3 recorded by Anon. Per. on Aeolian (piano roll) T 20844, London, ca. 1905 and for The Orchestrelle Coy AEOL 75929, London, 1905–1908.

No. 3 recorded by Rudolph Ganz on Duo-Art (piano roll) 5525.

No. 3 recorded by Carl Friedberg on Triphonola (piano roll) 50881.

No. 3 recorded by Arthur Klein on Welte-Mignon (piano roll) 6186.

No. 3 recorded by Paderewski in December 1926 on Victor 6633. Currently available on Pearl GEMM 9943, *The Art of Paderewski* Vol. II.

No. 3 recorded by Nina Sapiejewska for PR, PB-633A.

No. 3 recorded in an arrangement by Liberace and the George Liberace Orchestra on the album *Moonlight Sonata,* Columbia CL764, 1955.

Arnold Rezler's orchestration of no. 3 recorded for PR, R II 81226: PR Orchestra in Bydgoszcz, A. Rezler—conductor, 1953.

No. 3 recorded by an unknown organist for Skinner Rolls (Music rolls manufactured by Aeolian-Skinner Organ Co.) for the Hammond Organ Hammond model BA player organ), no. 131.

No. 3 recorded by members of the Aeolian Organ Guild based on previously released 116-note rolls interpreted for the Duo-Art system on *Aeolian Pipe Organ: Plays Duo-Art Salon Music*, XPMM1510596, MSS Studios, Rhiwlas, Cae Deintur, DOLGELLAU. Gwynedd LL40 2YS, Wales, 2005.

No. 4 recorded by Sidney Schachter, Carnegie Hall Recording Co., Station WNYC, Jan 12, 1947, 78-RPM and CD transfer, ZLSC.

No. 4 recorded on radio by ZS, October 15, 1944, NY: Desmar IPA 115, 1976.

No. 4 recorded by Zygmunt Lisicki for PR, 88716 B. 1957.

Nos. 3 and 4 recorded by Jonathan Plowright for Hyperion Records, CDA67437, *Stojowski, Music for Piano,* London: 2004.

Opus 27: *Fantaisie pour trombone ténor avec accompagnement de piano* **(1889)**

- **Dedication**
  À mon cher Maître Mr. Théodore Dubois, Directeur du Conservatoire de Paris.

- **Tempo Marking**
  Allegro risoluto

- **Editions**
  Evett et Schaefer, Paris, 1905: RPL, USC (ZLSC).

  PWM, Cracow, 1953: BL, BJ, BNW, WU; 2003 BNW.

Leduc, Paris, (reprint of the Evett et Schaefer edition) 1947 and 1953: USC.
Gos. Muzykalnoe Izdatelstvo, Moscow, 1958: UCN.

Leduc, Paris, 1967: ASU, EAST, SMU, UI.

Leduc, Paris, 1994.

International Music Co. (edited by Keith Brown), NY, 1972: ASU, LC,
MSM, UI.

The 1953 Polish edition also includes a transcription of the *Fantaisie* for viola
by Mieczysław Szaleski.

- **Orchestration**

  Arranged for trombone and orchestra by Arnold Rezler.
  Trb-2.2.2.2-4.2.0.0-timp.cym-str
  Manuscript Score and parts: PR
  Manuscript score: BNW. This score, however, is in Rezler's hand and not
  Stojowski's as claimed by the library.

- **Remarks**

  The work was written for the Conservatoire National's 1905 Trombone
  Competition. [*LMM*, "Aux Conservatoire Morceaux de Concours."]

  Usually found on required repertoire lists for trombonists pursuing a Doctor of
  Musical Arts degree in the United States.

  It is one of the few Stojowski works currently in print.

- **Recordings**

  Recorded by Leon Piwkowski for PR, 93482-B, 1961.

  Recorded by Annin Rosin for Telefunken LP 6.42828 AP, *Virtuose
  Kammermusik – Posaune.* Hamburg: 1980.

  Recorded by Roman Siwek for PR, P-5449-C, 1982.

  Recorded by Christian Lindberg for BIS CD-298 *The Romantic Trombone,*
  Germany: 1985.

  Orchestra version recording for PR, 93639-A, Leon Piwkowski, trombone, The
  Polish Radio Orchestra in Bydgoszcz, Arnold Rezler, conductor, 1977.

Opus 28: *2 Mazurkas pour Piano* **(1908)**

- **Dedication**

  1. *A Madame Agnes Johnson Holden.* Agnes Johnson Holden (1880–1968), was the daughter of Robert Underwood Johnson (1853-1937), poet, American ambassador to Italy (1920–1921), and the editor of the *Century Magazine*. Johnson's poem *The Housatonic at Stockbridge* was set to music by Charles Ives. Mr. Johnson was also a patron of Stojowski's series of historical New York piano music recitals in 1911. His daughter, Agnes, married the New York architect Frank Howell Holden in 1902. She was an authority on antique textiles. Stojowski performed Chopin's Funeral March at her father's burial service at New York University Chapel.

  2. *A Mademoiselle Barbara de Chłapowska.* Barbara Chłapowska (no dates available) was the daughter of Franciszek Chłapowski (d. 1928), a member of the Prussian Parliament, and Maria Teresa Lubieńska (d. 1906) who was the daughter of Count Edward Lubieński. Barbara's father was the brother of Karol B. Chłapowski (1841–1914), the second husband of Helena Modrzejewska (1840–1909), the famous Shakespearean actress known in English circles as Helena Modjeska. Helen's son from her first marriage, Ralph Modjeski, was an engineer remembered as "America's greatest bridge builder." Like the dedicatee's father of the first mazurka, Modjeski was a sponsor of Stojowski's five historical New York piano recitals in 1911.

- **Movements**

  No.1 *Mazurka fantasque— Molto vivace*
  No.2 *Mazurka brillante—Allegro con brio*

- **Editions**

  Arthur R. Schmidt, Leipzig & Boston, 1908: BL, BNW, EAST, LC, WU. A digitalized score can be downloaded at: http://hdl.handle.net/1802/1577

- **Recordings**

  No. 1 recorded by Véronique Briel for DUX 0265, *Pologne Romantique*, and also for PR PC 886, Warsaw: 1996.

Zwielicht.

Figure Cat-7. Sigfrid Karg-Elert's harmonium arrangement of Stojowski's

○ Registersignen für das Saugluftsystem (erweitertes Normalharmonium).
Signs indicating the registering on instruments built on the suction-system (enlarged Normal Harmonium).

F	Baßhälfte	. . . . h	c₁	Diskanthälfte	. . . . f₄
F	Bass-keys	. . . . b		Treble-keys	

(Teilung)
(Division)

① Diapason etc., ruhiger, mildvoller 8′
Diapason etc., soft, mellow 8′

①ₚ Diapason dolce etc., sehr still, mild-rund 8′
Diapason dolce etc., very quiet, mellow-round 8′

Melodia ①

8′ Melodia dolce ①ₚ

dunkel streichend 16′ Clarinette ②
resembling the sombre tone of strings 16′ Clarionet

③ Viola (od. Prinzipal) kräftig
Viola (or Principal) powerful

etwas spitz, hell 4′ Flöte ③
somewhat shrill, clear 4′ Flute

③ₚ Viola dolce, sehr dezentes Begleitregister
Viola dolce, very discreet obligato stop

mild-sonor, streichend 8′ Oboe ④
mellow-sonorous, resembling strings 8′ Seraphone

sehr scharf pronosziert 8′ Schalmei ④f
very sharply pronounced 8′ Musette

Summationsstim.v. ④+① füllig, schwebend 8′ Vox jubilans ⑤
Summation-stop of ④+① full, tremulant 8′ Vox celeste

⑥ Äolsharfe, ätherisch-schwebender 2′
Eolianharpe, ethereal tremulant 2′

⑦ Subbaß 16′, fundamental C—H (12 Töne)
Subbass 16′, fundamental C—B (12 tones)

Vh Vox humana — Vibrato

F Expression

OK Oktav-Koppel, **durchgehend** von unten nach oben
Octave-Coupler, having ascending effect throughout

☐ Registersignen für das doppelexpressive Druckluftsystem (Kunstharmonium).
Signes de registration pour le système à compression à double expression (Harmonium d'Art, Type Mustel).

C	Baßhälfte	. . . . e₁	f₁	Diskanthälfte	. . . . c₄
Ut	Moitié de basse	. . . . mi₁	fa₁	Moitié de soprano	. . . . ut₄

(Teilung)
(Division)

1ᴾ Percussion 8′, hochwichtiges Hammerspiel, origin. Mischstim.
Jeu de marteaux très important, Voix estompée originale

Percussion 8′ 1ᴾ

1 Cor anglais 8′, rund, etwas dick
rond, légèrement fort

flötenartiger Holzton, Flûte 8′ 1
ton de bois flûté,

2 Bourdon 16′, mächtig tubaartig
puissant, à la tuba

üppig, doch stumpf, Clarinette 16′ 2
riche mais émoussé,

3 Clairon 4′, sehr aparter Nasalklang
son nasal très original

flageolettartig, hell, pikant, Fifre 4′ 3
ton de flageolet, clair, piquant,

4 Basson 8′, sehr expressiver Celloklang
ton de violoncelle très expressif

expressiver, heller Oboeklang, Hautbois 8′ 4
ton de hautbois clair, expressif,

5 Harpe éolienne 2′, ätherisch, sehr expressiv
éthéré, très expressif

dünner, nobler Nasalklang, Musette 16′ 5
son nasal faible, noble,

weihevoll, mystisch, warm-schwebend, Voix céleste 16′ 6
solennel, mystique, trémulant,

Prol Prolongement, automatisch C—H (12 Töne)
Prolongement automatique Ut—Si (12 tons)

eminent wichtige, wundervolle Solo- u.Mischstim., Baryton 32′ 7
voix mêlée et de solo, merveilleuse, très importante,

ätherisch, sehr diskrete Violinschwebestim., Harpe éolienne 8′ 8
Voix trémulante de violon, très discret, éthéré,

0 Forte expressif (pneu-automatisch)
(pneu-automatique)

(pneu-automatisch) Forte expressif 0
(pneu-automatique)

F Forte fixe

(nur im Pianospiel zweckmäßig)
(seulement pratique dans le jeu piano)

Forte fixe F

Méta Métaphone

Klangwandler, der alle Streicher in Bläser umfärbt
Changeant de ton transformant tous les sons à cordes en sons à vent

Métaphone Méta

— Doppelexpression — Expression E — Doppelexpression —
— Double expression — Expression E — Double expression —

Figure Cat-8. Registration for Sigfrid Karg-Elert's harmonium arrangement of Stojowski's *Zwielicht*, Op. 29, no. 3.C. F. Peters, 1914/1915. Public domain

Opus 29: *Aus Sturm und Stille* **(190?)**

- **Dedication**

  1. *Fräulein Adele Aus der Ohe*. Adele Aus der Ohe (1864–1937), an American pianist and composer of Austrian descent. Ohe had the distinction of performing Tchaikovsky's First Piano Concerto with the composer conducting. A friend of Stojowski and Paderewski, she had to abandon her career because of ill health.

  2. *Herrn Mark Hamburg* [sic!]. Mark Hambourg (1879–1960), Russian pianist and a student of Leschetizky. In 1889, he relocated to England where he spent the remainder of his life.

  3. *Miss Ethel Parrish*.

  4. *A Monsieur Joseph Lhévinne*. Joseph Lhévinne (1874–1944), Russian pianist who studied with Safonov and immigrated to the United States after World War I. Lhévinne married the legendary pianist and master teacher, Rosina. They both taught at the Juilliard Graduate School (later the Juilliard School of Music).

  5. *Miss Mary Ruth Lockwood*. Possibly related to another dedicatee, Anna G. Lockwood

  6. *Seinem Freunde Theodore Hardt*.

- **Movements**

  No. 1 *Ballade—Allegro deciso*
  No. 2 *Aufschwung—Essor—Allegro appasionato*
  No. 3 *Zwielicht—Crépuscule—Twilight—Moderato*
  No. 4 *Capriccio—Presto*
  No. 5 *Sérénade—Allegretto grazioso*
  No. 6 *Valse—Impromptu—Allegro piacevole*

- **Editions**

  C. F. Peters, Leipzig, 1908: EAST, LC, PR, WU. A digitalized score can be downloaded at: http://hdl.handle.net/1802/2214
  C. F. Peters, Leipzig, 1928: BNW.

  No. 3 arranged and edited for harmonium by Sigfrid Karg-Elert. No. 12 in *Harmonium Album /28/ ausgewählte Stücke*. Leipzig: C. F. Peters, 1914/1915: HVU, SC.

- **Remarks**

  Six pieces in various styles, all rather difficult (with the exception of *Twilight*, which is musically one of the best). In these Stojowski is, perhaps, at his best, although his undoubted musicianship is never absent. [Rowley]
  The set of pieces *Aus Sturm und Stille*, six in number, are called *Ballade*,

Aufschwung, Zwielicht, Capriccio, Ständchen and *Valse Impromptu*. The *Ballade* is vividly dramatic in character, exceptionally free in harmonic utterance and splendidly adapted for exploitation on a recital program. It is dedicated to Adele aus der Ohe. *Aufschwung* is literally an uplifting conception, with a right hand employment that will bring joy to players of the virtuoso order. To Mark Hambourg falls the honor of the dedication. *Zwielicht* is a subtle study in shifting harmonic colors, beautifully tinted and toned. *Capriccio* is a whimsy as fantastical as Schumann's *Grillen*. The *Ständchen*, gracious and appealing, will be liked best of all by seekers after surface melody and moderate technical difficulty. As the title of the *Valse Impromptu* might imply, it is a brilliant concert number and reflects much of the spirit of Liszt, with no small share of that Polish charm of which Chopin was the greatest exponent. All of the Stojowski music has the Polish national coloring, and he is, in fact, the leading composer turned out by that melodious country within the past half century. ["Stojowski's Compositions." *Musical Courier,* 1908, Press clipping, ZLSC.]

No. 5:
This is not the serenade of a love-sick poet, but the tender avowal of the true affection of the lover of serious purpose. There is an honesty and sincerity in every beautiful note which he sings his heart's message, and makes his earnest appeal. [Bulletin: *New Ampico Recordings*, November 1921, ZLSC.]

- **Recordings**

  No. 5 recorded by the composer on Ampico (piano roll) Recordings 111001K, November 1921.

  No. 6 recorded by the composer on Ampico (piano roll) Recordings 62463H, October 1923.

Opus 30: *Trois Esquisses pour piano* **(1908)**

- **Dedication**

  1. *A Monsieur Rudolph Ganz.* Rudolph Ganz (1877–1972), Swiss pianist, composer and conductor. Ganz spent most of his life in the United States, where he joined the faculty of the Chicago Music College (now the Chicago College of the Performing Arts at Roosevelt University) in 1901. He first appeared as piano soloist with the Chicago Symphony Orchestra in 1903. From 1921 to 1927, he was the director of the St. Louis Symphony Orchestra. He later returned to Chicago to become the director of the Chicago Music College, a position that he held from 1934 to 1954. A friend and summertime neighbor of Paderewski, he was a regular guest at Paderewski's annual July 31 name-day party in Morges, Switzerland. Three short letters (two in French and one in English) from Stojowski to Ganz are

found in the Ganz Archive, Folder 327 at the Newberry Library in Chicago.

2. *Miss Anna G. Lockwood.* Anna G. Lockwood was a pupil of Stojowski's at the Institute of Music Art in New York at the beginning of his career in New York. Her name is found in an article listing her as one of the sponsors for Stojowski's five historical piano recitals in 1911.

3. *A Mademoiselle Hedvige de Wierzbicka.* Jadwiga Wierzbicka (ca. 1880–ca. 1945), Polish pianist. After studying with Aleksander Michałowski in Warsaw, Wierzbicka moved to Paris where she studied privately with Raul Pugno. In Paris, she befriended Stojowski and rented his apartment on Rue Léo Delibes when Stojowski moved to America. Based on advertisements for private lessons in *Le Monde musical*, she lived there until the summer of 1914. As a pianist she is credited for giving the first French performances of works by Szymanowski and Stojowski. In 1919, Wierzbicka returned to Poland and lived in Poznań until her death.

- **Movements**

  No.1 *Amourette de Pierrot—Andante con moto*
  No. 2 *Feuilles mortes (Autumn Leaves)—Lento ma non troppo*
  No. 3 *Près du ruisseau (By the Brookside)—Vivace*

- **Editions**

  Arthur P. Schmidt, Leipzig, 1908: BL, EAST, LC, WU; UTA no. 1; BNW no. 1; ASU, ICA no. 3; ZLSC nos. 1 and 2. A digitalized score can be downloaded at: http://hdl.handle.net/1802/1581.

  No. 3 was reissued by Schmidt in 1936 with corrections: EAST.

  No. 3 was reissued by MO, 198–: UC.

- **Remarks**

  Amourette de Pierrot [is] a story which speaks for itself. *Autumn Leaves* [is] a rather dry autumn! *By the Brookside* [is] one of his best pieces. Full of charm and delicate touches, we have a really musical brook, which widens into a river. The last line of all is a joy indeed." [Rowley]

  Mistakes in the first edition of *By the Brookside*: "Page 5, first system, measure 3 and in the five bars of the following two lines, a "B-flat" should be placed before the first "A" of each bar, the "A-natural" being correct only in the first bar of the fourth line of the staves." [Stojowski in a letter to Florence J. Emery of Arthur P. Schmidt in Boston, dated March 2, 1936.] There was also a French misspelling in the title of the first edition: "du" originally appeared as "de." [Arthur P. Schmidt Archive, Library of Congress, Washington, D.C.]

  No. 3 *By the Brookside* was one of Paderewski's favorite and frequently played encores..

- **Recordings**

  No. 1 recorded by Rudolph Ganz on Welte (piano roll) 3904.

  No. 3 recorded by Paderewski on December 1926 for Vic 1426. Currently available on Pearl GEMM CD 9943.

Opus 31: *Concertstück pour Violoncello et Orchestre* **(1913–1914)**

- **Dedication**

  A Monsieur Willem Willeke.

- **Tempo Markings**

  Allegro vivace
  Andante sostenuto
  Allegro come prima
  Allegro assai

- **Editions**

  Manuscript of Cello and Piano Score: Willem Willeke Collection, Williams College. The MS for the solo cello gives the title and dedication in French: *Pièce de Concert*; *A mon ami Willem Willeke.* The piano reduction of the orchestral score has the dedication in German, *Willem Willeke freundschaftlich gewidmet.* While the cover page refers to the work as *Konzert für Violoncello*, the first page of music uses the title *Concertstück.*

  Manuscript copies of the orchestral score and parts as well as a set of Photostat parts marked *Proprieté de la Maison Menestre*: ZLSC. See Appendix Inventory.

  Heugel & Cie., Paris: 1922.

  Cello/Piano score: BNP, GAM (photocopy), NYPLPA, ZLSC, LC, PWM.

- **Orchestration**

  3 (3rd alt. picc.).3*.2.2-4.2.3.0-timp.perc (1)-hp-str

- **Remarks**

  Concertstück is a one-movement Concerto, and the publicity flyer advertising its premiere listed the work as Concerto in D Major. The world premiere took place at the March 1, 1915 all-Stojowski concert at Carnegie Hall. The New York Philharmonic was led by Josef Stransky. Willem Willeke was the soloist.

The Cello Concerto (Op. 31) is being performed for the first time and will serve Mr. Willem Willeke, the popular cellist of the Kneisel Quartet, in what also is his "debut" with orchestra in New York. It is in one movement with three main themes and four sections, between which the motive in diminished fifths heard at the outset, serves as a connecting link. A novel formal feature is that the slow movement—*andante sostenuto*—is interpolated into the development of the first section, which is resumed after the episode, bringing back the second subject and leading on to a finale built upon the rhythmically transformed first theme. The finale is in condensed sonata form, the theme of the *andante* being used as a second subject and sounded emphatically by all cellos and horns before the close against briskly moving triplets in the upper strings. [From the Carnegie Hall Concert Program Notes, ZLSC]

Dutch cellist Willem Willeke was born in The Hague in 1880. At the age of 14 he had the distinction of performing cello works and other chamber music of Brahms with the composer at the piano. He also performed the cello sonatas of Grieg and Richard Strauss with the composers as the accompanists. Willeke was the principal cellist of the Hofoper in Dresden, a position he left in order to accept Gustav Mahler's invitation to become the principal cellist at the Royal Opera in Vienna, where he also performed with the Vienna Royal Philharmonic (1903–1907). The appointment in Vienna also included the position of soloist at the court of the Emperor Franz-Josef. He came to America in 1907 to become a member of the Kneisel String Quartet, a position he held until 1917, the year the quartet disbanded. In that same year he became the principal cellist and assistant conductor of the New York Symphony Orchestra, and also founded the Elshuco Trio. Willeke was the founding director of the summer Berkshire Festival of Chamber Music on South Mountain (Berkshire Music Colony) in Pittsfield, Massachusetts, in 1918. During the winter months he taught at the Institute of Musical Art. He died in 1950. [*Willem Willeke—The Distinguished Dutch Cellist*, publicity brochure by impresario John W. Frothingham, Inc., Aeolian Hall, New York; *Willem Willeke Collection of Music*, an address given by Douglas B. Moore; *60th Anniversary South Mountain 1918–1978*, an anniversary booklet. Courtesy of Douglas B. Moore, cellist and curator of the Willem Willeke Collection, Williams College, Williamstown, Massachusetts.]

Cellist Mila Wellerson, the recipient of the Naumburg Award in 1930, performed the *Concertstück* with the composer at the piano for the opening of the Polish Institute of Arts and Letters at the Roerich Museum in New York on April 7, 1932.

- **Recordings**

An August 2006 archival recording for Polish Radio was made with the National Polish Radio Symphony Orchestra (NOSPR) in Katowice with cellist Tomasz Strahl and conductor Łukasz Borowicz.

Recorded by cellist Jarosław Domżal and pianist Joanna Ławrynowicz or Acte Préable AP0144, *Complete Works for Cello*, November 2006.

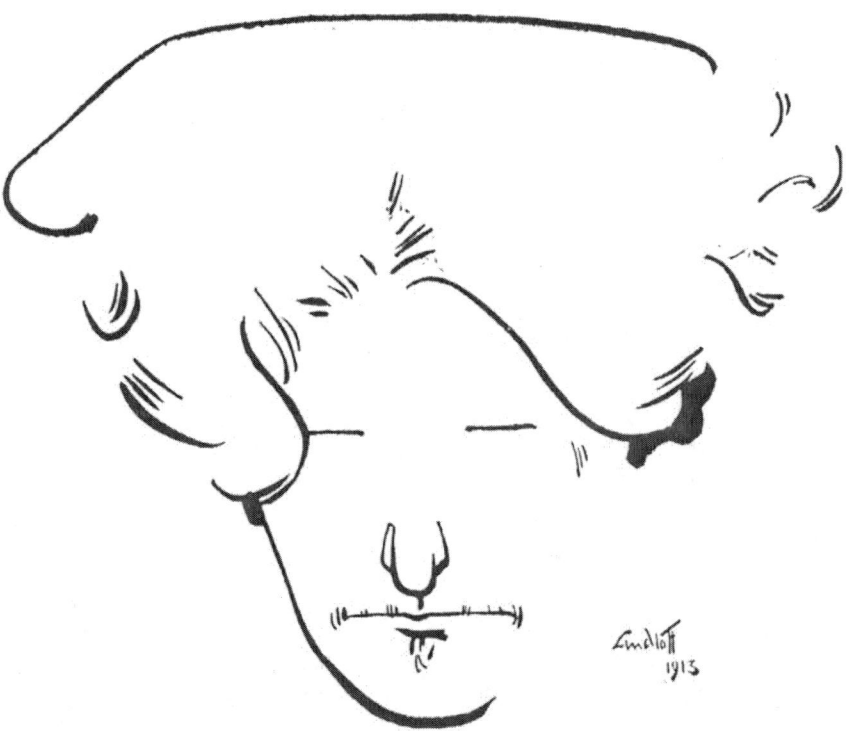

Figure Cat-9: A famous caricature of Paderewski by Adloff (1913). Courtesy of AAN, Warsaw.

Opus 32: *Prologue, Scherzo & Variations (2e Concerto) pour Piano et Orchestre* (Chamonix, summers of 1909–1910)

- **Dedication**

  Au Maître Paderewski, Hommage d'affection reconnaissante. See Opus 18 for biographical information.

- **Movements**

  Prologue—*Andante con moto*
  Scherzo—*Presto*
  Theme and Variations
  Tema: *Maëstoso e moderato molto*
  1. *Molto sostenuto*
  2. *Con espressione, poco rubato*
  3. *Più mosso*
  4. *Allegretto moderato*
  5. *Molto vivace*
  6. *Con fuoco agitato*
  7. *Con moto energico*
  8. *Andante sostenuto*
  9. *Andantino ben moderato*
  10. *Allegro molto*

- **Editions**

  Manuscript for the Scherzo of the piano duet version, first 21 measures, signed: EAST, Musical Autograph Collection, Box 2, Folder 26.

  Manuscript of the arrangement for two pianos: ZLSC. See Appendix Inventory.

  Manuscript sketches and 15 pages of the full score: ZLSC. See Appendix Inventory.

  Complete ink MS of the full score, 203 pages: ZLSC. See Appendix Inventory.

  Heugel & Cie., Paris: 1914.
  Full score: BNP, LC.
  Full score and parts: Alphonse Leduc, Paris; FLP; ZLSC.

  Arranged for two pianos by the composer: EAST, LC, NYPLPA, WU. A digitalized score can be downloaded at: http://hdl.handle.net/1802/2377

- **Orchestration**

  Pno—3(3rd alt. picc.).3*.2.2-4.2.3.0-timp.perc-hp-str

•   **Remarks**

The first performance took place with Arthur Nikisch conducting the London Symphony Orchestra with Stojowski as soloist on June 23, 1913, at Queen's Hall. This venerable concert hall was destroyed during the Nazi blitz in 1941.

A large effusive work with many effective moments. Influenced by Saint-Saëns. Thematic rhythmic transformation. [Hinson]

The title of *Prologue, Scherzo and Variations…* indicates that a radical departure has been made from the usual pattern of the concerto. Some of the variations are written for the orchestra alone, and it also is the first and only piano concerto which ends in a whisper. Here, again, the themes are several, but interwoven in the various sections which are played without interruption. The initial motive heard in the English horn appears in all the parts; the first cadenza of the pianoforte brings the first bars of what is going to be the theme of the variations, and the latter present the particularity of being evolved out of the two themes, one of the two belonging to the *Prologue*. This brings about the juxtaposition of two distant contrasting keys—that of E Minor, in which most of the variations are written, and that of A-flat, in which the works begins and concludes. The last (twelfth) variation, an elaborate finale dealing with both themes, starts in without transition in E Minor after the previous in A-flat, and after a long drawn climax, which brings back the amplified music of the *Prologue*, peace and serenity gradually replace the storm and stress until at the very close the two distant chords are mated together, providing a mysterious ending, suspended, as it were, in the clouds. [From the 1915 Carnegie Hall Concert Program Notes, ZLSC]

A review in the Aug 1, 1913 *The Musical Times,* vol. 54, stated that the British performance was shared with the music of Dr. Ethyl Smith. The critic wrote, "A wide gulf separated the styles shown by Dr. Smith in her songs and M. Stojowski in his Pianoforte Concerto, for the latter work contained scarcely a strong movement and little individuality, although one could observe the endeavour to achieve it."

Writing about the *Prologue* in the program notes for the British premiere, English musicologist F. Gilbert Webb wrote, "The writing….testifies to the composer's resource, imagination and contrapuntal skill."

You can never tell what a genius will do. Yesterday afternoon Paderewski punctured tradition by giving an encore at a Symphony concert. It happened that the great pianist's performance of the new Stojowski Concerto brought the concert to a close. The audience, instead of departing, remained en masse and drew the pianist out to bow a dozen times. Finally, Paderewski walked over to the piano, to the great surprise of the members of the orchestra, who were making for the exits, seated himself, and played enchantingly for about five minutes [Stojowski's *Chant d'amour*].

The Stojowski Concerto was given for the first time in this city. Stojowski is a Pole, like Paderewski, who came to New York a dozen years ago and is there now. He has a reputation as a pianist as well as a composer. This particular Concerto was written for Paderewski, and it is such a curious composition that it takes a Paderewski to perform it.

Even its form is unusual for the three movements are styled Prelude, Scherzo and Theme and Variations. As played by Paderewski, it was magnificently effective. The pianist evidently loves the work and played as though inspired by it. Stojowski, indeed, has a fine vein of melody and a most ingenious way of using an orchestra to assist the piano. [From a *Boston American* review by McIsaac of Paderewski's Boston performance, found in the Paderewski Scrapbooks at AAN in Warsaw.]

When Paderewski appears at the Symphony Concerts, the orchestra hitches its wagon to a star and consequently becomes a trailer...

Then came the magnetic Pole with his Stojowski offering. If we ventured to regret the Schumann Concerto, it would still be unjust to imagine Mr. Sigismond Stojowski as an unknown or inferior composer... We recall hearing him in Boston some ten ears ago, when he gave the impression of being a Jupiter Tonans of the piano, and his compositions left a good impression. This Concerto is a composition of real value.

It is the first time that we have heard one of Mr. Stojowski's works in the large forms. We are grateful that he keeps to symmetrical form and is not a disciple of tonal ugliness. It is needless to say that his work was played with all possible effect. Paderewski abundantly proved that he is still the greatest living pianist.

The Concerto is a free one, as the title in the above programme may show. It stands to the classical concerto about as the symphonic poem does to the Symphony. It begins and ends in free Fantasia. The orchestration is good and the piano well interwoven with it. There are notable climaxes, well worked up, and the pianist made the most of these.

The *Prologue* is long for such a prelude, but the work as a whole is of modest dimensions. The contrasts between pastoral and military effects in the *Scherzo* are finely arranged.

The theme of the *Finale* is a splendid one, both intrinsically and for variation purposes. But we scarcely like the variation form for a concerto finale: it generally puts ingenuity in the fore, and poetry in the background. Nevertheless, these variations were excellent contrast of power, rhythm, and general treatment, and the final pianissimo ending came as a real surprise.

Altogether then there was a real *raison d'être* for the Stojowski concerto, and when Paderewski brought forth the composer from the green-room there was intense enthusiasm. [From a *Boston Daily Advertiser* review Louis C. Elson of Paderewski's Boston performance, found in the Paderewski Scrapbooks at AAN in Warsaw.]

On June 14, 1910, *The Trenton Evening Times* (p. 12) reported that Paderewski was to premiere the Concerto at a concert in Lwów celebrating the centenary of Chopin's birth. It also reported that, "It has also been accepted for performance by composer Gustav Mahler with the New York Philharmonic next season. Mr. Stojowski has also been engaged by the New York Symphony Orchestra for one of its early concerts." Unfortunately, neither event happened. Paderewski kept insisting that Stojowski make changes in the concerto's *Scherzo*. In the end, Stojowski had to write several versions of the movement until Paderewski found one that was acceptable to his taste. Mahler died in the spring of 1911. The world premiere was delayed three years and the New York premiere had to wait for five years. Paderewski finally performed the Concerto in New York and Boston six years after the premiere had been originally discussed.

The Second Concerto had its American premiere with Stojowski and the New York Philharmonic under the direction of Josef Stransky on March 1, 1915. Victor Herbert, Józef Hofmann, Franz Kneisel, Mischa Elman and Leopold Godowsky were present in the audience. [*New York Herald*, March 2/3, 1915]

Of still greater interest and value is the piano concerto which Mr. Stojowski himself played. Here again there is experiment in form. The Concerto is in three movements... and use is made to some extent of the device called community of theme. The variations seem to be the finest portion of the work, and, indeed, in many respects, the finest of all that Stojowski presented yesterday. The theme has emphatic individuality and musical significance, and the variations show a rich fancy, abundant technical resource in the treatment of both the fortepiano and orchestra and originality of conception. Mr. Stojowski played the Concerto with assured mastery and evident conviction. [*NYT*, "Mr. Stojowski's Concert."]

At the beginning of March 1916, Paderewski performed the work under the title *Prologue, Scherzo & Variations* first with the New York Symphony conducted by Walter Damrosch at Carnegie Hall on March 2 & 4 and, one week later, with the Boston Symphony Orchestra under Karl Muck at Orchestra Hall on March 10 & 11. On the New York program the first American performances of Elgar's *Polonia* were given. There was such a demand for tickets for the March 4 concert that an open dress rehearsal had to be added on March 2. Paderewski also broke the Symphony Society's rule about not allowing soloists to play encores at orchestral concerts. After taking a dozen bows, Paderewski finally sat down at the piano and played Stojowski's *Chant d'amour* as an encore.

On Sunday afternoon, November 16, 1924, Stojowski once more played the Concerto with the New York Philharmonic Society under the baton of Willem van Hoogstraten (1884–1965) at Carnegie Hall, with the sixth variation cut from the last movement.

Stojowski also performed the Concerto with the Warsaw Philharmonic Orchestra under the baton of Jerzy Bojanowski on October 4, 1929, the opening concert of the 1929–1930 Season. Unfortunately, the performance with Stojowski was an artistic scandal. Although Artur Taube wrote to Szymanowski [See: Chylińska, *Karol Szymanowski Correspondence* vol. 3 * * 1929 letter 498, 300] that the music was "a mixed breed of romanticism" and that Stojowski "played poorly," the quality of his performance was the fault of the conductor and the orchestra. In the October 5 edition of the *Kurier Poranny*, music critic Zbigniew Domaniewski wrote that Bojanowski did not know the score, that he got completely lost a couple of times, and that the orchestra was totally disorientated and played as though they were sight reading at a rehearsal. Like Stojowski, Bojanowski (1893–1983) also immigrated to America. Prior to his emigration, Bojanowski was a conductor of the Warsaw Philharmonic (1928–1932). He first settled in Chicago in 1932, where he came to conduct—at the request of the Polish government—a concert with "members of" the Chicago Symphony Orchestra at the Chicago World's Fair and then remained as the cultural attaché at the Polish Consulate. In the early 1940s, he relocated to Milwaukee, where he spent the remainder of his life. He conducted the first American performance of Moniuszko's opera *Halka*. [Wisconsin Music Archives Online: http://music.library.wisc.edu/wma/papers/bojanowski/jbhome.htm]

Regarding Stojowski and the Warsaw Philharmonic, it is interesting to note that for nearly five consecutive years either Stojowski's music or a Stojowski pupil was featured at the beginning of each season:

> 1928: Inaugural Concert (Stojowski's Symphony in D Minor, Młynarski conducting)
> 1929: Inaugural Concert (Stojowski's Second Piano Concerto with the composer as soloist)
> 1930: Not represented
> 1931: Third Concert of the 30th Anniversary Season (conducted by Antonia Brico)
> 1932: Inaugural Concert (Alexander Brachocki, soloist, and Grzegorz Fitelberg, conductor)

There is a discrepancy between the full score and piano reduction. In Variation X of the last movement, from section 125 through to 126, there are six measures found in the reduction that do not appear in full score. Counting from the final bar and counting that bar as 1, it begins from the second quarter note of bar 46 to the first eight note of bar 41. These bars were orchestrated for the 2002 recording of the work on Hyperion Records.

While Hinson lists the playing time at 32 minutes, a 1916 review gives Paderewski's performance at 45 minutes. Jonathan Plowright's recording is 33 minutes long. In the *Note pour l'exécution* found in the full score, Stojowski writes that since this work is longer than the usual piano concerto, certain cuts can be made. Variations nos. I, VI and/or IX may be omitted. If Variation IX is cut, then the seven-bar transition from Variation VIII to IX supplied by the composer must be played. Paderewski, who was known for taking exceedingly slow tempi may be at fault here—many critics wrote that Stojowski's Concerto in Paderewski's intepretation, was much too long.

In his unpublished autobiography, Wiktor Łabuński includes a review of Paderewski's January 26, 1931, concert in Nashville, Tennessee, where Łabuński taught for three years. Łabuński only credits the critic as "W.K." and relates, "He was technically not perfect, played many things much too slowly and there was an aura of "old-fashionedness" [sic!] about his whole approach to the keyboard. And then there were magnificent moments of great climax, where he moved you to the depths of your heart." [Wiktor Łabuński, 226] George Bernard Shaw once went one step further by referring to Paderewski as the "harmonious blacksmith."

Paderewski's performances were usually accompanied by several strange rituals. Reportedly, he suffered from terrible stage fright and, as a result, his recitals always began 20 to 40 minutes late. While the audience waited, the auditorium was heated to the point where it would become unbearably hot. Windows could not be open while Paderewski played, because he was seriously worried about catching cold. When the concert finally begun, the stage was dimly lit, giving the impression that the artist was a priest sacrificing a victim on an altar, rather than a musician sitting at the piano.

Several reviews and a Letter to the Editor on Paderewski's January 1916 concert at Detroit's Arcadia Auditorium further describe the scene. Unfortunately, none of these reviews are identified, but they can be found on page 138 of the Stojowski Scrapbooks dealing with this period at the Paderewski Archive at the Archiwum Akt Nowych in Warsaw [Paderewski Archive 317] One reviewer wrote of the unbearable heat and of Paderewski's tendency to play louder and louder, powerful and more powerful to the point where it became neurotic, "an overwhelming desire to make a noise and make it continuously." Someone in the audience wrote a letter to one of Detroit's dailies, complaining of the suffering audience:

...The management of the building which shut up several thousand people in an airtight box and kept them there nearly three hours, breathing each other's breaths over and over again until the air of the place was hot enough for a Turkish bath and foul enough to sicken a goat. The air of our crowded streetcars about which we hear so much complaint is a rose geranium in comparison. What should [have been] an evening of refined enjoyment thus turned into a malarial debauch and a season of physical and mental misery. [From a 1916 Letter to the Editor, Detroit]

For Detroiters who remember riding the city's streetcars (sold in the 1950s to Mexico City), the reader's comment will certainly seem humorous and bring back a flood of fragrant memories.

- **Recordings**

Recorded by Jonathan Plowright and the BBC Scottish Symphony Orchestra, Martyn Brabbins conducting, for Hyperion Records CDA67314, 2002. Voted "Record of the Month" by *Muzyka 21* in March 2002; One of the Best of the Year CDs – 2002 by AUDIOPHILE AUDITION, http://www.audaud.com/ audaud/best2002.html; and one of the MusicWeb CDs of the Year, http://www.musicweb.uk.net/classrev/2002/Dec02/Record_of_the_Year/ Recordings_of_the_year_2002_2.htm

Opus 33: *Six Songs for Voice and Piano—Euphonies, Six Mélodies* (1910)

Polish poems by Kazimierz Tetmajer; French translation by Maurice Chassang, English translation by Henry Grafton Chapman.

- **Dedication**

To Mme. Marcella Sembrich (in Schirmer edition), *A Madame Marcella Sembrich* (in Heugel edition). For biographical information see Chapter 4, footnote no. 56.

- **Movements**

No. 1.   *Gdzie jest twój sen?—Où va ton rêve?—Where is Thy Dream?* [d#–g#']
No. 2   *Mów do mnie jeszcze—Parle de grâce!—Speak Once Again* [d#–g']
No. 3   *Gdybyś ty była szklanem jeziorem—Si tu étais un lac insondable — Wert Thou the Lake* [f–a']
No. 4   *Na mej duszy strunach—Comme un luth sonore, ô brise—On My Heart, Ye Wandr'ing Breezes* [f–f']
No. 5.   *Bądź zdrowa—Adieu—Farewell* [f–f']
No. 6.   *Niechaj jej niebo święci błękitnie—Invocation—Cloudless, Ye Skies* [e–g']

- **Editions**

Heugel & Cie., Paris, 1911 under the title of *Six melodies* with opus number printed in parentheses; Polish and French texts: BN, NYPLPA.

G. Schirmer, New York: 1921 under the title of *Euphonies* with French and English texts: BL, LC, TU, UI; ASU Nos. 1, 3, 4, 5 & 6.

- **Recordings**

Nos. 2, 3 and 5 recorded by soprano Maria Bogucka and pianist LS for station WNYC in New York: 78.26 RPM recording exists in ZLSC, ca. 1948.

Nos. 1 and 3 recorded by soprano Irena Lewińska for PR, R II 88716-D, 1957 and R II 88716-E, 1957 respectively.

Under the title *Les evocations de Sigismond*, the entire cycle was recorded by Paul Trépanier, tenor, and Janine Lachance, piano, Montreal: Radio Canada International, LP 470, (October 1977); BR, UG, UT.

- **Remarks**

On January 30, 1917, No. 3 was sung by Belgian tenor Paul Reimers at a party given by President and Mrs. Woodrow Wilson at the home of the Chief Justice and Mrs. White. [Anon. "White House Party at Concert."]

The confusion with the title of the cycle being the same as another French song published by Huegel in 1922 is the fault of the publisher, G. Schirmer, who selected the title without consulting the composer. In a letter dated January 12, 1921, from G. Schirmer to Stojowski, the publisher uses the excuses that the publisher never sends title-page proofs to composers and that they had found a process card from several year before, which listed the songs under *Euphonies*.

No. 3, *Gdybyś Ty była szklanem jeziorem*, was premiered in Polish in New York at Carnegie Hall on March 1, 1910 by Marcella Sembrich. She repeated it in another concert at Carnegie Hall on November 21, 1916.

No. 6 makes use of the incipit of the solemn version of the Gregorian chant *Salve Regina* in both the introduction and coda.

Several of the songs are marked by the use of ostinatos which dominate the accompaniment from beginning to end.

Opus 34[?]: *Deux Feuillets d'Album* [?]

Possibly a set of piano miniatures released without the opus number first by Stanley Lucas & Co, in London & Leipzig in 1895, and later by E. Ashdown in London in 1911.

Opus 35: *Trois Études de Concert pour piano* **(1912)**

- **Dedication**

  A Joseph Hofman. [sic!] See Opus 11 for biographical information.

- **Movements**

  No. 1 C Major—*Allegro molto*
  No. 2 F-sharp Major—*Presto*
  No. 3 A Minor—*Lento*

- **Editions**

  Manuscript score: ZLSC. See Appendix Inventory.

  Heugel & Cie., Paris, 1912: LC, WU.

- **Recordings**

  No. 2 recorded by Anon. Per. for Aeolian Co. AEOL T 30316, London, 1905.

Opus 36: *Poème d'été [Quatre Morceaux pour piano]* **(1910)**

- **Dedication**

  To Mrs. George Montgomery Tuttle in grateful friendship. Mrs. George Montgomery Tuttle, née Mabel Holden, (1874–1961), a patron of the arts and an American pianist who studied in Vienna at the turn of the century and then with Stojowski in New York. At the time of dedication, she was the widow of a New York surgeon. She is listed as one the "women prominent in the world of fashion and music" included in the list of sponsors for Stojowski's five historical New York concerts of 1911. Her name can be found on an all-Stojowski program performed at the Colony Club in New York in 1910. She did relief work during World War I and was an officer of The American Friends of the Musicians in France. She was also instrumental in founding parts of the Fontainebleau Summer School for Americans after World War I. She remarried and became Mrs. Randall-MacIver. The French government conferred upon her the Legion of Honor in 1923.

- **Movements**

  No.1 *Rêves (Dreams)—Andante non troppo, poco rubato e con espressione*
  No.2 *Rayons et reflets (Rays & Reflections)—Allegretto mosso e capriccioso assai*
  No.3 *Fleurettes (Flowerets)—Andantino espressivo ma con moto*
  No.4 *Bruissements (Forest Breezes)—Molto vivace*

And all at once it seems as tho' the wood were reeling
Above, like flying sparks, a swarm of bees is wheeling.

—H. Bouvele, *Le Royaume de la Terre*

• **Editions**

G. Schirmer, New York, 1910: BL, EAST, NYPLPA. A digitalized score can be downloaded at: http://hdl.handle.net/1802/2412
G. Schirmer, New York, 1912: ZLSC.

Heugel & Cie., Paris, c. 1914: WU.

• **Remarks**

Huegel uses the title *Quatre Morceaux pour piano,* while Schirmer uses the title *Poème d'été.*

The first is an introspective *legato* melody, rising at times to passionate intensity of expression; the second, a capricious *allegretto,* a shifting play of tonal lights and reflections. The third, an *andantino*, is a flower-song of subtly appealing simplicity, while the fourth, an exquisitely limned bit of programme-music, is a translation into tone of the inflections of the forest breeze, such a one as only the imagination of the true poet could conceive. [From an undated G. Schirmer advertisement found in ZLSC]

In a December 1920 or early January 1921 letter to publisher G. Schirmer, Stojowski asked about the possibility of reissuing No. 3 because it was out of print. The publisher's reply of January 12, 1921 was that *Flowerets* had only sold approximately 20 copies a year for the past several years. The publisher's representative, whose signature is illegible, writes, "That would not justify us in issuing a new edition which for practical technical reasons would have to be at least 300 copies. Our rule is in such cases to announce a piece is temporarily out of print and to accumulate sufficient back-orders (generally about 75) before we can risk the investment of further capital on the piece."

• **Recordings**

No. 3 recorded by LS, Desmar IPA 115, 1976.

Opus 37: *Deuxième Sonate (en mi majeur) pour Piano et Violon* **(Campobello, July 23, 1911)**

• **Dedication**

A Monsieur Arthur Argiewicz. Arthur Argiewicz (1881–1966), Polish violinist. A child prodigy, he gave his first public concert when he was only eight years old. With the support of Brahms and Josef Joachim, he appeared as a soloist with the Berlin Philharmonic, becoming a member of that ensemble at the age of 15. Argiewicz's talent came to the attention of Fritz Kreisler who accompanied him on the piano (!) at his first London concert. He immigrated to the United States prior to World War I and joined the faculty of the Institute of Musical Art where he befriended Stojowski and taught for seven years. In 1917, he became the assistant concertmaster of the San Francisco Symphony Orchestra, a position which he held for three decades. In San Francisco, he was also head of the violin department of the Ada Clement School of Music, now known as the San Francisco Conservatory of Music. Fritz Kreisler wrote the following recommendation for Argiewicz which the Polish violinist used in his publicity brochure, "I consider Mr. Arthur Argiewicz a splendid violinist of highly artistic attainments and a superior teacher, under whose guidance advanced pupils as well as beginners are sure to make rapid strides musically as well as instrumentally." His sister, Eugenia Argiewicz Bem, was also an accomplished violinist who, like her brother, settled in San Francisco. Together with her husband Stanislas Bem, a cellist, they formed a septet known as the Bem Little Symphony Orchestra which specialized in performing light classics and popular music. [Obituary. *San Francisco Chronicle*, May 10, 1966; Arthur Argiewicz Clipping File, San Francisco Public Library; Publicity Brochure, Argiewicz File, San Francisco Symphony Archives, San Francisco Performing Arts Library and Museum; Digitalized Publicity Brochure, *Stanislas Bem's Little Symphony Orchestra*, Redpath Chautauqua Collection, University of Iowa, Iowa City, http://sdrcdata.lib.uiowa.edu/libsdrc/details.jsp?id=/stanislas/1]

- **Movements**
  Allegro affetuoso
  Intermezzo—Poco vivace scherzando
  Arietta molto sostenuto
  Allegro giocoso

- **Editions**
  Manuscript score: ZLSC. See Appendix Inventory.
  Heugel & Cie., Paris; G. Schirmer, New York, 1912: BJ, BN, EAST, LC, NYPLPA, SAM.

  Arietta and *Intermezzo* edited by E. Umińska: PWM, Cracow, 1953 & 1988: BJ, BNW, EAST, LC, NYPLPA, WU, PR, USC.

- **Remarks**
  A very large audience attended the last of three recitals by Sigismond Stojowski and Arthur Argiewicz, who gave a programme of Polish Music in which the chief number of interest was a Sonata in E Major for Violin and Piano by Mr. Stojowski. This Polish pianist has frequently proved himself a composer of more

than ordinary merit, especially in music of the larger form, and the Sonata heard last night confirmed the impression of those who believe Mr. Stojowski to be one of the most talented men whose lot has been cast in our country. More than most writers he has a gift of warmth and of melody, he has a fine sense of values, and he is modern without being aggressive... The Sonata was received with spontaneous enthusiasm, and so it should be received by those who look so frequently in vain for works of a serious and dignified nature. [*New York Evening Mail*, March 19, 1912.]

The first performance took place with Argiewicz accompanied by the composer during a concert of Polish music for violin and piano at the MacDowell Club in New York on March 18, 1912. In one pre-concert notice, pianist Gaëtano Rummo was listed as the performer accompanying Argiewicz.

Following a performance of the Sonata on June 10, 1913 with violinist Georges Enesco and the composer on the piano, Frank Patterson of the *Musical Courier* of June 25 reported, "The Sonata, which was adequately played by Enesco and brilliantly accompanied by the composer, is a valuable addition to the literature of violin music and evidently strongly appealed to the audience." Stojowski also accompanied Enesco in concerts at Yale and Harvard during November 1924. The concerts were arranged by Elizabeth S. Coolidge and Stojowski's fee for two appearances was $500. [Stojowski. Letter to Elizabeth S. Coolidge.]

The Sonata was also performed by violinist Sascha Jacobsen and pianist Harry Kaufman (a former Stojowski student from the Institute of Musical Art) at Carnegie Hall on January 27, 1923. Jacobsen was a Russian-born violinist who played a Stradivarius most of his career. He eventually became the concertmaster of the Los Angeles Philharmonic Orchestra during 1947–1949. [Carnegie Hall and Los Angeles Philharmonic Orchestra Archives.] Regarding Stojowski's student Kaufman, he was also the first New York accompaninst to work with Mischa Mischakoff, another famous Russian violinist. Mischakoff escaped from communist Russia by Poland (and a season as concertmaster of the Warsaw Philharmonic) in 1921. [Mischakoff Heiles, 39–52, 60, 74, 75]
Polish violinist Paweł Kochański performed the work with Stojowski at a Town Hall recital on April 19, 1928. "The two ensemble works were interpreted with fine authority, impeccable taste and sound musicianship by the artists." [*NYT*, "Polish Artists in Recital."] The two Polish musicians played the Sonata once more in Washington, D.C. at the Polish Embassy on April 25, 1930. American Vice President Charles Curtis was in attendance. [*WP*, "Vice President Is Honor Guest of Ambassador."]

Figure Cat-10. Bernice Stochek-Friedson (b. 1929). Photograph courtesy of Mrs. Stochek-Friedson. All rights reserved

- **Recordings**

Recorded by violinist Bernice Stochek-Friedson and pianist Luisa Stojowska, for the WNYC-WOR Stojowski Memorial Program of April 30, 1952; Five 12-inch 78.26 RPM records as well as one 10-inch 33 RPM and a CD transfer: ZLSC. A native of New York, Stochek received her early musical training from her father, a violinist and violin maker, who ran a string repair shop in the city. Her violin teachers included Louis Persinger, Ivan Galamian and Joseph Fuchs, and she studied at the Mannes and Juilliard Schools of Music. In her teens she played with the City Center Opera Company Orchestra and made recordings under major conductors, such as Leopold Stokowski and Fritz Reiner. Since 1952, Mrs. Stochek-Friedson has lived in Connecticut, where she has been the concertmaster of several opera and symphony orchestras. She has been active as a teacher and performer, including directing a music school, and is currently the assistant conductor, concertmaster and the violin soloist with the Connecticut Chamber Orchestra.

Arietta and Intermezzo recorded by Henryk Tritt for PR, PB-7442 A and PB-7442 B, 1987.

Opus 38: *Fantaisie pour piano* (Maplewood, September 1911)

- **Dedication**

  A Monsieur Maurice Moszkowski. Moritz Moszkowski (1854–1925), German pianist and composer of Polish-Jewish descent. Moszkowski is best remembered for his piano miniatures and chamber music, especially the *Spanish Dances* for piano duet. He dedicated his Prelude and Fugue for String Orchestra, Op. 85 to Stojowski in 1911. Born in Breslau (now Wrocław, Poland), Moszkowski studied in Dresden and Berlin and later relocated to Paris, where he lost all his money on the German stock market and died a pauper. Stojowski was one of fourteen famous pianists who gave a benefit concert for Moszkowski at Carnegie Hall in 1921. Józef Hofmann and Wanda Landowska were among Moszkowski's Polish students. For more information on Moszkowski, see Chapter 3.

- **Tempo Marking**

  Sostenuto, molto cantabile e poco rubato

- **Editions**

  Manuscript: ZLSC. See Appendix Inventory.

  Heugel & Cie., Paris, 1912: WU

- **Remarks**

  Most of Stojowski's solo piano compositions are classified as piano miniatures. His *Fantasie* and his *Variations and Fugue* are, however, among the few major works for solo piano. The title *Fantasie* is misleading in that one might expect a free fantasy-like piece, improvisatory in style. Instead Stojowski shows his mettle by providing the listener with a solidly constructed musical form rich in melodic and rhythmic interest, reminiscent of Chopin's *Fantaisie* Op. 49.

The composition is divided into two main parts. The first (*Sostenuto, molto cantabile e poco rubato*) in quasi sonata-allegro form is characterized by a seemingly simple melody, which however, contains a key rhythmic motive repeated throughout the work:

The second section (*Allegro energico*) is in ABA form. It is immediately recognizable not only by a change of tempo and key change to the relative minor, but also by the change from triple to quadruple meter and, above all, by a heroic, rhythmically driving four-measure theme:

Following the exposition of this theme, Stojowski cleverly restates all of the thematic material of both sections.

When the above theme returns, the composer brilliantly transforms it into the subject of a three-voice fugue that forms the middle section (B). The fugue's exposition ends with a short transition based on the dotted rhythm found at the end of the subject. The development begins with the subject heard in the tenor range and then one octave lower in the bass register. A six-bar chromatic episode follows and once more the subject is heard, but this time two and three octaves higher. In the recapitulation, instead of returning—as might be expected—to the original key of the fugue's exposition, the composer opts for the key F Minor. Thus, he enables the fugue's coda to become the beginning of the third section (A1).

Having done this, Stojowski modulates to the parallel major (F Major) and presents the *appassionato* theme of the first section. As the work draws to a close, the composer masterfully combines a simultaneous restatement of the opening themes of both the first and second sections of the *Fantasie*. He briefly revisits the work's opening keys, after which he returns to F Major. The *Fantasie* quietly ends with thematic material from the first section, underlined by a subtle reminder of the second section's opening motive in the bass.

- **Recordings**

  Recorded by Jonathan Plowright for Hyperion Records, CDA67437, *Stojowski, Music for Piano,* London: 2004.

Opus 39: *Aspirations. Poèmes pour piano* **(1913)**

- **Dedication**

  1. *Mehr Licht (Goethe).*

  2. *A Donald Jonson.* Donald Jonson was a Canadian-born composer and one-handed pianist. He played an audition for Paderewski which resulted in his being sent to study with Stojowski at the Institute of Musical Art. Based on programs found in ZLSC, Jonson was assisted at concerts by Stojowski and Percy Grainger. On one program, Jonson accompanied soprano Greta Torpadie who sang one of his art songs. Jonson relocated to La Crosse, Wisconsin, where he taught for at least 26 years (1930–1956). One of his students was the composer Robert Moevs (b.1920). [[La Crosse City Directories, Courtesy of the University of Wisconsin's Murphy Library-Special Collections, La Crosse; Boros, 203–204.]

  3. *A Miss Elenore Altman.* See the entry on Elenore Altman in Chapter 4.

  4. *A Mrs. Ch. L. Scudder.*

  5. *A Ernest Schelling.* Ernest Schelling (1876–1939), American pianist, composer and conductor. Schelling worked with Moszkowski and Leschetizky before beginning three years of study with Paderewski in 1896. Schelling became a life-long friend of Stojowski and Paderewski. In 1924, Schelling was appointed the conductor of the Young Peoples Concerts of the New York Philharmonic Symphonic Society, which he conducted from its inception until his death. He was also the music director of the Baltimore Symphony Orchestra in 1935–1937. In both positions he programmed Stojowski's music on his concerts. Paderewski recorded Schelling's piano compositions. For more information on his collaboration with Marcella Sembrich and Stojowski for Polish relief during World War I, see Chapter 6.

- **Movements**

  No.1 *Vers l'azur (Prélude)—Andante non troppo, ma molto cantabile*
  No.2 *Vers la tombe (Elégie)—Lento e mesto*
  No.3 *Vers le caprice (Intermède)—Allegretto capriccioso*
  No.4 *Vers l'amour (Romance)—Andante appassionato*
  No.5 *Vers la joie (Rhapsodie)—Allegro molto quasi presto*

- **Editions**

Manuscripts of nos. 2, 3, 4 and 5: ZLSC. See Appendix Inventory.

Heugel & Cie., Paris, 1914: LC, WU, BJ no. 1.

No. 1 reissued in 1988 by Musica Obscura with the wrong opus number (Op. 30, instead of Op. 39) UMK, SMU.

- **Remarks**

No. 1 performed by Józef Hofmann and Ernest Schelling during 1916 recitals at Carnegie Hall.

Aspirations bears witness to Stojowski's studies in France. The music alternates between impressionism and post-romanticism. At times, Stojowski abandons the functional harmony of the romantic idiom and approaches the colourful harmonic palette of Debussy. The French titles of the five movements express the intangible and atmospheric impressions Stojowski wished to create. Fearing perhaps that this musical imagery would come across as unclear, he added typically romantic form-names for each movement in parentheses.

Stojowski's fascination with musical vibrations of colour and light can be clearly seen in the opening *Vers l'azur* (*Prélude*). The title itself—and the dedication—refer to Goethe's famous last words, "Mehr Licht." The piece is in duple metre and in the key of D-flat Major.

The following *Vers la tombe* (*Elégie*)—also in duple meter and in the key of F Minor—could be seen as a symbolic dialogue between life and death. The questioning *cantando* opening melody representing life (and using a descending tritone) is answered by the modal *misterioso* voice of death. The dialogue between the two continues passionately with death having the final word. However, *lux perpetua* suddenly appears as the piece ends with an ascending arpeggio in F Major.

Vers le caprice (*Intermède*) is in 5/4 and the key of D Minor. The descending tritone used forebodingly in the previous movement now forms a whimsical motive for the movement and is quoted throughout. The application of parallel major thirds, like the melodic use of the tritone, is one of many impressionistic techniques used by Stojowski.

The fourth movement, *Vers l'amour* (*Romance*), in 6/8 and D-flat Major, is thoroughly romantic in style. In this *Andante appassionato* Stojowski abandons his pretensions of impressionistic style and reveals himself as an imassioned conservative at heart.

The concluding *Vers la joie (Rhapsodie)* uses triple metre for its *Allegro molto quasi presto* sections and duple metre for the sections marked *Vivace*. Formally in the key of D Major, the work nonetheless begins with a daring, almost atonal melody, finally ending on the tonic D in the fifth bar. This theme returns four times, creating a quasi rondo form. The alternating *Vivace* sections are marked by the use of sixteenth-note triplets, suspiciously similar to figures used in Debussy's *Second Arabesque in G Major* (1888–1891). Like in the Debussy work, this motive serves to create an atmosphere of joyous celebration.

- **Recordings**

Nos. 1, 3, 4 and 5 recorded by Jonathan Plowright for Hyperion Records, CDA67437, *Stojowski, Music for Piano,* London: 2004.

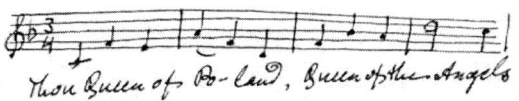

Figure Cat-11. Stojowski, *Modlitwa za Polskę,* Op. 40, dedication page. G. Schirmer, 1915. Public domain

Opus 40: *Modlitwa za Polskę* (*Prayer for Poland*)

Cantata for Soprano and Bass, Mixed Chorus, Orchestra and Organ. Text by Zygmunt Krasiński: *Modlitwa za Polskę* (1839), English text by George Harris, Jr.

- **Dedication**

To my beloved Mother, Ukochanej Matce. Maria (née Bogdańska) Stojowska (ca. 1850–1925). For biographical information on Maria Stojowska, see Chapter 1.

- **Editions**

Full score manuscript: ZLSC. See Appendix Inventory.
Piano/vocal manuscript: ZLSC. See Appendix Inventory.

G. Schirmer, New York: 1915
Piano/Vocal Score: BJ, BL, EAST, HVU, LC, NYPLPA, UM, photocopy at
BNW. During World War II, the publisher renewed the copyright in 1943 and
once more made copies of the Cantata available for sale. The Cantata was
withdrawn from the publisher's catalogue after the war in 1946.
A digitalized copy of the piano/vocal score may be downloaded at:
http://hdl.handle.net/1802/2732

Full score and parts: John Martin Hein from the University of North Florida in
Jacksonville prepared an edition of the full score and set of parts in 2003. It is
available on rental from the Polish Music Center at the University of Southern
California in Los Angeles.

- **Orchestration**

3*.3*3*.3*-4.4.3.1-timp-perc-celesta-org-sop. and bar. soloists-chorus SATB-
hp-str and optional antiphonal brass 0.4.4.0 used to support the organ where
needed

- **Remarks**

Written during the summer of 1915 in Cragsmoor, New York, *Modlitwa za Polskę*
was first performed at Carnegie Hall in New York on Tuesday, March 7, 1916,
with the *Schola Cantorum* and the Symphony Society of New York under the
direction of Kurt Schindler. Paderewski was in the audience. Soloists included
soprano Minnie Jovelli and baritone Bernado Olshansky (Bernard Olszański). The
program also included the first American performance of Sergei Rachmaninoff's
cantata *The Voice of Spring* and the world premiere of the orchestral version of
Deems Taylor's cantata *The Chambered Nautilus*. [Solomon]

Słownik muzyków polskich [The Dictionary of Polish Musicians] mistakenly gives
March 6, 1917, as the date of this concert.

The first orchestral performance of the cantata in 87 years took place on May
25, 2003, at Holy Cross Basilica in Warsaw, during the Zygmunt Stojowski May
Festival. It was performed by the *Szczecińskie Słowiki* [Szczecin Boys' Choir], the
Warsaw Archdiocesan Cathedral Boys' and Men's Choir, Cantores Minores, the
Stojowski May Festival Orchestra, soprano Anna Maćkowiak, and bass-baritone
Leopold Stawarz under the direction of Joseph A. Herter. It was also the first
performance of the Cantata with orchestra in Poland.

- **The Text**

Modlitwa za Polskę is based on a work of the romantic Polish poet, Zygmunt Krasiński (1812–1859). It is a hymn to the Blessed Virgin Mary, a litany which calls upon the Virgin as the "Queen of Poland" to "End… for Poland her deep anguish." The Marian appellation "Queen of Poland" dates from the seventeenth century following the defeat of the Swedish invaders at Częstochowa, the site of the shrine of Poland's miraculous icon of the Black Madonna. To celebrate that victory, King Jan Casmir dedicated the entire Polish nation to Mary as the Queen of Poland in a special ceremony at the Roman Catholic Cathedral of the Assumption in Lwów (now Lviv, Ukraine). Later the Vatican also gave its permission for the Church in Poland to use this appellation during the recitation of the Litany of the Blessed Virgin.

Although little known in Anglo-Saxon countries, Krasiński was one of Poland's great romantic writers of the early nineteenth century. His dramatic poems *The Undivine Comedy* and *Iridion* confront the plight of humanity and outline a philosophy which Poland's messianic role in history was born. In Prayer for Poland, the suffering of Poland becomes the suffering of Christ. During the soprano solo, the Queen of Poland is reminded of the role she played as the *mater dolorosa* at her son's passion. Likewise, the baritone solo symbolically recalls Christ's rising from the dead, and the cantata itself ends by asking Mary to have Poland share in the glory of her son's resurrection.

The English translation, which does not appear in the full score, is printed in the piano-vocal score, published by G. Schirmer in New York in 1916. Translated by George Harris, Jr., the poem reads as follows:

CHORUS

Thou Queen of Poland, thou Queen of the Angels,
Thou who beneath the deepest woe didst languish,
When thy Son to earth's dark valley descended,
End thou for bleeding Poland her deep anguish!
Thou Queen of Poland, thou Queen of Angels,
Let thy love's rainbow o'er her head be bending,
Her hands unloosen from the doomsman's scaffold:
Be thou her angel now and time unending!

SOPRANO SOLO

Thou Queen of Poland, thou Queen of the angels,
Stainless white lily, bright star of our morrow,
Seven times wounded with the sword of sorrow,
Like to lead boiling was the pain within thee.

CHORUS

Thorns, and the cross, and the driven nails thou knowest,
Thou knowest the blood and tears from Him descending,
And how the pangs of that hurt have no measure;
Be thou our angel now and time unending!

BARITONE SOLO

Thou Queen of Poland, thou Queen of the Angels,
Likewise thou knowest with what ardor glowed He,
When crucified, risen unto Heaven stood He:
Hurl us not into hell's infernal meshes.

CHORUS

Weapons immortal 'gainst death us defending,
Show unto death that death's power now is no longer;
Bring us, O Lady! Our resurrection's glory!
Be thou our angel now and time unending!
Thou Queen of Poland, thou Queen of the Angels,
This world is shattered, shattered into pieces!
No single one of its rent and ruptured fragments
Prays any more unto thee, O heavenly Virgin!
We, only we now, burning at the scaffold,
Forth into boundless space our prayers are sending;
Thou'lt know they subjects by their invocation:
Be thou our angel now and time unending!

The Music

Stylistically, Stojowski's music is romantic, very lyrical, highly chromatic and, at times, impressionistic. Thematic material recurring throughout the work provides a unifying formal element.

1. The opening motif of the Cantata's first subject, presented at b. 21 with the entrance of the chorus, returns at b. 57, 339, 402, 515 and 559.

2. The soprano and baritone solos are strophic in form but separated by a short contrasting choral transition which includes thematic material at b. 201 that was first heard at b. 88. The same thematic material is repeated at b. 381. With the exception of the opening interval, it is heard once more in canonic imitation at b. 529

3. The opening phrases of the soprano and baritone solos at b. 138 and b. 236 respectively as well as the choral part at b. 490 are based on a motif first sung by the choir at b. 71.

4. The theme found in the chorus with the text "Bring us, O Lady" at b. 353 is the same melody used in the Cantata's coda at b. 567.

5. Finally, the material used in the opening orchestral introduction is once more heard, first in a shorter eight-bar modulating transition at b. 394 and then during the coda at b. 551. In the two major contrasting sections of the Cantata, Stojowski proves himself to be a composer familiar with the harmonic palette of the twentieth century. The *Allegro feroce* section at b. 442 is based on a chord progression containing whole-tone pitch collections. Used as a harmonic ostinato, the chords are voiced so that parallel open tritones appear

in the bass throughout the entire section. Appropriately, the text in this part of the Cantata describes the anguish and turmoil of a world that has been "shattered to pieces." Stojowski, in his dramatic use of word painting, also shatters a world of tonality and any feeling for the key F Major (D Minor), the key signature given in the music.

Another highly chromatic section which stretches tonality to its ultimate border is the fugato found at the *Poco vivace* at b. 277. Again Stojowski makes a theatrical display of word painting with the text, "Hurl us not into hell's infernal meshes" by using a subject based on a chromatically altered, ascending minor scale. The subject is given two expositions. The first begins with the subject sung by the basses in B-flat Minor with the subject repeated at the fifth, entering in the following order: tenor, alto and soprano. In the second exposition, beginning in C-sharp Minor, the subject is first sung by the altos and then presented by the tenor, bass and soprano. Separating the two expositions is a modulatory episode highlighted by the choir which sings a descending harmonic progression twice on the words "Hurl us not." Each time it is answered by the orchestra with ascending runs and, finally, with a descending chromatic scale leading straight into the inferno.

Although the work begins and closes in post-romantic manner, the body of the Cantata uses Impressionist-style language, using tritones and whole tone scales melodically and harmonically. Based on Stojowski's copy of the piano/vocal score, the Cantata is to have a choral ending. This version of the Cantata's ending is included in the J. Hein edition of the full score.

Opus 41: (1921 & 1931)

No. 1 *Intermède lyrique pour piano* (1921)

- **Dedication**

  A la Señorita Luisa Morales-Macedo. For biographical information on Stojowski's wife, see Chapters 4 and 5.

- **Tempo marking**

  Andantino con moto

- **Editions**

  Manuscript score: ZLSC. See Appendix Inventory.

  Heugel & Cie., Paris, 1922: LC, OSU, WU.

Figure Cat-12. A photograph of one of Stojowski's students, Mildred Titcomb.
The inscription reads: "To Sigismond Stojowski in deepest appreciation, admiration
and gratitude and with the wish of continuing the years that have been my happiest.
Devotedly, Mildred Titcomb." Photograph courtesy of ZLSC. Used by permission. All
rights reserved

No. 2 *Scherzo-Caprice pour piano* (Newburgh, June 1931)

- **Dedication**

  A Mildred Titcomb (Mrs. William M. Rains). Mildred Titcomb was an American
  pianist from California who studied with Stojowski while attending high school in
  New York City. Titcomb made her Town Hall debut in 1929, and also performed
  in radio broadcasts for NBC. She later became the first wife of lawyer William M.

Rains after whom the Loyola University Law Library in Los Angeles is named. She made her debut in Los Angeles by playing the Schumann Concerto with the Los Angeles Symphony Club in 1934. While in Los Angeles, she also coached with Alfred Mirovitch.

- **Tempo Marking**

  Molto vivace

- **Editions**

  Manuscript at Alphonse Leduc in Paris as well as ZLSC. See Appendix Inventory. A color photocopy of the holograph can be found at BNW.

  Heugel & Cie., Paris, 1933: LC, OSU, WU.

- **Remarks**

  The MS found in ZLSC is an earlier version (1919) of the composition. See Appendix Inventory.

Opus 42: *Variations et fugue sur un thème original pour piano* **(1933)**

- **Dedication**

  A ma très chère femme. For biographical information on Stojowski's wife, see Chapters 4 and 5.

- **Movements**

  Theme: *Andante con moto* / (7/4)
  Variation 1: *Maestoso*
  Variation 2: *Poco più mosso*
  Variation 3: *Andante assai*
  Variation 4: *Allegro agitato* / (4/4–12/8)
  Variation 5: *Non troppo presto ma con fuoco* / (4/4)
  Variation 6: *Vivace* / (simultaneous use of 20/16 and 4/4 metres)
  Variation 7: *Presto* / B-flat Major / Canon at the fourth / (3/4)
  Variation 8: *Lento, ma non troppo, rubato* / E Minor / (4/2)
  Variation 9: *Andantino con moto* / E Major / (3/4)
  Variation 10: *Allegro moderato* / (7/4)

- **Editions**

  Manuscript : ZLSC. See Appendix Inventory.

  Heugel & Cie., Paris, 1933: CT, LC, WU

- **Remarks**

The *Variations and Fugue on an Original Theme* proves Stojowski to be a master of counterpoint and fugue. The jurors at the Conservatoire National, who awarded him the first prize in 1889, would be proud of this achievement.

The work is a set of ten variations based on an original theme and followed by a fugue. It begins in E Minor and ends in E Major. Easy to follow antecedent and consequent phrases enable the listener to keep track of the theme and its development throughout the work:

Here Stojowski proves himself to be a daring composer. His harmonies are bold, even shocking at times, and clearly signify Stojowski's advance into the language of twentieth-century modernism. The penultimate chord in the *coda*, for example, is a whole-tone chord that is spelled out as an augmented ninth chord. Played in the piano's lower register, its dissonant character has a stunning jazz-like effect.

The theme is written in the unusual metre of 7/4 that appears to have more in common with the written-in *rubato* typical of Brahms than with an effort to impress the listener with the unsettling effects of mixed meters. In the sixth variation there is the simultaneous use of 20/16 metre in the right hand with 4/4 metre in the left hand. In fact, this is merely an alternate way of notating an effect which other composers before him had simply rendered as five against four. In the ninth variation, Stojowski unexpectedly abandons modernist conventions and returns to his romantic roots in a section reminiscent of Chopin's Prelude in B-flat Major, Op. 28. At the end of the final variation, Stojowski uses harmonics by instructing the performer to hold an arpeggiated chord with the sostenuto pedal, depress the keys of certain notes without striking the strings, and then suddenly clear the pedal. This barely audible harmonic effect can probably be appreciated only by the front row of liseners. A similar effect was earlier employed by Debussy and Schoenberg.

The subject of the fugue, which begins in E Minor, is derived from the original theme.

- **Recordings**

Recorded by Jonathan Plowright for Hyperion Records, CDA67437: *Stojowski, Music for Piano,* London: 2004.

Romance

Sigismond Stojowski, Op. 43, No. 1

Figure Cat-13. First page of *Romance*, Stojowski's last composition with an opus number. Used by permission of G. Schirmer, Inc., New York; Peter Martin, Archivist

Opus 43, no. 1: *Romance for Piano* **(Sonthold, New York, September 1936)**

- **Dedication**

  Phyllida Ashley Everingham. See the entry on Everingham in Chapter 4.

- **Editions**

  Manuscript: ZLSC. On the MS it is listed as Op. 41, no. 3. See Appendix Inventory.

  G. Schirmer, New York, 1941: LC; Authorized photocopy: BNW, ZLSC.

- **Remarks**

  Having searched both published resources and electronic databases for library collections in the United States and Canada, no other bibliographic records for the Romance are listed other than the copy at the Library of Congress.

  Recordings

  A 1942 New York radio broadcast with ZS performing transferred onto LP: Desmar IPA 115, *Sigismond Stojowski Plays Chopin, Paderewski and Stojowski,* 1976.

II. Published Works without Opus Numbers

A. Songs

A Stella—An Stella **(ca. 1890)**

   French poem by P. R. Hirsch

- **Editions**

  Schott, Mainz:

Chanson de mer—Meereslied **(ca. 1890)**

   French poem by Sully Prudhomme

- **Editions**

  Schott, Mainz:

- **Remarks**

  Both of the above songs were performed at the February 19, 1892, Berlin Philharmonic concert. Copies of *A Stella, La flûte muette* and *Chanson de mer* have not been found in any library or with the publisher. There is a cover of another work published by Schott which showed the songs being prepared for publication. They are listed in Hofmeister and Stojowski clearly includes these works in his list of compositions "Published without Opus number" in a post World War I résumé entitled *Biographical Data.*

Euphonies—Ce furent là des heures douces [e–g']
French poem by Viellé-Griffin

- **Dedication**
  A Mademoiselle Greta Torpadie.

- **Tempo Marking**
  Andantino quasi allegretto

- **Editions**
  Heugel & Cie., Paris, 1922: PC

  The Canadian National Institute for the Blind also has this song available in Braille at 85 cents a page (2004 rates). http://www.cnib.ca/library/for_clients/music_library/vocal_catalogue/voclinkSte.htm

- **Remarks**
  Not to be confused with the song cycle *Euphonies,* Op. 33.

Krakowiak (Le Cracovien), *Wesoły, szczęśliwy Krakowiaczek—En Route gai Cracovien* **(for tenor)** [d–a']
Polish text by Edm. Wasilewski, French text by S. Bordése

- **Tempo marking**
  Vivace assai

- **Editions**
  Stanley Lucas & Co., London & Leipzig, 1895: BL, BJ.

  Schott, Mainz, 1910: Listed in Hofmeister.

La flûte muette
French poem by P. R. Hirsch

- **Editions**
  Schott, Mainz: 1898

Sérénade

Polish text by Adam Asnyk; French translation by Maurice Chassang
Patrz, patrz, oto wiosna—Viens, viens, le printemps râvi

- **Tempo marking**

    Allegretto

- **Editions**

    Heugel & Cie., Paris, 1913: BPL

B. Piano Works

Deux Feuillets d'Album

- **Editions**

    Stanley Lucas & Co., London & Leipzig, 1895: BL.
    E. Ashdown, London, 1911: BL.

- **Remarks**

    Deux Feuillets d'Album are simply full of charm and originality. Not difficult
    and thoroughly effective, these delightful little miniatures would make admirable
    encores, or would lighten a program. [Rowley]

Cadenza for Beethoven's Concerto No. 3

- **Editions**

    Heugel & Cie., Paris: 1913: BNP, LC

Twelve Exercises for Strengthening the 3rd, 4th and 5th Fingers

- **Editions**

    Carl Fischer, New York:, 1922: LC.

- **Remarks**

    Part of Alberto Jonás' *Master School of Modern Piano Playing and Virtuosity.*
    Sigismond Stojowski Album selected and edited by Alec Rowley (1892–1958).

- **Editions**

    Schott & Co., London, 1932, BL, BNW.

- **Remarks**

  The album consists of reprints of earlier Schott editions. Neither the dedications nor the opus numbers of the works are given in the album. The preface reads, "…Those who value beauty will find herein a treasury of delight." The collection contains:

  1. *Mélodie* [Op. 1, no. 1]
  2. *Berceuse* [Op. 5, no. 1]
  3. *Intermède* [Op. 4, no. 1]
  4. *Gondoliera* [Op. 5, no. 3]
  5. *Rêverie* [Op. 15, no. 1]
  6. *Serenade* [Op. 8, no. 3]

Lullaby—Cradle Song (1941)

- **Editions**

  Manuscript: ZLSC. The title on the MS reads, *Spanish American Berceuse*. See Appendix Inventory.

  Boosey & Hawkes, New York, 1942: BL. UM.

- **Remarks**

  Lullaby is part of an anthology entitled *Homage to Paderewski*. The collection was originally planned to be published in 1941 to mark the 50th anniversary of Paderewski's first American tour. His death during the summer of that year resulted in the *Lullaby* being published *in memoriam* of Paderewski. The lullaby is based on the Peruvian folk song *A larroro rito*. In addition to Stojowski, the collection contains 15 other works by Béla Bartók, Mario Castelnuovo-Tedesco, Bohuslav Martinu, Darius Milhaud, Ernest Schelling, Jaromir Weinberger, and other composers residing in America at that time. Benjamin Britten misunderstood the commission and submitted his *Mazurka Elegiaca* scored for two pianos. Although it did not make the anthology, it was published separately. The compositions by Britten and Bartók are the only two works from this anthology which are currently in print. The collection is available from Boosey & Hawkes custom reprint service for approximately £20.

  A benefit concert for the Paderewski Memorial Hospital in Edinburgh, which took place in the home of Mr. & Mrs. Samuel L. M. Barlow on February 27, 1942, was advertised as being the venue for the first performance of these works. Eight composers-pianists took part. Theodore Chanler, Feliks Łabuński, J. Nin-Culmell, Karol Rathaus, Vittorio Rieti and Stojowski performed their own works. Mr. Nin-Culmell also performed the pieces written by Arthur Benjamin, Eugene Goosens and Darius Milhaud. Colin McPhee played the pieces by Richard Hammond and Emerson Whithorne, while Rudolf Firkusny performed the work by Bohuslav Martinu. In the article, no mention was made of the remaining four works by

Béla Bartók, Mario Castlenuovo-Tedesco, Jaromir Weinberger and the late Ernest Schelling, leading one to believe that they were not played at all. [*NYT*, "Concert to Aid Hospital"]

There are current plans to finally reissue the anthology after over 60 years and to release a CD of the collection with pianist Jonathan Plowright on the German label EDA from Klassik Center Kassel.

Dumka (1945)

- **Dedication**

  To Guiomar Novaes-Pinto. See the entry for Novaes in Chapter 4.

- **Tempo Marking**

  Andante con moto

- **Editions**

  G. Schirmer, New York, 1945: BL, LC, QCC, TX, ZLSC.

- **Remarks**

  This piece is a revised version of Op. 17. Both works have the same music for the first fourteen bars, the only noticeable differences being discrepancies in pedalling and expression marks. In b. 15, a transition between the first and second sections, things begin to change. Although both transitions are the same length, the accent found on the first note in b. 15 and the g-sharp found in b. 16 are missing in the Schirmer edition. Also, in the Op. 17 transition, the music was played by the left hand alone, while in the Schirmer edition the composer has added a part for the right hand for its last three bars. After the next ten bars in the following section, the music in the Schirmer edition changes considerably, including a change of key not found in the earlier publication.

C. Violin

Sérénade for Solo Violin

- **Editions**

  Heugel (collection Selecta no. 95), Paris: c. 1920

- **Remarks**

  This is an arrangement of the *Serénade,* Op. 8, no. 3, which was earlier arranged for violin by A. Kaiser and published by Schott in 1910 under the title of *Aubade*: ZLSC.

D. Polish Song Collections

Chansons Polonaises

- **Polish Titles of Songs and Carols**

  Flis
  Owczarek
  Maciek
  Oj Chmielu
  Od Krakowa
  Gdzież to jedziesz Jasiu?
  Gdy w czystem polu
  Gaiczek zielony
  Pije Kuba
  Wysła na pole (duettino)
  Krakowiak
  Chałupeczka
  O, joj, joj
  Wezmę ja kontusz
  A w ogródeczku chmiel się wije
  Bóg się rodzi
  Lulajże, Jezuniu
  W żłobie leży
  Wśród nocnej ciszy
  Przybieżeli do Betleem

- **Editions**

  Heugel & Cie., Paris, 1927: BNP, BNW, EAST, ICA, LC

- **Remarks**

  Twenty selections, including fourteen Polish folksongs arranged for solo voice or unison chorus and piano, one duettino for soprano and tenor as well as five Polish Christmas carols arranged for mixed chorus and piano. Coincidentally, the same five carols were arranged by British composer Arnold Bax for unison chorus and orchestra during World War II.

  All songs and carols are printed with Polish, French and English texts, with the latter translated by Eleanor Hajue. The duettino is 12 pages long.

  Ukrainian-born Russian-Jewish baritone Igor Gorin (1904–1982) programmed some of the French versions of these folksongs in recitals during the 1940s. Gorin, who had been the head cantor at the Leopoldstrasse Synagogue in Vienna before moving to America in 1933, world premiered Mallote's famous setting of *The Lord's Prayer*. [*LAT,* March 27, 1941]

Memories of Poland

- **Dedication**

  To Mme. Marie Bogucka, Polish Prima-Donna, exquisite interpreter of folk-songs these songs are admiringly dedicated by Sigismond Stojowski.

- **Polish Titles of Songs**
  Albośmy-to-jacy-tacy
  A siadajże, siadaj!

  Boga Rodzico
  Boże coś Polskę
  Dalej bracia
  Dziewczyno kocham cię
  Hejże dalej do mazura
  Jeszcze Polska
  Koło mego ogródecka
  Kozak
  Krakowiak
  Lu lu, mój malutki
  Na polu wirzba
  Nie chcę cię Kasiuniu
  Obertas
  Oj, lu lu
  Pieśń weselna
  Porównaj Boże
  Przepióreczka (3/8 time)
  Przepióreczka (2/4 time)
  Przez czyśćcowe upalenia
  Siałem proso na zagonie
  Siedzi sobie zając pod miedzą
  Som, som, som w stawie rybecki
  Stoi jawor zielony
  W polu lipeńka
  Z dymem pożarów

- **Editions**

  Marks Music, New York, 1937: BL, LC, NYPLPA, PR, UMK, WTM.
  M. I. Kolin, London, 1941: BL.
  M. I. Kolin, London, 1942 reprint: BL.
  M. I. Kolin, London, ca. 1945 reprint: BJ, BNW.

- **Remarks**

Twenty-seven Polish folksongs, patriotic and religious hymns arranged for solo voice or unison chorus and piano with Polish and English texts. Stojowski provided many of the songs with commentaries.

The accompaniments by Sigismond Stojowski are well done, steering a middle course between dull purity and wilful intrusion of personal style. The English translations are less felicitous. The occasional annotations are helpful. Altogether, the book deserves a warm welcome. F. H. [From a review of "Memories of Poland" in *Music and Letters*, vol. 22 no. 4 (October 1941), 392.]

Autographed copy of the score at the Polish Museum of America in Chicago: "Na pamiątkę odwiedzin cennego i drogiego polskiemu sercu Muzeum Zjednoczenia Polskiego Rzymsko-Katolickiego." [signature] Chicago, 25/X/1943 r. [In commemoration of the visit to the important and dear to the Polish heart Museum of the Polish Roman-Catholic Society. Chicago, 25 October 1943.]

III. Unpublished, Lost Works

Cadenza for Beethoven's Piano Concerto No. 4

- **Remarks**

Mentioned in composer's résumé in ZLSC. "On December 9, [1902], a concert by Mr. Stojowski, pianist and composer took place. Here in France, this artist is considered an authority of the first rank as regards musical theory and execution... He performed the Fourth Concerto in G Major by Beethoven with cadenzas of his own composition. Mr. Stojowski acquitted himself in this audacious act in a fashion meriting the accolades of the most refined connoisseurs." [*LMM,* "Varsovie," vol. 14.]

Cello Sonata No. 2

- **Remarks**

Listed in *The New Grove*, 2001, it is most probably a mistake made by the author of the entry.

Fantazja polska [Polish Fantasy] for Piano and Orchestra

- **Remarks**

Based on Polish dance forms, it won first prize at the Maurice Zamoyski competition in Warsaw in 1901. Either Stojowski withdrew it from his catalogue or this is another name for *Rhapsodie symphonique,* Op. 23, premiered a year earlier. For more information on this topic see Stanisław Dybowski's article "*Rapsodia czy fantazja?*" [Rhapsody or Fantasy?] in the May 26, 2002 issue of *Ruch Muzyczny.*

Intermezzi for Piano

- **Remarks**

  Mentioned in Stojowski's *Biographical Data* and also in a December 23, 1918 review in *Musical America*: "Mr. Stojowski's own *Two Intermezzi*, played for the first time and as yet unpublished, had haunting moments. The first is hotly colored; its companion piece has much of that indefinable yearning and languor, the Polish *żal*."

Piano Concerto No. 3 in F Minor

- **Remarks**

  Mentioned in Groves, 1937; *Concerto pour piano avec accompagnement d'orchestre.* Also mentioned in Stojowski's *Biographical Data.*

Piano Quintet

- **Remarks**

  Listed in *The New Grove*, 2001, this is probably another mistake made by the author of the entry. There is, however, a short *Piano Quartet* as well as sketches for a piano trio. See Appendix Inventory.

Romance for Flute and Piano

- **Remarks**

  Mentioned in Reiss and in Stojowski's *Biographical Data.* Supposedly, it was intended as a competition piece for the National Conservatory in Paris.

Serenade 'Rigandon' [sic!] **for Piano Solo**

- **Remarks**

  Mentioned in the May 18, 1896 issue of *EMTA* as *Rigaudon* in the May 30, 1896 issue of *LMM.*

Symphony No. 2

- **Remarks**

Mentioned in *The Musical Courier*, April 26, 1911, and in the anononymous press clipping from June 1921, "Stojowski to Return to Concert Field after Six Years' Interval"; unfinished symphony. The unpublished *Scherzo* for orchestra is possibly a movement from the Symphony.

Three Songs

- **Remarks**

These art songs were set to the poetry of Edmund Wasilewski, including one entitled *Między nami nic nie było*, mentioned in *EMTA,* May 18, 1896. This does not include the *Krakowiak* mentioned as one of the printed art songs.

Inca Themes for Piano **by Peruvian composer Pablo Chávez Aguilar (1898–1950)**

- **Remarks**

Arranged by Stojowski as a four-movement suite in the following keys: A-flat Major, F Minor, D Minor and E Minor, they were performed by Luisa Stojowska at a Town Hall Recital on November 25, 1950.

IV. Unpublished Works in ZLSC

Ballade **for Orchestra**

- **Tempo Marking**

Andante non troppo

- **Edition**

Manuscript in ZLSC. See Appendix Inventory.

- **Orchestration**

3*.3*.3*.2.-4.2.3.1.-timp.-harp-strings

- **Remarks**

Mentioned in Grove's, 1937; 35 pages; Stojowski's first work for orchestra. Manuscript is marked in pencil as "Op. 1." First performed by Orchestre Colonne in Feb 1891.

Stojowski used the opening bass clarinet solo for the opening of his Symphony in D, Op. 21.

Cantata *Automne—Choeur à 4 parties, accompagnement d'orchestre* (May 1888) for Mixed Chorus and Orchestra

• **Edition**

Manuscript of the seven-page piano/vocal score: ZLSC. See Appendix Inventory.

• **Remarks**

Text: French poem by Lamartine. The work has probably never been performed.

Caprice-Étude pour le piano

• **Edition**

Manuscript: ZLSC. See Appendix Inventory.

• **Tempo Marking**

Allegro tempestuoso

• **Remarks**

Four pages. Dated May 3, 1888, this piece is not related to the other works bearing the same title in Opus 2 or Opus 16, nor is it related to the *Caprice Oriental* or the *Scherzo-Caprice*. It was written in Paris on the Polish holiday, Polish Constitution Day. Stojowski's name-day fell one day earlier, on May 2.

Dumka for solo voice and chamber orchestra

• **Edition**

Manuscript: ZLSC: See Appendix Inventory.

• **Remarks**

Incomplete, only the orchestral parts exist. The full score and solo vocal parts are missing. This very short piece was possibly intended for the 1915 pageant *A Night in Poland*.

Fugue de concours: Fugue du ton à quatre parties (July 25, 1889)

• **Dedication**

A Charles René, temoignage d'amitié et de reconnaissance. A student of Léo Delibes, Charles René won the *Prix de Rome* in 1884.

- **Edition**

  Manuscript: ZLSC. See Appendix Inventory.

- **Remarks**

  This is Stojowski's prize-winning (First Prize) composition at the Conservatoire in Paris on July 25, 1889.

Mazurka in F Major for Violin and Orchestra (unfinished)

- **Edition**

  Manuscript: ZLSC. See Appendix Inventory.

- **Remarks**

  The title is the author's; the MS is untitled.

Piano Quartet

- **Edition**

  Manuscript: ZLSC. See Appendix Inventory.

- **Remarks**

  Four-page sketch.

Scherzo for Orchestra

- **Edition**

  Manuscript: ZLSC. See Appendix Inventory.

- **Orchestration**

  3*.3*.2.2.-4.2.3.1.-1.-timp-harp-strings

- **Remarks**

  This is possibly the only movement from Stojowski's unfinished Second Symphony. The manuscript is marked in pencil as "Op. 10," 42 pages.

Six Musical Notebooks

- **Remarks**

  The first notebook has the following juvenilia works, presented in the order as found in the manuscript: See ZLSC, Appendix Inventory.

Tęsknota, song for high voice and piano, text by N. Zmichnowska.

- **Remarks**

  Written in Ischl in Aug 1884. Bad Ischl was the summer home of Theodore Leschetizky where he often vacationed with his friend, Johannes Brahms. *Tęsknota* was world premiered by Marta Zamoyska-Makowska, soprano, and Michael Oczko, pianist, on May 24, 2003, at the Paderewski Museum in Warsaw.

Feuille d'Album for piano (*Andantino quasi allegretto,* A-flat Major), Ischl, August 1884

- **Remarks**

  See Remarks for Opus 19, no. 1.

Waryacye [Theme and (13) Variations for piano in E Minor], Lwów, February 1885

- **Movements**

  Theme: *Grave*
  I *Un poco piu mosso*
  II *Piu mosso*
  III
  IV *Meno mosso*
  V *Un poco piu mosso*
  VI *Grave*
  VII
  VIII
  IX *Con moto*
  X
  XI
  XII *Animato*
  XIII *Meno mosso, energico*
  Coda *Tempo del Thema*

Trois morceaux en miniature for piano, Cracow: May 1885

- **Movements**

  Petite marche – Vivace (B-flat Major)
  Petite Barcarolle – Andante molto cantabile (F-sharp Major)
  Petit Scherzo (E-flat Major), Vienna, 1885.

Niegodziwy [Ungrateful] "Helenko, Helenko, żal szalony," a song for voice and piano, text by Rodoć (?), Cracow: March 1886.

Szkoda [Pity] for voice and piano, text by Adam Asnyk, Cracow: September 1886.

***Impromptu* for Piano** (First nine bars)

* **Tempo Marking**
  Presto

***Caprice* for Piano** (*Allegro con fuoco*—D Major), Cracow: September 1886.

***Phantaisie* for Piano** (*Andante sostenuto*), Cracow: June 1886.

* **Movements**
  Andante sustenuto
  Allegro assai

Romance sans paroles pour Violoncelle (no date)

* **Remarks**
  The piece is in A Major. World premiered by Henryk K. Grocholski, cello, and Michael Oczko, piano, at the Paderewski Museum in Warsaw on May 24, 2003.

Violin Concerto in D Minor

* **Movements**
  Allegro con fuoco, ma poco maestoso
  Andante con moto
  Allegro molto con fuoco, quasimente presto

* **Edition**
  Manuscript: ZLSC. See Appendix Inventory. The MS has the opus number as "15."

* **Remarks**
  Only the violin/piano score exists.

The Chopin Mazurkas edited by Zygmunt Stojowski

* **Remarks**
  This is the last project Stojowski completed before his death in 1946. Each mazurka, which contains Stojowski's fingering and pedaling, is accompanied by a lengthy (over 50 single-spaced typewritten pages) commentary and analysis. In 1970, one

of the Stojowski-edited mazurkas with commentary appeared in the American magazine *Clavier*, commemorating the centennial of Stojowski's birth.

V. Unpublished Works in Other Collections

Mazurka in D Major & Polonaise in F# Minor by Frederick Chopin

- **Orchestration**

  2.1.2.1.-2.2.1.0-timp.perc-pno.-str

- **Remarks**

  Orchestrated by Zygmunt Stojowski for Marcella Sembrich's 1915 musical pageant *A Night in Poland.*

  Full score and parts (manuscript): PIASA.

Figure Cat-14. "Please do not throw bottles in lake." Stojowski on the West Coast during the 1920s. Photograph courtesy of ZLSC. Used by permission. All rights reserved

Appendix 1

STOJOWSKI'S ORCHESTRAL PERFORMANCES

<u>Date</u>	<u>Location</u>	<u>Orchestra & Conductor</u>	<u>Repertoire</u>
<u>1885</u>			
?	Cracow Czartoryska Salon	ad hoc Jan N. Hock	Beethoven: Piano Concerto No. 3 in C Minor, Op. 37
<u>1887</u>			
Mar 25	Cracow Sala Saska	ad hoc Jan N. Hock	Beethoven: Piano Concerto No. 3 in C Minor, Op. 37
<u>1891</u>			
Feb 17	Paris Salle Erard	Orchestre Colonne Benjamin Godard	Stojowski: Piano Concerto in F-sharp Minor, Op. 3 (World Premiere)
<u>1892</u>			
Feb 19	Singakadmie	Berlin Philharmonic Rudolph Herfurth	Stojowski: Piano Concerto in F-sharp Minor, Op. 3
<u>1893</u>			
Jan 16	Cracow Sala Saska	13th Regiment Orchestra Jan N. Hock	Liszt: Concerto in E-flat Major R 455
<u>1894</u>			
Feb 22	Manchester Free Trade Hall	Hallé's Orchestra Sir Charles Hallé	Stojowski: Piano Concerto in F-sharp Minor, Op. 3
<u>1895</u>			
Mar 30	Paris	Orchestre Lamoureux	Stojowski: Piano Concerto in F-sharp Minor, Op. 3

1897

| ? | Berlin | | Stojowski: Piano Concerto in F-sharp Minor, Op. 3 |

189?

| Mar 25 | Berlin Beethoven-Saal | Berlin Philharmonic Josef Rebicek (Řebiček) | Saint-Saëns: Concerto No. 4 in C Minor, Op. 44 Rubinstein: Concerto No. 4 in D Minor, Op. 70 Chopin: Concerto No. 2 in F Minor, Op. 21 |

1900

| Nov 15 | Berlin Beethoven-Saal | Berlin Philharmonic Josef Rebicek (Řebiček) | Stojowski: Symphonic Rhapsody, Op. 23 |

1901

| ? | Warsaw | Teatr Wielki (Warsaw Opera House) Emil Młynarski | ? |
| Dec 20 | Warsaw | Warsaw Philharmonic Emil Młynarski | Saint-Saëns: Concerto No. 4 in C Minor, Op. 44 |

1902

Jan 8	Warsaw	Warsaw Philharmonic Emil Młynarski	Stojowski: Piano Concerto in F-sharp Minor, Op. 3 Stojowski: *Fantazja polska* (Symphonic Rhapsody, Op. 23)
Jan 27	Cracow Sala Saska		Saint-Saëns: Concerto No. 4 in C Minor, Op. 44 Stojowski: Piano Concerto in F-sharp Minor, Op. 3
Sep 27	Lwów Teatr Miejski	Lwów Philharmonic Orchestra – Inaugural Concert Ludwik Heller	Beethoven: Concerto No. 4 in G Major, Op. 58 Stojowski: Fantazja polska (Symphonic Rhapsody, Op. 23)

Oct 6	Cracow Teatr Miejski	ad hoc Jan N. Hock	Stojowski: Fantazja polska (Symphonic Rhapsody, Op. 23)
Dec 5	Munich	Musikalische orchestra Akademie Herman Zumpe	Beethoven: Concerto No. 4 in G Major, Op. 58
Dec 9	Warsaw	Warsaw Philharmonic Emil Młynarski	Beethoven: Concerto No. 4 in G Major, Op. 58

1905

Mar 29 Apr 8 13 & 19	Paris Salle Erard	Orchestre Colonne Edouard Colonne	Saint-Saëns: Concerto No. 4 in C Minor, Op. 44 Chopin: Concerto No. 2 in F Minor, Op. 21 Stojowski: Symphonic Rhapsody, Op. 23

1906

Jan 6	NY Carnegie Hall	NY Symphony Society Frank Damrosch	Beethoven: Piano Concerto No. 3 in C Minor, Op. 37
Nov 30	NY Carnegie Hall	NY Symphony Society Walter Damrosch	Chopin: Concerto No. 2 in F Minor, Op. 21

1907

Feb 19	New Haven, Yale Woolsey Hall	New Haven Symphony Horatio Parker	Saint-Saëns: Concerto No. 4 in C Minor, Op. 44

1908

Jun 7	London	London Symphony Orchestra Emil Młynarski	Stojowski: Symphonic Rhapsody, Op. 23

1911

Mar 19	NY New Theater	NY Symphony Society Walter Damrosch	Stojowski: Symphonic Rhapsody, Op. 23 (American Premiere)

Apr 2	NY MET Opera	MET Opera Orchestra Josef Pasternak	Stojowski: Concerto No. 1 in F-sharp Minor, Op. 3 (American Premiere)
Nov 20	Indianapolis German House	Indianapolis Musikverein Alexander Ernestinoff	Liszt: Concerto in E-flat Major R 455
Dec 1	NY Carnegie Hall	NY Symphony Society Walter Damrosch	Liszt: Concerto in E-flat Major R 455

1912

Feb 20	Pittsburgh Carnegie Music Hall	Cincinnati Orchestra Leopold Stokowski	Liszt: Concerto in E-flat Major R 455

1913

Jan 26	Boston	Boston Opera Company A. Dubois	Stojowski: Symphonic Rhapsody, Op. 23
Jun 23	London Queen's Hall	London Symphony Orchestra Arthur Nikisch	Stojowski: Concerto No. 2 in A-flat Major, Op. 32 (World Premiere)
Jul 2	Harrogate Kursaal	Municipal Orchestra Julian Clifford	Stojowski: Concerto No. 2 in A-flat Major, Op. 32

1915

Mar 1	NY Carnegie Hall	NY Philharmonic Josef Stransky	Stojowski: Concerto No. 2 in A-flat Major, Op. 32 (American Premiere)
Apr 18	NY Arion Society Club House	(Members of) NY Philharmonic Louis Koemmenich	Stojowski: Symphonic Rhapsody, Op. 23

1923

Nov 5	Albany, NY	Boston Symphony Pierre P. Monteux	Saint-Saëns: Concerto No. 4 in C Minor, Op. 44

1924

Nov 16	NY Carnegie Hall	NY Philharmonic W. van Hoogstraten	Stojowski: Concerto No. 2 in A-flat Major, Op. 32

1925

| Nov | Paris | Orchestre Colonne
Gabriel Pierné | Stojowski: Symphonic Rhapsody,
Op. 23 |

1929

| Oct 4 | Warsaw | Warsaw
Philharmonic
Jerzy Bojanowski | Stojowski: Concerto No. 2 in A-flat
Major, Op. 32 |

1930

| Aug 26 | San Francisco Civic
Auditorium | SF Symphony
Antonia Brico | Stojowski: Symphonic Rhapsody,
Op. 23 |

1934

| Feb 19 | Buffalo, Elmwood
Music Hall | Buffalo Community
Orchestra
Theophile Wendt | Stojowski: Symphonic Rhapsody,
Op. 23 |

1935

| Jan | Buffalo, Elmwood
Music Hall | Buffalo
Philharmonic
Lajos Shuk | Chopin: Concerto No. 2 in F Minor,
Op. 21 |
| Mar | NY Town Hall | NY Women's
Symphony
Antonia Brico | Chopin: Concerto No. 2 in F Minor,
Op. 21 |

1938

| Aug 16 | San Francisco | Bay Region Festival
Orchestra
Antonia Brico | Liszt: Concerto in E-flat Major R
455 |
| Oct 27 | Greenwich
Federal Music
Theater New York
City | Greenwich
Orchestra
Herman Neuman | Stojowski: Symphonic Rhapsody,
Op. 23 |

A p p e n d i x   I I

STOJOWSKI'S MANUSCRIPTS
ZYGMUNT AND LUISA STOJOWSKI COLLECTION
AT THE POLISH MUSIC CENTER, USC

(Represents partial accounting of the Collection as of August 15, 2006. [MZ])

CASE I: MUSIC SCORES A–C (TO VIOLIN CONCERTO)

1. Black hardbound music notebook 6.5 x 9 in. (16.5 x 24 cm). Approximately 95 continuous pages, not numbered. Contains clean copy of the following works:

   a. *Tęsknota – Pieśń do słów N. Żmichowskiej* [Longing – A Song to text by N. Żmichowska]. *Lento ma non troppo*. Inscribed top right: Ischl, *w sieprniu* 1884 [Ischl, in August 1884]. 4 pages

   b. *Feuille d'Album* [for piano]. *Andantino quasi allegretto*. Inscribed top right: Ischl, *sierpień* 1884 [Ischl,August 1884]. 2 pages

   c. *Waryacye* [Variations for piano in E Minor]. Inscribed top right: *we Lwowie w lutym* 1885 [in Lwów in February 1885]. *Thema. Grave*; I. *Un poco piu mosso*; II. *Piu mosso*; III.; IV *Meno mosso*; V. *Un poco piu mosso*; VI. *Grave*; VII.; VIII.; IX. *Con moto*; X.; XI.; XII. *Animato*; XIII. *Meno mosso, energico*; *Coda. Tempo del Thema*. 12 pages

   d. *Trois morceaux en miniature* [for piano]. Inscribed top right: *Kraków maj 1885* [Kraków May 1885]. 1. *Petite Marche: Vivace*. 4 pages; 2. *Petite Barcarolle: Andante molto cantabile*. 2.5 pages; 3. *Petit Scherzo*. Inscribed top right: *Wiedeń sierpień* 1885 [Vienna August 1885]. 3 pages

   e. *Niegodziwy. Słowa Rodocia* [Ungrateful. Words by Rodoć]. Inscribed top right: *Kraków marzec* 1886 [Cracow March 1886]. 2 pages

   f. *Szkoda. Pieśń do słów A. Asnyka* [Pity. A song to text by A. Asnyk]. *Andantino*. Inscribed top right: *Kraków czerwiec* 1886 [Cracow June 1886]. 4 pages

g. *Impromptu* [for piano]. *Presto*. First 9 bars only

h. *Caprice* [for piano]. *Allegro con fuoco*. Inscribed top right: *Kraków czerwiec* 1886 [Cracow June 1886]. 12 pages

i. *Phantaisie* [for piano]. Inscribed top right: *Kraków czerwiec* 1886 [Cracow June 1886].

j. *Andante sostenuto*. II. *Allegro assai*. 18 pages

k. *Berceuse*. Title only (no music) followed by 4 blank pages

l. *Romances sans paroles pour Violoncelle* [and piano] in A Major. 7 pages

2. Black softbound music notebook 6 x 9 in. (15 x 23 cm). Approximately 28 continuous pages, not numbered. Contains clean copy of the following works:

a. Untitled [String trio on an original theme? Possibly a study in fugue and counterpoint]. Includes annotations in French of various polyphonic techniques used in the composition. 14 pages

b. *Fugue du ton. Andante sostenuto* [in A-flat Major]. In 3 parts, on an original theme. Possibly a study in fugue and counterpoint]. Includes annotations in French of various polyphonic techniques used in the composition. 9 pages

3. Dark blue softbound music notebook 7.5 x 4.75 in. (20 x 12 cm). Approximately 20 continuous pages, not numbered. Contains sketches of various works, written in pencil, blue pencil, and ink

4. Light blue softbound music notebook 6 x 9 in. (15x 23 cm). Approximately 40 continuous pages, not numbered. Contains sketches of various works, written in pencil

5. Brown softbound music notebook 6 x 9 in. (15x 23 cm). Approximately 28 continuous pages, not numbered. Contains sketches of various works, written in pencil

6. Dark green softbound music notebook 6 x 9 in. (15x 23 cm). Approximately 43 continuous pages, not numbered. Contains fair copy in ink of counterpoint exercises (?) [fugues, canons, etc. with annotations in French of various polyphonic techniques used throughout the composition]

7. Folder: "Aspirations | (piano) | Op. 39." Contains fair copy scores on a 12-stave paper of the following works:

a. *Vers la tombe (Elegie)*. *Lento e mesto*. Top right: Sig. Stojowski Op. 39 no. 2. 4 pages

b. *Vers le caprice (Intermède)*. *Allegretto capriccioso*. Top right: Sig. Stojowski Op. 39 no. 3. 3 pages

8. Folder (no title). Inside leaf: "Op. 3 Concerto | First draft." Contains a fair copy score in ink on an 18-stave paper of the following work: *Concerto pour piano avec accompagnement d'orchestre* | Sigismond Stojowski. Top right (in blue ink, likely added later by the composer): "first draft of | 1 Concerto." A two-piano arrangement (with annotations by the composer in French in blue pencil to the engraver). 68 pages, numbered.

9. Folder (no title). Contains:

   a. A 4-page ink manuscript of various folk-songs and dances in a setting for piano: *Branle*; *Wolga Boatman's Song*; *Love-Song* (*Tatra mountains*); *Brigand's step* (*Tatra*) *Nehody Hryciu* (*Ukraina*); *Chanson triste* (*Tchaikovsky*); *Peruvian Lullaby*; *Lento*; *Andantino*; etc. Some excerpts have texts entered above the top RH part. 4 pages

   b. pencil sketch (solo part of the Violin Concerto?) – 5 lines of music

   c. fragments of piano unidentified piano pieces, in ink. 3 pages, manuscript very fragile and frayed at the edges

10. Folder (no title). Contains fair copy in ink of two songs for voice and piano on 4 pages of manuscript, 16-stave paper:

    a. *Ach jak mi smutno. Lento e mesto* [Ah, I'm so sad]. Upper right: Zygmunt Stojowski | Op. 11 no. 1. Text in Polish with French translation. Fair copy in ink (French text in pencil)

    b. *Letni wieczór. Andante con moto.* [Summer Evening]. Top right: Zygmunt Stojowski | Op. 11 no. 3. Texts in Polish and French.

11. Folder (no title). Contains several piano pieces in fair copy in ink on a 12-stave paper:

    a. *Berceuse. Lento.* [in A-flat Major] Top right. Sig. Stojowski | Op. 11 no. 1. 2 pages

    b. *Scherzo pour piano.* Title page: *A Monsieur Alexandre Michałowski | Professeur en Conservatoire de Varsovie | Scherzo | pour piano* | Sig. Stojowski | Op. 11 no. 2 [in A Major]. 6 pages with corrections and annotations

    c. *Gondoliera* [for piano]. Title page: *A Mademoiselle Augusta Benwick.* | Gondoliera | Sigismond Stojowski | Op. 11 no. 3 [in G-flat Major]. 2 pages with annotations

    d. *2e Mazurka.* Title page: *A Mademoiselle Hilda Thegerström | Professeur en Conservatoire de Stockholm | 2e Mazurka | pour Piano* | Sigismond Stojowski | Op. 11 no. 4 [in C Minor]. 3 pages

12. Folder (no title): Contains *Ballade, Andante non troppo* [for Orchestra] in full score. Fair copy in ink on a 20-stave paper. No title page. 35 pages, numbered

13. Folder (no title). Contains *Concerto pour violon et orchestre*, Op. 20:

   a. Arrangement for violin solo with piano reduction of the orchestral part. Fair copy in ink on a 15-stave paper, with annotations, corrections, etc. Title page: Concerto | pour violon et orchestre | Sig. Stojowski | Op. 20. 32 pages, not numbered, with rehearsal numbers only, containing all 3 movements

   b. Full orchestral score of the Violin Concerto Op. 20. In pencil on a 20-stave paper with frequent changes, corrections and blue pencil indications of rehearsal letters. Title page: *Concerto | pour violon et orchestre. | Sig. Stojowski | Op. 20. I. Allegro appassionato*: pp. 1–61; II. *Andante non troppo*, pp. 62–80. III. *Allegro giocoso*, pp. 81–138.

14. Folder (no title). Contains the following works in manuscript:

   a. Concerto Op. 15 [for Violin and orchestra? Piano reduction.] Fair copy in ink on a 20-stave paper. I. *Allegro con fuoco, ma poco maestoso* [in D Minor]. II. *Aria. Andante con moto.* [in A Major]. III. *Allegro molto con fuoco, quasimente presto* [in D Minor]. 20 pages

   b. *Caprice-Etude pour le piano. Allegro tempestuoso.* Title page: *Caprice-Etude | pour le piano* | Sigismond Stojowski. Clean copy in ink on an 18-stave paper. 3 pages. Dated at the end: "*3 mai 1888.*"

   c. *L'Automne* [for chorus and orchestra]. Title page: *L'Automne. | Choeur a 4 parties avec accompagnement d'orchestre. | Paroles de Lamartine.* | Sigismond Stojowski. Clean copy in ink on an 18-stave paper. Chorus with piano reduction. 7 pages, not numbered. Dated at the end: "*Fin. Mai 1888.*"

   d. A double-sided sheet of sketches [possibly for the Violin Concerto listed above] in pencil on a 15-stave paper

CASE II: MUSIC SCORES C–D (PIANO CONCERTO—CELLO CONCERTO)

1. Folder: Stojowski | 2nd Piano Concerto. Contains the following works:

   a. *2eme Concerto.* Signed Sig. Stojowski upper right. Clean copy of the full orchestral score, written in pencil on a 20-stave paper, 16 pages, numbered. I. *Allegro energico.* [Note by MZ: Incomplete—the MS. ends on p. 15 of the score]

   b. *2eme Concerto.* In composer's hand, unsigned. Upper right: "Opus 32" added later, possibly by the composer. A two-piano arrangement (orchestral accompaniment written above the solo part). Fair copy with occasional corrections and crossing out (pages 12–14, part of p. 15, etc.) written in pencil on a 15-stave paper. 48 pages, numbered 1–45 (the MS ends on p. 45). Allegro energico (p. 1); *Molto vivace, scherzando* (p. 15); *Andante* (p. 25), *Allegro* (p. 32); *Animato* (p. 35); The MS ends on p. 45 with a change of key (from F Major to F Minor) indicated at the very end of the page

c. Untitled. *2eme Concerto* [?] MS in composer's hand, written in pencil on a 16-stave paper. A sketch—continuation [?] of the Concerto's 2-piano arrangement (change to 4 flats indicated at top left of the page and the indication of orchestration: "Fl."). 4 pages, not numbered. Fair copy, with corrections and crossed-out bars. The soloist's part begins on p. 2 with an octave passage. Top of p. 3 (upper right corner) and p. 4 (upper left corner) are torn out. Incomplete

2. Folder: *Dumka* (parts), containing orchestral parts only for Dumka [for Voice and Orchestra, Op. 14?]. Fair copy (with occasional corrections and annotations, some in composer's hand), written in ink on a 10-stave paper, unsigned. Flute; Oboe; Clarinets I & II in B-flat; Bassoon; Horns I & II in F; Violin I (also called Violin I^{mo}) – 3 sets of parts; Violin II^{do}; Viola; Cello; Bass

3. Folder: *Concertstück pour Violoncelle et Orchestre*, containing the full orchestral score of the work. Title page: *Concertstück* | pour | *Violoncelle et Orchestre* | Sig. Stojowski | Op. 31. Clean copy, in pencil, 72 pages, numbered. Occasional annotations [to the engraver/publisher] in German on the margins. No tempo designation at the beginning

4. Folder: *Concertstück pour Violoncelle et Orchestre*, containing pencil sketch for the work with the orchestral part notated as piano reduction below the solo part. Title: *Concerto p. violoncello et orchestre*. Top right: "Sig. Stojowski | Op. 31." Written in pencil on a 12-stave paper, 22 pages, not numbered. Incomplete *Allegro vivace* (opening tempo). The MS ends with a portion of the *Animato* section in 2/4 (in the full score in Folder no. 3 it is marked: *Allegro assai*). Compare with p. 59 of the full score

5. Folder: *Concertstück pour Violoncelle et Orchestre*, containing an envelope with photostatic copies of the orchestral parts (incomplete). All written on a 12-stave paper in composer's hand and stamped with the Maison du Ménestrel hire library stamp. Piccolo & 3rd flute; Flute I; Flute II; Oboe I; Oboe II & Corno inglese; Clarinetto I in A & B; Clarinetto II in A & B; Fagotto I; Fagotto II; Arpa; Corno I in F; Corno II in F; Corno III in F; Corno IV in F; Tromba I in F; Tromba II in F; Trombone I; Trombone II; Trombone basso; Timpani in A, C, E et Piatti; Piatti

6. Folder: *Concertstück pour Violoncelle et Orchestre*, containing an envelope with the orchestral parts (incomplete). Clean copy in ink on a 12-stave paper [likely in composer's hand] with numerous additions, corrections and interpretative markings [some in composer's hand; others from musicians rehearsing and performing the work]. Violino I, 8 pages (4 sets of parts); Violino II, 8 pages (4 sets of parts); Viola, 8 pages (3 sets of parts); Cello I, 8 pages; Cello II, 8 pages; Basso (ou Cello), 6 pages; Basso II, 6 pages.

CASE III: MUSIC SCORES E–SO

1. Folder: *Fugue de concours* [for string quartet]. Contains clean copy of the score, in ink on a 14-stave paper. Title page: *A | Charles René | témoinage d'amitié et de reconnaissance. |* Sigismond Stojowski *| 1er prix de fugue en 1889. | Paris, le 25 juillet 1889.* Inside title page: Fugue du ton | a quatre parties. | Sigismond Stojowski | [with a musical quotation of the fugue subject below]. 8 pages, written on one side only, with comments in French of the polyphonic techniques used

2. Folder: *In Tempo di minuetto* [for piano]. Clean copy, in ink, with a few corrections and indications in pencil [at the end of the piece for the Da capo], 4 pages, written on a 14-stave paper. Top left: *Moderato con anima.* Top right: Sig. Stojowski | Op. 26 no. 2

3. Folder: 2 Piano pieces [Op. 41 no. 1], containing:

   a. *Intermède lyrique pour piano.* Clean copy in ink on a 12-stave paper, 8 pages (including the title page), not numbered. Title page: *A Señorita Luisa Morales-Macedo | Intermède lyrique | pour Piano |* Sigismond Stojowski | Op. 41 no. 1 | Copyright by Heugel 1921 | 27742. Inside title: Intermezzo. Top: left: *Andantino con moto.* Top right: Stojowski, Op. 41 no. 1

   b. *Intermède.* (Op. 41 no. 2). Clean copy in ink on a 12-stave paper, 8 pages (including the title page), not numbered. Numerous indications of fingering in ink and pencil as well as remarks on performing grace notes at the end of the piece. Further inscription at the end: Bakeloo Cottage, Twilight Park, Catskills, N.Y., July 1916. Although numbered Op. 41 no. 2, it is probably an earlier version of the item a. above

4. Folder: Piano Quartet. Contains sketches for a Piano Quartet, in pencil on a 15-stave paper. Undated and unsigned. Incomplete (4 pages of full score) [opening movement?]

5. Folder: *Romanza* [for Violin and Orchestra, Op. 15?]. Contains a clean copy of the full orchestral score, in ink, on a 20-stave paper. Title: Romanza; top left: Andante non troppo. Top right: Sig. Stojowski | Op. 15. 22 pages, numbered

6. Folder: 2 Piano pieces, containing:

   a. *Scherzo-Caprice.* Clean copy (with a few corrections and annotations) in ink on a 12-stave paper, 8 pages. Top left: *To Mildred Titcomb.* Top right: Sig. Stojowski | Op. 41 no. 2. Inscribed at the end: "June 1931 | Newburgh."

   b. *Romance.* Clean copy (with a few corrections and annotations) in ink on a 12-stave paper, 4 pages. Top left: *Andante con moto.* Top right: "S. Stojowski | Op. 41 no. 3." Inscribed at the end: "Sonthold, N. Y. | Sept. 1936."

7. Folder: *Prayer for Poland*, containing a choral score with orchestral accompaniment in orchestral reduction. Fair copy in ink on a 15-stave paper, with numerous annotations, corrections, and performance directives in ink, pencil and color pencil. 24 pages, including title page. Title page: *Sigismond Stojowski | Op. 40 | Prayer for Poland | Poem by | Sigismond Krasinski | (Translation by George Harris, Jr.) | for mixed chorus, Soprano solo, Baritone solo, Organ and orchestra | Modlitwa za Polskę. | Hymn | do słów | Zygmunta Krasińskiego. | Na sopran solo, baryton solo, chór mięszany, orkiestrę i organy | Zygmunt Stojowski | Op. 40*

8. Folder: *Pageant* (*Wedding*) *Wesele*. Contains various solo sheets of Polish folk songs and dances, some with words in Polish (occasionally transliterated into the English) with stage directions, involving roles for the performers (incl. Madame Sembrich!)

9. Folder: *Fantaisie pour piano*, Op. 38. Clean copy in ink on a 22-stave paper. Title page: *Fantaisie | pour piano | Sigismond Stojowski | Op. 38.* 16 pages, numbered [the piece ends on p. 9, but there is a passage of 4 bars with fingering on the following blank page – to be inserted at the spot marked with an "x" on p. 7]. Inscribed at the end: "Maplewood | Sept. 1911."

10. Folder: *Siedzi ptaszek na drzewie* [*Bird on a Tree*]. Fair copy of a song *Siedzi ptaszek na drzewie*, in ink on a 12-stave paper, with corrections in pencil and colored pencil, 2 pages. Also contains a French translation of the text, written in pencil above the Polish original as well as a separate leaf with the French translation written out in ink in the composer's hand. Top left: *Andantino con moto*. Top right: *Zygmunt Stojowski | Op. 14 no. 1*

11. Folder: *Le Printemps*. Clean copy of the orchestral score with some corrections and additions, in ink on a 24-stave paper. 24 pages, numbered. Title page: *A la Mémoire de mon bien aimé Maître | Léo Delibes | Le Printemps | d'après une Ode d'Horace | pour | Chœur et Orchestre | Sigismond Stojowski | Op. 7.* On inside of title page, pencil text in German: *Der Frühling | Nach einer Ode der Horaz | Deutscher Text von Dr. A. Nossig | Musik von | Sig. Stojowski | Op. 7.*

12. Folder: *Modlitwa za Polskę. Prayer for Poland*. Contains a fair copy of the orchestral score, with numerous corrections, additions and changes, in ink on a 34-stave paper. 31 pages, numbered. Top left: *Andante con moto*. Top right: *S. Stojowski | Op. 40*

NOTE: The manuscript was folded in half and is in extremely fragile condition [MZ]

CASE IV: SCORES SY–Z

1. Folder: Symphony [in D Minor, Op. 21]. Contains a full orchestral score in pencil, on a 22-stave paper. First movement—*Andante mesto-Allegro*; 67 pages, numbered. (Several pages that were cut from the final version of the score but are included here, are not numbered). Second movement—*Andante*, 27 pages, numbered (also included a clean copy in ink on a 20-stave paper of the last 12 bars of the movement). Third movement—*Molto vivace*, 77 pages, only partially numbered 1–7, with bar numbers in lower right running throughout—1–617. Ending of the movement in sketches, with bar numbers continuing from 618 to the final chord in 656. Fourth movement—*Allegro con fuoco*, 59 pages, numbered. Title page: from top left: *Andante mesto.* | *Symphonie* | *I* | *Sig. Stojowski*

2. Folder: *Variations et Fugue pour Piano*. Fair copy in ink on a 12-stave paper. 16 pages, numbered, plus a title page: *A ma très chère femme* | *Variations et Fugue* | *sur un thème original* | *pour Piano* | *Sigismond Stojowski* | *Op. 42*. Below, in red ink, "Copyright by Heugel 1923 | 28279."

3. Folder: *Thème cracovien varié* [for piano]. Fair copy of *Thème cracovien varié*, Op. 26, no. 4, in ink on a 12-stave paper. 10 pages, numbered. Another, possibly definitive version of the final section, *Allegro vivo*, and the 16 opening bars of the *Allegretto capriccioso, ma non vivace* variation on a separate sheet. A further sheet of a 12-stave paper has a 17 bar long fragment of an unidentified piano piece in A Major.

4. Folder: *Scherzo* [for orchestra]. Clean copy in ink on a 20-stave paper of the third movement for a symphony. From top left: III. *Scherzo.*| *Vivacissimo.* | *Symphonie* | *Sig. Stojowski* | Op. 10 [added in faintly visible pencil]. 50 pages, numbered.

5. Symphony in D Minor, Op. 21. A bound manuscript copy of the score. Inscribed *To be or not to be* above the title, *Symphonie*, and the composer's signature underneath. On the inside cover, left side page: *Adresse: Sig. Stojowski* | *Paris, 12 rue Leo Delibes.* 236 pages, numbered.

6. Folder: *Spanish American Berceuse* [for piano]. Clean copy on a 9-stave paper, 2 pages, not numbered. Top left: *Andantino poco mosso*. Top right: arr. by *S. Stojowski*.

7. Folder: Untitled work for violin and orchestra in F Major. Clean copy in ink on a 20-stave paper. 15 pages, numbered.

8. Folder: Sketches for Piano Trio. Contains two fragments:

   a. Fragment 1: pencil on a 12-stave paper, 3 pages, not numbered. [Possibly the opening movement in G Minor, *Agitato*]. At the bottom of p. 3, an 8-bar opening of a fugue, in ink, not necessarily related to the sketches of the trio.

   b. Fragment [possibly for a second movement] in E-flat Major, marked *Moderato*. 1 page, in pencil, on a 12-stave paper

9. Folder: miscellaneous writings:

   a. Contains several loose sheets of paper with Stojowski's thoughts, remarks and observations on various composers and their music. Some in English, some in Polish, some in ink, some in pencil.

   b. green, leather-bound address book

CASE V: ORCHESTRAL WORKS:

1. Folder: Contains the score for *Prologue, Scherzo & Variations* [for Piano and Orchestra]. Title page, written on an 11-stave paper: *Partition Orchestre | Prologue, Scherzo, & Variations. | Sig. Stojowski | Op. 32*. The full orchestral score, written in ink on a 24-stave paper. 203 pages, numbered. Includes added pages and indications for deleting sections of varying lengths throughout the score.

CASE V-a: VARIOUS MANUSCRIPTS:

1. Folder: *Chant d'amour*. Manuscript score in pen and ink on a 14-stave paper. Top right, signed: *Sig. Stojowski | Op. 26 no. 3*

2. Folder: *Trois Etudes de Concert*. Manuscript in pen and ink on a 14-stave paper. Title page: *Trois Etudes de Concert | 1. en ut | 2. en f♯ | 3. en la min.| Cop. 1912 | Sigismond Stojowski | Op. 35*. 18 pages, numbered by the composer in pencil.

3. Folder: *Sonate pour piano et violoncelle*. Manuscript in pen and ink on a 15-stave paper. Title page: *Sonate | pour piano et violoncelle | Sig. Stojowski | Op. 17*. 31 pages, numbered in pen and ink and in pencil by the composer. Several sections contain crossing out, ossia passages and a section stapled together between pages 25 and 26. One extra page with ossias, other inserts, and composer's explanations (in French) of text changes. At the last bar, the following inscription: "Kissingen | wrzesień 1895 | Paryż listopad 95 | Zygmunt Stojowski." Manuscript in a fragile condition.

4. Folder: Two piano pieces from Aspirations:

   a. *Vers l'amour* (*Romance*) [for piano]. Manuscript in pen and ink on a 12-stave paper, 4 pages, not numbered. Top right, signed: *Sig. Stojowski | Op. 39 no. 4*. Bottom (in ink and pencil): *Copyright__1913*

b. *Vers la joie* (*Rhapsodie*) [for piano]. Manuscript in pen and ink on a 12-stave paper, 4 pages, not numbered. Top right, signed: *Sig. Stojowski | Op. 39 no. 5.* Bottom (in ink and pencil): *Copyright__1913*

5. Folder: Deux Orientales [for piano]. Contains 2 pieces:

a. No. 1. *Romance.* Manuscript in pen and ink on a 16-stave paper, 2 pages, not numbered. Top right, signed: *Sig. Stojowski | Op. 10 no. 1*

b. No. 2. *Caprice.* Manuscript in pen and ink on a 14-stave paper, 5 loose pages, not numbered, with the exception of *Seite 5* entered in blue pencil by the composer on the last page. Last page is smaller-sized, 12-stave paper. Top right, signed: *Sig. Stojowski | Op. 10 no. 2.* Manuscript in fragile condition.

6. Folder: *Deuxième Sonate (E-dur – Mi majeur) pour Piano et Violon Op. 37.* Manuscript in pen and ink with numerous pencil additions on a 20-stave paper. Title page: *Deuxième Sonate | (E-dur – Mi majeur)| pour Piano et Violon | Op. 37 |.* 34 pages, numbered in pencil, in composer's hand. Contains also a solo violin part—manuscript on a 22-stave paper, 15 pages, not numbered. Top right, signed: *Sig. Stojowski | Op. 37*

7. Folder (no title). Contains:

a. Second Mazurka [for piano] by Gustave L. Becker. Manuscript in pen and ink on a 12-stave paper, 3 pages. Inscription on top of first page: "Cordially dedicated to Sigismond J. Stojowski."

b. *Allah* [for voice and piano] by Harry Meyerowitz. Two mimeographed copies of the engraved manuscript. 3 pages.

CASE VI: STOJOWSKI—PUBLISHED WORKS (1)

1. Folder: *Berceuse* [Op. 5 no. 1] for piano. Two copies:

a. Published by Stanley Lucas, Weber, Pitt & Hatzfeld Ltd. London and Leipzig. Color cover, in extremely fragile condition

b. Published by Schott & Co., London. Good condition

2. Folder: *Bruissements* (Forest Breezes), Op. 36 no. 4 for piano. Published by Schirmer. Good condition

3. Folder: *Amourette de Pierrot,* Op. 30 no. 1 for piano. Two copies:

a. Published by Arthur R. Schmidt—Boston, Leipzig, New York. Fair condition, with a stamp "Luisa Morales Macedo" on the cover

b. Same publisher, slightly smaller score size. Good condition

4. Folder: *Aspirations* [for piano] Op. 39. Black leather front cover: "Album | Sig. Stojowski."

   a. *Vers l'azur*, Op. 39. no. 1. Published by Heugel & Cie, Paris. In extremely fragile condition

   b. *Vers la tombe*, Op. 39 no. 2. Published by Heugel & Cie, Paris. In extremely fragile condition. The last stave of the second page of the piece (p. 9) has one bar added in ink in composer's hand

   c. *Vers le caprice*, Op. 39 no. 3. Published by Heugel & Cie, Paris. In extremely fragile condition. Contains pencil markings of fingering throughout

   d. *Vers l'amour*, Op. 39 no. 4. Published by Heugel & Cie, Paris. In extremely fragile condition. Contains pencil markings of fingering throughout

   e. *Vers la joie*, Op. 39 no. 5. Published by Heugel & Cie, Paris. In extremely fragile condition. Contains pencil markings of fingering throughout and text changes in pencil and ink on the last 3 pages of the piece, entered in composer's hand

   f. *Aspirations* Op. 39 [complete]. With title page: *Aspirations | Poèmes pour piano etc.* Published by Heugel & Cie, Paris (large-size edition). Cover in fragile condition, the remaining score in fair condition

   g. *Aspirations* Op. 39: single copy edition of *Vers l'amour*. Published by Heugel & Cie, Paris (large-size edition). In fragile condition

   h. *Aspirations* Op. 39: single copy edition of *Vers la joie*. Published by Heugel & Cie, Paris (large-size edition). In fragile condition

   i. An incomplete score of *Aspirations* Op. 39, containing *Vers l'azur* Op. 39 no. 1, and the first page of *Vers la tombe*, Op. 39 no. 2. Smaller version of the Heugel & Cie, Paris edition above. In very fragile condition. Includes pencil markings of fingering throughout

   j. A series of stapled sets of photocopies of *Aspirations* Op. 39 with the original title page

5. Folder: *Au soir pour piano*, Op. 15 no. 3. Published by Stanley Lucas, Weber, Pitt & Hatzfeld Ltd. London and Leipzig. Color title pages (2 copies); the score and cover in extremely fragile condition

6. Folder: *Aus Sturm und Stille*, Op. 29. *Sechs Klavierstücke*. Published by Peters, Leipzig. Fragile condition

7. Folder: *Chant d'amour*, Op. 26 no. 3 for piano. Contains several copies of different editions and versions of the work:

   a. Published by B.F. Wood, Boston. On the cover: "not correct" in composer's hand. Annotations in blue and red pencil. Fair condition

   b. Published by Schirmer, Inc., New York. Revised edition. In very fragile condition. Contains pencil markings, fingering, pedal, and other annotations

      c. Published by Schirmer, Inc., New York. Revised edition. In fragile condition. Contains pencil markings, fingering, pedal, and other annotations, including "3'30" at the end [possibly timing for a recording]

      d. Published by Schirmer, Inc., New York. Revised edition. Green cover, score in fragile condition. Contains pencil markings, fingering, pedal, and other annotations, including "4.35" at the end

      e. Published by Schirmer, Inc., New York. Revised edition. Red cover, score in fragile condition. Contains an annotation "3'25" at the end

      f. Published by Schirmer, Inc., New York. Revised edition, more modern cover (1939?) with red border. Good condition, no annotations

      g. Published by Carl Fischer, New York. Contains fingering and other marking and the new ending, entered in pencil on the score in composer's hand

8. Folder: *Aubade pour Violon et Piano*. Published by Schott & Co., London. Arrangement by A. Kaiser for violin and piano of Stojowski's Op. 8 no. 3. Contains the vn & pf score and the solo violin part. Fair condition

9. Folder: *Concert in G für Violine von Sigismond Stojowski*, Op. 22. Contains two items:

      a. Small orchestral score (ca. 8 x 11 in / 19 x 27 cm), published by Arthur P. Schmidt—Boston, Leipzig, New York. Fair condition

      b. Piano-violin reduction with the violin solo part, published as above. Fragile condition

10. Folder: *Dumka* for piano. Contains two copies of the 1945 single work edition by Schirmer, New York. Fair condition

11. Folder: *Cinq Miniatures* Op. 19 [for piano]. Contains 1 copy of the set of five pieces (*Feuillet d'Album* | *Moment musical* | *Arabesque* | *Barcarolle* | *Mazurka*). Published by Heugel & Cie, Paris. Extremely fragile condition

12. Folder: *Concerto en fa # pour Piano et Orchestre par Sigismond Stojowski*, Op. 3. Two piano score. Includes fingering, penciled in by the composer [?]. Published by Stanley Lucas, Weber, Pitt & Hatzfeld Ltd., London & Leipzig. Outside cover missing—on the inside title page an ink stamp "Luisa Morales Macedo." Fair condition

CASE VII: STOJOWSKI—PUBLISHED WORKS (2)

1. Folder: *Prologue, Scherzo et Variations* (*2eme Concerto*), Op. 32. Contains full orchestral score, published by Heugel, Paris, with interpretative remarks, annotations and changes of text entered into the score. Very fragile, with the front cover torn. Paper clips indicate a cut in the last movement

2. Folder: *Prologue, Scherzo et Variations* (*2eme Concerto*). Contains orchestral parts (strings) – most are in fair condition:

   a. Violins I (8 copies)

   b. Violins II (8 copies)

   c. Violas (6 copies)

   d. Cellos (6 copies)

   e. Double-basses (8 copies)

3. Folder: *Prologue, Scherzo et Variations* (*2eme Concerto*). Contains orchestral parts (winds, percussion and harp) – most are in fair condition:

   a. Flutes 1-2-3, and Piccolo (2 copies)

   b. Oboe (1 copy)

   c. English Horn (1 copy)

   d. Clarinets (1 copy)

   e. Bassoons (1 copy)

   f. Horns 1–4 (2 copies)

   g. Trumpets 1–2 in F (1 copy)

   h. Trombones 1-2-3 (2 copies)

   i. Percussion (3 copies: Drum/Cymbals-Triangle-Snare Drums/Bells)

   j. Harp (1 copy)

CASE VIII: STOJOWSKI—PUBLISHED WORKS (3)

1. Folder: *Prologue, Scherzo et Variations* (*2eme Concerto*). Contains 5 copies of the 2 piano score – most are in poor condition, with covers torn, loose pages, etc.

2. Folder: *Prologue, Scherzo et Variations* (*2eme Concerto*). Contains orchestral parts (strings) – most are in fair condition:

   a. Violins I (4 copies)

   b. Violins II (4 copies)

   c. Violas (1 copy)

   d. Cellos (2 copies)

   e. Double-basses (3 copies)

3. Folder: *Prologue, Scherzo et Variations* (*2eme Concerto*). Contains orchestral parts (winds, percussion and harp) – most are in fair condition:

   a. Flutes 1-2-3, and Piccolo (2 copies)

   b. Oboe (1 copy)

c. English Horn (1 copy)

d. Clarinets (1 copy)

e. Bassoons (1 copy)

f. Horns 1–4 (2 copies)

g. Trumpets 1–2 in F (1 copy)

h. Trombones 1-2-3 (2 copies)

i. Percussion (3 copies: Drum/Cymbals-Triangle-Snare Drums/Bells)

j. Harp (1 copy)

CASE IX: STOJOWSKI—PUBLISHED WORKS (4)

1. Folder: *Danses Humoresques pour Piano*, Op. 12. Contains single editions of the following:

   a. Mazurka, Op. 12 no. 3

   b. *Cracovienne*, Op. 12 no. 4, published by Stanley Lucas, Weber, Pitt & Hatzfeld Ltd., London and Leipzig. In poor condition. (3 copies, one bound; one with extensive fingering markings)

   c. *Cracovienne*, Op. 12 no. 4, published by Stanley Lucas, Weber, Pitt & Hatzfeld Ltd., London and Leipzig. In poor condition

   d. *Cosaque fantastique*, Op. 12 no. 6, published by Stanley Lucas, Weber, Pitt & Hatzfeld Ltd., London and Leipzig. In poor condition

   e. *Cracovienne*, Op. 12 no. 4, published by Augener & Co., London. In fair condition

2. Folder: *Fantaisie pour Trombone Ténor avec accompagnement de Piano*. Published by Evette & Schaeffer, Paris. Written for the 1905 Conservatoire National de Musique competition. 2 copies of the piano-trombone score. Extremely fragile condition

3. Folder: *Deux Caprices pour Piano*, Op. 16. Published by Stanley Lucas, Weber, Pitt & Hatzfeld Ltd., London and Leipzig. In fragile condition. Contains 3 copies (one copy bound) of Op. 16 no. 2 only

4. Folder: *Fantaisie pour Piano*, Op. 38. Published by Heugel & Cie., Paris. Contains three copies of the work, two with blue pencil markings indicating corrections for the engraver. In fragile condition

5. Folder: *Quatre Morceaux*, Op. 5. Contains three copies of Mazurka, Op. 5 no. 4. Published by Stanley Lucas, Weber, Pitt & Hatzfeld Ltd., London and Leipzig; 2 copies in poor condition. One copy (published by Schott?) in fair condition

6. Folder: [Piano pieces] Op. 8. Contains:

   a. Two copies of *Légende,* Op. 8 no. 1 (large and small sized scores), published by Stanley Lucas, Weber, Pitt & Hatzfeld Ltd., London and Leipzig; in fair condition

   b. One copy of Mazurka, Op. 8 no. 2, published by Stanley Lucas, Weber, Pitt & Hatzfeld Ltd., London and Leipzig. In fair condition

7. Folder: *Deux Pensées musicales pour Piano*, Op. 1. Contains:

   a. Two copies of *Mélodie,* Op. 1 no. 1, published by Schott & Co. In fragile condition

   b. One copy of *Mélodie,* Op. 1 no. 1, transcribed by Reginald Goss Custard for organ. Published by Schott, Mainz. Contains pencil corrections and amendments to the arrangement, entered possibly by the composer. In fair condition

8. Folder: *Deux Caprices-Etudes pour Piano*, Op. 2. Contains one copy of *Fileuse*, Op. 2 no. 1, published by Augener Ltd. In fair condition

9. Folder: *Poème d'Eté—Quatre Morceaux pour Piano*, Op. 36. Contains two copies of *Fleurettes*, Op. 36 no. 3, published by Schirmer, New York. Both versions have hand-entered fingering indications, the smaller score is signed "Stojowski" [possibly in Stojowski's hand] top right. In fair condition

10. Folder: *Morceaux pour Piano*. Contains three copies of *Gondoliera*, Op. 5 no. 3

    a. Published by Theodore Presser, Philadelphia (illustrated cover)
    b. Published by Theodore Presser, Philadelphia (plain cover)
    c. Published by Stanley Lucas, Weber, Pitt & Hatzfeld Ltd., London and Leipzig. In fragile condition

11. Folder: *3 Esquisses pour Piano*, Op. 30. Contains two copies of *Feuilles mortes*, Op. 30 no. 2. Published by Arthur P. Schmidt, Boston, Leipzig, New York, and Alfred Lengnick, London.

12. Folder: *Cinq Mélodies | Pięć Pieśni* Op. 11. Contains the piano-vocal score of the entire set, published by Schott & Co. Inscribed in Polish and dated Paris, 28 September 1908, on the inside cover to Madame Marcellina Sembich-Stengel by the composer. In fair condition

Bibliography

WRITINGS BY ZYGMUNT STOJOWSKI

- Stojowski, Zygmunt (Sigismond). *The Art of Chopin* (Unpublished lecture notes). Six typewritten pages, ZLSC.
- ——. "Chopin." *The Polish Review* vol. 3 no. 18 (May 17, 1943), 8–10, 14.
- ——. "Chopin and Liszt Still Supreme" (Interview). *Musical America* (December 3, 1910). Stojowski Clipping File, IPAM.
- ——. *The Chopin Mazurkas*. (Annotated commentary to an unpublished edition of the *Mazurkas*), (1945–1946); ca. 50 single-spaced typewritten pages, ZLSC.
- ——. "Chopin Program Address" (An address given for Polish Relief Benefit at the Syracuse Museum of Fine Arts after an All-Chopin Program on December 9, 1939). *Bulletin of the Stojowski Students' Association.* (January 1940), 3–4, ZLSC and PIASA Archives, collection no. 43 folder no. 24.
- ——. "Chopin's 'First Impromptu'" (A Master Lesson). *The Etude* vol. 33 no. 2 (February 1915), 107–109.
- ——. "Chopin's 'Military Polonaise'" (A Master Lesson). *The Etude* vol. 44 no. 2 (February 1926), 110–113; also in Johnson as "Polonaise in A Major, Op. 40, no. 1."
- ——. *Chopin's Piano Music* [author's title]. (The lecture notes for one of Stojowski's Juilliard Summer School lecture-recital courses, dating from ca. 1943–1946.) ca. 100 typewritten pages; first two pages missing, ZLSC.
- ——. "Day of Mediocrity in Piano Music" (Interview). *Musical America* (November 23, 1912), Stojowski Clipping File, DPL.
- ——. Death Certificate. Slonimsky Collection, Box 236 Folder 14. Library of Congress, Washington, D.C.
- ——. "Dwa oblicza postępu w muzyce" [Two Aspects of Progress in Music]. *Muzyka* vol. 14 no. 6 (June 1937), 186–188.

- ———. "Eastern Europe and the American Dream." Five-page typewritten speech with handwritten addition on sixth page (December 4, 1944), ZLSC.
- ———. "Evolution of Style and Interpretation in Piano Literature" (Summary of a course given at the summer session of the Juilliard Institute of Musical Art). *Keyboard* vol. 2 no. 4 (November 1940), 2–3, 43–44, 47.
- ———. "The Future of Futurism?" *The Etude* vol. 34 no. 5 (May 1916), 332.
- ·· ———. "German Schemes vs. Polish Aims" (written under the pseudonym Anthony D. Jordan). Free Poland [a semi-monthly published by the Polish National Council in Washington, DC], December 16, 1917, Lineback Collection. ZLSC.
- ———. *Glimpses of Polish History* (A prologue to the historical pageant *A Night in Poland* given at the Hotel Biltmore on Thursday, April 8, 1915, by the American Relief Committee of New York). New York Public Library, microfilm of printed program: 7 pages.
- ———. "The Greatness That Was Paderewski." *The Polish Review* vol. 5 no. 2? (August 9, 1943), 13–14.
- ———. "Greetings to Paderewski from the 'Koło Polskie'" [Polish Circle], in *An Album of Greetings to Paderewski on the Tenth Anniversary of the Independence of Poland.* New York: The Kosciuszko Foundation, 1928.
- ———. "Has the Art of the Piano Reached Its Zenith or Is It Capable of Further Development?" (Conference of a group of the foremost pianists of the day, including Stojowski, Jonás, Grainger, Bauer, Hofmann, Gabrilowitsch, Hutcheson and Lambert). *The Etude* vol. 37 no. 2 (February 1919), 79.
- ———. "Ignacy Jan Paderewski," in *Piano Mastery: Talks with Master Pianists and Teachers* by Harriette Brower. New York: Frederick A. Stokes Co., 1915, 2–11.
- ———. "In Honor of Paderewski." (An address given at the Cosmopolitan Club in Montclair, NJ, on October 18, 1941). *Bulletin of the Stojowski Students' Association* (December 1941), 1–2. PIASA Archives, collection no. 43 no. 24.
- ———. Interview with Stojowski from *El Comercio*, Lima: August 1934, in *Stojowski Students' Bulletin* (Feb 1935), 1, 4, ZLSC.
- ———. Letter to Coolidge, Elizabeth S. 1924. Elizabeth S. Coolidge Archive, Box 96. Library of Congress, Washington, D.C.
- ———. Letter to Grainger, Percy. November 28, 1923, two-page handwritten. Percy Grainger Collection, Library of Congress, Washington, D.C.
- ———. Letters to Hofmann, Józef. Undated ca. 1915, four-page handwritten; November 20, 1918, four-page handwritten; March 19, 1926, four-page handwritten; June 9, 1927, two-page handwritten; April 3, 1935, two-page handwritten; International Piano Archives at Maryland (Letters on loan to Gregor Benko), University of Maryland, College Park.
- ———. Letters to Loesser, Arthur (Short handwritten notes). May 17, 1910; Jan 27, 1912; May 3, 1916; Arthur Loesser Collection, International Piano Archives at Maryland, University of Maryland, College Park.

- ———. Letters to Łabuński, Feliks. K-LXXXIII/40, K-LXXXIII/65 and K-LXXXIII/68 (1945–1946). Warsaw University Library, Archives of Twentieth-Century Polish Composers.

- ———. Letters to Mickiewicz, Maria (Mariotka). Twenty-six letters from Zygmunt, two of which are concluded by the composer's wife Luisa, and one letter from Władysław Stojowski. The Polish Library in Paris, Call No. 2272. The letters are addressed to Mlle Marie Mickiewicz, 7, Rue Guénégand, Paris and date from 1906 to 1939.

- ———. Letter to Paderewski, Ignacy J. October 19, 1905, Paderewski Archives, File 3702, AAN.

- ———. Letter to Paderewski, Ignacy J. April 20, 1938, Paderewski Archives, File 3702, AAN.

- ———. Letters to Schmidt, Arthur P. Arthur P. Schmidt Company Archive, General Correspondence, Box 71, Library of Congress, Washington, D.C.

- ———. Letter to Stojowski, Ignatius. April 11, 1946, ZLSC.

- ———. "Mendelssohn's 'Rondo Capriccioso' " (A Master Lesson). *The Etude*, vol. 31 no. 12 (December 1913), 864–871.

- ———. "Mendelssohn's 'Spinning Song, Op. 67, No. 4'" (A Master Lesson). *The Etude* vol. 34 no. 11 (November 1916), 783–784; also in Johnson.

- ———. "Mind in Piano Study," in *Piano Mastery: Talks with Master Pianists and Teachers* by Harriette Brower. New York: Frederick A. Stokes Co., 1915, 25–31.

- ———. "Mozart's 'Fantasia in D Minor'" (A Master Lesson). *The Etude*, vol. 32 no. 5 (May 1914), 346–349.

- ———. "The Music of Poland." *Poland America,* vol. 6 no. 8 (August 1925) and vol. 6, no. 9 (September 1925), 455–458, 486–490, 527–529, and 558–561.

- ———. "On Performing a Chopin Mazurka" (Commentary on *Mazurka in C Minor*, Op. 30, No. 1). *Clavier,* vol. 9 no. 9 (December 1970), 20–21.

- ———. "An Open Letter" (to the Students' Association about his 1929 trip to Poland). *Stojowski Students' Association Bulletin.* (1929): only the typewritten manuscript could be found in ZLSC.

- ———. "Our Music Culture Due to Women" (Interview with K.C.). *Musical America* (March 30, 1912). Stojowski Clipping File, IPAM.

- ———. "Outline of Polish Music." *Poland America*, vol. 13 no. 5 (May 1932), 204–213.

- ———. *Paderewski Anniversary 1945* (A five-page typewritten text of a radio interview with Stojowski and Mr. Milo). ZLSC, 5 typewritten pages.

- ———. "Paderewski as I Knew Him (1884–1941)," in *Intimate Memories of Paderewski* by Marguerite Merington. (An unpublished biography) New York: Polish Institute of Arts and Sciences of America Archives (PIASA), Marguerite Merington Papers, Collection No. 43, Folder No. 16, 18 pages. Later edited and annotated by Joseph A. Herter and presented as a paper at the 62nd Annual

Meeting of PIASA at Northeastern University in Boston on June 4, 2004.
Later published in *The Polish Review*, vol. 49 no. 4 (2004), 1027–1043. Later
published in a shortened Polish edition as "Paderewski jakim go znałem."*Ruch
Muzyczny*, vol. 50 no. 8 (April 16, 2006), 28–33.

- ———. "Paderewski, the Unique" (Written on Paderewski's 75th Anniversary).
Poland America, vol. 13 no. 5 (May 1932), 221–223.

- ———. "Paderewski w świetle moich wspomnień i wierzeń" [Paderewski in
the Light of My Recollections and Beliefs]. Życie Muzyczne i Teatralne no.
5/6 (1935), 5–11. English translation by Marek Żebrowski in *Polish Music
Journal* vol. 5 no. 2, Winter 2002: http://www.usc.edu/dept/polish_music/PMJ/
issue/5.2.02/paderewskistojowski.html

- ———. *Poland and the Present War.* Nineteen typewritten pages, London,
September 22, 1914, Harold Lineback Collection. ZLSC.

- ———. *Poland at War*. Ten typewritten pages, Harold Lineback Collection.
ZLSC.

- ———. "Poland's Right at Peace Table" (written under the pseudonym Anthony
D. Jordan). Free Poland [a semi-monthly published by the Polish National
Council in Washington, DC], (January 1, 1918), 83–85. Lineback Collection.
ZLSC.

- ———. *Poland's Share in War and Peace.* Twelve typewritten pages, Harold
Lineback Collection. ZLSC.

- ———. "Poland's Struggle." *The North American Review* (January-June 1920).

- ———. "Polish Music Festival at Carnegie Hall" (Excerpt of an address given on
May 4, 1944). *The Polish Review* vol. 4 no. 17 (May 3, 1944), 15.

- ———. "Polish Musicians Relief." (Zestawienie wpływów i wydatków, 1941–
1942) [Summary of Income and Spending, 1941–1942]. ZLSC.

- ———. "Postęp prawdziwy i urojony" [Real and Imaginary Progress]. *Muzyka*
vol. 9 no. 3/4 (March-April 1932), 74–76.

- ———. *The Poles, the Jews and the World's Peace.* An address, eight typewritten
pages, (May 25, 1919), Lineback Collection. ZLSC.

- ———. "Practice as Art." *The Etude* vol. 55 no. 9 (September 1937), 565–566,
614, 616.

- ———. "Prawda psychologiczna w muzyce" [The Psychological Truth in Music].
Muzyka vol. 6 no. 4 (April 20, 1929), 197–200.

- ———. Program Notes for the Philharmonic-Symphony Society of New York's
4th Young People's Concert, December 29, 1930, with pianist Ignacy J.
Paderewski, Ernest Schilling conducting, Carnegie Hall. Program: Noskowski,
Symphonic Poem *Step,* Op. 66; Stojowski *Intermède Polonaise* from *Suite,* Op.
9; Paderewski (arr. Henryk Opieński) *Deux Danses Montagnardes* from *Tatra
Album,* Op. 12 & *Concerto in A Minor,* Op. 17; Chopin Selected Piano Pieces.

- ——. *Quelques Reflections sur la Symbole en Musique*. Nine typewritten pages, Mills College, 1934, Harold Lineback Collection. ZLSC.

- ——. "Recollections of Brahms." *Musical Quarterly* vol. 19 (April 1933), 143–150.

- ——. *Reminiscences of Sigismond Stojowski*. Five-page typewritten manuscript, Harold Lineback Collection. ZLSC.

- ——. Résumé. *Biographical Data* (ca. 1919), four typewritten pages with hand-entered corrections and additions in the margins. ZLSC.

- ——. Résumé. *Biographical Note* (posthumous, ca. 1947), two typewritten pages. ZLSC.

- ——. Résumé. *Untitled Résumé* (ca. 1940), one typewritten page intended for the U.S. Immigration Service.

- ——. "Revealing the Composer's Hidden Meaning" (An interview). *The Etude* vol. 29 no. 9 (September 1911), 591–592; also in Johnson.

- ——. "Romantyzm w dobie współczesnej" [Romanticism in Contemporary Times]. *Muzyka* vol. 5 no. 7/9 (July-September 1932), 99–100.

- ——. "Rubinstein's 'Barcarole in F Minor'" (A Master Lesson). *The Etude* vol. 31 no 1 (January 1913), 28, 72; also in Johnson.

- ——. "Schubert-Liszt's 'Hark, Hark, the Lark' " (A Master Lesson). *The Etude* vol. 33 no. 2 (February 1914): pp. 106, 135; also in Johnson.

- ——. "Schubert's 'Moment Musical in F Minor'" (A Master Lesson). *The Etude* vol. 31 no. 4 (April 1913), 258: also in Johnson.

- ——. "Schumann's 'Nachtstück in F Major'" (A Master Lesson). *The Etude* vol. 31 no. 5 (May 1913).

- ——. Telegram to President Franklin D. Roosevelt. (December 16, 1944), ZLSC.

- ——. "A Tribute to Ernest Schelling." *Bulletin of Stojowski Students' Association.* (January 1940), 2–3, ZLSC and PIASA Archives, collection no. 43 folder no. 24.

- ——. *W 95. Rocznicę. Słowo wstępne do rekordów muzyki Chopina nadanych przez Office of War Information do Polskiej Walczącej ku uczczeniu pamięci Chopina zmarłego dnia 17. października 1849 roku.* [On the 95th Anniversary. An Introduction to the Recordings of Chopin's Music Broadcast by the Office of War Information to Poland-at-War, in Honor of the Memory of Chopin, who Passed Away on October 17, 1849.] (October 1944), 4 typewritten pages, ZLSC.

- ——. "Wezwanie na koncert 4 maja" [An Appeal for the May 4th Concert]. *Tygodnik Polski –The Polish Weekly* vol. 2 no. 18 [70] (April 30, 1944), 11.

- ——."What Interpretation Really Is," in *Great Pianists on Piano Playing* by Francis Cooke. Philadelphia: Theo. Presser Co., ca. 1917, (Reprint. New York: AMS Press, 1966), 279–287. [Preceded on p. 278 with a biographical sketch followed by a one-page, unnumbered portraiture photograph of ZS.]

- ——. *What is Music?*, 2 typewritten pages, ZLSC.
- ——. "What the Pianist of Tomorrow Must Posses—A Conference with Sigismond Stojowski Secured Expressly for *The Etude* by Benjamin Brooke." *The Etude* vol. 53 no. 11 (November 1940), 730, 771.
- ——. "Wherever There Is No Music, Life Also Ceases" (An address given in April 1944 at the Polish Consulate in NY). *Bulletin of the Polish Institute of Arts and Sciences in America,* vol. 2 no. 4 (July 1944), 1197–1200.
- ——. "Why Poland Must Be Free." The New York Evening Post, January 18, 1919, Harold Lineback Collection. ZLSC.
- ——. "W imię prawdy w dźwiękach" [In the Name of Truth in Sound]. [Part 1] *Muzyka* vol. 5 no. 10 (January 20, 1928), 15–18; [Part 2] vol. 7 no. 10 (October 20, 1929), 430–435.
- ——. "Względność prawdy a szczerość ideału" [The Relativity of Truth and the Sincerity of the Ideal]. *Muzyka* vol. 5 no. 3 (March 20, 1928), 104–111.

OTHER SOURCES

- Adrianowska, Kazimiera A. "Zygmunt Stojowski." *Biały Orzeł* vol. 6 (June 1944): 6–7.
- Aldrich, Richard. *Concert Life in New York.* New York: G. P. Putnam's Sons, 1941.
- Anon. "Antonia Brico, pierwszy dyrygent-kobieta w Warszawskiej Filharmonii" [Antonia Brico, the First Woman Conductor at the Warsaw Philharmonic]." *Bluszcz* no. 43 (October 24, 1931), 12–13.
- ____. "Chwila Bieżąca" [The Current Moment]. *Biesiada Literacka* no. 43 (October 25, 1901), 334.
- ——. "Colony Club Hears Stojowski Program." *Musical America* (March 19, 1910), 27, Stojowski Clipping File, NYPLPA.
- ____. "Conservatoire de Fontainebleau." *Le Ménestrel* vol. 83 no. 39 (September 30, 1921), 384.
- ——. "Fourteen Pianists Join Forces to Aid Moszkowski." *Musical America* (January 1922), 5, ZLSC.
- ——. "In the Realms of Music." *Christian Science Monitor* (January 28, 1910), 9.
- ——. "The Lady and the Fan." Undated clipping [between November 1946 and 1952?]. Scrapbook, Marcella Sembrich Opera Museum, Lake George, New York.
- ——. "Metropolitan Sunday Evening Concert, Apr 2." *Musical Courier* (April 1911), Stojowski Clipping File, NYPLPA.

- ——. "A New Cultural Endeavor, Polish Institute of Arts and Letters Formally Opened at the Roerich Museum in New York." *Poland America* vol. 13 no. 5 (May 1932), 219.
- ——. "New Haven Hears Stojowski Play." *Musical America* (March 2, 1907), Stojowski Clipping File, NYPLPA.
- ——. "Paris et Départaments" [Chopin Anniversary]. *Le Ménestrel* vol. 66 no. 1 (January 7, 1900), 6.
- ——. "Paul Kochanski, Noted Violinist, Passes Away after Long Illness." *Musical America* vol. 54 no. 1 (January 25, 1934), 33.
- ——. "Polish Pianist Greets Old Pupils after Concert at Albany Institute." (November 1923), ZLSC.
- ——. "Polska w Ameryce" [Poland in America]. *Świat* no. 3 (January 17, 1920), 8.
- ——. "Popular Pacific Coast Piano Duo." *Christian Science Monitor* (January 10. 1931), 14.
- ——. "Press Comments on Concerts of Compositions by Sigismond Stojowski Given at Carnegie Hall New York with the New York Philharmonic Orchestra March 1, 1915." *Musical Courier* (March 17, 1915), 33.
- ——. "A Priceless Fan." *International Music and Drama* (January 21, 1915), 8–9, ZLSC.
- ——. *Program Notes for 'Rapsodie symphonique, Op. 23.'* London Symphony Orchestra (June 7, 1908), ZLSC.
- ——. *Program Notes for 'Rapsodie symphonique, Op. 23.'* San Francisco Symphony Orchestra (August 26, 1930), ZLSC.
- ——. Publicity poster: *Here and There with Stojowski, Celebrated Composer Pianist*, Season 1921–1922, ZLSC.
- ——. "Sigismond Stojowski's Tour." *Musical America* (October 14, 1911), Stojowski Clipping File, NYPLPA.
- ——. "Society Revives Poland's Past as Spectacle, Proceeds for War Sufferers $10,000." *The New York City Herald* (April 9, 1915), Marcella Sembrich Scrapbooks, NYPLPA.
- ——. "Stojowski Admires American Energy: Distinguished Pianist and Composer a Man of Broad Intellectual Development." *Musical America* (November 3, 1906), Stojowski Clipping File, NYPLPA.
- ——. "Stojowski Artist-Pupil Recital for Polish Victims Relief Fund." *Musical Courier* (May 25, 1916), Stojowski Clipping File, NYPLPA.
- ——. "Stojowski Conducts Class at Mills College." *Musical America* vol. 54 no. 12 (1934), 30.
- ——. "Stojowski Heard in Cornish School Recital." *Musical America* vol. 51 no. 14 (September 1931), 11.

- ———. "Stojowski Historical Piano Recitals." *The Musical Courier* (February 8, 1911), 47, ZLSC, Stojowski Clipping File, NYPLPA.
- ———. "Stojowski in Anniversary Recital." *Musical America* vol. 51 no. 5 (March 10, 1931), 39.
- ———. "Stojowski Reopens NY Studio." *Musical America* vol. 54 no. 17 (November 10, 1934), 30.
- ———. "Stojowski Symphony Played in Boston." *The Christian Science Monitor* (January 17, 1920), 14.
- ———. "Stojowski to Mark Twenty-fifth Year in America with NY Recital." *Musical America* vol. 51 no. 4 (February 25, 1931), 30.
- ———. "Stojowski to Return to Concert Field after Six Years' Interval" (June 1921). Unidentified press clipping. Stojowski Clipping File, DPL.
- ———. "Stojowski wygłosił odczyt o Chopinie i grał utwory Chopinowskie" [Stojowski Lectured on Chopin and Performed Chopin's Compositions]. Press clipping from one of the Chicago Polish newspapers ca. April 17, 1945, ZLSC.
- ———. "Woman's [sic!] Symphony under Brico in Debut before Invited Audience." *Musical America,* vol. 55 no. 4 (February 25, 1935), 11.
- ———. "Z listów do 'Bluszczu'" [From Letters to 'Bluszcz']. *Bluszcz* no. 49 (November 24, 1902), 585.
- Anthony, Dr. James R. *A History of the School of Music 1893–1985.* Tucson: University of Arizona School of Music, 1986.
- Armstrong, William. "Sigismond Stojowski and His Views on Piano Study." *The Etude* (ca. 1906), ZLSC.
- Balchin, Robert (ed.). "Stojowski, Zygmunt" in *The Catalogue of Printed Music in the British Library to 1980* vol. 54. London, Munich: K. G. Saur, 1986, 285–286.
- Bank Polski (London). Letter to Zygmunt Stojowski, September 12, 1941, Box 3 ZLSC.
- Baumann-Szulakowska, Jolanta. "Synteza uniwersalizmu i stylu narodowego w polskiej muzyce kameralnej przełomu XIX i XX w." [The Synthesis of Universalism and National Style in Polish Chamber Music at the Turn of the Nineteenth and Twentieth Centuries], in *Warsztat kompozytorski, wykonawstwo, koncepcje polityczne Ignacego Jana Paderewskiego,* eds. Wojciech Maria Marchwica and Andrzej Sitarz. Cracow: Musica Jagiellonica, 1991, 161–180.
- Bias, Iwona, Monika Bieda and Anna Stachura. Józef Stompel, moje życia z muzyką [Józef Stompel, My Life with Music]. Katowice: Akademia Muzyczna im. K. Szymanowskiego, 2003.
- Blejwas, Stanislaus A. *The Polish Singers Alliance of America, Choral Patriotism.* Rochester, New York: University of Rochester Press, 2005.
- Boehm, Jan. *Feliks Nowowiejski, Zarys Biograficzny* [Feliks Nowowiejski, A Biographical Outline]. Olsztyn: Pojezierze, 1968.

- Bongrain, Anne and Alain Porter in collaboration with Marie-Hélène Coudray-Saghaï. *Le Conservatoire de Paris, Deux cents ans de pédagogie 1795–1995.* Paris: Bucht/Chastel, 1999.

- Boros, James and Robert Moevs. "A Conversation with Robert Moevs." *Perspectives of New Music,* vol. 28 no. 1 (Winter 1990), 324–335.

- Boston, Margie Viola. *An Essay on the Life and Works of Léo Delibes.* Dissertation, Iowa City: The University of Iowa, 1981 (Ann Arbor: University Microfilms International, 2001).

- Bowers, Jane and Judith Task. *Women Making Music.* Urbana, Illinois: University of Illinois Press, 1987.

- Brachocki, Alexander. "Here Comes the Bride" in Herter's Aleksander Brachocki, protegowany Stojowskiego i polsko-amerykański uczeń Paderewskiego. *Ruch Muzyczny* vol. 50, no. 18, Part two (September 3, 2006).

- Brown, David. *Tchaikovsky, the Final Years (1885–1893), A Biographical and Critical Study, Vol. 4.* London: Victor Gollancz Ltd., 1991.

- Burgone, Arthur. G. "Stokowski and Stojowski," in the column "All to the Point," in *The Pittsburgh Chronicle Telegraph* (ca. February 20, 1912), ZLSC; reprinted in the *Musical Courier* (March 6, 1912).

- Bychowska, Maria and Henryk Schiller (eds.). *100 Lat Filharmonii w Warszawie* [100 Years of the Philharmonic in Warsaw]. Warsaw: Filharmonia Narodowa, 2001.

- Centkiewicz, Stanisław L. "In Memoriam Sigismond Stojowski." *The Polish Review* vol. 6 no. 20 (November 28, 1946), 4.

- Chasins, Abram. *Leopold Stojowski—A Profile.* New York: Hawthorn Books, 1979.

- Cherkassky, Shura. Letter of Condolence to Luisa Stojowska, two pages, undated, ca. end of 1946, ZLSC.

- Chomiński, Józef (ed.). *Słowik muzyków polskich* [Dictionary of Polish Musicians] vols. 1–2. Cracow: Polskie Wydawnictwo Muzyczne, 1964.

- Chybiński, Adolf. *Chopin a muzyka polska* [Chopin and Polish Music]. *Widnokręgi,* 1910 no. 1 in *Antologia Polskiej Krytyki Muzycznej XIX i XX w.* ed. Stefan Jarociński, Polskie Wydawnictwo Muzyczne. Cracow: 1955, p. 322.

- Chylińska, Teresa. *Karol Szymanowski Correspondence, Vol. 1 1903–1919.* Cracow: Polish Music Publishers (PWM), 1994.

- ——. *Karol Szymanowski Correspondence, Vol. 2 1920–1926 * to 1923.* Cracow: Polish Music Publications (PWM), 1994.

- ——. *Karol Szymanowski Correspondence, Vol. 3 1927–1931 ** 1929.* Cracow: Musica Jagiellonica, 1997.

- Clark, Kenneth S. "Hopes of Poland Crystallized in Stojowski's New Cantata." *Musical America* (February 26, 1916), Stojowski Clipping File, NYPLPA.

- Coleman, Arthur and Marion. *Mickiewicz in Song, 25 Songs to Poems of Mickiewicz*. New York: Klub Polski/Columbia University, 1947.

- Collins, Judy (Writer, director and producer). *Antonia: A Portrait of the Woman*. DVD Pioneer Artists PA-11982, a 2003 reissue of the 1974 documentary film.

- Conrad, Joseph. "Prince Roman" in *The Complete Short Fiction of Joseph Conrad,* Volume 2. New York: ECCO Press, ca. 1991.

- Cooke James E. *Great Pianists on Piano Playing, Study Talks with Foremost Virtuosos*. Philadelphia: T. Presser Co., 1917.

- Cooper, Frank. Liner notes for *Sigismond Stojowski plays Chopin, Paderewski and Stojowski; Luisa Stojowska Plays the Music of Stojowski*. New York: International Piano Archives (IPA) 115, 1976.

- ——. "100 Years Later, the Centenary of an Extraordinary Musician." *Clavier* IX no. 9 (1970), 14–19.

- Curzon, Henri de. *Léo Delibes: sa vie et ses oeuvres*. Paris: G. Legouix, 1926.

- Cushing, Edward. "Musical Censorship." *The Brooklyn Eagle* (March 27, 1932).

- Damrosch, Frank. *Institute of Musical Art 1904–1926*. New York: Juilliard School of Music, 1936.

- ——. *History of the Institute of Musical Art, Appendix*. New York: Juilliard School of Music, ca. 1936.

- Dandelot, A. "L'Exposition d'Autographes de Bibliothèque de l'Opera, Compositeurs Anciens." *Le Monde musical* vol. 12 no. 22 (December 15, 1900), 355.

- ——. "L'Exposition d'Autographes de Bibliothèque de l'Opera, Russie-Pologne." *Le Monde musical* vol. 12 nos. 23–24 (December 30, 1900), 57.

- Dane, Jeffrey. *Notes on Film Music*. 2001: http://inditer.com/dane/movies/music.intro

- Davies, Norman. *A History of Poland Vol. II—1795 to the Present*. Oxford: Clarendon Press, 1981.

- Debussy, Claude. *Debussy on Music: The Critical Writings of the Great French Composer Claude Debussy* / collected and introduced by François Lesure / translated and edited by Richard Langham Smith. New York: A. A. Knopf (first American edition), 1977.

- Delibes, Léo. Three Letters to Paderewski, March 23, 1889; June 13?; undated. Warsaw: Paderewski Archives 3492, 186–189, 192–194, 198–200, AAN. (N.B. Delibes' name is misspelled in the archives' catalogue.)

- ——. Letter to Stojowski. Undated ca. 1887. Property of the composer's great-granddaughter Lisa Stojowski.

- Detroit Foundation Music School. *Brochure for Summer Master Classes with Sigismond Stojowski* (July 27–August 22, 1942), ZLSC.

- Downes, Olin. "Sigismond Stojowski's Recital." *The New York Times* (February 22, 1925).

- Drobner, Mieczysław. *Wspomnienia o początkach życia muzycznego w Polsce Ludowej 1944–1946* [Remembering the Beginnings of Musical Life in the Peoples' Republic of Poland 1944–1946]. Cracow: Polskie Wydawnictwo Muzyczne, 1985.

- Dubal, David. *The Art of the Piano*. New York: Summit Books, 1989.

- Dunham, Charlotte. Letter to Werner Fuchs, founder of Musée Paderewski in Morges, Switzerland. Aug 12, 1981. R.189, Paderewski Museum, Morges.

- Dybowski, Stanisław. *Aleksander Michałowski, Rzecz o wielkim chopiniście i muzycznej Warszawie jego czasów*. [On Alexander Michałowski, the Great Interpreter of Chopin and Warsaw of his Era] Warsaw: Selene, 2005.

- ———. *Laureaci konkursów chopinowskich* [Laureates of the Chopin Competitions]. Warszawa: Selene, 2005.

- ———. "Rapsodia czy fantazja?" [Rhapsody or Fantasia?] *Ruch Muzyczny* vol. 46 no. 11 (May 26, 2002), 34.

- ———."Zapomniany Zygmunt Stojowski" [The Forgotten Zygmunt Stojowski]. *Ruch Muzyczny* vol. 46 no. 9 (April 28, 2002), 34–38.

- ———. "Zygmunt Stojowski" in *Słownik pianistów polskich* [Dictionary of Polish Pianists]. Warsaw: Selene, 2003.

- Echo Muzyczne, Teatralne i Artystyczne. Unsigned articles.

Title:	Issue:
Z Filharmonii	no. 951 (December 8, 1901), 561–562.
(Interview with Stojowski)	
'Kasia,' Opera Leona Delibes'a	no. 396 (May 2, 1891), 242.
Koncerty symfoniczne	no. 884 (August 26, 1900), 428.
Konkurs Paderewskiego	no. 779 (August 22, 1898), 442–443.
Kronika.	no. 396 (May 2, 1891), 242.
Konserwatoryum paryzkie	no. 309 (August 31, 1889), 441.
Listy z Paryża	no. 661 (May 18, 1896), 264.
Muzyka w roku 1897	no. 745 (December 27, 1897), 17.
Nasi artyści za granicą	no. 977 (June 8, 1902), 258.
Recenzja	no. 183 (1887),178.

- Ellis Island Passenger Records, Ship Manifests: S.S. La Provence, October 4,1907;

  S.S. La Savoie, October 8, 1910: http://www.ellisisland.org/search/matchMore. asp?MID=13543668000183090624&FNM=SIGISMOND&LNM=STOJOWSKI &PLNM=STOJOWSKI&CGD=M&bSYR=1869&bEYR=1871&first_kind=1&ki nd=exact&offset=0&dwpdone=1;

S.S. Amerika, October 18, 1913: http://www.ellisisland.org/search/passRecord.asp
?MID=13543668000183090624&FNM=SIGISMOND&LNM=STOJOWSKI&P
LNM=STOJOWSKI&CGD=M&bSYR=1869&bEYR=1871&first_kind=1&last_
kind=0&TOWN=null&SHIP=null&RF=3&ALTS=97%7Cstogowski&ALTS=97
%7Cstojouski&pID=100773010251;

S.S. Caronia, September 12, 1920: http://www.ellisisland.org/search/shipManifest.
asp?MID=13543668000183090624&FNM=MARY&LNM=STOJOWSKI&PLN
M=STOJOWSKI&CGD=F&bSYR=1849&bEYR=1851&first_kind=1&last_kind
=0&RF=1&pID=100254130344&.

- Elson, Louis Charles. *The History of American Music,* (Revised by Arthur Nelson). New York: McMillan Co., 1925.

- ———. "Paderewski and Symphony Concert—Pianist Triumphant and Crowd Adoring" (Review of Stojowski's Second Piano Concerto). *Boston Daily Advertiser* (March 1916), Press clipping from Paderewski Scrapbooks, Archiwum Akt Nowych, Warsaw.

- Eversman, Alice. "Piano Recitals Dominate Recent Musical Events: Master Class in Interpretation Performed Last Night under Direction of Sigismond Stojowski." *The Evening Star* (June 6, 1933), Washington, D.C.

- Filharmonia Warszawska. *Filharmonja Warszawska 1901–1931* [Warsaw Philharmonic's 30th Anniversary Booklet]. Warsaw: Filharmonia Warszawska, 1931.

- Fitelberg, Grzegorz. *Korespondencja Grzegorza Fitelberga z lat 1941–1953* [Leon Markiewicz (ed.)] [The Correspondence of Grzegorz Fitelberg from the Years 1941–1953]. Katowice: Fundacja Muzyczna Międzynarodowego Konkursu Dyrygentów im. Grzegorza Fitelberga, 2003.

- Frączkiewicz, Aleksander. "Koncert instrumentalny w II połowie XIX wieku" [The Instrumental Concerto during the Second Half of the Nineteenth Century], in *Z dziejów polskiej kultury muzyczny Vol. II*, eds. Stefania Łobaczewska et al. Cracow: Polskie Wydawnictwo Muzyczne, 1966, 445–462.

- Friskin, James and Irwin Freundlich. *Music for the Piano, A Handbook of Concert and Teaching Materials from 1580 to 1952.* New York: Dover Publications, 1973.

- Gamble, Frederick. Letter to Mr. Locklair. March 6, 1982. Stojowski File, Juilliard School Archives.

- Gillespie, John. *Notable Twentieth-Century Pianists.* Westport, Conn.: Greenwood Press, 1995.

- Gliński, Mateusz (ed.) "Romantyzm w muzyce" (Romanticism in Music) [Comments by Stojowski]. *Muzyka* vol. 7–9 (1928), 99–100.

- Gliński, Mateusz. "Z opery i sal koncertowych, Warsawa." *Muzyka* vol. 6 no. 10 (October 20, 1929), 445.

- Goldberg, Albert. "Abundant Concert Fare in Chicago." *Musical America* vol. 55 no. 18 (November 25, 1935), 30.

- Gooch, Bryan N.S. "Barbara Custance" in *Encyclopedia of Music in Canada*, 2nd edition, Toronto: University of Toronto Press, 1992. Online: http://www.thecanadianencyclopedia.com/index.cfm?PgNm=EMCSubjects&TCE_Version=U&mState=2

- Górecki, Tadeusz. "Zygmunt Stojowski," *Gazeta Literacka* vol. 4 no. 1 (October 1932), 12–13.

- Gottlieb, Jane, Stephen E. Novak and Taras Pavlovsky (eds.). *Guide to the Juillard School Archives*. New York. The Juillard School, 1992.

- Gronowicz, Antoni. *Paderewski, Pianist and Patriot*. Edinburgh: Thomas Nelson and Sons, 1944.

- Hale, Philip. *Program Notes for 'Piano Concerto No. 2, Op. 32.'* Boston Symphony Orchestra Concert of March 10 & 11, 1916, 1044–1050, Paderewski Archives, Warsaw, AAN.

- Halski, Czesław R. "Sigismond Stojowski," in *Grove's Dictionary of Music and Musicians* 5th ed. vol. 8. London: Macmillan, 1954, 97–98.

- Haughton, John Alan. "Marcella Sembrich: The Close of a Life of Triumphs." *Musical America*, vol. 55 no. 2 (January 25, 1935), 5, 17.

- Herter, Joseph A. "Aleksander Brachocki, protegowany Stojowskiego i polsko-amerykański uczeń Paderewskiego" [Alexander Brachocki, Stojowski Protégé and the Polish-American Pupil of Paderewski's]. *Ruch Muzyczny* vol. 50, Part one, no. 17 (August 20, 2006); Part two, no. 18, (September 3, 2006).

- ——. "Annotated Catalogue of Music by Zygmunt Stojowski." *Polish Music Journal* vol. 5 no. 2 (Winter 2002), online: http://www.usc.edu/dept/polish_music/PMJ/issue/5.2.02/stojowskiworks.html

- ——. "Elgar's 'Polonia' Updated," in *The Elgar Society Journal* vol. 12 no. 4 (March 2002), 156–159.

- ——. "The Etude's 1915 Musical Salute to Poland." *Polish Music Newsletter* vol. 7 no. 11 (November 2001), http://www.usc.edu/dept/polish_music/news/nov01.html

- ——. "The Life of Zygmunt Stojowski." *Polish Music Journal* vol. 5 no. 2 (Winter 2002), online: http://www.usc.edu/dept/polish_music/PMJ/issue/5.2.02/herterstojowski.html

- ——. Liner notes. Jonathan Plowright, pianist; Martyn Brabbins, cond. BBC Scottish Symphony Orchestra. *Piano Concertos Nos. 1 & 2* by Zygmunt Stojowski. London: Hyperion CDA67314, 2002.

- ——. Liner notes. Jonathan Plowright, pianist: *Stojowski Music for Piano*. London: Hyperion CDA67437, 2004.

- ——. "Schelling's 'A Night in Poland.'" *Polish Music Newsletter* vol. 7 no. 12 (December 2001), http://www.usc.edu/dept/polish_music/news/dec01.html

- ——. (ed.) "Stojowski and Stokowski: A Poem by Arthur G. Burgoyne." *Polish Music Journal* vol. 4 no. 1 (Summer 2001), http://www.usc.edu/dept/polish_music/PMJ/issue/4.1.01/stojowskipoem.html

• ——. "Stojowski: The Polish Patriot." *Polish Music Newsletter* vol. 9 no. 2 (February 2002), http://www.usc.edu/dept/polish_music/news/feb02. html#stojowski

• ——. "Zygmunt Stojowski and 'Piotr Czajkowski'." *Polish Music Newsletter* vol. 8 no. 3 (April 2001), http://www.usc.edu/dept/polish_music/news/apr01. html

• ——. *Zygmunt Stojowski—From Warsaw to the New York Polonia by Way of Paris.* A paper delivered at the International Symposium *Polen in Herzen – Komponieren in der Fremde* at the Universität der Künste in Berlin, 21–24 October 2004.

• ——. *Zygmunt Stojowski: Polish Patriot and Composer.* Paper delivered at the 60th Annual Meeting of the Polish Institute of Arts and Sciences of America at Georgetown University in Washington, D. C., June 7, 2002.

• Herx, Stephen. "Marcella Sembrich—A Legendary Singer's Career Rediscovered." *The Record Collector,* vol. 44 no 1, (March 1999), 2–28.

• ——. *Sembrich in America* (an unpublished biography of Marcella Sembrich), chapter 10.

• Himonet, A. "Rapsodie symphonique de M. Stojowski." *Le Courrier Musical* vol. 27 no. 19 (November 15, 1925), 539.

• Hinson, Maurice. *Music for Piano and Orchestra, an Annotated Guide.* Bloomington: Indiana University, 1981.

• Hofmann, Józef. Letters to Zygmunt Stojowski: August 9, 1915, four-page handwritten; January 8, 1919, two-page handwritten; April 4, 1924, one-page handwritten; February 18, 1926, one-page handwritten; March 3, 1926, two-page handwritten; June 9, 1927; September 13, 1931, one-page typewritten; International Piano Archives at Maryland, College Park, (Letters on loan to Gregor Benko).

• Hofmeister, Friedrich. *Handbuch der Musikalischen Literatur,* 1886–1891, 1892–1897, 1898–1908 L–Z. Leipzig: Friedrich Hofmeister.

• ——. *Verzeich erschienen Musikalen,* 1905, 1907, 1909–1911. Leipzig: Friedrich Hofmeister.

• Horszowski, Mieczysław. *Mieco—Remembrances of Mieczysław Horszowski.* Genova: Erga edizioni, 2002.

• Howard, John Tasker. *Our American Music.* New York: Thomas Y. Crowell Co., 1939.

• Huneker, James Gibbons. *The Philharmonic Society of New York and Its Seventy-Fifth Anniversary—A Retrospect—Early Histories of the New York Philharmonic.* New York: Da Capo Press, 1979.

• Hutcheson, Ernest and revised by Rudolph Ganz. *The Literature of the Piano, a Guide for Amateur and Student.* London: Hutchinson of London, 1969.

- Jachimecki, Zdzisław. *Żeleński*. Cracow: Polskie Wydawnictwo Muzyczne, 1956.

- Janaczewska-Sołomko, Katarzyna. *Dyskopedia poloników do roku 1918, v. 1–3*. [The Recording Catalogue of Polonica before 1918, vols. 1–3]. Warsaw: Biblioteka Narodowa, 2002.

- Jarociński, Stefan. *Antologia Polskiej krytyki muzycznej XIX wieku (do roku 1939)* [An Anthology of Nineteenth Century Polish Musical Criticism (to 1939)]. Cracow: Polskie Wydawnictwo Muzyczne, 1955.

- Jasieński, Jerzy. *Ignacy Jan Paderewski Antologia*. Poznań: Ars Nova, 1996.

- Jasiński, Roman. *Koniec epoki, muzyka w Warszawie (1927–1939)* [The End of an Epoch, Music in Warsaw 1927–1939]. Warsaw: Państwowy Instytut Wydawniczy, 1986.

- ———. Na przełomie epok, Muzyka w Warszawie (1910–1927) [At the End of an Era, Music in Warsaw 1910–1927]. Warsaw: Państwowy Instytut Wydawniczy, 1979.)

- Johnson, Jeffrey. *Piano Lessons in the Grand Style: from the Golden Age of 'The Etude' Music Magazine*. Mineola, New York: Dover Publications, 2003. (Contains four Stojowski "Master Lessons" cross-referenced in the Writings by Stojowski Bibliography.)

- Jonás, Alberto. *Master School of Modern Piano Playing and Virtuosity, Vol. 1*. New York: Carl Fischer, 1922.

- Juilliard School of Music. *Summer School Catalogues*. New York: Juilliard School of Music, 1932, 1940–1946.

- Juilliard School of Music. *Summer School Scrapbooks*. New York: Juilliard School of Music, 1932–1946.

- Kassern, Tadeusz. Letter to Luisa Stojowska, April 24, 1949, one-page handwritten, ZLSC.

- ———. "Poznań—koncerty symfoniczne—recitale [Poznań—Symphonic Concerts—Recitals]. *Muzyka* vol. 9 nos. 1–2 (January and February 1932), 38.

- Kipnis, Igor. "Archive Piano Recordings in Near Miracles of Restoration." *Stereo Review* 40 (April 1978), 126–127.

- Klein, Walther. "Polnisches Symphonie Konzert" (Review of Stojowski's Symphony in Vienna). *Musikblätter des Ansbruch* 6 (March 2, 1921), 121–122.

- Komorowska, Małgorzata. *Kobieta z głosem* [A Woman with a Voice], an unpublished biography of Marcella Sembrich.

- Kosciuszko Foundation Archives. The Edith Cullis Williams Papers, Box 38 Folders 1–11, New York.

- Kramarz, Henryka. *Tadeusz Rutkowski—Portret pozytywisty i demokraty galicyjskiego* [Tadeusz Rutkowski—A Positivistic and Democratic Portrait of Galicia]. Cracow: Wydawnictwo Naukowe Akademii Pedagogicznej, 2001.

- Krehbiel, H. E. "Program Notes for *Chant d'amour*, Op. 26, no 3." in *Analytical Notes on Mr. Paderewski's Programmes*, (American Tour of 1907–1908), Paderewski Archives, Warsaw, AAN.

- *Księga Heraldyczna Królestwa Polskiego* [Heraldic Register of the Kingdom of Poland], November 5/17, 1838, certificate no. 3234, page S, consecutive no. 420, signed January 12/24, 1840: ZLSC.

- *Księga Kawalerów 'Odrodzenia Polski', Obywatele Cudzoziemscy* [The Register of Commanders of the 'Polonia Restituta' Order, Foreign Citizens]. Warsaw: AAN, 1921–1937, 110.

- Kutsch, K. J. and Leo Riemens. *Grosses Sänger-Lexikon*, vols. 1–6, Munich: K. G. Sauer, 2003.

- Labunski, see: Łabuński.

- Landau, Roman. *Ignacy Paderewski, Musician and Statesman*. New York: Thomas Y. Crowell Co., 1932.

- Lednicki, Wacław. Letter to Stojowski. 1941. ZLSC.

- Leedy, Denoe. "Harold Randolph: The Man and Musician." *Musical Quarterly* vol. 30 no. 2 (April 1944), 198–204.

- Leichtentritt, Hugo. *Serge Koussevitzky.* Cambridge, Massachusetts: Harvard University Press, 1947.

- Levant, Oscar. *The Memoirs of an Amnesiac.* New York: G. P. Putnam's Sons, 1965.

- ——. "The Odyssey of Oscar Levant," *The Etude,* Vol. 58, May 1940, 316.

- ——. *A Smattering of Ignorance.* New York: Doubleday, Doran, 1940.

- Los Angeles Times. Articles: ProQuest Historical Newspapers, Online.

Title:	Issue:
Gorin and Rabinowitch... (by Shirley Boyes).	March 27, 1941, 13.
Mrs. Rains Will Make Debut with Symphony Club.	May 20, 1934, A5.
Noted Artists Play and Sing for Charity (by Isabel Morse Jones).	October 20, 1939, 13.
Noted Pianist Here on Visit.	July 18, 1926, C34.
Paderewski Indorses Stojowski.	June 15, 1924, 34.
Polish Benefit Concert Aided by Famous Artists.	October 8, 1939, C5.
Stojowski Classes Visited.	August 24, 1924, B34.
Stojowski Teaches Variety.	May 13, 1928, B15.
Stokowski Will Conduct Polish Relief Concert.	September 27, 1939, A15.
Teacher of Pianists Here for Class.	June 17, 1928, C15.
Woman Scores as Conductor.	August 4, 1930, A7.

- Łabuński, Feliks Roderick. *Correspondence*, K-LXXXIV. Warsaw University Library, Archives of Twentieth-Century Polish Composers.

- ——. "Poland's Contribution to Music." *The Polish Review* vol. 4 no 17 (May 3, 1944), 8–10.

- Łabuński, Wiktor. *Memoirs* (an untitled and unpublished 902-page typewritten manuscript written during the 1960s). University of Missouri-Kansas City Archives.

- Macharska-Wolańska, Maria. *Twórczość fortepianowa Zygmunta Stojowskiego* [Zygmunt Stojowski's Piano Compositions]. Thesis. Cracow: Jagiellonian University, 1950.

- Malherbe, Charles. *Program Notes for 'Symphony in D Minor, Op. 21.'* French version: Concerts Colonne, 31st year, program for March 30, 1903, Stojowski Clipping File, Music Reading Room, Bibliothèque Nationale, Paris. English version: Boston Symphony Orchestra Program of January 16–17, 1920, 739–740, ZLSC.

- Marchwica, Wojciech Maria and Andrzej Sitarz (eds.). *Warsztat kompozytorski, wykonawstwo, koncepcje polityczne Ignacego Jana Paderewskiego* [The Compositional Style, Performances, and Political Concepts of Ignacy Jan Paderewski]. Cracow: Musica Jagiellonica, 1991.

- Markiewicz, Leon. *Grzegorz Fitelberg 1870–1953—Życie i dzieło* [Grzegorz Filtelberg 1870–1953—His Life and Work]. Katowice: Fibak Marquard Press S.A., 1995.

- Marriage Certificate (*Akt Ślubny*) of Władyslaw Górski and Helena Maria Rosen. The Marriage Registry of St. John the Baptist Cathedral in Warsaw, Year 1872 no. 69. Notarized translation from Russian into Polish, April 18, 1934, Morges: the Paderewski Museum, doc. 37.

- McIsaac, Fred J. "Symphony Gets Precedent Blow from Paderewski" (Review of Stojowski's Second Piano Concerto). *Boston American*, (March 1916), Press clipping from the Paderewski Scrapbooks, Archiwum Akt Nowych, Warsaw.

- McKellar, Annabel F. "A Tribute to Mischa Levitzki." *Bulletin of the Stojowski Students' Association* (February 1941), not paginated, PIASA Archives, Collection no. 43 folder 24.

- Mechanisz, Janusz. *Poczet Kompozytorów* [A Galaxy of Composers]. Warsaw: Wydawnictwo Szkolne i Pedagogiczne, 1993.

- Melcer, Wanda. *Henryk Melcer—mój ojciec* [Henryk Melcer—My Father]. Warsaw: Akademia Muzyczna im. Fryderyka Chopina w Warszawie, 1994.

- Methuen-Campbell, James. *Chopin Playing: From The Composer to The Present Day.* New York: Taplinger Publishing Company, 1981.

- Mills College. *Mills College Bulletin, Summer Sessions for Men and Women.* Oakland, California: Mills College, 1934.

- Milne, Mary Jo. "Piano Makes Debut." *Wenatchee (Wa.) World* (August 19, 1973).

- Mischakoff Heiles, Anne. *Mischa Mischakoff, Journeys of a Concertmaster.* Sterling Heights, Michigan: Harmonie Park Press, 2006.
- Le Monde musical, Articles and Reviews:

Title:	**Issue:**
Advertisements (ZS' Paris addresses).	vol. 7 (May 1895), 323; vol. 7 (October 15, 1895), 194.
Aux Conservatoire Morceaux de Concours. [*Fantasie pour trombone*].	vol. 17 no. 12 (June 30, 1905), 159.
Aux Mathurins [1ˢᵗ Piano Concerto].	vol. 12 no. 4 (February 28, 1900), 57.
Cinquantenaire de Frédérick Chopin.	vol. 12 no. 1 (January 15, 1900), 5.
Concerts Colonne.	vol. 36 nos. 21–22 (November 1925), 380–381.
Conservatoire de Musique.	vol. 1 [?] (July 15, 1889), 8
Conservatoire de Musique.	vol. 1 [?] (July 30, 1889), 9.
Correspondence de Londres.	vol. 3 no. 54 (July 30, 1891), 2.
Deuxième et troisième recitals Paderewski.	vol. 11 no. 9 (May 15, 1899), 202.
Diémer Obituary.	vol. 31 nos. 1 and 2 (January 15 and 30, 1920), 38.
Edition Mackar et Noël.	vol. 6 no. 18 (January 30, 1895), 349.
L'Exposition Universelle Française en 1900.	vol. 4 no. 6 (July 30, 1892), 96.
Fontainebleau. [Brachocki.]	vol. 32 nos. 11 and 12 (June 1921), 191.
M. H. Opienski [accompanied by ZS].	vol. 12 no. 10 (June 15, 1900), 181.
M. Ladislas Gorski.	vol. 6 no. 23 (April 15, 1895), 446.
M. Ladislas Gorski.	vol. 7 no. 24 (April 30, 1896), 482.
M. Ladislas Gorski.	vol. 8 no. 24 (April 30, 1897), 446.
M. Ladislas Gorski.	vol. 9 no. 22 (March 30, 1898), 443.
M. Ladislas Gorski.	vol. 13 no. 5 (March 15, 1901), 78.
M. Ladislas Gorski [Violin concerto].	vol. 12 no. 6 (March 30, 1900), 93.
M. L. Diémer.	vol. 4 no. 22 (March 30, 1893), 383.
M. L. Gorski.	vol. 13 no. 5 (March 15, 1901), 78.
Mlle. A. Anderson.	vol. 12 no. 11 (June 30, 1900), 203.
Mlle. H. Wierzbicka.	vol. 20 no. 3 (February 15, 1908), 56–57.
M. Louis Diémer. [Performs Stojowski].	vol. 5 no. 23 (April 15, 1894), 412.
M. Sigismond Stojowski [With Górski].	vol. 7 no. 24, (May 30, 1895), 31.
M. Sigismond Stojowski [Cello Sonata].	vol. 8 no. 2 (May 30, 1896), 31.
M. Sig. Stojowski.	vol. 4 no. 1 (May 15, 1892), 9.
M. Sig. Stojowski [Suite, Op. 9 and Górski].	vol. 6 no. 23 (April 15, 1895), 446.
M. Sig. Stojowski [Casals].	vol. 12 no. 9 (May 15. 1900), 144.
M. S. Jordan de Stojowski [Debut].	vol. 2 no. 44 (February 28, 1891). 6.
M. S. Stojowski.	vol. 4 no. 24 (April 30, 1893), 424.
M. S. Stojowski.	vol. 5 no. 1 (May 15, 1893), 9–10.

M. S. Stojowski.	vol. 13 no. 9 (May 15, 1901), 152.
M. S. Stojowski.	vol. 14 no. 9 (May 15, 1902), 158.
Nouvelles Diverses.	vol. 2 no. 43 (February 15, 1891), 11.
Nouvelles Diverses.	vol. 5 no. 12 (October 30, 1893), 200.
Nouvelles Diverses.	vol. 6 no. 13 (November 15, 1894), 253.
Nouvelles Diverses [Father's obituary].	vol. 7 no. 16 (December 30, 1895), 308.
Nouvelles Diverses.	vol. 8 no. 12 (Oct 30, 1896), 210.
Salle Erard, Mme Conneau.	vol. 7 no. 2 (May 30, 1895), 25.
Salle Erard, M. S. Stojowski.	vol. 13 no. 9 (May 15, 1901), 152.
Salle Pleyel, M. Sig. Stojowski.	vol. 4 no. 1 (May 15, 1892), 9.
Varsovie (by J. Rosenzweig) [Beethoven].	vol. 14 no. 24 (December 30, 1902), 401.
Varsovie (by J. Rosenzweig)[All-Stojowski].	vol. 15 no.27 (February 15, 1903), 47.
Wierzbicka Advertisements:	
Cours et leçons.	vol. 20 no. 3 (February 15, 1908), VIII.
Concert Advertisement.	vol. 26 no. 9 (May 15, 1914), VI.

- Morawska, Katarzyna. "Opieński" in *Encyklopedia Muzyczna* vol. 7. Cracow: Polskie Wydawnictwo Muzyczne, 2002, 164–166.
- The Musical Times. Unsigned reviews of printed editions and concerts:

Title:	**Issue:**
Concert in fa sharp. Pour piano et orchestre. Par Sigismond Stojowski.	vol. 34 no. 608 (October 1, 1893), 613.
Cosaque fantastique. Pour piano par Sigismond Stojowski.	vol. 36 no. 623 (January 1, 1895), 30.
Deux Orientales (No. 1, Romance; no. 2, Caprice), Mazurka, Gondoliera, Berceuse, Scherzo. For pianoforte solo by Sig. Stojowski.	vol. 36 no. 628 (June 1, 1895), 386.
Elgar's Symphonic Prelude 'Polonia': Performance at Queen's Hall.	vol. 56 no. 870 (August 1, 1915), 491.
Music in Glasgow.	vol. 50 no. 792 (February 1, 1909), p. 118.
Music in the Provinces.	vol. 83 no. 1192 (June 1942).
Piano Concerto No. 2 [Review]	vol. 54 no. 846 (August 1, 1913), 538.
Pianoforte recitals.	vol. 32 no. 582 (August 1, 1891), 474.
Pianoforte recitals.	vol. 34 no. 605 (July 1, 1893), 408–409.
Suite en mi bémol pour grand orchestre par Sigismond Stojowski.	vol. 35 no. 618 (August 1, 1894), 547.
The Wreck of the Hesperus...Spring-Time.	vol. 46 no. 754 (December 1, 1905), 800.

- Neuls-Bates, Carol. *Women in Music*. Boston: Northeastern University Press, 1996.

- ———. *Women in Music, An Anthology of Source Reading from the Middle Ages to the Present.* New York: Harper and Row, 1982.
- The New York Times. Unsigned articles: ProQuest Historical Newspapers Online.

Title	Issue
Activities of Musicians [Tempo Magazine].	November 26, 1933, X6.
Activities of Musicians, Winners Named...	November 3, 1935, X7.
Arthur Loesser, 74, A Concert Pianist [Obit.]	January 6, 1969), 47.
Benefit for Kosciuszko Foundation.	March 13, 1937, E8.
Brico Orchestra at Carnegie Hall.	January 26, 1939, 23.
Brico Orchestra Heard.	March 17, 1935, N8.
Concerts, Recitals...Musical Notes.	December 31, 1905, X2.
Concert to Aid Hospital [*Homage to Paderewski*].	February 27, 1942, 21.
Composers Form Promotion Group.	May 15, 1936, 28.
Cornelius Bliss, 74, Financier, Is Dead.	April 6, 1949,
Drive Begun Here for Polish Relief.	February 26, 1940, 2.
Elenore Altman, Pianist, Plays.	November 14, 1926, 28.
For Children of French Musicians.	July 21, 1918, 22.
France Again Honors Mrs. Tuttle.	November 4, 1923, E1.
Free Concerts by WPA [Schachter concert].	November 24, 1935, X6.
A 'Gala Concert' [Second Piano Concerto].	March 5, 1916, 3.
Harriet Ware, Concert Pianist and Composer Is Dead at 84.	February 11, 1962, 86.
Heifetz Plays to Crowd.	January 12, 1920, 7.
In Aid of Paris Musicians.	March 12, 1916, X7.
Jacobsen Plays Local Composers.	October 28. 1923, S8.
A Matinee of New Music.	December 12, 1912, 10.
Mildred Titcomb Heard.	November 25, 1930, 34.
Mischa Levitzki, Noted Pianist, Dies.	January 3, 1941, 19.
Mme. Sembrich Must Rest.	November 17, 1915, 6.
Mme. Sembrich's Recital.	March 2, 1910, 3.
Mrs. Frank H. Holden [Obituary].	November 26, 1968, 47.
Mrs. Randall-MacIver, 87, Dies; Music Patron Cited by France.	May 17, 1961, 37.
Mr. Stojowski's Concert.	March 2, 1915, 9.
Mr. Stojowski's Recital [Cello Sonata].	January 24, 1907, 9.
Mr. Stojowski's Recital [Historical Piano Recitals].	February 5, 1911, 11.
Music and Music Makers.	December 5, 1905, XI.
Music for Young People [First NY Orch. Concert].	January 7, 1906, 7.
Music Notes [Brachocki/Windheim concert].	February 25, 1933, 20.

Philharmonic Concert [Suite, Op. 9].	February 6, 1915, 11.
Polish Artists in Recital.	April 20, 1928, 32.
The Schola Cantorum [Prayer for Poland].	March 8, 1916, 9.
Simple Rites Held for R.U. Johnson	October 18, 1937, 17.
Stojowski Is Dead; Polish Pianist, 76.	November 6, 1946, 22.
Stojowski, Pianist, Heard.	April 27, 1936, 19.
Stojowski Plays His Own Piano Concerto.	November 17, 1924, 17.
Two Composers Win $1,000.	October 29, 1939, 42.
Woman to Conduct Musicians' Symphony.	December 28, 1932, 15.
Women's Symphony Orchestra of 80 Will Make Its Debut Here Monday.	January 24, 1935, 21.

- Ney, Elly. *Ein Leben für die Musik.* Darmstadt: Franz Schneekluth-Verlag GmbH, 1952.

- Noskowski, Witold (ed.). *Tydzień Muzyki Polskiej* [Program for the Festival 'Week of Polish Music']. Poznań: October 2–9, 1938 [Biblioteka Narodowa, Czytelnia Dokumentów Życia Społecznego, Warsaw].

- Nowowiejski, Feliks M. and Kazimierz. *Dookoła kompozytora* [In the Composer's Circle]. Poznań: Wydawnictwo Poznańskie, 1971.

- Oakley, Lansdale. "'Rays and Reflections' from Stojowski's Western Trip." *Bulletin of the Stojowski Students' Association* (January 1940), 6–7. PIASA Archives, collection no. 43 folder no. 24.

- Obituary: "Sigismond Stojowski." *Musical America* (November 25, 1946).

- Obituary: "Sigismond Stojowski Has Died." *The Polish Review* vol. 6 no. 20 (November 28, 1946), 3, 15.

- Obituary: "Zgon Zygmunta Stojowskiego." Życie Warszawy vol. 3 no. 307 (November 8, 1946), 1.

- Oliver, George Edgar. Review of Stojowski's performance in Albany, New York. "Concert of the Boston Symphony Orchestra." *The Albany Evening Journal* (November 6, 1923). Press clipping, ZLSC.

- Opieński, Henryk. "Walkirie" in *Echo Muzyczne, Teatralne i Artystyczne* no. 956 (January 25, 1902), 39.

- Orgelbranda, S. "Stojowski," in *Encyklopedia Powszechna* vol. 14. Warsaw: Wydawnictwo Towarzystwa Akcyjnego, 1903, 98.

- Owen, H. Goddard. *A Recollection of Marcella Sembrich.* New York: Da Capo Press, 1982.

- Paderewski, Ignacy Jan. *Hej, Orle biały, hymn bojowy* [Hey, White Eagle, a Battle Hymn] [piano/vocal score]. New York: Echo z Ziemi Rodzinnej, 1918.

- ——. *Hej, Orle biały.* [Hey, White Eagle] [Vocal score]. Chicago: B. J. Zalewski Publisher, 1931.

- ——. Letter to Maria Stojowska, December 5, 1884. Morges: Paderewski Museum, De 65-2.

- ———. *May 13, 1924 Letter of Recommendation for Stojowski*. Morges, Switzerland: Paderewski Museum, De 65-1.
- Paderewski, Ignacy and Helena. Telegram of condolence on the death of Stojowski's mother, Maria, April 7, 1925. Stanford: Paderewski Collection, Hoover Institution, Stanford University.
- Perkowska, Małgorzata. "Delibes" in *Encyklopedia Muzyczna* vol. 2. Cracow: Polskie Wydawnictwo Muzyczne, 1984, 390–391.
- ———. *Diariusz Koncertowy Ignacego Jana Paderewskiego* [The Concert Diary of Ignacy Jan Paderewski]. Cracow: Polskie Wydawnictwo Muzyczne, 1990.
- Perkowska-Waszek, Małgorzata. "O Paderewskim — pedagogu" [About Paderewski—the Pedagogue] in *Muzyka wobec tradycji*, ed. Szymon Paczkowski. Warsaw: Instytut Muzykologii, Warsaw University, 2004, 619–631.
- Petrak, Albert M. (ed.) *Ampico Piano Roll Catalog*. The Reproducing Piano Roll Foundation, 1998. http://www.rprf.org/PDF/Ampico_Catalog.pdf
- ———. *Welte Piano Roll Catalog*. The Reproducing Piano Roll Foundation, 1998. http://www.rprf.org/PDF/Welte_Catalog.pdf
- Peyser, Ethel. *The House that Music Built, Carnegie Hall*. New York: Robert M. McBride & Co., 1936.
- Philipp, Isidore (trans. Frederick H. Martens). "The French National Conservatory." *The Music Quarterly,* vol. 6 no. 2 (April 1920), 214–226.
- Phillips, Charles. *Paderewski, the Story of a Modern Immortal*. New York: The Macmillan Co., 1933.
- Piber, Andrzej. *Droga do sławy, Ignacy Paderewski w latach 1860–1902* [The Road to Fame, Ignacy Paderewski during the Years 1860–1902]. Warsaw: Państwowy Instytut Wydawniczy, 1982.
- Pierre, Constant. *Le Conservatoire National et de déclamation—Documents Historiques et Admistratifs*. Paris: Heugel et Cie., 1900.
- Pływawko, Danuta. *Polonia Devastata, Polonia i Amerykanie z pomocą dla Polski (1914–1918)* [Poland Devasted, Polonia and Americans in Aid of Poland (1914–1918)]. Poznań: Wydawnictwo Poznańskie, 2003.
- Poe, Elisabeth P. "Among Musicians." *The Washington Post* (September 21, 1930), A4.
- Polish Institute of Arts and Letters. *Report of the Polish Institute of Arts and Letters: 1932–1933, 1933–1934*, ZLSC and BNW.
- Polish Institute of Arts and Sciences. Sigismond Stojowski Papers, Collection No. 046, Folders 1–51, New York.
- Poznansky, Alexander. *Tchaikovsky's Last Days*. Oxford: Clarendon Press, 1996.
- Poźniak, Włodzimierz. "Muzyka fortepianowa po Chopinie" [Piano Music after Chopin], in *Z dziejów polskiej kultury muzycznej Vol. II*, eds. Stefania Łobaczewska et al. Cracow: Polskie Wydawnictwo Muzyczne, 1966, 510–552.

- ———. "Muzyka kameralna i skrzypcowa" [Chamber and Violin Music], in *Z dziejów polskiej kultury muzycznej Vol. II*, eds. Stefania Łobaczewska et al. Cracow: Polskie Wydawnictwo Muzyczne, 1966, 463–510.

- ———. "Pieśń solowa po Moniuszce" [Art Song after Moniuszko], in *Z dziejów polskiej kultury muzycznej Vol. II*, eds. Stefania Łobaczewska et al. Cracow: Polskie Wydawnictwo Muzyczne, 1966, 355–400.

- Pratt, Waldo Selden (ed.). "Sigismond Denis Antoine Stojowski" in *Grove's Dictionary of Music and Musicians,* 3rd edition, American Supplement vol. 6. London: The Macmillan Co., 1937, 376.

- Prendergast, Alan. "The Brico Requiem." *Westword* (November 1, 1995): Part 1 https://den.secure.newtimes.com/issues/1995–11–01/news/feature4_print.html; Part 2 http://www.westword.com/search/results.php?issue_date=1995–11–01

- Preyss, Adele and Joanne Stefanik. "Sigismond Stojowski." *The New American, A Monthly Digest of Polish-American Life and Culture* Vol. 5 no. 6 (June-July 1938), 1, 5.

- Program for Buckingham Palace Concert of July 5, 1895, including Stojowski's cantata *Spring,* Op. 7. The Choral Class of the Royal College of Music, Her Majesty's Private Band, Sir Walter Parratt conducting. The Royal Archives at Windsor Castle.

- Program notes for *Prayer for Poland*, the Chorus of the Schola Cantorum of New York, Second Subscription Concert… March 7, 1916, with the Orchestra of the Symphony Society of New York, ZLSC.

- Reiss, Józef. *Almanach muzyczny Krakowa 1780–1914* [A Musical Almanac of Cracow 1780–1914], Vol. II. Cracow: Towarzystwo miłośników i zabytków, 1939.

- ———. *Najpiękniejsza ze wszystkich jest Muzyka Polska* [The Most Beautiful of All Is Polish Music]. Cracow: T. Gieszczykiewicz, 1946.

- ———. *Statkowski, Melcer, Młynarski, Stojowski*. Łódź: Wiedza Powszechna Wydawnictwo Popularno-Naukowe, 1949.

- Roberts, Don. "Noted in Europe, Antonia Brico Returns to Win Distinction as Orchestra Leader." *Newark Advocate and American Tribune* (September 2, 1930), 7.

- Rodziński, Artur. Letter to Stojowski (December 30, 1944). Rodziński Collection, Box 3, Library of Congress, Washington, D.C.

- Rosenblatt, Roger. *Everlasting Art,* October 9, 1997: http://www.pbs.org/newshour/essays/october97/rosenblatt_10-9.html

- Rostworowski, Emanuel (editor-in-chief). *Polski Słownik Biograficzny* [Polish Biographical Dictionary] vols. 7 and 11. Wrocław, Warsaw and Cracow: Polska Akademia Nauk Instytut Historii, 1964–1965.

- Rothstein, Edward. *Arthur Loesser in Recital* (CD liner notes). Swarthmore, Pennsylvania: Marston Records, 2001.

- Rowley, Alec. "The Pianoforte Works of Siegmund [sic!] Stojowski, A Short Survey." *The Musical Mirror* (July 1928), 177.

- Rubinstein, Artur. *My Many Years.* New York: Alfred A. Knopf, Inc., 1980.

- ———. *My Young Years.* New York: Alfred A. Knopf, Inc., 1973.

- Schaeffner, André. "Concerts—Colonne." *Le Ménestrel* vol. 87 no. 5 (November 6, 1925), 449.

- Schelling, Ernest. Letter to Sigismond Stojowski, April 1, 1926, ZLSC.

- ———. *A Victory Ball, Fantasy for Orchestra* [Full score]. New York: Carl Fischer, ca. 1923.

- Schelling, Mrs. Ernest (Julia). Letter to Marguerite Merington. August 17, 1945. PIASA Marguerite Merington Papers, No. 43.7.

- Sęp. "Z Warszawy" [From Warsaw]. *Biesiada Literacka* no. 4 (January 17, 1902), 42.

- Shaw, G. Bernard. *Music in London, 1890–1894.* London: Constable and Company Limited, [1932] reprinted 1949–1950.

- Sienkiewicz, Henryk. *Listy* [Letters], Vol. II Part 1, Letter to Jadwiga Janczewska, no. 135, Paris (October 25, 1988), Warsaw: Państwowy Instytut Wydawniczy, 1996, 595–596.

- Śledziński, Stefan. "Zarys dziejów symfonii polskiej w XIX wieku" [A Musical Outline of the Polish Symphony in the Nineteenth Century], in *Z dziejów polskiej kultury muzycznej Vol. II*, eds. Stefania Łobaczewska et al. Cracow: Polskie Wydawnictwo Muzyczne, 1966, 401–462.

- Slonimsky, Nicolas. Stojowski File. Slonimsky Collection, Box 236, Folder 14, Library of Congress, Washington, D.C.

- Soloman, Abraham. "Concerts and Recitals, Schola Cantorum in Second Concert." *International Music and Drama* (March 11, 1916), 7–8.

- Stojowski, Alfred J. "Biographical Information" in *Wenatchee 'Meet a Rotarian' –Week 52* (February 2002), http://www.crcwnet.com/~rotary/stojowski.htm

- Stojowski, Henry J. *Curriculum vitae: Henry J. Stojowski Architect* (2002), 10 typewritten pages, ZLSC.

- Stojowski, Ignatius L. *Data Sheet* (ca. 1978), one typewritten page, ZLSC.

- ———. Letter to Paderewski. Warsaw: Paderewski Archives, 3702, AAN.

- Stokowski, Leopold. Two Letters to Stojowski, September 12 and 14, 1939. The Leopold Stokowski Archives, Manuscript Collection 381, Folder 175, two one-sided typewritten pages, The University of Pennsylvania, Philadelphia

- Stojowski, Luisa. "Mme. Stojowski Tells the Secret of Practicing." *The Southwestern Musician* 15 (July 1949), 16.

- Suchecki, Krystyna and Roman. "Polska Sonata Wiolonczelowa" [Polish Cello Sonatas], in *Zeszyty Naukowe X.* Gdańsk: Wyższa Szkoła Muzyczna w Gdańsku, 1972, 203–223.

- Sullivan & Cromwell. Letter to Stojowski and Roman J. Majewski informing them of the return of Poland's U.S. gold deposits to the Bank Polski (March 23, 1944), ZLSC.
- Szopski, Felicjan. "Z Filharmonii." *Kurjer Warszawski* (October 5, 1929), 9–10.
- Talma-Davous, Eva. "O ekspozycji autografów muzycznych na paryskiej Wystawie Powszechnej w 1900 roku" [About the Exhibit of Musical Autographs at the Parisian Universal Exposition in 1900] in *Muzyka wobec tradycji*, ed. Szymon Paczkowski. Warsaw: Instytut Muzykologii, Warsaw University, 2004, 611–618.
- Thirteenth Census of the United States: 1910—Population. New York City, Borough of Manhattan, Ward 22, Enumeration District (ED) 1389, Sheet no. 14 B, 249 West 74th Street.
- Transcript of *Stojowski Memorial Broadcast*, Station WNYC, Sunday, May 1, 1949, ZLSC.
- Trochimczyk, Maja. "Music at PIASA's 60th Meeting." *Polish Music Newsletter* vol. 8 no. 6 (June 2002), online: http://www.usc.edu/dept/polish_music/news/june02.html
- ——. (ed.). *Selected Reviews of Stojowski's Music (1907–1943)*. Polish Music Journal vol. 5 no. 2 (Winter 2002), online: http://www.usc.edu/dept/polish_music/PMJ/issue/5.2.02/stojowskireviews.html#1907
- ——. "Stojowski Manuscripts at PIASA." *Polish Music Letter* vol. 7 no. 8 (August 2001), online: http://www.usc.edu/dept/polish_music/news/aug01.html
- University of Washington—Seattle. *Brochure for Summer Master Classes with Sigismond Stojowski,* July 23-August 24, 1928, ZLSC.
- *Von Ende School of Music Bulletin*. New York: 1915–1916, ZLSC.
- The Washington Post. Unsigned Articles: ProQuest Historical Newspapers Online.

Title:	Date and Page:
Sigismond Stojowski.	December 24, 1905, E1.
Stojowski to Appear in Capital This Week.	March 14, 1917, TR6.
Vice President Is HonorGuest [sic!] of Ambassador.	April 26, 1930, 8
White House Party at Concert.	January 31, 1917, 7.

- Wallace, Robert K. *A Century of Music Making, The Lives of Josef and Rosina Lhevinne*. Bloomington: Indiana University Press, 1976.
- Watkins, Glenn. *Proof through the Night, Music and the Great War.* Berkeley: University of California Press, 2003.
- ____. *Soundings—Music in the Twentieth Century*. New York: Schirmer Books, 1988.

- Webb, F. Gilbert. *Program Notes for Piano Concerto No. 2, Op. 32.* London Symphony Orchestra, World Premiere, June 13, 1913, ZLSC.

- Wier, Albert E. "Sigismond Denis Antoine Stojowski," in *The Macmillan Encyclopedia of Music and Musicians.* New York: The Macmillan Co., 1938, 1800.

- Westney, William. *Program Notes for Stojowski's Piano Concerto in F-sharp Minor, Op. 3.* Jackson (Michigan) Symphony Orchestra, (October 6, 1990).

- Wissel, Jean [Stojowski's impresario in the 1930s]. *List of Stojowski Students.* One-page typewritten list of names, ZLSC.

- Woollett, Henry. "European Export Supplement of 'The Presto.'" *Le Monde musical* (April 30, 1900), A-D.

- Wroński, Thaddeus. *The Singer and His Art.* New York: D. Appleton & Co., 1922.

- Zamoyski, Adam. *Paderewski.* New York: Atheneum, 1982.

MENDELSSOHN HALL, 119 WEST 40th STREET

Five Historical Piano Recitals by

Sigismond Stojowski

Saturday afternoons, at 2.30

FEBRUARY 4th   FEBRUARY18th   MARCH 4th
MARCH 18th   APRIL 1st

MASON & HAMLIN PIANO

Subscription $7.00 :: :: :: Single Tickets $1.50, $1.00
at 1 West 34th Street: Room 1105 Telephone 3540 Murray Hill

DIRECTION   FRANCES SEAVER
(by arrangement with Haensel & Jones)

1911

Patrons

Mrs. Andrew Carnegie
Dr. Frank Damrosch
Mrs. Charles Healy Ditson
Mr. John W. Frothingham
Mrs. Ben Ali Haggin
Mrs. Edith Jayne
Mrs. Robert Underwood Johnson
Mrs. Otto H. Kahn
Mr. Franz Kneisel
Mr. Alexander Lambert
Miss Anna G. Lockwood
Mr. James Loeb
Mrs. Morris Loeb
Mrs. Edward MacDowell
Mr. Ralph Modjeski
Miss Florence Pease
Mr. Rudolph E. Schirmer
Mme. Marcella Sembrich
Mrs. Harriet Seymour
Mrs. George Montgomery Tuttle
Mrs. Samuel Untermyer
Mrs. Paul M. Warburg
Mrs. Richard G. Wiener
Mrs. J. A. H. Worthington

V. April 1st

Modern Epigones and Forerunners

Programme

JOHANNES BRAHMS   Variations and Fugue on a
1833–1897   theme by HAENDEL

CÉSAR FRANCK   Prelude, Choral and Fugue
1822–1890

CAMILLE SAINT-SAËNS Romance in B minor
1835

EDWARD GRIEG   Danse—Caprice
1843–1907

CLAUDE DEBUSSY   Reflets dans l'eau
1862

EDWARD MacDOWELL   In Autumn
1861–1908

MORITZ MOSZKOWSKI   Etude en doubles notes in G
1854   minor

I. J. PADEREWSKI   Theme varié, op. 16
1860–

ANTON RUBINSTEIN   Barcarolle in A minor
1829–1894

FRANZ LISZT   Etude de Concert in F minor
1811–1886   (La Leggierezza).
                   Hungarian Rhapsody. No. 2

Plates I & II. Stojowski's five historical recitals, presented in New York City during the early spring of 1911, show the considerable breadth of his solo repertoire. The chronological choice, beginning with the Baroque masters and concluding with a selection of contemporary composers, also reflected upon Stojowski's approach as a renowned New York piano teacher.

I. February 4th

German, French and Italian masters of the clavichord and the polyphonic forms

Programme

G. F. HAENDEL Suite in D minor
1685-1759
  Prelude and Fugue—Courante—Air et Doubles—Presto

PIETRO DOMENICO PARADISI Sonata in A major
1710-1792
  Vivace—Allegro

FRANÇOIS COUPERIN Les Roseaux
1668-1733 Les Barricades mystérieuses

CLAUDE DAQUIN Le Coucou
1694-1772

DOMENICO SCARLATTI Pastorale
1683-1757 Capriccio

JEAN PHILLIPPE RAMEAU Gavotte variée
1683-1764

J. S. BACH Bourrées from English Suite in A major
1685-1750 Sarabande from French Suite in D minor
  Gigue from first Partita
  Chromatic Fantasy and Fugue

II. February 18th

Masters of the Classical Sonata

Programme

JOSEPH HAYDN Andante in F minor
1732-1809

W. A. MOZART Rondo in A minor
1756-1791 Sonata in A major
  Andante con variazioni—Minuetto—Allegrino alla Turca

LUDWIG VAN BEETHOVEN Sonata in C minor, op. 111
1770-1827 Maëstoso—Allegro con brio ed
    appassionato—Arietta
  Sonata in F minor, op. 57
    (Appassionata)
  Allegro assai—Andante con
    moto, Allegro ma non troppo
    —Presto

III. March 4th

Romantic Classics and Classic Romantics

Programme

CARL MARIA von WEBER Sonata in A flat major, op. 39
1786-1826 Allegro moderato—Andante—Menuetto capriccioso—Rondo

FRANZ SCHUBERT Three Musical Moments, op. 94, No's 2, 3, 4
1797-1828 Minuetto from G major Fantasy
  Two Impromptus, B flat major, op. 142, No 3
    A flat minor, op. 90, No. 4

FELIX MENDELSSOHN BARTHOLDY Variations serieuses
1809-1847 Four Songs without words
  Hunting Song—F major, No. 22
  Spinning Song—G minor. No.46

JOHN FIELD Rondo in E flat major
1782-1837

IV. March 18th

The Two Romantic Masters

Programme

ROBERT SCHUMANN Fantasie in C major, op. 17
1810-1856 Durchaus energisch und leidenschaftlich, Im Legendenton—Mässig durchaus energisch—Langsam, getragen

  Aufschwung

  Warum

  Carnaval, op. 9
  Préambule, Pierrot, Arlequin, Valse noble, Eusebius, Florestan, Coquette, Réplique, Papillons, Lettres dansantes, Chiarina, Chopin, Estrella, Reconnaissance, Pantalon et Colombine, Valse allemande, Paganini, Aveu, Promenade, Pause, Marinc des Davidsbündler contre les Philistins

FREDERICK CHOPIN Fantasie in F minor, op. 49
1810-1849 Polonaise in C minor, op. 40, No. 1
  Two Nocturnes (G major, op.37, No.2
    C minor, op. 48, No.1)
  Three Mazurkas (G major, op. 50, No.
    1—C sharp minor, op. 41, No. 1
    —C major, op. 56, No. 2)
  Two Studies (op. 10, No. 8—op. 25,
    No. 7)
  Scherzo in C sharp minor, op. 39

The New York Times reviewer favorably commented on Stojowski's virtuosity and the remarks he made to the audience before each program

Plate IVa. Stojowski in action at his New York studio in the late 1920s

PADEREWSKI ENDORSES STOJOWSKI.

Hotel Gotham, New York.
May 13th, 1924.

It has been my privilege and my joy to assist Mr. Sigismond Stojowski in his studies as a pianist for a number of years. Remarkable pianist and composer, extraordinary musician, highly educated and refined man, he has done me the honor of adopting my method and style to such an extent that, whenever listening to some young people who had enjoyed his guidance and tuition, I have the impression to hear my own pupils.

Among the few really great piano pedagogues of the present day, Mr. Stojowski occupies a very prominent position, for he has no superior.

Plate IVb. This important tribute to Stojowski by his teacher, mentor and close friend confirms Stojowski's stature among the pianists of his day

Columbia University
in the City of New York

UNIVERSITY EXTENSION
THE INSTITUTE OF ARTS
AND SCIENCES

IN COOPERATION WITH THE
DEPARTMENT OF SLAVONIC LANGUAGES

AN EVENING OF POLISH MUSIC

MR. ADAM DIDUR, *Basso*
of the Metropolitan Opera Company

MR. PAUL KOCHANSKI, *Violin*

MR. SIGISMOND STOJOWSKI, *Piano*

MR. KAROL SZYMANOWSKI, *Composer*

TUESDAY, DECEMBER 13, 1921, 8:15 p. m.
HORACE MANN AUDITORIUM

Program

1. a) MÉLODIE ....*Stojowski*
   b) VALSE HUMORESQUE ....*Stojowski*
   c) MAZURKA ....*Stojowski*
                         MR. STOJOWSKI

2. SONGS OF POLISH COMPOSERS
                         MR. DIDUR

3. a) NOCTURNE ....*Chopin*
   b) MAZUR ....*Wieniawski*
   c) FONTAINE D'ARETHUSE............................*Szymanowski*
                 (The Composer at the Piano)
   d) NOTTURNO ....*Szymanowski*
                 (The Composer at the Piano)
                         MR. KOCHANSKI

4. POLISH NATIONAL DANCES IN COSTUME
   a) MAZUR
   b) OBEREK

   Under the direction of Miss Halina Bruzovna, of the Warsaw Municipal Theater, danced by the Misses Maciejevska, Mysliviec, Swieza, York, and Messrs. Adryanovski, Leszynski, Michalevicz, and Winogrodzki.

NOTE

Poland can be surpassed by no nation in the greatness of her music. Her composers and musicians, to which number belongs the immortal Chopin, have been many, and their genius and brilliancy in their art have been rivalled only by the patriotism and loyalty which they have always showed to their country. Columbia University is happy to present this program which is designed to bring to the American people some appreciation of the greatness of this art, and the University feels itself highly honored in that the artists who have consented to appear are not only world renowned masters, unexcelled in their particular spheres of music, but also natives of Poland and most distinguished representatives of the cultural greatness of their native land.

The Steinway Piano Used

Plate V. At this important December 1921 concert at the Columbia University Stojowski and Szymanowski shared the stage in performances of their compositions

AEOLIAN HALL, 34 West 43rd Street
Saturday Evening, February 21, 1925 at 8:15

Piano
Recital

by

Sigismond
Stojowski

PROGRAM

I.

Andante F major .... BEETHOVEN
Sonata in F sharp minor, Op. 11 .... SCHUMANN
    Introduzione. Un poco adagio. Allegro vivace.
    Aria. Scherzo e Intermezzo. Finale.

II.

Fantaisie, Op. 38   }
Polish Idyls, Op. 24 } .... STOJOWSKI
    Solitude. L'Appel des Moissonneurs.
    Coquette de Village. Vision de Danse.
    Souvenirs de Fête.

III.

Ballade G minor   }
Nocturne G major   } .... CHOPIN
Scherzo C sharp minor }

Tickets: 55c to $2.20. Boxes $16.50. On Sale at Aeolian Hall Box Office

STEINWAY PIANO   AMPICO RECORDS

Management: JEAN WISWELL

FISK BUILDING   NEW YORK

Plate VI. A romantic at heart, Stojowski eagerly programmed works by Schumann and Chopin. After hearing Stojowski perform the Schumann's Sonata Op. 11 in 1905, Frank Damrosch, founder and director of the newly formed Institute of Musical Arts in New York City, immediately offered Stojowski a chairmanship of the piano department

POLISH MUSIC

FESTIVAL

TO COMMEMORATE THE POLISH CONSTITUTION OF MAY 3rd, 1791

Eighty Members of the

NEW YORK PHILHARMONIC-SYMPHONY

GREGOR

FITTELBERG

CONDUCTOR

BRONISLAW

HUBERMAN

VIOLINIST

*Assisting
Artists*

WITOLD

MALCUZYNSKI

PIANIST

Carnegie Hall

THURSDAY EVE., MAY 4, 1944 at 8:30

[OVERLEAF]

THE POLISH INSTITUTE OF ARTS AND SCIENCES IN AMERICA

Presents

FESTIVAL
OF
POLISH MUSIC

THURSDAY MAY 4 at 8:30 P. M. ★ CARNEGIE HALL

Program

♪ STOJOWSKI . . . . SUITE OP. 9

♪ LABUNSKI . . . . SUITE FOR STRINGS
(FIRST TIME IN NEW YORK)

♪ PADEREWSKI . . . . . POLISH FANTASY OP. 19
(FOR PIANO AND ORCHESTRA)
Soloist: WITOLD MALCUZYNSKI

♪ SZYMANOWSKI . . . . . "HARNASIE" OP. 55

♪ SZYMANOWSKI . . . FIRST VIOLIN CONCERTO OP. 35
(FOR VIOLIN AND ORCHESTRA)
Soloist: BRONISLAW HUBERMAN

Steinway Piano

Tickets: Parquet $3.00, $2.40; Dress Circle $2.40, $1.80; Balcony $1.80, $1.20;
Boxes, seating eight, (lower tier) $28.80, (upper tier) $19.20

(PRICES INCLUDE THE NEW 20% TAX)

CONCERT MANAGEMENT ARTHUR JUDSON, Inc.
Division of COLUMBIA CONCERTS, Inc.
113 West 57th Street   New York 19, N. Y.

Plates VII & VIII. Throughout his life Stojowski was a great patriot and a dedicated ambassador of Polish culture. He organized and participated in a multitude of concerts presenting the most prominent artists, as in this 1944 concert in New York

Plate IX. Henry Stojowski, the middle son of Zygmunt, opening the Stojowski Room at the Polish Music Center, during a special ceremony on October 11, 2006

Plate X. October 11, 2006. Robert Cutietta, Dean of Thornton School of Music (left) with Diane Wilk-Burch, daughter of the Polish Music Center's founder, Wanda Wilk. Next to Diane is her husband, Michael Burch. Henry Stojowski, on the right, delivers his remarks, celebrating the donation of the Zygmunt and Luisa Stojowski Collection (ZLSC) to the Polish Music Center at USC

Plate XI. Dean Cutietta and the book's author, Joseph A. Herter, at the Stojowski Room dedication. Polish Music Center, October 11, 2006

Plate XII. A group photo of special guests at the Polish Music Center, October 11, 2006. From left to right: Dean Cutietta, Henry Stojowski, Nancy Harris, Joseph Herter, Dean Susan Lopez, Esther Sahl, Alice Stojowski, Alfred Stojowski, Lars Hoefs, Dorothy Ditmer, and Steven Stojowski. In the back, Ljiljana Grubisic and Marek Żebrowski

Plate XIII. October 12, 2006. Alfred, Steven and Henry Stojowski following the 2006 Paderewski Lecture-Recital at the Alfred Newman Recital Hall, USC. This event, organized annually by the Polish Music Center, celebrated the legacy of Zygmunt Stojowski on the 60th anniversary of his death. Joseph A. Herter delivered a lecture on the life and opus of Z. Stojowski, and Jonathan Plowright performed a recital of works by Z. Stojowski and I. J. Paderewski

Plate XIVa. After concert reception at the Herklotz Courtyard, October 12, 2006. From left to right: Nancy Harris, Alfred, and Henry Stojowski with pianist Jonathan Plowright

Plate XIVb. Jonathan Plowright receives a firm handshake from Henry Stojowski as Steven and Alfred Stojowski look on. October 12, 2006

Index

Contains names of individuals, institutions, geographical places, and major international events found in the Introduction and the subsequent ten chapters of the book. Also includes references to works by composers other than Zygmunt Stojowski, and information found in the Endnotes to all chapters. The Catalogue, Appendix I & II, and the Illustration sections of this book are not covered by this index.

G

H

M

N

SYMPHONY CONCERTS

LAST CONCERT OF NINTH SERIES

(SEASON 1912-1913).

MONDAY, JUNE 23rd, 1913, at 8 p.m.

Symphonic Poem	" Les Hommages " (BY DESIRE)	*Holbrooke*
Pianoforte Concerto No. 2 (Prologue, Scherzo and Variations) (First Performance in London).		*Stojowski*

Soloist - M. SIGISMUND STOJOWSKI

(a). **Three Moods of the Sea**

    (1.—Requies ; 2.—Before the Squall ; 3.—After Sunset).

(b). **" On the Road "** (a marching tune)

    (With Orchestral accompaniment).

Dr. Ethel Smyth

(First time of performance),

Vocalist - Mr. HERBERT HEYNER.

Symphony No. 4, in F minor   Tschaikowsky

Conductor—Herr ARTHUR NIKISCH

TICKETS—

Sofa Stalls and Grand Circle (Reserved) 7s. 6d. & 5s.

Balcony (Unreserved) 2s. 6d.   **Area** 1s. (All Sold).

Tickets can be obtained at CHAPPELL'S BOX OFFICE, QUEEN'S HALL (10 to 8), and 50 New Bond Street, W.; Ashton & Mitchell, 33 Old Bond Street, W., & 35 Sloane Street, S.W.; Army & Navy Stores, 105 Victoria Street, Westminster, S.W.; Augener Limited, 63, Conduit Street (Regent Street Corner), W. (Tel. No. Mayfair 3030); Box Office, Cafe Royal, 48 Regent Street, W.; Civil Service Supply Stores, 138 Queen Victoria Street, E.C ; Cramer & Co., Ltd., 126 New Bond Street, W.; District Messenger & Theatre Ticket Co., 133 Piccadilly, W. & Branches; Alfred Hays, 26 Old Bond St., W., and 4 Royal Exchange Buildings, E.C.; S Hermitage & Sons, 23 Clapham Road, S.W.; Lester James, Fira Parade, Muswell Hill, N.; Keith, Prowse & Co., Ltd., 162 New Bond St., W., High Street, Kensington, W., Carlton Hotel, Pall Mall, S.W., 3 Grand Hotel Buildings, Trafalgar Square, 42 Poland Street, Oxford Street, W., 1 Prince of Wales's Buildings, Coventry Street, 48 Cheapside, E.C., 4 First Avenue Hotel Buildings, Holborn, 148 Fenchurch Street, E.C.; Lacon & Ollier, 2, Burlington Gardens, W.; Leader & Co., 13 Royal Arcade, Old Bond Street, W.; Cecil Roy, 15 Sussex Place, South Kensington, S.W.; Webster & Girling, 44 Upper Baker Street, W.; Webster & Waddington, Ltd., 304 Regent Street, W.; White's Box Office, 27 High Street, Kensington W.; Messrs. Etherington's Box Office, Hill Street, Richmond Telephone 140); and of

Telephone 5564 Gerrard.   **L. G. SHARPE, 61, Regent Street, W.**

VAIL AND CO., LONDON, E.C.

Plate III. As a pianist, Stojowski performed with some of the best conductors of his era. Arthur Nikisch also championed Stojowski's orchestral works, including his prize-winning Symphony in D-minor, Op. 21, dating from 1898

Joseph A. Herter, a native of Detroit, is a graduate of the University of Michigan's School of Music in Ann Arbor, where he studied voice with Rosemary Russell, conducting with Thomas Hilbish and Gustav Meier, and musicology with Glenn Watkins. Mr. Herter continued his education with summer choral studies at Westminster Choir College in Princeton. He also studied orchestral conducting as a member of the 1984 conductors' seminar at Tanglewood.

At the beginning of his career, Joseph Herter worked as music teacher and music director in several Detroit Roman Catholic schools and churches, including downtown's historic Old St. Mary's Church, known for its outstanding music program and orchestral Latin Masses. After going to Poland in 1974 as a Kosciuszko Foundation grantee, he relocated there and has lived in Poland ever since.

In his adopted homeland, Mr. Herter has been very active as a teacher and conductor, with numerous engagements leading the philharmonic orchestras of Częstochowa, Jelenia Góra, Kielce, Koszalin, Lublin, Łódź, Olsztyn, Opole, and Szczecin, as well as the Warsaw National Philharmonic, with whom he also has recorded the soundtrack for feature films and TV serials. For nearly twenty years Maestro Herter has been working at the Teatr Rozrywki, a music theater in northern Silesia, conducting American musicals such as West Side Story and Fiddler on the Roof. Joseph Herter is also the founder and conductor of Cantores Minores, the Warsaw Archdiocesan Cathedral Boys' and Men's Choir. Together they have traveled to seventeen countries and taken part in twenty-eight festivals. Under Mr. Herter's direction, Cantores Minores has won top prizes at competitions in Lecco, Prague, Moscow, and Międzydroje.

In addition to his busy performing schedule, Joseph Herter is widely respected as a writer for such international publications as *The Polish Review*, *Polish Music Journal*, *Polish Music Newsletter*, and *Elgar Society Journal*. In Poland, he is a frequent contributor to *Muzyka 21* and *Ruch Muzyczny*. Mr. Herter has been invited to deliver papers and lectures at various conferences and symposia in Berlin, Los Angeles, New York and Washington, D.C.

The long and distinguished record of Joseph Herter's musical activities has been universally recognized: he is a recipient of awards from the City of Warsaw (1999), the Polish Ministry of Culture (2003) and the Polish Union of Choirs and Orchestras (2005). In 2004, Joseph Herter was elected an Honorary Member of the Polish Singers' Alliance of America, North America's oldest Polish cultural society. Since November 2006, he has been the Warsaw representative of the Kosciuszko Foundation.

Joseph Herter's pioneering research of pianist and composer Zygmunt Stojowski led to the reintroduction of Stojowski's music to the concert stage and the release of several commercial recordings over the past few years.